Pro Team Foundation Service

Mathias Olausson
Joachim Rossberg
Jakob Ehn
Mattias Sköld

Apress·

Pro Team Foundation Service

ISBN 978-1-4302-5995-4

ISBN 978-1-4302-5996-1 (eBook)

Trademarked names, logos, and images may appear in this book. Rather than use a trademark symbol with every occurrence of a trademarked name, logo, or image we use the names, logos, and images only in an editorial fashion and to the benefit of the trademark owner, with no intention of infringement of the trademark.

The use in this publication of trade names, trademarks, service marks, and similar terms, even if they are not identified as such, is not to be taken as an expression of opinion as to whether or not they are subject to proprietary rights.

While the advice and information in this book are believed to be true and accurate at the date of publication, neither the authors nor the editors nor the publisher can accept any legal responsibility for any errors or omissions that may be made. The publisher makes no warranty, express or implied, with respect to the material contained herein.

President and Publisher: Paul Manning
Lead Editor: Matthew Moodie
Technical Reviewers: Terje Sandstrøm, Will Smythe, and Ravi Shanker
Editorial Board: Steve Anglin, Ewan Buckingham, Gary Cornell, Louise Corrigan, Morgan Ertel, Jonathan Gennick, Jonathan Hassell, Robert Hutchinson, Michelle Lowman, James Markham, Matthew Moodie, Jeff Olson, Jeffrey Pepper, Douglas Pundick, Ben Renow-Clarke, Dominic Shakeshaft, Gwenan Spearing, Matt Wade, Coordinating Editor: Mark Powers
Copy Editor: Mary Bearden
Compositor: SPi Global
Indexer: SPi Global
Artist: SPi Global
Cover Designer: Anna Ishchenko

Distributed to the book trade worldwide by Springer Science+Business Media New York, 233 Spring Street, 6th Floor, New York, NY 10013. Phone 1-800-SPRINGER, fax (201) 348-4505, e-mail orders-ny@springer-sbm.com,or visit www.springeronline.com. Apress Media, LLC is a California LLC and the sole member (owner) is Springer Science + Business Media Finance Inc (SSBM Finance Inc). SSBM Finance Inc is a Delaware corporation.

For information on translations, please e-mail rights@apress.com,o rv isit www.apress.com.

Apress and friends of ED books may be purchased in bulk for academic, corporate, or promotional use. eBook versions and licenses are also available for most titles. For more information, reference our Special Bulk Sales–eBook Licensing web page at www.apress.com/bulk-sales.

Any source code or other supplementary materials referenced by the author in this text is available to readers at www.apress.com/9781430259954. For detailed information about how to locate your book's source code, go to www.apress.com/source-code/.

Contents at a Glance

Foreword xix

About the Authors... xxi

About the Technical Reviewers xxiii

Acknowledgments... xxv

Introduction xxvii

■Chapter 1: Introduction to Application Lifecycle Management 1

■Chapter 2: Introduction to Agile Planning, Development, and Testing 9

■Chapter 3: Deciding on a Hosted Service 21

■Chapter 4: Getting Started 27

■Chapter 5: Working with the Initial Product Backlog 43

■Chapter 6: Managing Teams and Alerts.. 59

■Chapter 7: Initial Sprint Planning 69

■Chapter 8: Running the Sprint 79

■Chapter 9: Kanban 91

■Chapter 10: Engaging the Customer 101

■Chapter 11: Choosing Source Control Options.. 115

■Chapter 12: Working with Team Foundation Version Control in Visual Studio 123

■Chapter 13: Working with Git in Visual Studio 157

■Chapter 14: Working in Heterogeneous Environments................................. 177

■Chapter 15: Configuring Build Services.. 201

■**Chapter 16: Working with Builds**..**215**

■**Chapter 17: Customizing Builds** **245**

■**Chapter 18: Continuous Deployment** **271**

■**Chapter 19: Agile Testing**...**293**

■**Chapter 20: Test Management**...**313**

■**Chapter 21: Lab Management** **339**

Index...**367**

Contents

Foreword xix

About the Authors.. xxi

About the Technical Reviewers xxiii

Acknowledgments xxv

Introduction xxvii

■Chapter 1: Introduction to Application Lifecycle Management 1

Modern Business Challenges 1

Competences in the ALM Process 1

Three Pillars of Traditional Application Lifecycle Management 4

Traceability of Relationships Between Artifacts 5

Automation of Processes..5

Visibility into the Progress of Development Efforts 5

A Brief History of ALM Tools 5

Application Lifecycle Management 2.0+ 6

Summary..7

■Chapter 2: Introduction to Agile Planning, Development, and Testing 9

The Scrum Process 9

Roles in Scrum 10

Product Owner..11

Scrum Master 12

Development Team 12

Definition of Done..12

Agile Requirements and Estimation 13

    Requirements 13

    Estimation...15

    Backlog...16

Agile Development Using eXtreme Programming 17

Agile Testing 18

Summary..19

■Chapter 3: Deciding on a Hosted Service 21

Why Use Microsoft Team Foundation Service? 21

    Zero Friction Start...21

    Always On, Trouble-Free Operations...21

    Always Updated..21

    Access for External Users..22

    Build as a Service 22

    Deployment to Azure 22

    Use On-Premises or Cloud Resources..22

Why Use an On-Premises Team Foundation Server? 22

    Customizations...22

    Legal Requirements and Policies 23

    Identities and Authentication...23

    Control of Operations..23

    Migration of Data..23

    Reporting 24

    SharePoint..24

    Dependencies to Local Environments 24

Organization Dependent Factors 25

    Cost...25

    Organizational Strategies 25

    Security 25

The Decision...25

    Other Hosting or Servicing Options 25

    Situation-Based Approach 26

Summary...26

■Chapter 4: Getting Started 27

Before You Begin 27

What Is a Team Foundation Service Account?..27

    Naming the Account 28

    Creating the Account 29

Creating Your First Team Project 30

    Selecting the Name of the Team Project 31

    Selecting Type of Version Control Repository 32

    Selecting Process Template..32

Connecting to Your Team Project..35

    Quick Connect..35

    Connecting Through Team Explorer 36

Moving into Your Project...39

    Inviting People 39

    Roles and Permissions 40

Summary...41

■Chapter 5: Working with the Initial Product Backlog 43

Case Study 43

    Company Background 43

    The Pilot Project 44

    The People 44

Scrum Process Template...44

    Work Items 45

    TF Service Web Access..46

    Charts and Queries 46

Project Startup Phase..**49**

    PO Sets Off to Work 49

    Building the Initial Team 49

    Requirements 51

    Building the Backlog.. 52

    Adding Backlog Items in TF Service 52

    Definition of Done 53

    Estimation... 55

    Risk Assessment 56

    Updating the Backlog Order... 57

    Grooming the Backlog 57

    Building the Team 57

Summary...**58**

■**Chapter 6: Managing Teams and Alerts**..**59**

Adding Team Members..**59**

Creating New Teams **61**

Managing TF Service Groups, Teams, and User's Permission **63**

Managing Alerts **65**

Summary...**68**

■**Chapter 7: Initial Sprint Planning** **69**

Initial Velocity...**69**

    Available Time... 69

    Capacity Planning in TF Service 70

    Initial Sprint Planning 71

    Updating Backlog and PBI 72

    Forecast in TF Service 73

Release Planning...**75**

    Themes.. 75

    Estimated Time Plan 75

Creating the Sprints in TF Service 76

Estimated Project Cost 77

Summary 78

■Chapter 8: Running the Sprint 79

Scrum Meetings During the Sprint 79

Sprint Planning 79

Daily Standup 85

Retrieving Data from TF Service 87

Backlog Grooming 89

Sprint Review 89

Sprint Retrospective 90

Summary 90

■Chapter 9: Kanban 91

The Kanban Method 91

Start with What You Do Now 92

Agree to Pursue Incremental, Evolutionary Change 92

Respect the Current Process, Roles, Responsibilities, and Titles 92

The Five Core Properties 92

Visualize the Workflow 92

Work-in-Process Limit 94

Manage Flow 94

Make Process Policies Explicit 94

Improve Collaboratively 95

Common Models Used to Understand Work in Kanban 95

Kanban in Team Foundation Service 95

Setting Up the Kanban Board 96

How to Use the Board 97

Summary 99

■Chapter 10: Engaging the Customer 101

Creating Application Mockups 101

Storyboarding a User Story 102

Sharing Your Storyboards 105

Creating Reusable Storyboard Shapes 107

Getting Customer Feedback 108

Sending a Feedback Request 108

Responding to a Feedback Request 110

Following Up on Feedback Responses 112

Summary 113

■Chapter 11: Choosing Source Control Options 115

Overview of Team Foundation Version Control 115

Atomic Check-In 116

Check-In Policies 116

Shelving 116

Team Visibility 116

Locks 116

Labeling 117

Branching 117

Branch Visualization and Tracking 117

Cross-Platform Support 118

Disconnected Work 118

Overview of Git 119

Disconnected Work 119

Distributed Development 119

Rewriting History 119

Workflows 120

Tagging 120

Rebasing 120

Branching 120

Branch Visualization 121

Cross-Platform Clients...121

Git-TF: A Third Option 121

Choice of Source Control System..122

Advantages of Team Foundation Version Control...122

Advantages of Git...122

Summary..122

■Chapter 12: Working with Team Foundation Version Control in Visual Studio 123

Team Explorer...123

Team Members Extension 125

Connecting to a Team Project..125

Source Control Operations 126

Using Source Control Explorer...127

Mapping Workspaces 128

Different Kinds of Workspaces 129

Check Out 130

View History...130

Compare File Versions 131

Annotate 132

View Pending Changes 133

Shelving..135

Retrieving Shelvesets 136

Branching..138

Creating a Branch 139

Visualize Branch Structure 140

Merging 140

Performing a Merge Between Branches...141

Forward and Reverse Integration 145

Branch Visualization and Tracking..145

    Track Changeset...145

    Track Work Item...147

    My Work..150

    Starting New Work...151

    Suspending Your Current Work...151

    Resuming Your Suspended Work...152

Code Reviews..152

    Requesting a Code Review..152

    Responding to a Code Review Request...154

    Viewing and Responding to a Review...154

    Finalizing a Code Review..156

Summary...156

■Chapter 13: Working with Git in Visual Studio 157

Installing Git Extensions to Visual Studio 2012 157

Using Team Explorer...158

    Team Members Extension 159

    Connecting to a Team Project..159

    Connecting to a Remote Git Repository..160

    Browsing the Source Code..163

    View History..163

    Committing Changes to Your Local Repository..165

    Pulling Changes from the Server...166

    Pushing Changes to the Server...166

Branching..167

    Create a New Local Branch...168

    Switching Branches...169

    Merging Branches...169

    Resolve Conflicts..170

    Publishing a Branch to the Server...173

Viewing the Server Repository 173

Using Non-Microsoft Git Tools 174

Using Git Command Line Utilities 176

Summary 176

■Chapter 14: Working in Heterogeneous Environments 177

Working with Eclipse 177

Installing Team Explorer Everywhere 178

Adding an Eclipse Project to Source Control 181

Using Work Items 186

Using Builds 188

Working with Xcode 189

Cloning a TF Service Repository 190

Adding an Xcode project to Source Control 193

Working with Git-TF 196

Setting Up Git-TF 197

Cloning a TF Service Repository 197

Summary 199

■Chapter 15: Configuring Build Services 201

About Build Automation 201

Team Foundation Build 202

Configuring Hosted Build Server 203

Software on the Hosted Build Server 205

Hosted Build Server Limitations 206

Managing Dependencies 207

Using Source Control 207

Using NuGet Restore Packages 207

Other Options 209

Adding On Premises Build Servers 209

Summary 214

Chapter 16: Working with Builds...**215**

Build Artifacts...215

Creating a Build Definition...215

Running a Build...221

Executing Tests...225

    Configuring Unit Tests for Automated Builds 226

    Specifying Test Filters... 227

    Enabling Different Test Adapters 229

Building Git Projects..232

Tracking Build Status..235

    View Build Status.. 236

    Build Favorites... 237

    Build Alerts 239

    Build Notification Power Tool.. 242

Summary..243

Chapter 17: Customizing Builds **245**

About Windows Workflow Foundation...245

Customizing Build Process Templates..247

    Modify the Build Process Template 247

    Parameterize the Build Process Template 252

Using External Custom Activities..255

    Getting Custom Activities into Visual Studio 255

    Deploying Custom Activities to the Hosted Build Server 258

    Adding Custom Activities to the Build Process Template... 259

Creating Custom Activities 262

    Solution for Developing Custom Activities... 263

    Developing a Custom Activity 264

Summary..269

■**Chapter 18: Continuous Deployment** **271**

Automatic Deployment to Windows Azure...271

Setting It Up 271

How It Works 278

Troubleshooting Azure Deployments 281

Deploy On Premises Using Web Deploy 283

Installing Web Deploy 284

Creating a Publish Profile 285

Web Deployment in Automated Builds 288

Deploying SSDT Database Projects 289

Creating a SSDT Publish Profile 289

Deploy SSDT Projects in Automated Builds 290

Summary 291

■**Chapter 19: Agile Testing** **293**

Acceptance Criteria 293

Evolving Tests 295

Clients for Managing Tests 295

Microsoft Test Manager 296

Microsoft Web Test Manager 297

Getting Started 298

Adding a Test Plan 298

Creating a Test Case with WTM 299

Working with WTM 300

Running a Test Case with WTM 301

Exploratory Testing 305

Creating a Test Case from an Exploratory Test 308

Summary 311

■Chapter 20: Test Management **313**

Planning the Tests 313

What Is a Test Plan? 313

Test Suites 313

Test Plan Properties 316

Designing Test Cases 317

What Is a Test Case? 317

Creating Test Cases 319

Test Configurations 322

Assign to Tester 323

Grouping and Adding Fields 324

Test Suite Status 324

Running Tests 325

Filtering Tests to Run 325

Using with the MTM Test Runner 326

Analyze Test Runs 330

Test Settings 331

Data Collection 331

Reporting Bugs and Validating Fixes 333

Creating a Bug 333

Verifying Bugs 335

Fast-Forward Playback 336

Summary 337

■Chapter 21: Lab Management **339**

Architecture 339

Capabilities 339

Components 341

Setting up the Lab 343

Topology 343

Installing the Test Controller 344

Installing an On-Premises Build Service 345

Creating a Standard Environment 345

Testing with Lab Management 348

Running Manual Tests 348

Selecting an Environment to Use 349

Connecting to an Environment for Testing 349

Automated Testing 351

Running Automated Tests from MTM 353

Running Automated Tests from the Command Line 355

Build-Deploy-Test Workflow 357

Implementing a BDT Workflow 357

Running the BDT Workflow 364

Summary 365

Index 367

Foreword

Team Foundation Server has been a popular Application Lifecycle Management platform in enterprises for years. It provides a comprehensive set of capabilities for planning, developing, testing, releasing, and collecting feedback on high-quality, agile software projects. Team Foundation Server scales from very small teams collaborating in tight iterations to large organizations managing a portfolio of projects.

The introduction of Team Foundation Service—a Cloud-based offering—makes TF Service more accessible than ever. With teams becoming more distributed and innovation happening faster than ever, TF Service enables you to get started in just a few minutes, without worrying about purchasing infrastructure, installing software, configuring network access, creating a high availability plan, and everything else that goes along with setting up a mission critical on-premises service. TF Service takes care of all of that for you and enables access quickly and easily from anywhere in the world. It also grows as you grow. You can start with just source control or scrum planning and gradually grow to the full ALM feature set as your needs develop.

Another advantage to TF Service is that it is "always up to date." TF Service is constantly evolving and improving based on your feedback. We too are an agile team and release new capabilities to the service every sprint (which is three weeks for us). The service not only allows you to get access to these improvements sooner but also eliminates the need to worry about finding time to do server updates.

Software development practices are evolving rapidly. The age of "agile" has matured and the age of "DevOps" and "Build-Measure-Learn" is beginning to take shape. We'll strive to make TF Service the best solution for helping you adopt these evolving practices. We'll continue to add capabilities to TF Service to help you build "modern" Cloud-connected device applications. We'll continue to work to ensure you can engage with your users to understand their needs and respond quickly and deliver an experience that delights them. And we're always eager to hear your feedback on how we can help you more.

This book is a great overview of TF Service, its capabilities, and how to get started. I encourage you to give it a try and share feedback on your experience. We look forward to working with you.

Brian Harry
Visual Studio Cloud Services

About the Authors

Mathias Olausson works as the ALM practice lead for Transcendent Group, specializing in software craftsmanship and application lifecycle management. With over 15 years of experience as a software consultant and trainer, he has worked in numerous projects and organizations. Mathias has been a Microsoft Visual Studio ALM MVP for five years and is also active as a Visual Studio ALM Ranger. Mathias is a frequent speaker on Visual Studio and Team Foundation Server at conferences and industry events and blogs at `http://msmvps.com/blogs/molausson`.

Joachim Rossberg has worked as an IT consultant since 1998. He is primarily a product owner, Scrum master, and project manager but has an extensive history as a system developer and designer. He has demonstrated his technical background with various achievements over the years: MCSD, MCDBA, MCSA, and MCSE. His specialties include project management, ALM process, and Team Foundation Server. Joachim is now working for Know IT Systems Development in Gothenburg, Sweden.

Jakob Ehn is currently a Microsoft Visual Studio ALM MVP and also a Visual Studio ALM Ranger. Jakob has 15 years' experience in the IT industry and currently works as a solution architect at Inmeta Crayon ASA, specializing in Visual Studio ALM. Jakob is coauthor of Team Foundation Server 2012 Starter (Packt Publishing, 2012), and he actively participates in the MSDN forums and contributes to different open source projects, such as the Community TFS Build Extensions and the Community TFS Build Manager. Jakob's blog: http://geekswithblogs.net/Jakob and Jakob's Twitter: @JakobEhn

Mattias Sköld is the ALM practice manager for Sogeti in Sweden, focusing on the Microsoft platform. Mattias has been working in the software industry for 20 years and as an ALM Consultant the past five years, helping developer teams and organizations improve the software development process. Mattias is a Microsoft ALM MVP and was awarded the ALM MVP of the Year 2013. Mattias is also an active ALM Ranger, working together with Microsoft, lately as the project lead for the ALM Rangers Branching Tooling project. Mattias blogs at http://mskold.blogspot.com.

About the Technical Reviewers

Terje Sandstrom works as the chief software architect at InmetaCrayon in Norway, in the consulting division, and has been a Microsoft Visual Studio ALM MVP since 2008. Most of his time is spent advising developers, architects, project managers, and testers in larger companies. He is interested in all aspects of software development, although coding principles are a favorite.

Terje has worked with professional and industrial design and development for many more years than he wants to remember, moving gradually from electronic design to software design. He holds an MSc in physics from the University in Oslo, graduating with a mixture of physics and informatics and software background.

Terje has programmed in a lot of different computer languages, but is very fond of the object-oriented ones, from his early exposure to Simula at the university. He is very interested in the theoretical aspects of programming languages, design patterns, and everything that has a higher level of complexity. His interests range from areas of development process like Agile, Lean, Scrum, and Kanban to development practices in object-oriented programming, databases, OLAP, UML, functional programming, graphics, 3D, and more. He has yet to learn that there is probably a limit as to how much one person can possibly do.

Terje has worked with Microsoft technology since the late 1980s and is familiar with many of the products made by Microsoft. He has worked with the TF Service family since the product appeared. Terje has run courses, seminars, and workshops and he speaks not only at public events but also at internal company events for larger Norwegian companies. He is blogging actively at http://geekswithblogs.net/terje. Follow him at Twitter @OsirisTerje.

Will Smythe is currently a Program Manager at Microsoft on Team Foundation Service and is primarily responsible for the core services that Team Foundation Service is built on. Although Will is fairly new to Microsoft, he has over 10 years of experience delivering software for developers, including development and application lifecycle management tools.

Ravi Shanker has around 19 years' experience in software industry, about 15 years of which, is at Microsoft Corporation. He has held multiple roles of a developer, a support engineer, an escalation engineer and finally a program manager in his career, spanning different geographies from Delhi, Dallas, Redmond and finally Hyderabad. As a Principal Program Manager in the Visual Studio India team, he is the product owner for Microsoft Test Manager & Microsoft Feedback Client and has helped ship two versions of the boxed product, Microsoft Test Professional 2010 and Microsoft Test Professional 2012. With the shift to frequent ship cycles, he has been involved in shipping the Test related capabilities on the Hosted TFS Service, every 3 weeks. He is passionate about the manual testing space and strives to deliver products that solve real customer problems.

Acknowledgments

First we would like to thank our technical reviewers Terje Sandstrom, Will Smythe, and Ravi Shanker, the time you spent giving us feedback has been invaluable to the finished result. We would also like to thank Jamie Cool, Brian Harry, Anutthara Bharadwaj, Ed Blankenship and Vijay Machiraju for your valuable input to the book.

Thanks to everyone at Apress, it's been a pleasure working with all of you. A special thanks to our coordinating editor Mark Powers for the close collaboration during the tight schedule to deliver this book.

Last but not least, thanks to our families and colleagues for your support during this project.

Introduction

Pro Team Foundation Service is a scenario-based book that takes you through the different stages of software development. Every project needs to plan, develop, test, and release software, and with agile practices often at a higher pace than ever before. With Microsoft Team Foundation Service (TF Service) comes a collaboration platform that gives us as a team the tools to better perform our tasks and nicely integrated as well.

TF Service is a Cloud-based platform that gives us tools for agile planning and work tracking. It has a code repository that can be used not only from Visual Studio but also from Java platforms and iOS. The testing tools allow testers to start testing at the same time as the developer starts developing. The book also covers how to set up automated practices, such as build, deploy, and test workflows. This book will:

- Take you through the major stages in a software development project.
- Give practical development guidance to the whole team.
- Enable you to quickly get started with modern development practices.

Who This Book Is For

This book is for anyone interested in improving their software development process. Regardless of whether you are a development manager, stakeholder, developer, or tester, there is a common goal in the development process—deliver software with the right features with great quality on time. The Application Lifecycle Management (ALM) principles bring the team together by looking at how to optimize the end-to-end flow rather than focusing on fine tuning the individual practices. In this book you will learn how the TF Service can be a great platform to build an effective ALM process that improves the whole process as well as each of the roles in the process.

Contacting the Authors

Should you have any questions or comments or spot a mistake you think we should know about, you can contact the authors at mathias@olausson.net, rossberg@gmail.com, jakobehn@gmail.com, and mattias.skold@sogeti.se.

■ ■ ■

CHAPTER 1

Introductiont o Application LifecycleMan agement

What comes to mind when you hear the term *Application Lifecycle Management* (ALM)? During a seminar tour in Sweden to present the Microsoft Visual Studio Team System, we asked people what ALM was and whether they cared about it. To our surprise, many people equated ALM with operations and maintenance. This is still often the case today when we visit companies, but more companies are aware of the term these days.

Maybe that was your answer as well? Doesn't ALM include more than just operations? Yes, it does. ALM is the thread that ties together an application's lifecycle from its conception to its retirement. It involves all the steps necessary to coordinate the activities that make up an application's lifecycle. Operations are just one part of the ALM process; ALM is the glue that binds the development processes and defines the efforts necessary to coordinate the process, including requirements management, the development lifecycle, testing, and so on. Before we dive into ALM, let's consider some challenges for companies these days so that we understand why a flexible ALM process is necessary.

Modern Business Challenges

Modern organizations depend on software and software systems in many ways. Business processes are often implemented digitally and without software to support this, and even small companies could experience problems as a result. For most companies, the world and the way we do business have changed quickly in the past few years. Most companies have to offer online services and purchases, which they did not have to do 10 to 15 years ago. This change has come rather rapidly and is constantly in movement, which leads to constant changes in the business processes. It is clear that if business processes do not change with the surrounding world, business opportunities will suffer.

For companies, development of software has changed as well. Nowadays many organizations have large development teams working on software to support the business. Often the teams are spread globally. This poses many potential problems, such as collaboration issues, maintaining shared source code storage, and handling effective requirements management. Without processes to support modern software development, business will likely be affected.

Competences in the ALM Process

All software development includes various steps performed by people who have specific competences that are necessary in the ALM process. In agile practice, we should not confuse these competences with roles. Scrum, for instance, only has three roles defined, but they incorporate different competences into these roles.

There are many competences involved in the ALM process, and we define some of them in this section. Take a look at Figure 1-1, which illustrates the ALM process starting with the business needs. When the need for new software or applications arises in a company, we need to figure out if the software fits into its application portfolio.

If it does, we request that the development team build our software and once ready we deploy it into production where it gives us business value. During its lifetime the software might need bug fixes and new releases are implemented, and later we probably retire the system.

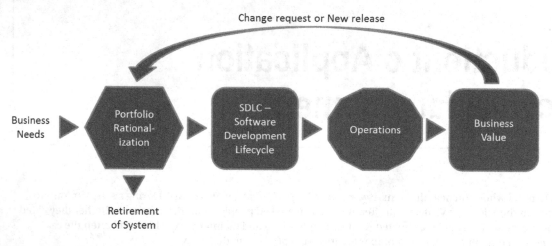

Figure 1-1. *The Application Lifecycle Management process from an overview perspective*

It is essential to understand that all business software development is a team effort. Different competences collaborate on projects to deliver business value to the organization. If we don't have this collaboration, the value of the system most likely will be considerably lower than it could be. If we look at it one step up from the actual project level, it is also important to have collaboration among everyone involved in the ALM process to ensure this process is performed optimally.

The competences in the ALM process include, but are not limited to, the following:

- *Business manager*: Somebody has to make the decision that development activity is going to start. After initial analysis of the business needs, a business manager decides to initiate a project for the development of an application or system that will deliver the expected business value. A business manager will have to be involved in the approval process for the new suggested project, including portfolio rationalization, before a decision to go ahead is reached. Other people involved in this process are of course IT managers, because the IT staff will probably be involved in the project's development and deployment into the infrastructure.

- *Project manager, product owner, or scrum master*: Suitable individuals are selected to fill these roles and set to work on the project after the decision to go ahead is made. Ideally, these people continue leading the project all the way through, so there is continuity in project management.

- *Program management office decision makers*: A project management office (PMO) is a group or department within a business, agency, or enterprise that defines and maintains standards for project management within the organization. The PMO is the source of documentation, guidance, and metrics on the practice of project management and execution (http://en.wikipedia.org/wiki/Project_management_office). These individuals are also involved in planning because a new project might very well change or expand the company's portfolio.

- *Business analyst*: A business analyst is responsible for analyzing the business needs and requirements of the stakeholders to help identify business problems and propose solutions. Within the system's development lifecycle, the business analyst typically performs a collaborative function between the business side of an enterprise and the providers of services to the enterprise.

- *Architect*: The architect starts drawing the initial picture of the solution. Briefly, the architect draws the blueprint of the system, and the system designers or engineers use this blueprint to move forward. The blueprint includes the level of freedom necessary in the system (e.g., scalability, hardware replacement, new user interfaces, and so on). All of these issues must be considered by the architect.

- *User experience design experts*: The user experience (UX) design is a core deliverable and not something that is left to the developers to handle. The UX experts make sure that the design is consistent and follows any rules and regulations that must be followed (e.g., rules for UX to better adjust the UX for those with vision impairment). The UX experts also ensure that the company profile is met in the UX. UX design is sadly often overlooked and should definitely have more consideration. It is important to have close collaboration between the UX team (which could be just one person) and the development team. The best solution is obviously to have a UX expert in the development team throughout the project, but that is sometimes not possible. The UX design is extremely important in making sure users can really perceive the value of the system. We can write the best business logic in the world, but if the UX is badly designed, the users will probably never think the system is any good.

- *Database administrators*: Almost every business system or application uses a database in some way. The database administrators (DBAs) are the ones who can make our databases run like lightning with good up-time, so it is essential to use their expertise in any project involving a database. Be nice to them! They can give you lots of tips on how to make a smarter system. What we have seen lately is that more and more of the DBA's role is being filled by developers, however, since many modern developer tools also offer great DBA support.

- *Developers*: Developers, developers, developers, as Microsoft CEO Steve Ballmer shouted in a famous video. And who can blame him? These are the people doing their magic to realize the system that we are building by using the architecture blueprint drawn from the requirements. Moreover, these are the people who have to modify or extend the code when change requests come in.

- *Tester*: I would rather not see testing as a separate activity, although we have the designated tester capability in most projects. Testing is something we should consider from the first time we write down a requirement and continue doing this during the whole process.

- *Operations and maintenance staff*: Here it is. When an application or system is finished, it is handed over to operations. The operations staff takes care of it until it is retired, often with the help of the original developers who come in to do bug fixes and add new upgrades. Don't forget to involve these people early in the process, at the point when the initial architecture is considered, and keep them in the project until it is completed. They can give great input as to what can and can't be done in the company infrastructure. So operations is just one part, but an important one, of ALM. In the past few years, the term *DevOps* has become very popular. DevOps aims to bring developers and operations much closer, both in collaboration as well as physical location.

All project efforts are done as collaborative work. No person can act separate from any of the others.

In a scrum project, there may be only three roles: product owner, scrum master, and team members. This does not mean that the capabilities described above do not apply! They are all essential in most projects; it's just that in an agile project you may not be labeled a developer or an architect. Rather, you are there as a team member and as such you and your comembers share responsibility for the work you have committed to. We will go deeper into the agile world later in the book.

ONE WAY OF LOOKING AT APPLICATION LIFECYCLE MANAGEMENT

ALM is the glue that ties together all of these competences and the activities they perform. Let's consider one way of looking at ALM. There can be more viewpoints of ALM, of course, but we think this is the best way to look at it, and this is called the *unified view*.

In the unified view, we do as the chief information officer would do: we focus on the business needs, not on separate views. We do this to improve the capacity and agility of the project from start to end.

Three Pillars of Traditional Application Lifecycle Management

Let's look at some important pillars that are found in ALM, as shown in Figure 1-2.

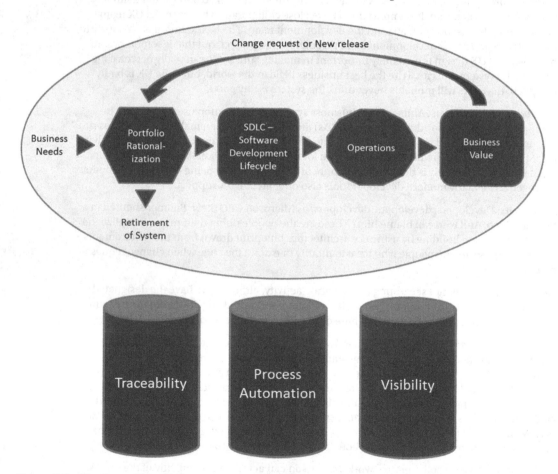

Figure 1-2. *The three pillars of ALM*

Let's examine these three pillars in more detail.

Traceability of Relationships Between Artifacts

Traceability is important. In software development, we benefit from a high level of traceability, as the requirements can flow down through the design and code and can then be traced back up at every stage of the process. *Traceability* basically means that we should be able to follow the requirements from when they were created to when and where they were implemented in code. This means that we should be able to follow the requirement through the whole ALM lifecycle, including builds, tests, check-ins, and so on.

Some customers we have encountered have stopped doing upgrades on their systems that are running in production because these customers had poor or even no traceability in their systems. For these customers, it was far too expensive to do upgrades because of the unexpected effects even a small change could have. If the company implemented a bug fix in one part of the code, suddenly they might find that the bug fix caused a new bug in a different part of the system. The company had no way of knowing which original requirements were implemented at which area in the application and hence had no way of knowing the full effect of the bug fix, all because they lacked traceability in their development efforts. These customers claimed, and we have seen and heard this in discussions with many other customers, that traceability can be a major cost driver in any enterprise if not done correctly.

There must be a way of tracing the requirements all the way to delivered code—through architect models, design models, build scripts, unit tests, test cases, and so on—not only to make it easier to go back into the system when implementing bug fixes, but also to demonstrate that the system has delivered the things the business wanted.

Another reason for traceability is internal as well as external compliance with rules and regulations. If we develop applications for the medical industry, for example, we need to have compliance with Food and Drug Administration regulations. We also need to have traceability when change requests are coming in so we know where we updated the system and in which version we performed the update.

Automation ofP rocesses

The next pillar is automation of various processes. All organizations have processes of some kind. For example, there are approval processes to control hand-offs between the analysis and design or build steps or between deployment and testing. Much of this is done manually in many projects, and ALM stresses the importance of automating these tasks for a more effective and less time-consuming process. Having an automated process also decreases the error rate when compared with handling the process manually.

Visibility into the Progress of Development Efforts

The third and last pillar provides visibility into the progress of development efforts. Many managers and stakeholders have limited visibility into the progress of development projects. The visibility they have often comes from steering group meetings, during which the project manager reviews the current situation. Some would argue that this limitation is good, but if we want to have an effective process, we must ensure visibility.

Other interest groups such as project members also have limited visibility of the whole project despite being part of the project. This often stems from the fact that reporting is hard to do and often involves a lot of manual work. Daily status reports would quite simply take too much time and effort to produce, especially when we have information in manyr epositories.

A Brief History of ALM Tools

We can resolve these three pillars manually without the use of tools or automation. ALM is not a new process description, although Microsoft, IBM, HP, Atlassian, and the other big software houses right now are pushing ALM to drive sales of their respective ALM solutions. We can, for instance, continue to use Excel spreadsheets, or as one of my most dedicated agile colleagues does, use sticky notes and a pad of paper, to track requirements through use cases or scenarios, test cases, code, build, and so on to delivered code. It works, but this process takes a lot of time and requires much manual effort. With constant pressure to keep costs down, we need to make tracking requirements more effective.

Of course, project members can simplify the process by keeping reporting to the bare minimum. With a good tool, or set of tools, we can cut time (and thus costs) and effort and still get the required traceability we want in our projects. The same goes for reporting and all those other activities we have. Tools can help us be more effective and also help us to automate much of the ALM process right into the tool.

By having the process built directly into our tools, it is much easier for those involved to avoid missing any important step by simplifying anything. For instance, one of our agile friends could definitely gain much from this, and he has now started looking into Microsoft Team Foundation Server to see how that set of tools can help him and his teams be more productive. So process automation and the use of tools to support and simplify our daily jobs are great things because they can keep us from making unnecessary mistakes. Imagine the Herculean task of keeping all those things in order manually. That would be impossible if we wanted to get something right and keep an eye on the status of projects.

This has led to increasing awareness of the ALM process among enterprises. We can certainly see this among the customers we have. ALM is much more important now than it was only five years ago.

Application Lifecycle Management 2.0+

The field of ALM has evolved over the years: From solutions with brittle integration among different tools (developer tools, testing tools, requirements management tools, work-item tools, and so on) to more full-fledged tools like Team Foundation Server from Microsoft. So far not all the ALM features have been implemented by tools vendors, and there are various reasons for this. One of these is the fact that it is not really easy for any company to move to a single integrated suite, no matter how promising the benefits might look. To make such a switch would mean changing the way they work in their development processes and even within their company. Companies have invested in tools and practices, and spending time and money on a new platform can require a lot more investment.

For Microsoft-focused development organizations, the switch might not be as difficult, however, at least not for the developers. They already use Visual Studio, SharePoint, and many other applications daily and the switch would not be that big. But Microsoft is not the only platform out there, and competitors like IBM, Serena, and HP still have some work to do to convince the market.

The growth of agile development and project management in recent years has also changed the way ALM must support development teams and organizations. We can see a clear change from requirements specs to backlog-driven work, and the tooling we use needs to support this in a good way.

Agile practices such as build-and-test automation become critical for our ALM tools to support. Test-driven development (TDD) continues to rise, and more and more developers require that their tools support this way of working. If the tools don't do this, they will be of little use for an agile organization. Microsoft has really taken the agile way of working to heart in the development of the Team Foundation Service. We will explain all you need to know about support for agile practices in Team Foundation Service throughout this book.

We can also see a move from traditional project management toward an agile view, where the product owner and scrum master require support from the tools as well. Backlog grooming (the art of grooming our requirements in the agile world), agile estimation and planning, and reporting—all important to these roles—need to be integrated into the overall ALM solution.

The connection between operations and maintenance has become increasingly more important. Our ALM tools should integrate with the tools used by these parts of the organization.

In the report "The Time is right for ALM 2.0+," Forrester Research presented the ALM 2.0+ concept as shown in Figure 1-3. In their report, Forrester extended traditional ALM with what they called ALM 2.0+. Traditional ALM covers traceability, reporting, and process automation, as discussed earlier. Forrester envisions the future of ALM to also include collaboration and work planning.

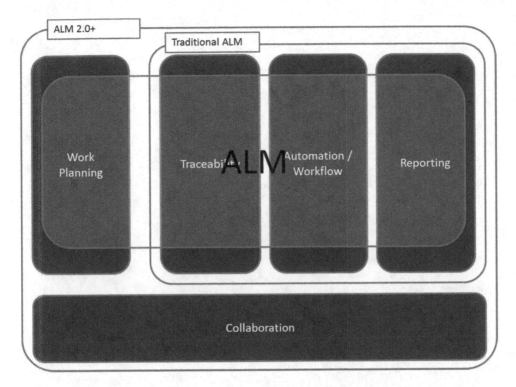

Figure 1-3. *Future ALM according to Forrester Research (Forrester Research, Inc., The Time Is Right For ALM 2.0+, October 19, 2010)*

These concepts will be essential throughout the rest of this book so let's take a quick look at them.

- *Work planning*: In this concept, Forrester adds planning functions (e.g., the possibility to define tasks and allocate them to resources). The planning functions should not replace the strategic planning functions that enterprise architecture and portfolio management tools provide. Instead they help us execute and provide feedback on those strategic plans. Integration of planning into ALM 2.0+ helps us follow up on our projects so we can get estimates and effort statistics, essential to all projects.

- *Collaboration*: Collaboration is essential these days. An ALM 2.0+ tool needs to support the distributed development environment that many organizations have. The tools must help us work effectively, sharing, collaborating, and interacting as if they were colocated. They should also do this without adding complexity to the work environment of our resources.

We will take a closer look at these topics in later chapters.

Summary

This chapter has presented an overview of what ALM is and explained how ALM is the coordination and synchronization of all development lifecycle activities.

We know that traceability, automation of high-level processes, and visibility into development processes are three pillars of ALM. Other important key components are collaboration and work planning. A good ALM tool should help us implement and automate these pillars and components to deliver better business value to our company or organization.

Let's continue with the next chapter where we will look at agile planning, development, and testing.

CHAPTER 2

Introduction to Agile Planning, Development,an d Testing

Through our experience, we have seen a great deal of improvement in the management of projects over the past few years. To be more specific, we have seen that the agile influence is making an impact on how projects deliver business value.

The focus of this book, when it comes to processes and frameworks, is on scrum and eXtreme Programming (XP), partly because we like these ourselves and partly because Microsoft strongly focuses on implementing support in Visual Studio and Team Foundation Service (TF Service) for these practices. Microsoft, for example, includes a great template for running scrum projects straight out of the box.

This chapter discusses how to use scrum as an agile project management model to deliver software using TF Service. We cover the scrum process briefly, adding how in practice you could use scrum and agile practices such as agile estimation and planning in combination with TF Service.

We will also discuss some of the agile development and testing practices that are essential for a successful project.

The Scrum Process

Let's start with the scrum process itself. It is important that you have a common understanding of this process because there are a lot of adjustments to the process in various organizations. Figure 2-1 shows the scrum process.

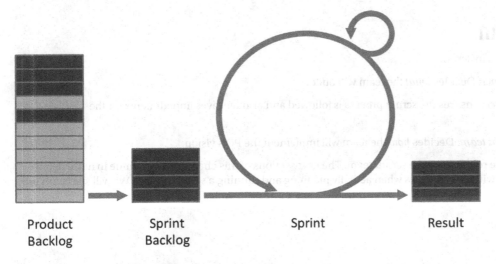

Product Backlog   Sprint Backlog   Sprint   Result

Figure 2-1. The scrum process

The requirements from the business side of an organization are put on a backlog as product backlog items (PBIs). The backlog itself is an ordered (former prioritized) list with the (currently) most important requirements at the top. The product owner (PO) is responsible for ordering the backlog (we'll explain more about scrum roles in the next section). When the first sprint starts, the development team, together with the PO, selects a number of PBIs for the sprint backlog (SP) in the sprint planning meeting. During the sprint planning the team breaks these backlog items into smaller, more manageable tasks that are then time estimated. Based on the time estimates and the available working time for the sprint, the team continues to select new backlog items for the SB until it is full. The team commits to delivering these sprint backlog items (SBIs) and starts working on them.

A sprint usually lasts between 2 and 4 weeks and is divided into 24-hour increments (the smaller loop in Figure 2-1). Every day the development team and the scrum master (SM) meet in a daily scrum meeting (time boxed to 15 minutes) going over the three magic questions:

- What have you done since the last meeting?

- What will you do until the next meeting?

- Do you have any impediments stopping your work?

The end result of a sprint should be a potentially shippable increment of the software. At the end of each sprint, there are also two meetings:

- *Sprint review*: During this meeting the team shows the PO and maybe stakeholders what they have done by demonstrating the software. The PO signs off on the delivery (unless something has not met the expectations).

- *Sprint retrospective*: During this meeting the team assesses what was good, what can be improved, or what needs to be changed for the next sprint.

That's it. No more than that. Seriously. The process is extremely easy to use and learn, but it is hard to master. But as we said, we have seen great improvements in our companies and with our customers' projects taking an agile approach compared with a traditional project approach using waterfall or Rational Unified Process (RUP).

Let's take a look at the roles in scrum and what their responsibilities are. Many of the following sections of this chapter are short and concise. Keep in mind that there are books and trainings covering these topics in depth, so this book does not give you everything you need to know about this. What we aim to do in this part of the book is to exemplify how TF Service can support agile project management, and to do that we need to know a little bit more about some important concepts.

Roles in Scrum

There are only three roles in scrum:

- *Product owner*: Decides *what* the team will build.

- *Scrum master*: Ensures the scrum process is followed and also removes impediments for the team.

- *Development team*: Decides *how* the team will implement the PO's vision.

Together these three roles create the scrum team. The next sections of this chapter will examine in more detail what responsibilities lie within these roles when actually planning and running a scrum project. We will start with the product owner.

ProductO wner

The PO is the role that most equals traditional project managers (PMs). The full truth is that the responsibilities of the PM have been divided among all three roles in scrum, but a good part of the responsibilities lands on the PO role. Much of what the PO is responsible for ends up in TF Service, especially at the beginning of a project. Here are a few things the PO is responsible for:

- *What to build and who should create the vision for the project*: The PO is the one who must have the business domain competence; if this doesn't happen, it will be difficult for the PO to fulfill their role. It is only the PO who decides what the project should build and deliver. The PO has final say in all decisions regarding the "what" question.

- *Project delivery*: The PO is responsible for the delivery (software/business value etc.) of the project. A PO should never have to say that the development team did not build what the PO wanted. If that situation occurs, the PO has done a bad job and probably has not been as present and dedicated as they should have been. It is essential that the PO is available for the team during the sprints. The team should never find itself blocked because of unavailability of the PO.

- *Requirements and estimation*: When the need for a new system (as an example) comes up in the organization, the PO should be responsible for gathering the initial requirements and estimating these. We look at this in more detail later in this chapter.

- *Creating the initial backlog and continually grooming it*: Based on the requirements, the PO creates the initial backlog. During the project, the PO is responsible for keeping the backlog in good shape (also known as backlog grooming), which the PO does together with the team. Included here is the art of breaking down the backlog into manageable pieces, which is something the PO also does with the help of the rest of the team.

- *Prioritizing the backlog*: In order for the team to build the right thing, it is important that the backlog is ordered in some way. By prioritizing the product backlog, the team knows what tasks to take on first. It is the PO who is responsible for this prioritization. The PO probably cannot do this by him- or herself, so the team is welcome to help and give input.

- *Calculate the estimated budget and return on investment*: With the initial requirements and estimation completed, the PO can calculate the estimated budget and return on investment (ROI) of the project so they can convince stakeholders that the project is necessary.

- *Product management*: The PO should know what and why something should be built. All requirements and requests that come into the project should be filtered through the PO. After looking at the incoming requests, the PO decides what to place on the backlog. Nobody else decidest hat.

- *Stakeholder management*: The PO is of course not alone with all of these responsibilities. The PO needs to manage all stakeholders and end-user input so they know what the organization wants; otherwise it is hard to make the decisions. One way of doing this is to schedule repeated stakeholder meetings where the needs and priorities of the organization ared iscussed.

- *Release management*: It is important early on in a project to get an overview of the releases in the project. Is there a specific theme that drives a release or a certain set of functions that should be a release? The PO should make sure this is done early on and then follow up on this.

- *Team manager/staff project*: The PO is responsible for staffing the project. Initially, the PO needs experienced people who can help with requirements and initial estimation. These people should, in the best of worlds, follow the project until it ends. Once the project starts, the PO, together with the initial team, makes sure it is scaled up in the best possible way.

These are some of the PO responsibilities. We will soon see how many of these are mapped into TF Service. First, let's look at the other two roles.

ScrumM aster

We have kept this short because the PO's responsibilities affect the backlog more, but the responsibilities of the SM include (among many others):

- *Protecting the team*: The team should be able to work without being interrupted by anything. For example, the team should not be disturbed by managers asking them to spend time on other (nonproject) related tasks. If that happens, the SM needs to explain to the manager why the team (or team member) cannot do the things the manager asks for. This is essential for the team to deliver what it has committed to deliver.

- *Resolving problems*: If the team or a team member is blocked by an obstacle and cannot continue working on a user story, it is the SM who needs to resolve the problem. The SM needs to clarify what the problem is, why the block happened, and how it can be solved.

- *Maintaining process integrity*: The SM must ensure that the team (including PO) understands and complies with the scrum process in the right way. It is also the SM who needs to ensure that the rest of the organization outside the scrum team understands the process and why it is importantt os tickt oi t.

DevelopmentT eam

So now we have come to the team, the ones producing the actual code. Here are some responsibilities of the developmentt eam:

- *Deciding how to build what the PO has decided to build*: The team is responsible for coming up with the solution, breaking down user stories, and giving feedback and suggestions to the PO. This happens during backlog grooming, sprint planning, daily stand-up, and other scrum meetings.

- *Delivering quality code*: This means that the team needs to comply with the requirements in the definition of done (DoD), which we will discuss in the next section. It also means that the software must be tested properly.

- *Giving estimates of user stories, both before and during a sprint*: The team needs to estimate the best it can to give input to the PO. It also needs to have a good dialog with the PO so the team can point out alternative ways for the project. If the team feels that the PO should make another decision, it is obliged to point out and argue for a better way.

- *Following the principles of XP*: This might not be in the scrum guide, but we recommend this fromo uro wne xperience.

Definition of Done

DoD is really important, but it is also something we often tend to forget. (Do not confuse DoD with Department of Defense! That is something entirely different and way out of the scope of this book.) DoD is a quality document that states what must be fulfilled before we can say that a project backlog item is finished. Both the PO and the development team must agree on this document. In many projects we have seen, arguments have arisen between the delivering development organization and the person ordering the project as to whether a task has been done at the end of (and also during) a sprint or project. It could be that testing has not been done the way the client assumed it would be or that the software does not comply with certain regulations. The following conversation is typical:

> The product owner Sofia stops by the developer Mike to check on how things are going.
>
> S: Hi. How's the cool new feature you are working on coming along?
>
> M: It's going great. I am done with it right now and will start the next feature soon.
>
> S: Great! Then I can show it to our customer who's coming here after lunch. He will be very excited!
>
> M: No, no. Hold on. I am not "done" done with it. I still need to fix some test cases, do some refactoring, get it into the build process, and so on. I just thought you wondered if I had gotten somewhere with it.

For the most part, this conversation could have been avoided if they had sat down together in the beginning and written and signed a DoD.

There are other reasons for having a DoD as well. In order for the team to estimate a user story, it needs to know when it is done with it. Otherwise, it is very hard to complete the estimate. For a specific user story, we know it is done when we have fulfilled the acceptance criteria for it. But where do all those general things like style guides, code analysis, build automation, test automation, regulatory compliance, governance, nonfunctional requirements, and so on fit in? They affect the estimate of a user story as well.

Here is where the DoD comes into play again. The DoD tells us what other requirements besides the acceptance criteria of the user story itself we need to fulfill in order to be done with the story. We include the general requirements into the DoD because they affect all user stories in the end.

We can say that DoD is our primary quality document. If we do not fulfill what is in it, we do not deliver quality. It is essential that the PO and the team agree on the DoD. The DoD is part of the agreement between the team and the PO.

There should not be an argument over this concept during the project. If the PO thinks it is too costly to use pair programming or TDD, have the PO sign the DoD where you specify that these things have been removed. If at the end of a sprint the PO complains about the number of bugs, just present the document and say that the PO has removed essential parts of the testing and hence bugs will be present.

Agile Requirements and Estimation

This topic is huge, but important. We will cover some of the most important areas here and show you how they are implemented in TF Service. But if you want to master this, there are several training courses you can take and books you could read. The training from Mountain Goat Software is really good, and we recommend both their online training as well as their physical training. Check out http://www.mountaingoatsoftware.com for more information.

Most of the agile planning and estimation tips and tricks of this chapter come from the agile community but are not specific to scrum. Scrum really does not tell us how to do specific things like planning, estimation, and so on. Scrum is the process framework or process method we use for running our agile projects. However, scrum works excellent together with these concepts, which we will look at now.

Requirements

In agile projects, we usually represent our requirements in something called *user stories*. These can initially be viewed as fluffy requirements—a little bit like use cases actually. The higher into the backlog order they end up, the more they are broken down and specified, but initially they should always be written on a business level, not on a technical level. The reason for this is that the initial user stories are often captured by talking to stakeholders, end-users, businesspeople, and others who do not have to worry about technical implementation. We write user stories like this:

As a <type of user> I want <some functionality> so I may have <some business value>.

Another example would be:

As a manager I want my consultants to be able to send in expense reports through the Internet so that we can be more efficient in our expense report process.

Figure 2-2 shows how Microsoft has implemented the user story into the work item type Product Backlog Item. The terminology is a little different from my previous description, but it works.

Figure 2-2. *The user story implementation in the scrum template Microsoft provides with TF Service*

User stories capture requirements at a high level and will not get tangled up with detailed functions or implementation details. The details and nonfunctional requirements are instead captured as acceptance criteria for the user story. Based on these acceptance criteria, we can also develop acceptance tests at the same time we write the requirements.

The DoD is also important at this stage because it describes other important requirements all user stories need to fulfill before they are done. These requirements are not expressly included in a user story, but they affect the estimates of a user story because they must always be fulfilled.

So, how can we go ahead with gathering requirements before we start a project? The PO should use any method they think is suitable. We often use story-writing workshops where important stakeholders, end-users, business analysts, experienced developers, and others can participate to brainstorm the user stories they create. During such a workshop we focus on the big picture and do not dive into details. These big user stories are often called *epics* because they are big and not broken down into details yet.

In TF Service we can use the storyboarding features using PowerPoint as a base for discussing the flow of the software. The storyboarding features are a powerful way to take your ideas and goals and turn them into something visual that others can more easily understand, which gives you the opportunity to get more feedback from stakeholders and others sooner. This way you can graphically discuss the requirements with the customer without bothering with the technical implementation.

But don't we need to determine all of the requirements at the beginning? No. And that is what makes agile so great. The agile concept builds on acknowledgment that we don't know and cannot know all the requirements early in the project. New requirements and changes to early requirements will pop up throughout the process, and that is okay because the agile approach takes care of this for us. We start with what we have initially and continue handling requirements throughout the project. So the short version is to get started right away and be aware that changes and new requirements will come. It is essential that the PO is aware of this and can explain this to stakeholders and managers.

When the initial requirements are done, we have the embryo for the product backlog. However, before we can prioritize and estimate these user stories, we need to perform a risk assessment of them so we can get a grip on any risk associated with each and every one of them. A user story with a great risk associated with it usually takes more effort to finish and should probably be done early in development. The risk assessment is usually done at backlog grooming or at sprint planning so the PO can make decisions based on prioritization.

Estimation

In order to determine the effort that will be required for a user story, we need to estimate it. The sum of all initial estimates gives us a (very) rough estimate of how much time the whole project might take. But because we know things usually change over time, we do not take this estimate as if it were written in stone.

So, how do we do estimation? We have what we need to do this, we know the requirements, we have a DoD, and we have acceptance criteria. In the agile world it is recommended to estimate time in *story points*. Story points are not an exact size—instead they are relative.

Here is an easy example we use when running agile training. Take four animals, for instance: let's say a cat, a pig, a zebra, and an elephant. Without being a zoologist, most can say that the pig is three times the size of the cat, the zebra is twice the size of a pig, and the elephant is maybe four times the size of the zebra. If we sit down a couple of people and discuss these animal sizes, we will pretty soon come up with an agreement on their relative sizes.

The same goes for user stories. Most developers will come up with an agreement pretty quickly about the relative size of the user stories. User story A is twice as big as user story B, and so on. We do not need to be very experienced in the details of each user story to come up with this agreement. Novice developers usually end up with the same estimates as those who are experienced. Keep in mind that we are not talking exact time yet, only relative size.

The most common scale for expressing story points is a modified Fibonacci scale. This scale follows the following sequence: 1, 2, 3, 5, 8, 13, 20, 40, and 100. We could use other scales as well, but for us this works very well.

Very often teams use a technique called *planning poker* when doing estimates. The deck of cards each player has contains the numbers from the modified Fibonacci scale. Here is how it goes:

1. PO/SM reads the first user story.

2. The team briefly considers the user story and selects a card each, without showing it to the others.

3. The team members show their cards at the same time.

4. If the result varies much, those with the highest and lowest cards explain how they reasoned.

5. After a short discussion, the team plays again.

6. When consensus is reached (or the team members are only one step from one another), you are done.

7. If you still disagree, the team should pick the highest value.

Then someone asks "But what about time?" How can we get down to time? There are several things we need to know to estimate time. The first is the team capacity. Consider the following when calculating the team capacity:

- Howl ongi st hes print?

- How many working days are available in the sprint?

- How many days does each team member work during the sprint (minus planned vacation or other days off, planned meetings, and so on)?

- Deduct the time for sprint planning, review, or retrospective meetings.

- The result of this is the capacity before drag (*drag* is wasted time or unknown activities).

- We should measure drag in each sprint, but at the initial planning we really don't know how much we should calculate for. The longer the project, the more accurate the drag will be.

- If you don't know from experience what the drag is, 25 percent can be a good landmark. Included in this is 10 percent backlog grooming.

- Now we have the available number of hours in the sprint.

We now should connect points and time. We need to know the *team velocity*, which is the number of story points the team can handle in a sprint. Initially this is impossible to know. The easiest way to figure it out is to perform a sprint planning meeting. This is the meeting where the team breaks down a user story into manageable tasks. And this is where time becomes interesting. During this meeting the team estimates the tasks in hours so that it can plan the sprint and decide how many user stories it can take on in the sprint. This is usually the way team performs this:

1. Estimate the first user story in detail.

2. Break down what the team needs to do to deliver the story.

3. Estimate the hours for each task and summarize.

4. Deduct the summary from the available time the team has in the sprint.

5. Ist heres tillt ime left?

6. Take a new user story and repeat the process until no available time is left.

7. Summarize the number of story points from the stories that were included in the sprint.

8. Noww eh avea the oreticalve locity.

Now that we know the velocity of the team, we can make a rough time plan for the entire (at that point known) project. This is good input for the PO in their discussions with stakeholders and also input for ROI calculations.

The sprint planning process then continues throughout the project, and the theoretical velocity can soon be replaced with one based on experience instead.

Backlog

When the initial user stories are in place and estimated with story points, the PO can start prioritizing the backlog. In scrum this is called *ordering the backlog*. Based on the business needs, the PO makes sure that the order of the backlog reflects what the business wants. In Figure 2-3 we can see the initial backlog we used for writing a previous book. We did a rough estimate on each backlog item and then a velocity planning. After that we could see what backlog items should be completed during which sprint (two-week sprints were used).

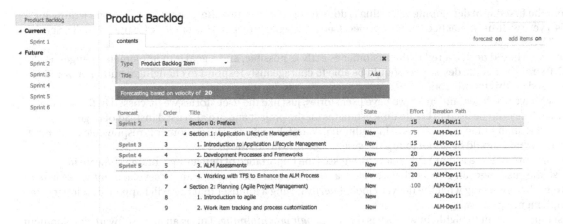

Figure 2-3. *The backlog we used for writing a previous book*

The PO needs to keep the backlog in good shape throughout the project. This means that it needs to be ordered. It also needs to have fine granularity at the top (maybe three or four sprints down the list) and rougher granularity farther down.

The PO can also start to look at release planning at this point. It is important to get an overview of coming releases in the project especially if you have a larger project. Release planning can be done on the epics (the larger user stories). A good way is to look for themes among the user stories. What could be useful to release at the same time? If we find such features, we could make a theme of it and plan the theme for a certain release. Keep in mind that release planning does not mean that a sprint should not deliver something. What is produced in the sprint should be potentially shippable. This does not mean it will be shipped after the sprint; however, it could very well be shipped in a specific release.

When this is done we could also do a very rough time estimate on the releases, and suddenly we also have a rough time plan for the project.

Now we have as much information as we could possibly ask for this early in a project. The next step will be the sprint planning meeting when the team (as we showed earlier) has a planning meeting and selects the backlog items it feels it can commit to during the sprint.

Agile Development Using eXtreme Programming

XP is a software development methodology for improving software quality and responsiveness to changes in customer requirements. XP is a flavor of agile software development and as such emphasizes frequent releases in short development cycles, just like scrum. This improves productivity and introduces checkpoints where new customer requirements can be adopted.

Most agile teams use some or all of the parts of the XP practices. XP is a deliberate and disciplined approach to software development. It stresses customer satisfaction, an important part of the agile manifesto. The methodology is designed to deliver the software the customer needs and do this when it is needed. XP focuses on responding to changing customer requirements, even late in the lifecycle, so that customer satisfaction (business value) is met.

XP also emphasizes teamwork. Managers, customers, and developers are all part of a team dedicated to delivering high-quality software. XP implements a simple and effective way to handle teamwork.

There are four ways XP improves software teamwork: communication, simplicity, feedback, and courage. Courage, by the way, is an interesting subject. It means don't be afraid to kill your darlings—in other words, be prepared to redo (refactor) what you have coded and be prepared to change what you have done after a review. It also means be prepared to be persistent and not give up. It is essential that XP programmers communicate with their customers and fellow programmers. The design should be simple and clean. Feedback is supplied by testing the software from the first day of development. Testing is done using TDD (writing the unit tests before even writing the code) and is a very well-used practice in many projects, not only agile projects. This book will explain how TF Service implements TDD.

The software should be delivered to the customer as early as possible, and a goal is to implement changes as suggested. XP stresses that the developers should be able to courageously respond to changing requirements and technology based on this foundation.

In RUP we have use cases, and in XP we have user stories, just like the user stories we discussed in the scrum sections earlier. They can be used to create time estimates for the project and are also used instead of large requirements' documentation, which we see in traditional waterfall projects. The customer is responsible for writing the user stories, which should be about things the system needs to do for the users.

Another important issue is that XP, like scrum, stresses the importance of delivering working software in increments so the customer can give feedback as early as possible and not have to wait for several months like in a waterfall project before seeing what the delivery looks like. By having a mindset that this will happen, developers are ready for implementing changes.

The last topic we want to highlight with XP is the use of *pair programming*. This is an agile software development technique where two developers work at one development computer; all code to be included in a production release is created by these two people on this one machine. One person, referred to as the *driver*, writes the code while the other, usually called the *observer* or navigator, reviews each line of code as the driver writes it. The two programmers switch roles frequently.

The observer considers the strategic direction of the work while observing, coming up with ideas for improvements and possible future problems to address. This enables the driver to focus all of their attention on completing the current task, using the observer as a safety net and guide. The aim is to increase software quality without impacting the time to delivery.

To learn more about XP, I encourage you to visit www.extremeprogramming.org.

CONTINUOUS INTEGRATION

There is also a very popular agile method called Continuous Integration (CI). CI is the practice of frequently integrating new or changed code into the existing code repository. By running automated unit tests at, for example, a build or a check-in, we can verify that existing code is not broken by the new or changed code. We can also run static and dynamic code tests as well as measure and profile the performance of our application or system. Using CI we can improve the quality of our software, which will facilitate our quality assurance process. CI will be discussed in detail in Chapters 15 and 16.

Agile Testing

One of the most important principles of agile testing is that testing is not a phase. It is something that is done continuously. Traditionally, testing has been a phase, often at the end of a project, but unfortunately often used as a buffer that was shortened when development took longer than expected.

In agile projects, testing requires all members of the team and testers to contribute with their special knowledge. Everyone, from the PO responsible for the backlog to the development team, is responsible for delivering the business value the organization wants. This means that testing and test case development should be part of everything from requirements (i.e., acceptance criteria in user stories) to coding. Testing and coding are done incrementally and iteratively, building up each feature until it provides enough value to be released into production.

Often agile teams use the Agile Testing Quadrants (Figure 2-4) to plan and execute their testing. Lisa Crispin's PDF document explains more about these quadrants (http://lisacrispin.com/downloads/AdpTestPlanning.pdf).

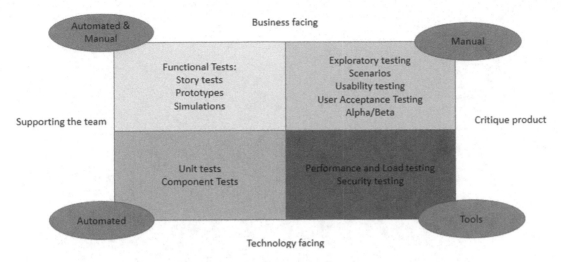

Figure 2-4. The Agile Testing Quadrants

The goal of this book is not to explain all these tests in detail. It suffices to say that TF Service supports a multitude of these tests, and we will explain how you can implement some of these in Chapters 19 and 20. Both automated tests and manual tests can be supported using TF Service.

Summary

This chapter has discussed many of the agile practices that influence modern software development. We have seen what agile project management using scrum looks like as well as how XP and agile testing affect development. Most agile practices aim to handle change during a project so we can better deliver high-quality software to our stakeholders.

Before we continue this topic in Chapter 5, the next two chapters cover the details of the hosted TF Service and how to get started using it. With that in place, in Chapter 5 we will explain how to start adding the user stories into the TF Service. We will also explain how to manage users and teams in a TF Service project, which is explained further in Chapter 6.

In Chapters 7 and 8 we will also explain how you can support the agile process during the sprint. We will explain not only how the PO benefits from the agile project management features of TF Service, but also how the SM and the team can use these features to enhance their work.

On to Chapter 3 and a discussion of why we should use a hosted TF Service instead of an on-premises one. We will discuss some pros and cons regarding the use of a service.

CHAPTER 3

■ ■ ■

Deciding on a Hosted Service

Whether you have already decided to use Team Foundation Service (TF Service) or are still in the process of making a decision about that, you need to understand the differences between hosted TF Service and an on-premises installation of Team Foundation Server (TFS). This chapter will help you understand the benefits and trade-offs with the hosted TF Service and assist you in making (or verifying) a decision whether to go with a hosted service.

As you might suspect, both Microsoft's hosted TF Service and a self-hosted on premises TFS installation each have their own benefits and drawbacks. If neither TF Service nor an on-premises TFS is suitable for you, there are other options for running TFS, ranging from other service providers to consulting firms offering both managed services and projects.

Why Use Microsoft Team Foundation Service?

Let's start by looking at the reasons for using TF Service.

Zero Friction Start

One of the first and most obvious advantages of a hosted service is the zero friction start. No investment decisions and no lead time for acquisitions and provisioning of environments or installation. With TF Service, it's just a couple of clicks and a few minutes time and you're ready to go.

Always On, Trouble-Free Operations

As a hosted service, Microsoft takes care of all operations and maintenance tasks, keeping the service alive and healthy. Microsoft will also make sure that the TF Service scales as your usage grows, provisioning resources as needed to scale out the TF Service. You don't need to worry about backups, emergency recovery testing, or patching. These are provided to you by a team focused on and dedicated to provide a good service 24/7.

Always Updated

One of the advantages (and perhaps risks) with TF Service is that Microsoft continuously deploys its newest features every 3 weeks. Not only does Microsoft deploy a new version of the services, they also take care of the upgrade process for you. This way you will always be running on the latest and greatest bits without having to do any planning or work for upgrades. If you want to provide the equivalent service for your on-premises TFS, Microsoft's current plan is to provide quarterly updates, and a major upgrade each year, so if you want to keep up with the releases, you need to plan for at least four updates each year.

Accessf or ExternalU sers

With the TF Service already in the Cloud and accessible from most places, it's very easy to add external parties and contributors, as long as they have, or can get, a Microsoft account (formerly known as Live ID).

Setting up an on-premises installation of Team Foundation Server and publishing it to external parties is in most organizations a lengthy and painful process, even if there is an extranet solution for external partners in place already. With TF Service you can add and mix contractors, customers, and your own staff as long as they have Internet access and a Microsoft Account.

On the other hand, what in some cases is a great advantage is in other cases a big disadvantage. TF Service will require all users to logon using their Microsoft Account, because there is still no ADFS (Active Directory Federation Services)i ntegration.

Builda sa Service

TF Service offers both a build as a service solution and the option to run your own on-premises build servers.

For the build as a service solution, Microsoft takes care of provisioning, installing, and running build servers for you, enabling you to always have a build server available within minutes, regardless of how many builds or projects you have.

Deploymentt o Azure

If your team is targeting an Azure environment, using TF Service gives you fast and easy deployment options. Microsoft integrates Azure web sites and TF Service to enable a quick and easy deployment using a prepackaged build-deployp rocess.

UseO n-Premiseso r CloudR esources

With TF Service you have, in most cases, the choice between using a Cloud resource or service or using your own on-premises resources. You can also combine them as you see fit for your needs. This is a very important advantage as using Cloud resources or services can eliminate adoption blockers fast and take care of the extreme situations when you don't want to reserve capabilities for your on-premise resources. The ability to use your own on-premises resources opens up the door to adapt the service to your organization's special needs.

Why Use an On-Premises Team Foundation Server?

Now let's examine reasons for hosting your own TFS installation. These will naturally exclude some drawbacks of TF Service that are not present in an on-premises TFS installation.

Customizations

The ability to adapt TFS to the process of a team or organization has always been one of the advantages with a Team Foundation Server. TFS on premises offers many customization points like:

1. Processt emplates

2. Buildt emplates

3. Modificationof w orkite mty pes

4. Servera ndc lients idee vents

5. TFSA PI

As with other capabilities, this capability has also been a trade-off when moving to a hosted service. The only customization option left in the hosted TF Service is to use the TFS API to connect and modify data in the TF Service. Because this is a potential deal breaker for many teams and organizations, Microsoft wants to offer some capabilities to modify and adopt their service to the team's process, but at the time of writing no real plans or features have been revealed.

LegalR equirementsa ndP olicies

Currently TF Service is only hosted in U.S.-based datacenters, which may be a problem for customers located in other countries, because of the current laws affecting Microsoft and the data stored by Microsoft inside the United States.

Microsoft has declared its intention to provide the option to select which datacenter your TF Service account should be hosted, but currently the only datacenter hosting TF Service data is located in the United States.

For example, within the European Union there are requirements that governmental data must reside within the European Union. There are also other legal requirements prohibiting data transfer to parties not meeting European standards for data protection.

The legal requirements and policies can be a direct deal breaker, so it is therefore important for you to take appropriate actions to investigate the requirements that affect you and to ensure if the TF Service is in compliance.

Identitiesa ndA uthentication

Having multiple sets of identities for an individual is not a dream for any organization. Adding yet another identity provider that needs to be managed adds extra costs, work, and security issues to organizations. Most organizations use Active Directory (AD) to manage their users and TFS on premises integrates directly with AD, which is a big advantage. Until TF Service can make use of the identities managed by organizations, most likely through Active Directory Federation Services (ADFS), an on-premises TFS installation is the only available choice for large-scale adoption in most organizations.

Controlo fO perations

Although having all operations activities magically taken care of by an external, focused professional team sounds like a dream, it still has drawbacks. One of them is control. With an on-premises TFS you have the option to add to or use your own services, apart from maintaining and keeping the services alive. You can control and manage backup routines to make them compliant with company policies.

A practical example of the benefit of controlling the operations is the ability to restore data in case of user errors. Let's say a user destroys a file or deletes a team project by "accident;" in the hosted TF Service that file is gone forever. In an on-premises situation, where you have control of operations, you have an option to recover the lost data. It might very well be too costly or too complex and require external help, but it's an option you have.

Migrationo fD ata

This is closely related to control of operations. For your on-premises TFS you can always export data to another TFS instance if needed without data loss. This can be useful if you need to ship some projects to another location or company. This could, for example, be useful in cases of outsourcing or acquisitions.

Unfortunately, currently this capability is not available with TF Service, although Microsoft has announced it is working on a solution. But for now, there is no simple way to get an existing project with history to, or even from, TF Service. What you can do is use the TFS integration platform to make a move, but it's a complicated process and it's does have some drawbacks like compressed history. You can of course take a snapshot of your code at any time.

Reporting

One of the strongest advantages with an integrated ALM platform is the ability to gather and report on different data from the lifecycle. This is still true for TFS on premises, but for the hosted TF Service there is no reporting solution in place. To compensate for this, Microsoft has built a few of the most common reports into web access of the hosted TF Service one of which is shown in Figure 3-1.

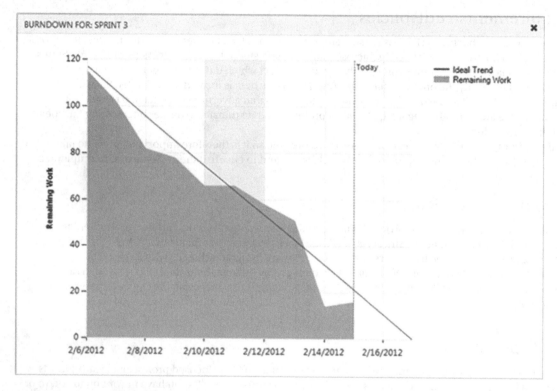

Figure 3-1. *Example of a built-in report*

This is an ongoing investment from Microsoft, but currently there are only a couple of those built-in reports. If you have need for deep or customized reporting, you should really think twice whether the hosted TF Service is right for you.

SharePoint

SharePoint, or rather SharePoint integration, is another feature of on-premises TFS that currently is not available in TF Service. This might not be a big deal to some customers, but it might be a key feature for other customers.

Dependenciest oL ocalE nvironments

If your system has strong dependencies to on-premises environments, it will be easier to do build-deploy-test workflows with an on-premises TFS deployment. It still might be possible to use TF Service, and perhaps to even build-deploy workflows, but you will face a number of barriers ranging from security to network speed.

If you plan to use TF Service and you do build and deploy to an on-premises environment, you need to investigate whether you will be able to get it to work and if it will be a reasonable path to follow.

Organization Dependent Factors

When you are trying to decide whether you should use TF Service or an on-premises TFS, there are some factors that will mainly depend on the situation of your organization. They will be the deciding factors as to whether you go with the hosted service or the on-premises services. These involve cost, organizational strategies, and security.

Cost

The total cost of the solution will most certainly be a motivator in your organization. The question is whether your organization will find the cost of TF Service favorable when compared to the cost of an on-premises TFS installation.

All of the details about Microsoft pricing are not know at the moment, but the ones that are known cover most organizations and make it fairly simple to calculate the direct cost for the TF Service. Calculating the direct cost for an on-premises TFS might be tricky for some organizations (and very simple at others).

There are also indirect costs, such as user administration and support, for both the TF Service and the on-premises hosted TFS. Those costs needs to be quantified and put into the equation and provide a fair basis for a decision.

OrganizationalS trategies

If your organization has a hosted or Cloud strategy, whether expressed or implied by actions, it might be a key factor for the decision about TF Service. If, for example, your organization moves to Office 365 (or other solutions), the factors behind that decision should be studied closely to determine whether it affects the TF Service decision.

Security

Putting all policies aside, security is or should be a very important capability for all organizations. Security is also a very large and complex topic that should ideally be analyzed both for the hosted TF Service and an on-premises TFS to provide a fair basis for a decision.

The Decision

Now that we've gone through the key advantages of both the TF Service and an on-premises TFS, it's time to weight them together and reach a decision. In some cases it might actually be a clear and easy decision to go all in on TF Service or a self-hosted on-premises TFS installation.

Other Hosting or Servicing Options

In most cases, this isn't a black or white decision, and for those real-life situations there are alternatives to be considered. One option is to look for other solutions that better match your needs. There are other hosting partners that offer a more customizable hosted TFS that could be suitable for your organization. You could also look for companies that provide TFS/ALM services, effectively buying TFS as a service, but hosted in your own environment.

Situation-BasedA pproach

You could also think about this decision through a situation-based approach. In which situations is the hosted TF Service right for a project?

Perhaps some projects with a very agile approach and high degree of external dependencies should be hosted on the TF Service, while your core enterprise applications with a large amount of internal decencies should be hosted on an on-premises TFS.

The situation-based approach will let you and your organization evaluate the best TFS solution for your needs. It is also a less drastic approach to the decision and might be the best model in the long term.

Summary

This chapter examined the different benefits and trade-offs with Microsoft's hosted Team Foundation Service. The TF Service is an excellent choice for a small, independent agile team, but currently it lacks some of the capabilities that might be required for large-scale enterprise use. Microsoft is hard at work to address these issues, so expect this to change in the near future.

Even if TF Service isn't right for you, it might be worth evaluating other TFS hosts or other service scenarios.

Looking at the hosted TF Service question from a situation-based approach is a less drastic approach and will probably allow you to evaluate the TF Service within a context for your organization so it makes sense.

The next chapter will take a closer look at how to get started using TF Service if you have decided to go ahead withthe hoste dT FS ervice.

CHAPTER 4

■ ■ ■

Getting Started

Once you have decided to use Microsoft's Team Foundation Service (TF Service), it's then time to create an TF Service account and get started. This chapter will guide you through the process of getting up and running with your project, including topics such as:

- Creating an TF Service account
- Creating a team project choosing process templates and source control system
- Invitingpe opleto j ointe am

Before You Begin

In order to use Microsoft's TF Service, you need to have a Microsoft account, formerly known as Windows Live ID. If you don't have a Microsoft account, you can sign up for one for free and then create your TF Service account. TF Service currently only supports Microsoft accounts as identities.

The next thing you need to do before creating a TF Service account is read and understand the pricing and license information for TF Services. At the time of writing, not all details are set, but Microsoft states that TF Services:

- Will be free for accounts with five users or less
- Unlimited number of team projects
- Will be included in most Microsoft Developer Network (MSDN) subscriptions (currently MSDN Test Professional, Premium, and Ultimate).

What Is a Team Foundation Service Account?

If you are experienced with Team Foundation Server on premises, it's quite simple: a TF Service account is in most aspects the equivalent of a Team Project Collection. In fact a TF Service account has one collection named DefaultCollection.

If you don't know what a Team Project Collection is, it's the repository or container for your TF Service account data. The structure for a Team Project Collection is shown in Figure 4-1.

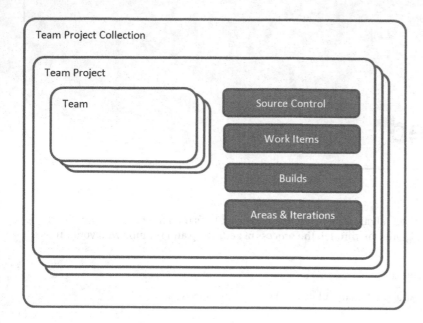

Figure 4-1. *The structure of a TF Service account*

- A *team project collection* is a repository or container for a number of team projects.

- A *team project* is a container for all definitions and instances for source control, requirements, tests, and builds. Each team project can have multiple teams.

- A *team* is a group of people who work together on a certain area of the team project's backlog. Each team has its own capacity, velocity and view of the team's backlog and virtual boards.

- *Areas* is used to break down the project into team or functional areas. Areas has a hierarchical structure that you can modify for your project.

- *Iterations* is used to break down the project in time, normally deliveries and iterations.

Namingt heA ccount

The first decision you need to make is what your TF Service account should be named. Because a TF Service account is at the top of the structure, it's probably a good thing to try to name it accordingly. If your account is used for the first pilot of your organization, naming it with the organization's name is a better idea than naming it with the project's name. It is possible to rename a TF Service account once it has been created, assuming the name is available, but it is associated with a lot of work for an ongoing project.

■ **Caution** Renaming a TF Service account will break existing links and force all users to change their environments. It's therefore advisable to make sure the account name will not change early in the process.

Creatingt heA ccount

Use the following steps to create a TF Service account:

1. Start you browser and browse to `https://tfs.visualstudio.com`.

2. On the Welcome screen, click Sign up for free, and you will be presented with the Account Creationp age,a ss howni nF igure 4-2.

Figure 4-2. *Account Creation page*

Type in the name you want for your account and click the Create Account button. If the account name isn't available, you will get an error message and it will ask you to try another name.

3. If the account name is available, the TF Service will start to create your account and show you the Creating Your Account page, as shown in Figure 4-3, during the process.

Figure 4-3. *Creating Your Account page*

4. A moment later your account is created and you're shown your account's home screen (Figure 4-4).

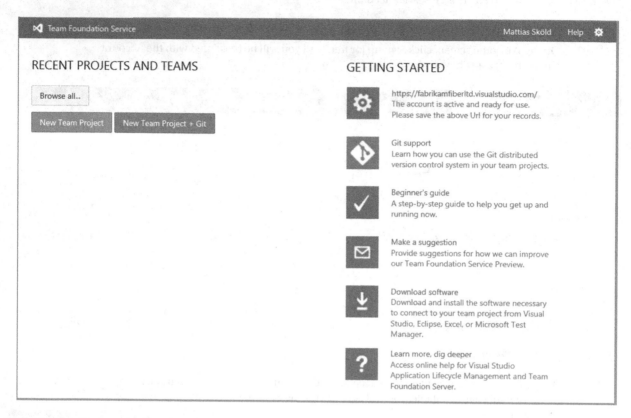

Figure 4-4. Your account home page

Now that you have created your account, you need to create a team project to associate with that account.

Creating Your First Team Project

When creating a new team project, you need to make three decisions that you can't change once you created your teamp roject:

- Nameo ft hep roject
- Type of version control repository
- Processt emplate

You create a new team project by clicking one of the buttons on the account home page (as shown in Figure 4-4):

- NewT eamP roject
- NewT eamP roject+ G it

■ **Note**   Both the buttons take you to the same page, but with the selected choice of source control system selected.

You're then presented with the page as shown in Figure 4-5, with your choice of version control system set (you can still change your mind at this stage).

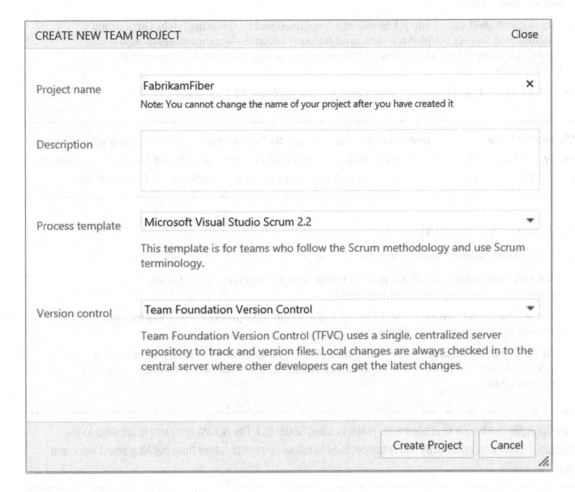

CREATE NEW TEAM PROJECT	Close

Project name   FabrikamFiber   ✕

Note: You cannot change the name of your project after you have created it

Description

Process template   Microsoft Visual Studio Scrum 2.2   ▼

This template is for teams who follow the Scrum methodology and use Scrum terminology.

Version control   Team Foundation Version Control   ▼

Team Foundation Version Control (TFVC) uses a single, centralized server repository to track and version files. Local changes are always checked in to the central server where other developers can get the latest changes.

Create Project   Cancel

Figure 4-5. Create new team project page

Now let's see what's involved in each of the three decisions shown in Figure 4-5.

Selecting the Name of the Team Project

Then deciding on a name for your new team project it's important to remember that you can't change the name latero n.

Selecting Type of Version Control Repository

TF Service offers two different kind of source control systems:

- Team Foundation Version Control (TFVC) is a centralized source control system that was developed for a controlled enterprise environment and offers good features for defined teams following a common process. Visual Studio and Eclipse offer a great integrated experience for working with TFVC.

- Git is a distributed source control system that has gained much popularity lately. Git is strong in distributed, loosely coupled scenarios and supports advanced workflows regarding source control. Git is supported across most platforms and integrates with XCode, Eclipse, and VisualS tudio.

For more information about choosing a source control system, please refer to Chapter 11.

■ **Note**   Microsoft is in the process of developing first-class support for Git in its tooling, including integration in Visual Studio. Currently, Git is only available in TF Service (not in the on-premises product), and offered as a Preview extension in Visual Studio 2012. Git integration will be part of the next major release of Visual Studio and TFS on premises.

SelectingP rocessT emplate

TF Service offers three development process templates:

- Microsoft Visual Studio Scrum is a process template for those following the Scrum methodology and using the Scrum terminology.

- Microsoft Solution Framework (MSF) for Agile is a flexible agile process that works for most teams doing agile planning and development.

- MSF for Capability Maturity Model Integration (CMMI) Process Improvement is a process for formal projects with requirements to provide auditable decisions and a framework for process improvements.

■ **Note**   MSF for Agile can be the best choice for projects doing ScrumBut. The Scrum template is adopted to the Scrum methodology and focus on velocity and retrospectives to follow up results rather than tracking spent work and doing prognosis.

Once you have decided, type the name and select the process template and type of version control and click the Create Project button.

You'll see the screen shown in Figure 4-6, which monitors the progress of your team project creation.

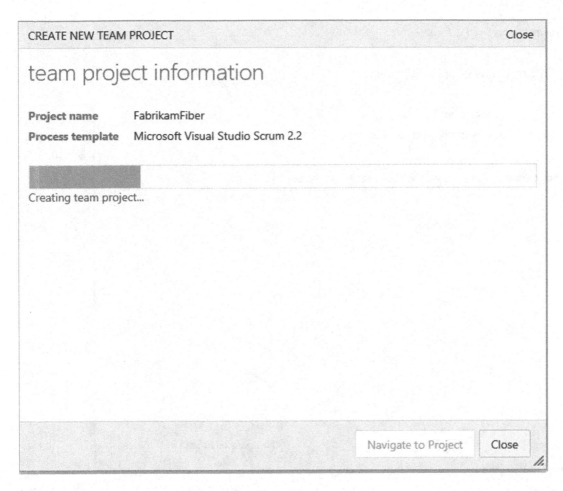

Figure 4-6. *Team project creation progress window*

In a moment your new project will be ready, and once the project is created, you'll see the screen shown inF igure 4-7.

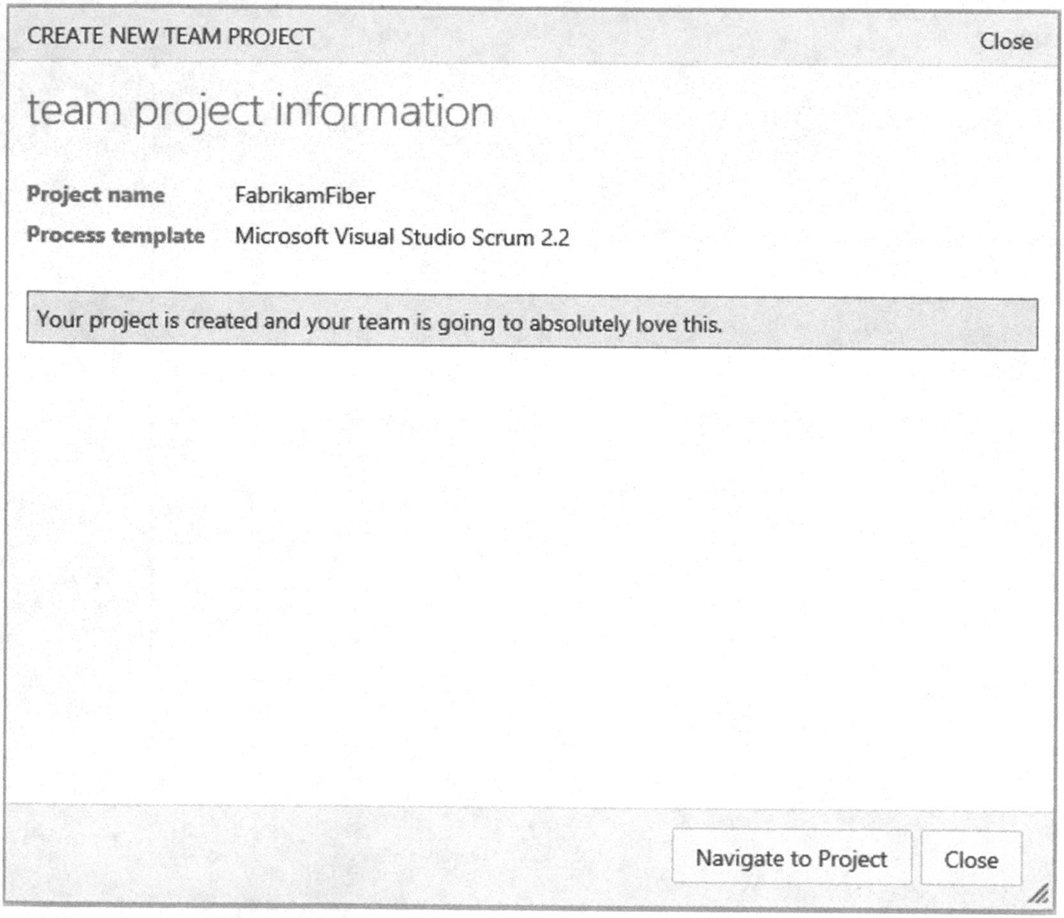

CREATE NEW TEAM PROJECT   Close

team project information

Project name   FabrikamFiber

Process template   Microsoft Visual Studio Scrum 2.2

Your project is created and your team is going to absolutely love this.

Navigate to Project   Close

Figure 4-7. *Team project created message*

You can navigate to your new project by clicking the Navigate to Project button, which will take you to your new teampr ojecthom epa ge,a ss howninF igure 4-8.

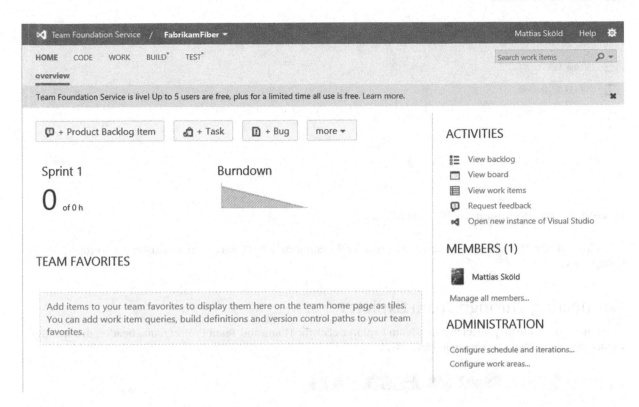

Figure 4-8. *Home page of your new team project*

Connecting to Your Team Project

One of the first things you might want to do is open your new team project in Visual Studio and take a peek at your new project. Team Explorer is the central place where most TF Service -related operations start. The Team Explorer view is built up with Sections and Pages, and it is built dynamically based on the installed capabilities of your Visual Studio, TF Service, and team project capabilities. For example, the Team Explorer window connected to a team project with TFVC as the source control system looks different from a team project with Git as the source control system.

QuickC onnect

To quickly connect to your team project you can simply click the Open new instance of Visual Studio link in your team project home page, as shown in Figure 4-9.

ACTIVITIES

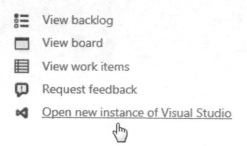

- View backlog
- View board
- View work items
- Request feedback
- Open new instance of Visual Studio

Figure 4-9. *Open new instance of Visual Studio link*

This will start Visual Studio, automatically register the connection to TF Service and connect you to your teamp roject.

Connecting Through Team Explorer

To connect to your team project through Team Explorer, click the Home and Team Project name header; this will give you a drop-down menu, as shown in Figure 4-10.

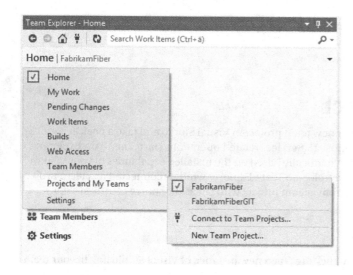

Figure 4-10. *Connecting to a team project*

If you have previously connected to a team project on the current server, it will appear in the list and you can select it directly. If you haven't connected to a TFS server or if you need to connect to team projects on another server, click the Connect to Team Projects menu. That will take you to the Connect page, as shown in Figure 4-11.

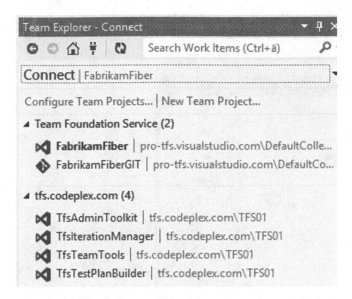

Figure 4-11. *Connect page*

In the Connect page, you can see your recently used team projects grouped by servers. You can also identify which team projects have TFVC as their source control system by looking at the icon to the left of the project name, as shown in Figure 4-11. Team Projects with TFVC repositories have the Visual Studio icon.

You can also add projects or connect to a new server by clicking the Configure Team Projects link. It will show you the Connect to Team Foundation dialog box, as shown in Figure 4-12. In this menu you can select which team project you want to connect to on the selected server.

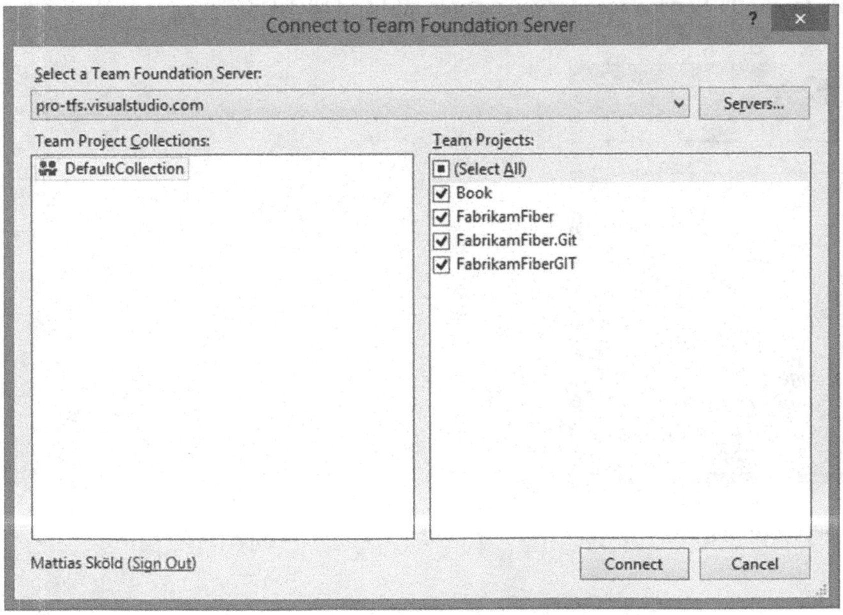

Figure 4-12. *Connect to Team Foundation Server dialog box*

CHAPTER 4 ■ GETTING STARTED

You can change the server you're connecting to by changing the selection in the Select a Team Foundation Server drop-down menu. To connect to a new server, click the Servers button, which will show you the list of available servers, as shown in Figure 4-13.

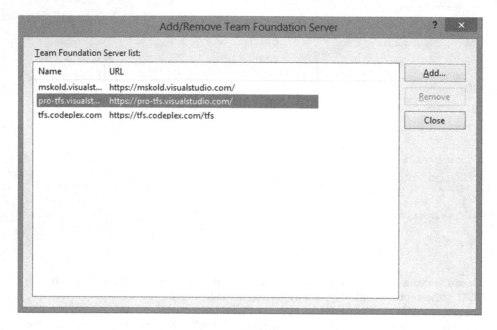

Figure 4-13. *Add/Remove Team Foundation Server dialog box*

If you want to add a new server, click the Add button. This will show the Add Team Foundation Server form, as shown in Figure 4-14. Type the URL for the TF Service account you want to add and click OK.

Figure 4-14. *Add Team Foundation Server dialog box*

Once you have connected to the server and selected the team projects you want, they will appear in the list of servers and projects on the Connect page (Figure 4-11).

You can now connect to your team project simply by clicking its name. Note that when doing this, Visual Studio will close any open solutions that are connected to the currently selected team project.

Moving into Your Project

By default a new *team* is created in your new project (the team being a group of people who can work on the project). A team project can have multiple teams if you like, and a user can be part of multiple teams. Each team works on a part of the team project's backlog defined by the Area field, which identifies which team a specific requirement or task belongs to.

InvitingP eople

You can invite other people to join your team by clicking the Manage all members link on the Team Start page. You will be taken to the screen shown in Figure 4-15.

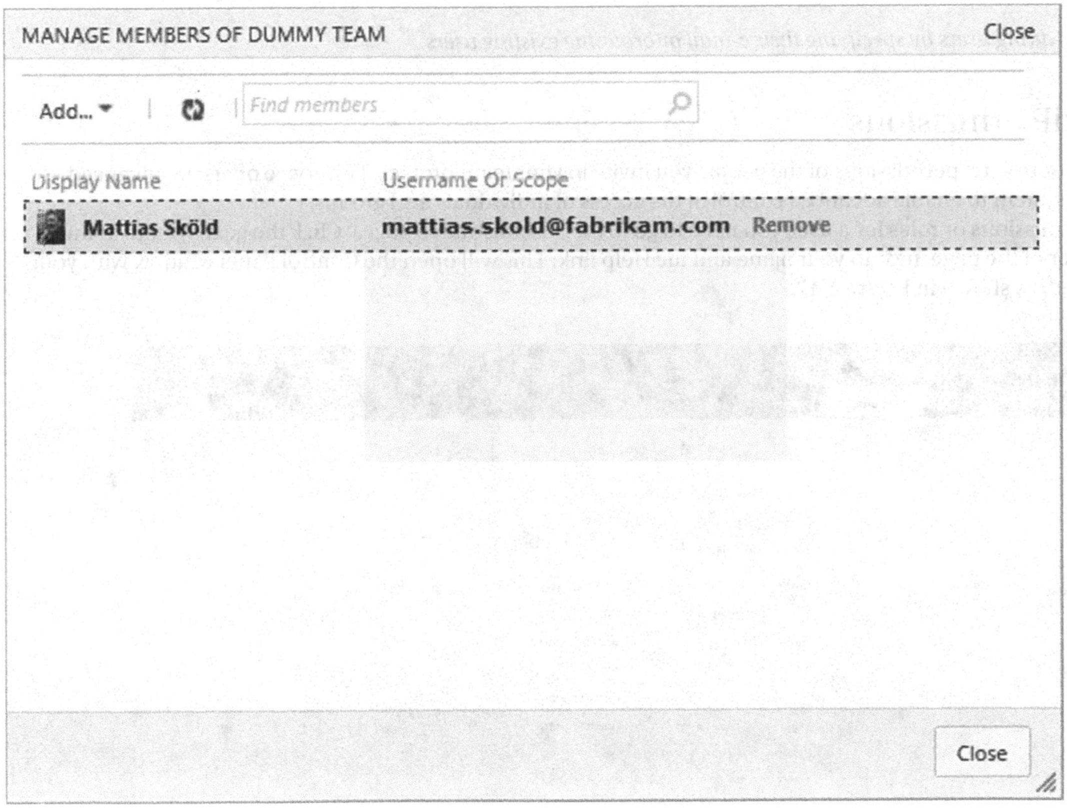

```
MANAGE MEMBERS OF DUMMY TEAM                                      Close

  Add... ▼    |    ⟳    | Find members                         🔍

  Display Name                Username Or Scope
  👤 Mattias Sköld            mattias.skold@fabrikam.com   Remove




                                                              Close
```

Figure 4-15. Manage team members window

Then click Add ➤ Add User to add a new person by submitting the e-mail address for their Microsoft account, or you can search to add an existing user of your TF Account to a new team, as shown in Figure 4-16. You can also use the Browse link or use the drop-down menu to show the existing members of your TF Service account.

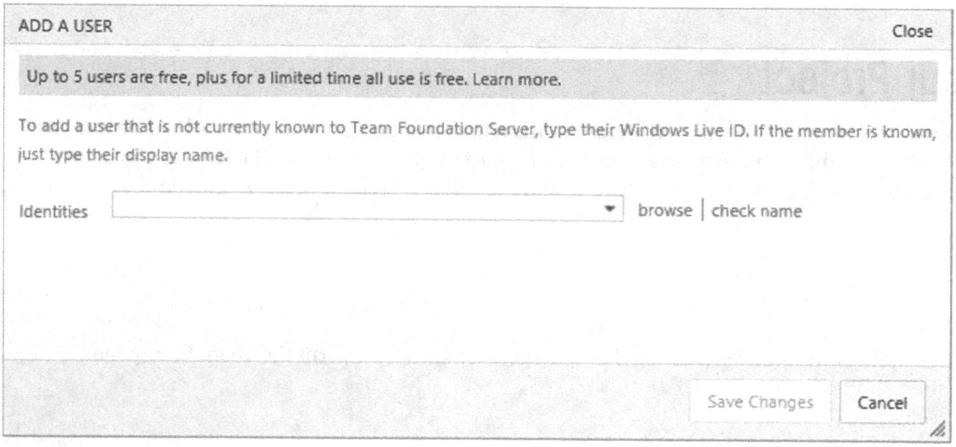

Figure 4-16. *Adding users by specifying their e-mail or browsing existing users*

Rolesa ndP ermissions

You can also control the permissions of the people you invite to your team project. TF Service offers an advanced authorization system to enable advanced control of the access of individuals and groups.

To set permissions or roles for a user, you need to go to the administrative pages. Click the gear symbol at the top right corner of the page, next to your name and the Help link. This will open the Control Panel window with your project selected, as shown in Figure 4-17.

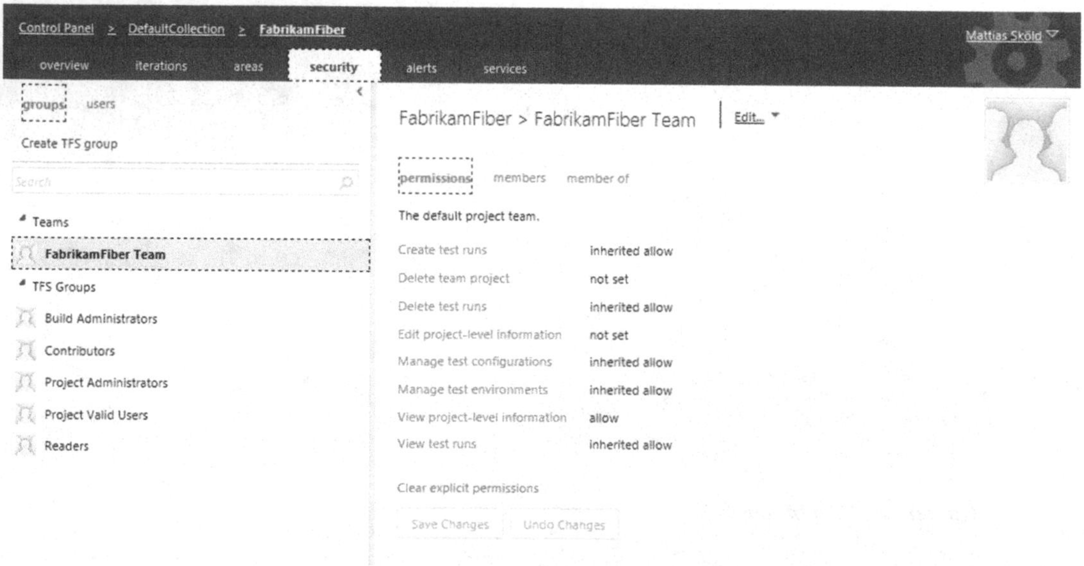

Figure 4-17. *TF Service Control Panel showing the project's security page*

■ **Note**   The Control Panel is the place where you manage the settings for your TF Service account. It will launch the Account, Collection, or Project level, depending on the context from which it was launched.

On the Security tab, you can choose if you want to work with roles in the form of TFS groups or if you want to view or work with individual user's permissions.

You can grant users access either by adding the user to a group or by setting permissions directly on a user. To do so, navigate to the Users tab and click a user's name, and then change the permission directly.

For more information about permissions and how to manage the team, please refer to Chapter 6.

Summary

This chapter has guided you through the steps of creating your Microsoft account, creating your first team project, and connecting to it with Visual Studio. We also showed you how you can invite other people to join your team project.

The next chapter will take a closer look at how to get started with agile planning in TF Service.

CHAPTER 5

■ ■ ■

Working with the Initial Product Backlog

In this chapter we will complete the startup of an agile project using TF Service. Many of the concepts covered in Chapter 3 are exemplified in this chapter, so you can see how we move from planning to implementation. We also look at how TF Service can support the agile project management process during sprints.

In this chapter and throughout the rest of the book, we will use a fictitious company in our examples. This way we use a common denominator in the things we present so we can more easily understand the process and how TF Service supports our development organization.

This chapter focuses on the project management parts of a project. Support for agile development practices such as continuous integration, test-driven development, test automation, and so on will be explained in subsequent chapters.

The main part of this chapter is written from the perspective of the PO, whom we will meet shortly. There will be a personal touch on some parts. The reason for this is because part of a project focuses so much on collaboration and interaction between people.

Case Study

Let's start with the company we will use as an example. Any similarities to real companies are totally unintentional.

Company Background

Fabrikam Fiber is a cable television provider in the United States. They are growing rapidly and are using Windows Azure to scale their customer-facing web site; this will allow end users to use a self-service ticket system and a technician tracking system. They also use an on-premises ASP.NET MVC application for their customer service representatives to administer customer orders.

Fabrikam development manager, Cindy Crafoord, has decided to implement a pilot project using the ALM features of TF Service to bridge the gap between what they have today and what they can benefit from in TF Service. If the pilot is successful, Fabrikam will migrate all its development to the TF Service platform.

Cindy and Bob Peak (the IT manager) have decided to use Scrum as the preferred project management method, and the developers agree on using XP practices to enhance the quality of the software and therefore increase business value to the company.

ThePilotPr oject

The project Fabrikam has decided to use as a pilot for the ALM implementation is an expense reporting application (Fabrikam Expense Reporting). In the early days, expenses were handled easily by the administrative staff, but since the company has grown quickly and salespeople are located and traveling all over the United States, things have become a little more complicated. The admin staff wants an application that will make their jobs easier and at the same time make sure employees will get reimbursement for expenses quickly. The requirements for this application are covered in the section "Requirements" later in this chapter.

Because this project will be using Scrum as a project management process, Cindy and Bob have appointed Fiona Gallos as PO for the application. Fiona has only been working with Fabrikam for six months. She is experienced as a PO because her previous employer used Scrum extensively. Fiona also has PO certification from both Scrum Alliance and scrum.org.

Important stakeholders for the project are Bob Peak, Cindy Crafoord, and Karen Guckenheimer. Karen is manager for the admin department and will represent the end users as well as the admin organization. Because the project aims to be a pilot program for an ALM implementation, Dave Applemust from the infrastructure side and Harry Bryan from the development organization are also considered important stakeholders.

TheP eople

- AliceM iller,C EO
- Bob Peak,I Tm anager
- CindyCr afoord,de velopmentm anager
- KarenG uckenheimer,a dminm anager
- DaveA pplemust,i nfrastructures pecialist
- Eric Parrot, businessa nalyst
- FionaG allos,p roducto wner
- GuillioP eters,S crumm aster
- HarryB ryan,s eniord eveloper
- MikaelP ersbrandt,d eveloper
- Petter Ivarsson, user experience (UX)
- IngridS vensson, seniort ester

Scrum Process Template

Before we follow Fiona as she begins this project, we want to have a look at the Scrum Process Template. This template is supplied out of the box by Microsoft and is a good implementation of Scrum. We will use this template for our sample project (Fabrikam Expense Reporting) in this book.

WorkI tems

There are five work item types in the Scrum template (Figure 5-1):

- *Bug*: Self-explanatory perhaps, but this is used to report bugs.

- *Impediment*: Based on the outcome of the daily Scrum, we may have one or more impediments blocking the team or a team member. This work item type is used for thei mpediments.

- *Product backlog item*: All requirements should be in a user-story format and this work item type is used to document them.

- *Task*: This could be anything that needs to be done. If we use PBIs for user stories, we could use tasks for all detailed work that needs to be done to solve the user story based on the outcome of the sprint planning meeting.

- *Test case*: Just what it sounds like. Use these for documenting your test cases. They can also be linked directly to a user story so that we can have traceability from story to test.

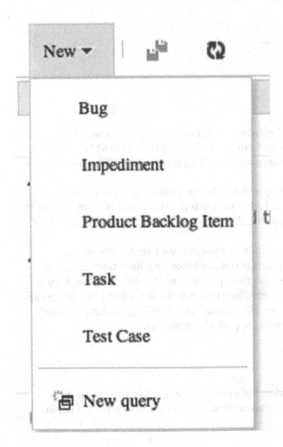

Figure 5-1. *The five work item types in the Scrum template*

TF Service Web Access

A TF Service web access portal is created for all new TF Service projects (Figure 5-2).

Figure 5-2. *TF Service web access*

We can use the TF Service web access if we want to let nontechnical users add reports of bugs or new PBIs. From this we can view reports, create new work items, view builds, and much more. Often the PO or SM prefers to use the portal so he or she doesn't have to use Visual Studio to access these features. If we have a PO or SM who prefers a Mac, web access is the best way to access the power of TF Service.

We can set access control for the web access in Settings for the project. By controlling the access to the portal, we can let certain users or groups of users only see (and do) what we want them to see. This way we can let customers (if we are consultants) into TF Service with limited functionality. The portal is great for different kinds of collaboration.

In the web access we can find quick links to important information in our project. We can directly see the burndown chart for the current sprint. We can also see how many hours of our available time have been assigned to a story. Team Favorites is a customizable placeholder that we can use to display the information we want for our team. We can add information here about our builds, bugs, impediments, and much more so we can provide a good overview for team members and stakeholders alike. Below Activities we find links to the backlog, the Scrum board, work items, and so on. We can also see a list of the team members who are part of our project.

Chartsa ndQ ueries

There are a few out-of-the-box charts with the templates in TF Service. Let's just say that the burndown chart (Figure 5-3) is maybe the most common status report used. The burndown shows how many hours are still left in the sprint and is useful to determine if we are on track.

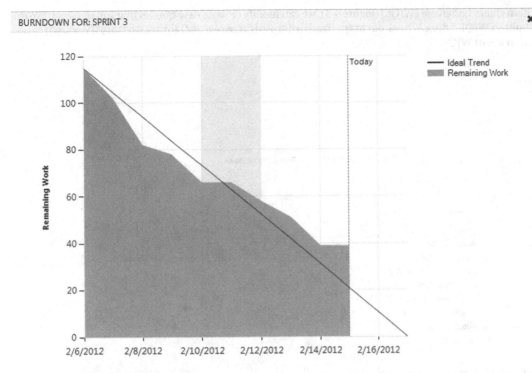

Figure 5-3. *The burndown chart*

There are also queries we can use to retrieve information from TF Service: One query that is always supplied in the Scrum template is the "Assigned to me" query (Figure 5-4), which shows all of the work items assigned to me.

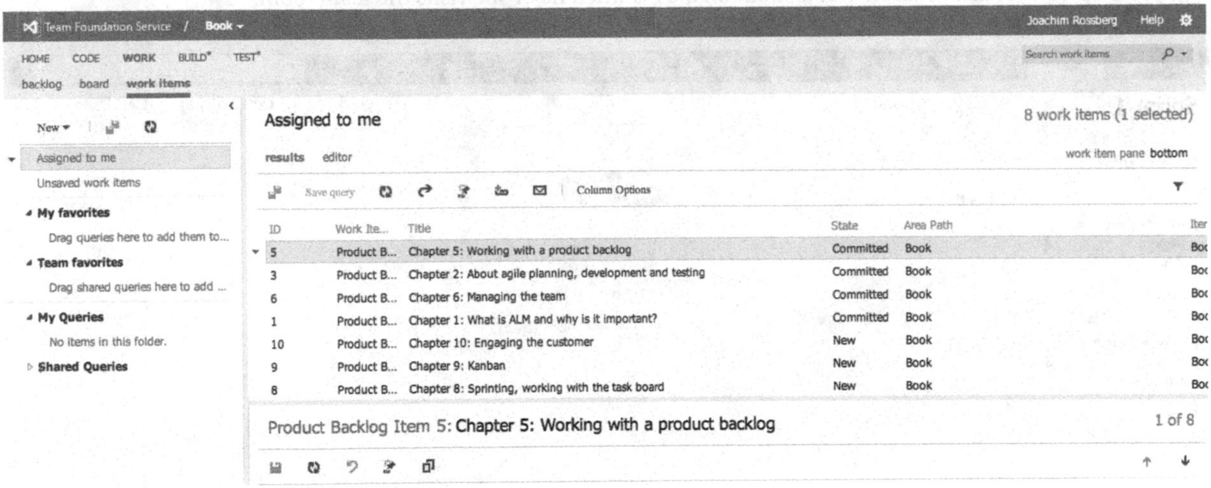

Figure 5-4. *The Assigned to me query in TF Service*

Using Work Item Query Language (WIQL) (Figure 5-5), we can modify or write new queries that suit us better. We do this by using the built-in WIQL Editor. Check out `http://msdn.microsoft.com/en-us/library/bb130198(v=vs.90).aspx` for more information about WIQL.

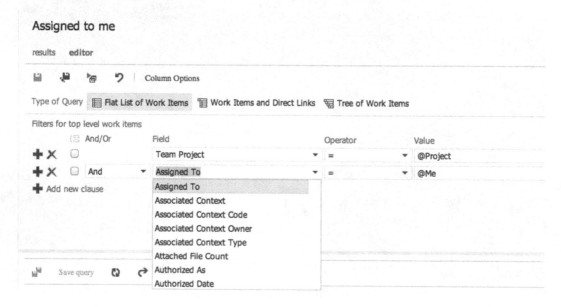

Figure 5-5. *Modifying the Assigned to me query in TF Service*

Another nice addition to TF Service is the possibility of having an electronic task board showing the state of the work items on the sprint backlog (Figure 5-6). Here we can see what has been done, what is in progress, and so on, instead of using sticky notes on a wall! Having a big screen on the wall that shows progress provides all of the team members up-to-date information, not to mention the PO when he or she visits the team room.

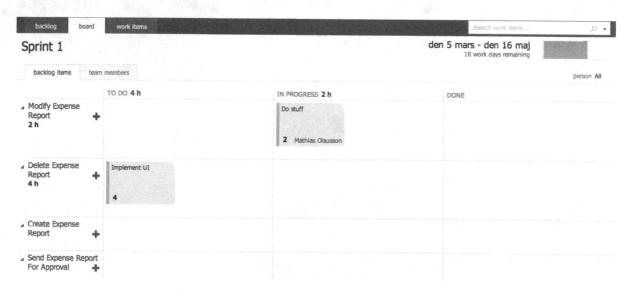

Figure 5-6. *The task board showing sprint backlog items and their status in TF Service*

There is also a new board in TF Service; the Kanban board. In Chapter 9 we will have a look at both Kanban and the Kanban board.

Project Startup Phase

This section follows the PO, Fiona Gallos, during the startup phase of the project. We will see how TF Service is used to insert the information Fiona collects during this phase.

PO Sets Off to Work

The idea for this project started when Fabrikam noticed that bug fixes created new bugs and that the new bugs sometimes appeared in parts of the system considered not to be affected by the original bug fix. Fabrikam soon realized it lacked traceability and had no way of knowing where a bug fix would have its impact besides the actual code change.

Fiona had just attended a conference and learned a great deal about ALM and TF Service. She came up with the idea of getting a better grip on the ALM process and at the same time started using agile practices at Fabrikam. Both of these efforts would greatly improve things at Fabrikam so it could avoid embarrassing situations such as when customers found new bugs that had been caused by bug fixes.

At the same time, Fiona saw that collaboration between the two developer teams could improve if they started to use TF Service. Fiona wrote down a business case and presented it to the management team. After a few discussions they agreed to try this on a pilot project. Because the expense report project was in the pipeline, they decided to use it for the pilot.

At this point it was hard to calculate ROI, but anything that could improve how the customers viewed them would be worth going for.

Building the Initial Team

It is recommended that the PO starts with a small team during initial planning of the project. Fiona selected Cindy Crafoord, Harry Bryan, and Eric Parrot because they were experienced within the company and were also senior members with experience from other companies as well. They were also available for the whole pilot project, which was an important aspect for Fiona. She knew the importance of having consistency among the team members during a project. Guillio Peters would be the SM for the entire project. The rest of the team would be selected a bit later in the project.

Fiona created the project in TF Service (Figure 5-7) from the web portal using the Scrum template. She named it Fabrikam Pilot, chose Scrum 2.2, and also Team Foundation Version Control. They had discussed which version control to use, Git or Team Foundation Version Control, and decided to go for the latter.

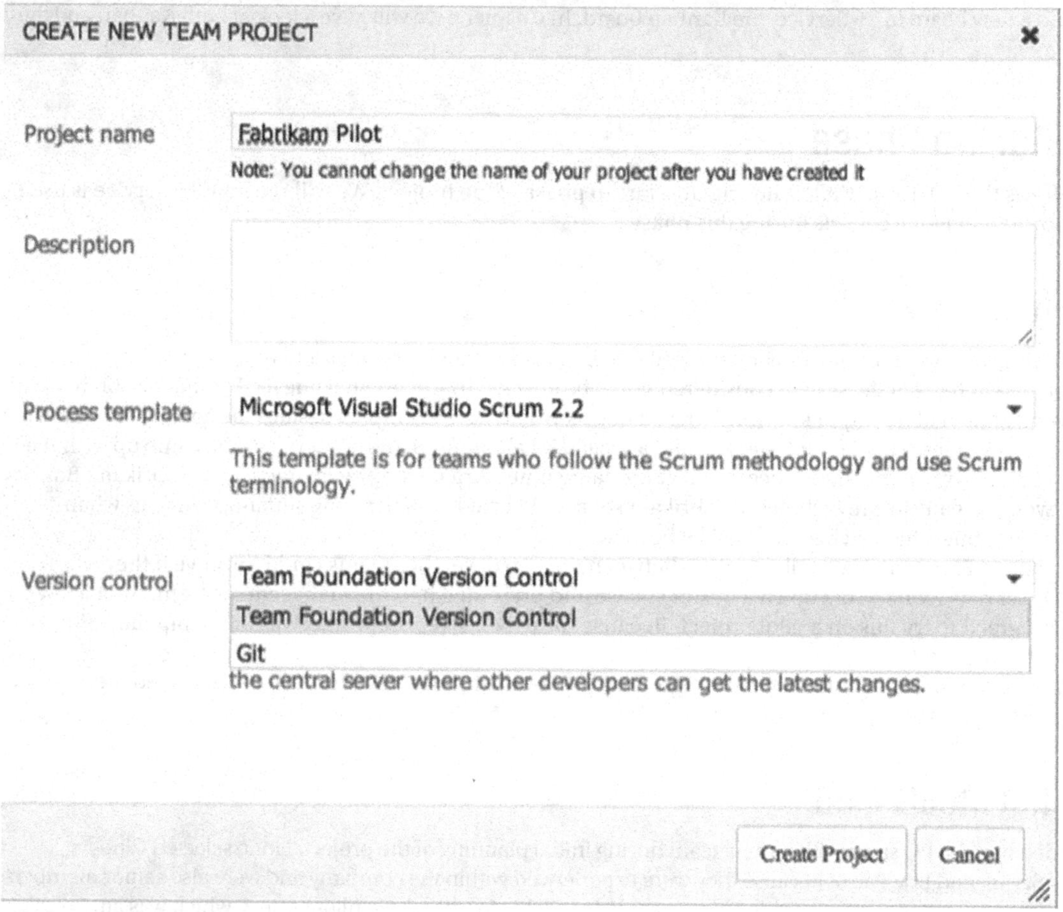

| CREATE NEW TEAM PROJECT | ✖ |

Project name   Fabrikam Pilot

Note: You cannot change the name of your project after you have created it

Description

Process template   Microsoft Visual Studio Scrum 2.2   ▼

This template is for teams who follow the Scrum methodology and use Scrum terminology.

Version control   Team Foundation Version Control   ▼

Team Foundation Version Control

Git

the central server where other developers can get the latest changes.

Create Project   Cancel

Figure 5-7. *Creating the Fabrikam pilot project in TF Service*

Then she started to add the users to the project (Figure 5-8).

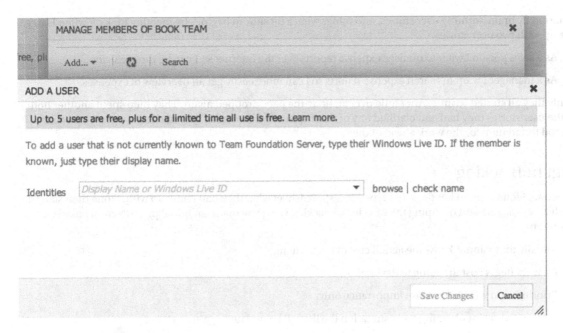

Figure 5-8. *Adding users to the project*

After adding the users and creating the TF Service project, Fiona was ready to go. She had what was necessary to start requirements' gathering.

Requirements

Requirements gathering was the fun part of the project in Fiona's eyes. Discussions with traditional project managers and stakeholders about requirements always came up, and she enjoyed that. Traditionally all requirements had to be determined at the beginning of the project, and it was hard for many to accept that it is okay to start a project even without specifying everything. The fact that so many of these requirements were wrong or unnecessary in the end didn't seem to bother traditionalists. They still went head first into projects that often failed or were flawed.

Fiona had run so many successful agile projects she knew that catching higher-level requirements in the beginning was okay. They could start without all of the details because they would be clarified at each sprint planning meeting and also during the sprints.

Fiona called the initial team together for a requirements workshop. She also added Karen Guckenheimer to the workshop because she was one of the main stakeholders from the business side. Because Guillio (SM) was not present, Fiona explained what they were going to do. She stressed that they should look for higher-level requirements in the sense that they did not have to detail them yet. There would not be any discussions about solutions or technicalities at this point. That would be left for the development team to decide when the sprints started.

To avoid any confusion, she then explained the concept of a user story for the requirements team. Fiona wanted all requirements in this form:

As a <type of user>, I want <some goal> so that <some reason>.

Fiona had calculated three hours for this meeting and booked a room with a large whiteboard. She also supplied sticky notes and pens for everyone.

They started by brainstorming user stories, and things were a bit slow to begin. The meeting took off when Harry Bryan came up with two user stories:

- As a sales person I want to manage expense reports over the Internet so I can be more efficient.

- As a manager I want to search expense reports so I can more easily get an overview of expenses.

Suddenly they all started writing. After little over an hour, the pace dropped again. They then spent another hour going over the user stories they had and clarified any of them as needed. Fiona felt they had done a great job so far and had a good foundation for the work ahead of them.

Buildingt heB acklog

After the meeting, Fiona went to her desk and typed in a spreadsheet what they had come up with. Fiona then started to order the list by dragging and dropping the PBIs in the backlog view. She made an initial prioritization based on some assumptions:

- Initially they cannot know the actual cost of a work item.

- All work items cost the same to develop.

- Prioritization will be based on importance only.

- After initial sprint planning and estimation the list will be updated again.

It took Fiona roughly 30 minutes to complete the initial sorting. Now she really had something to start with. It was still early afternoon and she wanted to add the user stories to TF Service before going home for the day.

AddingB acklogI temsi nT FS ervice

Fiona opened the project web access in Safari and felt a little bit of excitement as she saw the empty project that soon would be filled with activities. She had lots of input for the backlog.

She took a long look at the results of the initial story writing workshop she had in front of her and started by going to the Work Items tab on the web page (Figure 5-9). She could have gone to the Backlog tab, which has a quick-add feature for adding work items (Figure 5-10) that can be turned on or off.

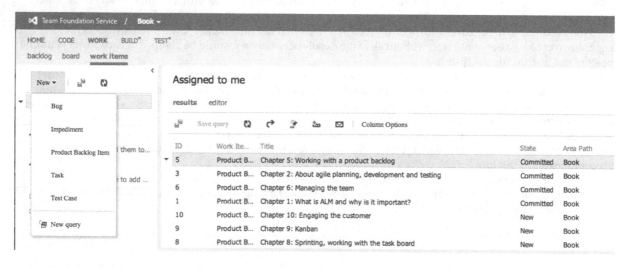

Figure 5-9. The Work Items tab

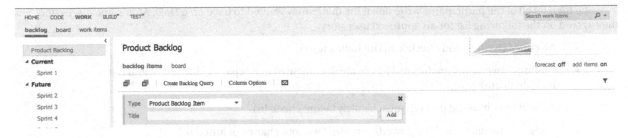

Figure 5-10. *Adding a PBI from the Backlog tab using the quick-add feature*

From the drop-down menu on the left she selected New ➤ Product Backlog Item. This opened the form shown in Figure 5-11. If Fiona had created a backlog item from the Backlog tab using the quick-add feature, the new backlog item would have ended up at the top of the backlog. Fiona would have had to click it and then she would have had the work item form seen in Figure 5-11.

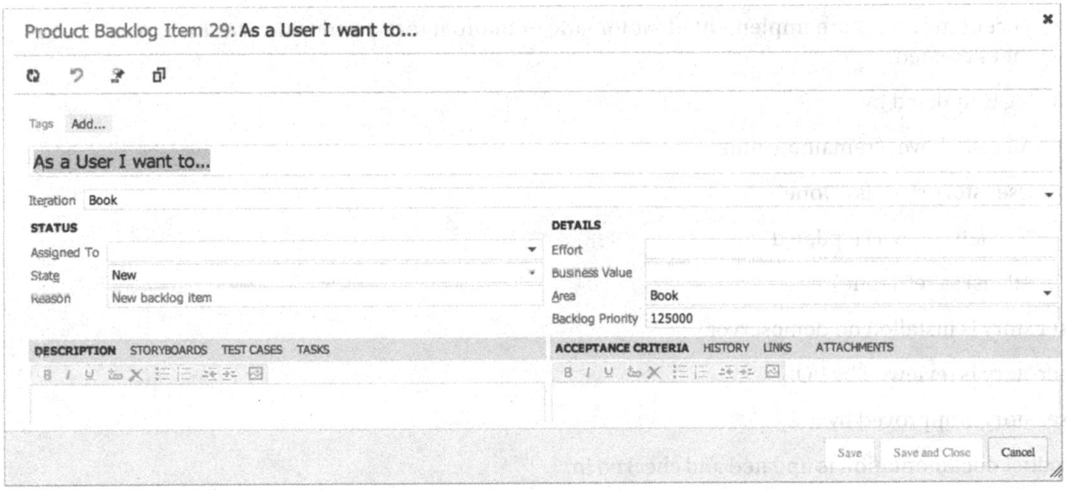

Figure 5-11. *The first PBI*

She took the first PBI on her backlog and started filling in the fields. She left a lot as it was for now and only filled in the PBI name and description.

Fiona then continued with the rest of the higher-level use cases until they were all in the TF Service.

Definitiono fD one

Before going home that day Fiona set up a date for a new meeting with the team to establish DoD. She included infrastructure specialist Dave Applemust for this meeting as there are constraints from the infrastructure team when building and deploying new projects.

She wanted to discuss the DoD so that they all had a common view on this before starting the actual coding. Many times she had experienced problems when a DoD was not in place for a project, so she knew this was important.

Two days later they met for the DoD meeting. Fiona explained the importance of this concept and spoke about issues she had experienced when there was no DoD. There were nods of recognition among the participants as she spoke.

She then let all of the participants write down the things they wanted to have on a DoD. After some discussion, they agreed on the following list for an approved user story:

- All code is written and checked in (including tests).

- Coding conventions are fulfilled (these are documented in a separate document and not includedh ere).

- All unit tests must be passed (must be okay before check-in).

- Code is to be refactored (improved/optimized without change of function).

- All code must be reviewed by at least two people (peer programming or peer review).

- The user story is included in the build (build scripts updated, all new modules included).

- The user story is installable (build scripts updated so that story is included in the automatic install).

- All acceptance tests are passed:

  - Acceptancec riteriam uste xist.

  - Acceptance tests are implemented (automatic or manual tests) and test cases for them created.

- Backlog is updated by:

  - All tasks have a remaining time = 0

  - User story state is "Done"

  - "ActualH ours"i su pdated

  - Allt asksa re" Done"

- User story is installed on demoserver.

- User story is reviewed by PO.

- User story is approved by PO.

- Product documentation is updated and checked in.

- Userm anuali sw ritten.

- Administrativem anuali su pdated.

- Helpt extsh aveb eenw ritten.

The team also came up with the following DoD for when the sprint is approved:

- All user stories in the sprint fulfill the DoD.

- Product is versioned (release management/rollback).

- All accepted bugs are corrected.

- New bugs that have been identified are closed or parked.

- Eighty percent code coverage from automated tests is fulfilled.

- All tasks are done and approved.

- All integration tests have passed.

- Sprint retrospective is performed and actions for improvements are identified.

- Sprint review, with PO present, has been performed.

- Performance test of the complete system has been done.

Estimation

After establishing the DoD, they had what they needed to begin some initial estimation of the work. Fiona needed to come up with a rough budget for the project to show the stakeholders and also an initial release plan. She decided to use planning poker for this. She had used it previously and was happy with the result.

Poker Planning/Story Points

Again they met in the same conference room. This time the entire team was there, not just the initial team. Fiona had purchased planning poker decks for everybody. She started by explaining the rules for everybody:

- Fiona started by reading the first user story.

- After a short time participants each selected a card without showing it to the others.

- When Fiona asked them to show their cards, they turned them over.

- Cindy and Harry were the farthest apart and they both explained their thoughts on the user story and then the team played again.

- This time they were closer to each other's points (only one step apart) and the higher value was selected for the story.

- They continued through the user stories until they were finished.

Updating the PBI

After they were done, Fiona went to her desk and started to update the PBIs. She now inserted the story points for each PBI into the work items in the Effort field. During sprint planning these would be broken down into more manageable pieces and each task would get a time estimate instead of story points (Figure 5-12).

Product Backlog

backlog items   board

⬜   ⬜ | Create Backlog Query | Column Options

Forecasting based on velocity of **40**					
Forecast	Order	ID	Title	State	Effort
▾	1	326	Test migration of ALL team sites.	New	
	2	43	Create Term store	New	5
	3	80	Set Up Basic Continous Integration for SharePoint	New	13
	4	38	◂ As an Editor I want to publish an information page	New	
Sprint 03	5	162	Set up search to be able to index Information pages and all of thei...	New	13
	6	329	As an editor, I want to create an information pages and fill it with ...	New	13
	7	407	As an editor, I want to add Metadata to an information page	New	20
	8	488	Set up ViaWorks search for SharePoint	New	5
	9	461	As a user, I want to navigate between information pages in a left menu	New	5
Sprint 04	10	466	As an editor, I want to add information (body) on an information page	New	2

Figure 5-12. *Storypoints (effort) in the backlog*

So story points were now done, but before continuing to sprint planning and time estimates, Fiona wanted to do an initial risk assessment.

Risk Assessment

Risk assessment is part of all estimation in agile projects and should be done throughout the whole project. If any PBI is considered very risky, it might need to be prioritized higher on the backlog. It is always better to address high-risk items as early as possible to avoid surprises later. Fiona knew the surprises would come anyway.

There are different ways of performing risk assessments. We suggest you choose the one you are familiar with. Fiona chose to do a traditional risk assessment by using the following parameters:

- Severity(1-5)

- Probability(1-5)

- Risk

- Risk assessment score (severity ×p robability)

- Mitigations

- Probabilitya fterm itigation

- Risk assessment score after mitigation (severity ×p robabilitya fterm itigation)

They went through this analysis for each user story on the backlog. Fiona ended up with an Excel sheet looking like the one in Figure 5-13. Fiona checked this document into source control so everyone had access to it.

User Story	Risk	Severity	Probability	Score	Mitigation	Probability after Mitigation	Score after Mitigation
As a Sales person I want to manage expense reports so that I can be more efficient	Expense reports cannot be created	5	3	15	Some Mitigation	1	5
As a Manager I want to Search Expense Reports so that I can							

Figure 5-13. *Risk mitigation*

Updatingt heB acklogO rder

The team found no risks that were exceptional at the initial risk assessment, so Fiona left the backlog almost untouched. She only moved two stories a little higher in the list because the developers had recommended that she develop these a little earlier.

Groomingt heB acklog

Throughout the sprints the PO needs to groom the backlog. The PO does not do this work alone, so the team needs to be part of this as well. This is an excellent way to get the team's views on the upcoming features and for them to give feedback and new ideas to the PO. Fiona decided to estimate about 10 percent of the team's time for backlog grooming. This number had worked well in the past.

Grooming the backlog also means that the PO has to order (prioritize) the backlog. Using TF Service we can easily order the backlog by dragging a PBI up and down in the backlog view and thus change the order of that PBI.

■ **Note** A new feature in TF Service is the possibility to tag our PBIs. This way we can get much finer granularity into how we can organize our PBIs. We can use the tags any way we want, for instance tagging work items that are going to be included in a specific release with a tag for the release and so on.

Buildingt heT eam

Now the team was close to getting started. Fiona had Cindy Crafoord, Harry Bryan, Eric Parrot, and Guillio Peters in the team so far. She talked to the other team members and they decided they needed three more people to enhance the development and testing competences even more. She also got feedback from the initial team that they needed an experienced UX person onboard. They selected the following:

- MikaelP ersbrandt,d eveloper

- IngridS vensson,s eniort ester

- PetterI varsson,U X

Fiona then contacted each person's manager and made sure he or she would be available for the project. Luckily, they all were, and when she approached the potential team members, they were happy to come aboard.

Fiona was going to go for two-week sprints because that was a good time box based on her experience. She once had a team who complained that they could not finish their PBIs during the four-week sprints they used. They always seemed to be late or failed to deliver everything they had committed to, complaining they needed more time in the sprints. She then said: "Okay, then we use two-week sprints instead." The team was very confused, as Fiona had decreased the number of days in the sprints, not increased them. Once they started working on the two-week sprints, however, they soon found they delivered more in two weeks than they had in four weeks. The team was more focused and did not postpone anything until the end of the sprint, hence, they were more effective.

With the team in place Fiona was ready to start sprint planning. We will follow this in Chapter 8, but first we'll look at how we can use TF Service to manage the team.

Summary

This chapter has shown how we can use the web access of TF Service to manage our backlog. We have followed an example of how we can start planning our project as a PO and end up with an initial backlog. In Chapter 7 we will continue following Fiona as she starts planning for the first sprint.

Before that, the next chapter will examine how we can manage our team using TF Service.

■ ■ ■

CHAPTER 6

ManagingT eams and Alerts

In Chapter 5 we followed a product owner (PO) preparing the backlog for a project. One part of the responsibilities of the PO is to staff the project, at least initially. After an initial team has been created, it is up to the team members to inform the PO about which competences they need to fulfill the project vision.

This chapter will discuss how we can create and build teams in TF Service. We will show how we can add new team members, create new teams, and set user access rights for team members. We will also see how we as team members can set up alerts so we can be notified when important events occur. Such an event could be that we have a work item assigned to us or that a work item we have created has been changed. This chapter will be more hands-on than Chapter 5, giving direct instruction to manage your team.

Adding Team Members

Once the project has been created, navigate to the web access front page. One team is created by default, so we can start adding members right away. However, it could be a good practice to consider creating teams other than the default team so you get more flexibility in how you manage the project. We will explain more on how to create teams later in this chapter, but now we will focus on adding members to the default team. Click the Manage all members link, as shown in Figure 6-1.

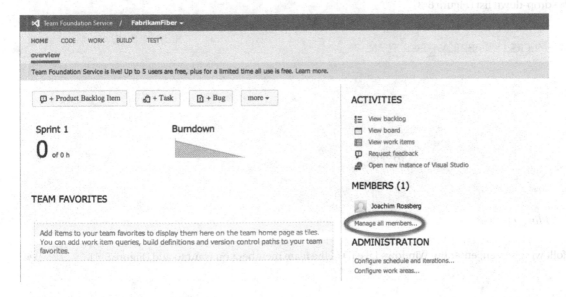

Figure 6-1. *Managing team members*

This will open the dialog box shown in Figure 6-2.

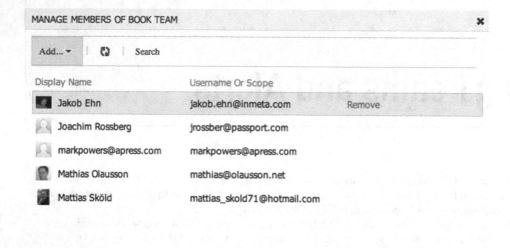

Figure 6-2. *Adding and removing team members*

From this screen we can add or remove team members and team groups. To add a new team member, select Add user from the drop-down list (Figure 6-3).

Figure 6-3. *Adding a new user*

In the following screen, enter the Windows Live ID of the team member you want to add (Figure 6-4).

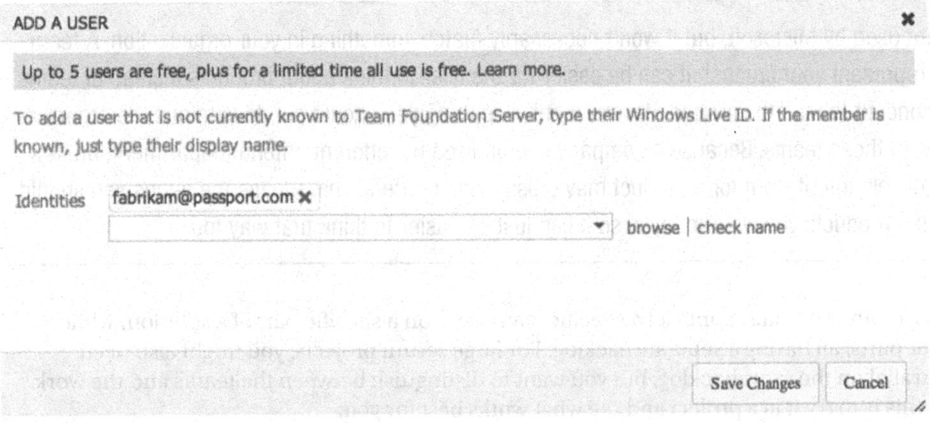

ADD A USER   ✖

Up to 5 users are free, plus for a limited time all use is free. Learn more.

To add a user that is not currently known to Team Foundation Server, type their Windows Live ID. If the member is
known, just type their display name.

Identities   fabrikam@passport.com ✖

                                              ▼ browse | check name

                                                    Save Changes   Cancel

Figure 6-4. *Add a valid Windows Live ID of the user you want to add*

The fact that TF Service only uses Windows Live ID as authentication might be a problem in some organizations.
Many organizations want to use their Active Directory for all authentications, and not being able to use that might be
a showstopper for using TF Service. Keep that in mind before implementing the service in your organization so you
don't invest a lot of time and effort into setting up a TF Service you cannot use in the end.

■ **Note** There are ways we could use the Active Directory and still use Windows Live ID. For instance, you can add the
Windows Live ID as a record in the Active Directory. But discuss this with your IT organization first.

TF Service security is based on users and groups. You can use this to ensure the security of your TF Service
deployment by correctly assigning permissions to users and groups. You should only add users to groups if those users
need the permissions that are part of that group. These permissions let users access only the data and functionality
they require for their jobs based on their roles and responsibilities on your team, which will help you protect sensitive
data. The default groups in TF Service will meet the needs of most organizations. If they do not meet your security
needs, you will have to edit existing groups or even create new ones.

■ **Note** Windows Live ID is free to use. You can use it to log in to web sites that use either Microsoft Passport Network
or Windows Live ID like Office365, MSN Messenger, MSN Hotmail, and `tfs.visualstudio.com`. Just create your ID and
you are ready to go. You can register your Windows Live ID account using your own e-mail address as well.

After the user has been successfully added, you send the URL of the team project to the user and he or she is
ready to log on and start working.

Creating New Teams

In TF Service, a team is simply a way of recognizing the team or teams you have, whether that is one team working on a
project or several. One person can be a member of several teams. Using area paths, we can describe the development
work that belongs to a specific team. We can easily look at which work items the team is responsible for. If a work item
is assigned to an area path that is assigned to a team, that work item is placed into the backlog for the team.

■ **Note**   A team is a concept used by Microsoft, but it won't necessarily match something in your organization. A team can be anything; it can also represent your product. It can be easier for the user to think about products instead of teams, and then just use the team concept to staff the product development. One thing you should not do is mimic the organizational structure of a company in these teams. Because a company is organized by different criteria (department, broken down into subject teams), a development team for a product may cross these borders. That means the teams you should consider here are based on the products you want to build, so it can just be easier to think that way too.

There are several ways we can use teams. Some let a specific team work on a specific part of a solution, while another team works on other parts, all having a separate backlog. For large scrum projects, you might also need several teams working in parallel on the same backlog, but you want to distinguish between the teams and the work they do. The best way to do this is to try it in a project and see what works best for you.

The default team has an area path and an iteration path configured for it automatically when you create a new team project. As soon as you choose areas and iterations for a team, a backlog is also generated for it automatically. If your project will use more than one team, you can easily add new teams by opening the Control Panel from the top right corner of the web access page (Figure 6-5).

Figure 6-5. *Opening the Control Panel*

In the Control Panel (Figure 6-6), we can create a new team by clicking the New team link.

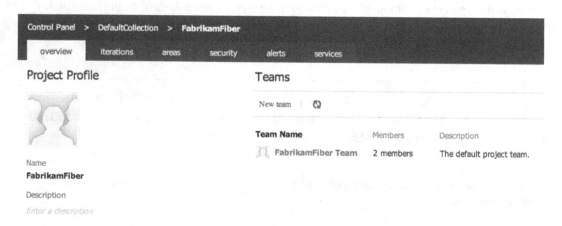

Figure 6-6. *Creating a new team from the Project Profile page in the Control Panel*

Fill in all of the information about the team (Figure 6-7). In this screen you can also select permissions for the team by adding it to an existing security group (more about this in the next section). We can also create a team area at this time, but if we don't do that now, we can also associate it with an area later. When you are done, click Create Team, and in a few seconds the new team is created and you can start adding users to it.

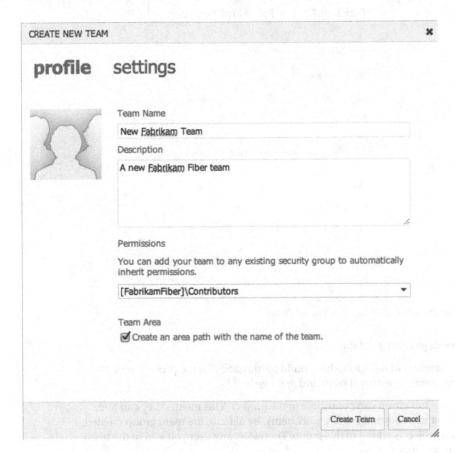

Figure 6-7. *Entering values for the new team*

Managing TF Service Groups, Teams, and User's Permission

From Control Panel you can change permissions for both teams and team groups by going to the Security tab (Figure 6-8) and selecting the Groups link.

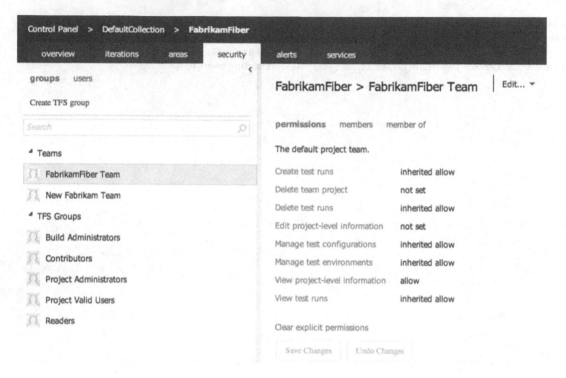

Figure 6-8. *Viewing permissions for groups and teams in Control Panel*

There are five different TF Service groups by default:

- *Build Administrators*: Members of this group have build permissions for the project. Members can manage test environments, create test runs, and manage builds.

- *Contributors*: Members of this group can contribute to the project. This means they can add, modify, and delete code and create and modify work items. By default, the team group created when you create a team project is added to this group. Therefore, any user you add to the team will be a member of this group.

- *Project Administrators*: Members of this group can administer the team project, however, they cannot create projects.

- *Project Valid Users*: Members of this group have access to TF Service. This group automatically contains all users and groups that have been added anywhere within TF Service. You cannot modify the membership of this group.

- *Readers*: Members of this group can view the project, but they may not modify it.

There are various permissions you can set for the groups and teams. We will not go over them all here, please refer to the TFS documentation if you need more information on this (http://msdn.microsoft.com/en-us/library/vstudio/ms252587.aspx is a good place to start).

For managing user permissions, click the Users link. Here we can change the existing permissions for this user and manage the group membership (Figure 6-9).

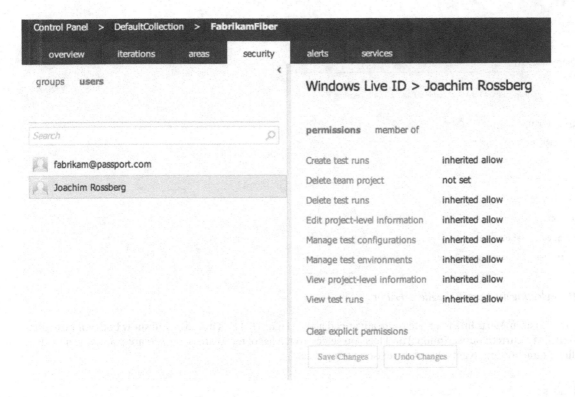

Figure 6-9. *Viewing permissions for users*

Note that by default most permissions are inherited. You can also break the inheritance and define custom permissions here. One common scenario is when you bring in external people who are only allowed to see parts of the work item structure. It can quickly become hard to keep track of these specialized permissions, however, so use it with care.

Managing Alerts

Most activities that occur in TF Service are exposed as events. For example, every time a build completes or a changeset is checked in, TF Service will notify all interested parties about this. As a user, I might be interested in getting notifications when a specific event occurs. I can accomplish this by configuring alerts in TF Service.

To configure the alerts, you use the Alert Editor in the web access. You can also access this from Team Explorer, by selecting Team ➤ Project Alerts. The Alerts Editor (Figure 6-10) lets you quickly select from a list of predefined basic alerts that are common, such as Any build completes.

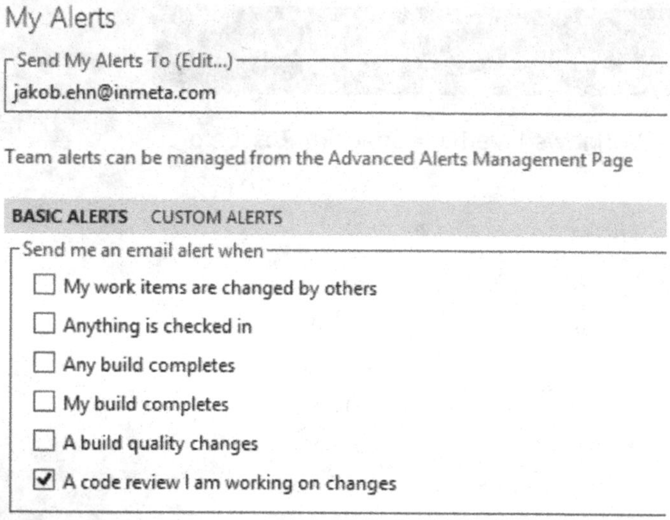

My Alerts

Send My Alerts To (Edit...)
jakob.ehn@inmeta.com

Team alerts can be managed from the Advanced Alerts Management Page

BASIC ALERTS   CUSTOM ALERTS

Send me an email alert when

- ☐ My work items are changed by others
- ☐ Anything is checked in
- ☐ Any build completes
- ☐ My build completes
- ☐ A build quality changes
- ☑ A code review I am working on changes

Figure 6-10. Selecting an alert in the Alerts Editor

Select the Custom Alerts link to create more advanced alerts (Figure 6-11). This page will show both your existing personal alerts (My Current Subscriptions) and lets you select from a list of templates when creating a new alert. Click the Other link at the bottom to get a list of the existing templates.

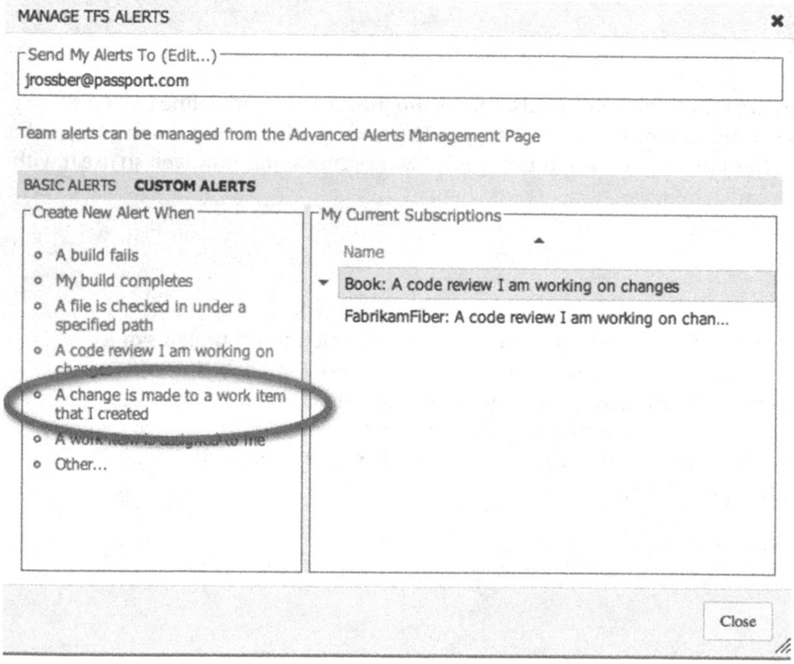

MANAGE TFS ALERTS   ✖

Send My Alerts To (Edit...)
jrossber@passport.com

Team alerts can be managed from the Advanced Alerts Management Page

BASIC ALERTS   **CUSTOM ALERTS**

Create New Alert When

- ○ A build fails
- ○ My build completes
- ○ A file is checked in under a specified path
- ○ A code review I am working on changes
- ○ A change is made to a work item that I created
- ○ A work item is assigned to me
- ○ Other...

My Current Subscriptions

Name   ▲

▼ Book: A code review I am working on changes

FabrikamFiber: A code review I am working on chan...

Close

Figure 6-11. Selecting a custom alert in the Alerts Editor

Let's create an alert that will notify you anytime a work item you have created is changed.

Select the link A Change is made to a work item that I created from the list, as shown in Figure 6-11. In the Alerts Editor (Figure 6-12), make any modification you might need.

BOOK: A CHANGE IS MADE TO A WORK ITEM THAT I CREATED ✖

| Name | Book: A change is made to a work item that I created | | | Subscriber | Joachim Rossberg |
| Send To | jrossber@passport.com [Default] | | Edit... | Format | HTML |

Alert Filters

	And/Or	Field	Operator	Value	
➕ ✖		Team Project	=	Book	
➕ ✖	And	Created By	=	[Me]	
➕ ✖	And	Authorized As	<>	[Me]	
➕ Add new clause					

Figure 6-12. *Creating a custom alert in the Alerts Editor*

By default all alerts are sent using e-mail. In the Format drop-down, you can select either HTML or Plain Text as the format for the e-mails.

> ■ **Note** The third option, SOAP, is used for triggering external services using standard WCF/ASP.NET web services. This is currently not supported in TF Service, so you will need an on-premises installation to use this.

For an overview of the TF Server Event Service, MSDN has an article that will explain this further (http://msdn.microsoft.com/en-us/magazine/cc507647.aspx).

From the Alerts Editor, you can also access the Advanced Alerts Management page (Figure 6-13), which is part of the Administration pages. Here you can view all existing alert subscriptions, but you can also create team alerts. They work exactly like personal alerts but instead they apply to all members of the team. This makes it easy to set up alerts for all members of the team without having to create them individually.

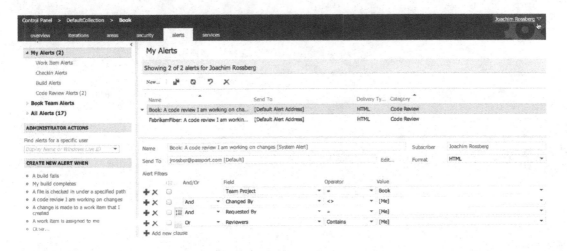

Figure 6-13. *Advanced Alerts Management page*

A nice feature here is that you can easily view subscriptions for a specific user or team. Select a user in the drop-down list and the alerts will appear above, as shown in Figure 6-14.

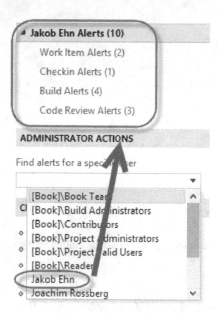

Figure 6-14. *Viewing alerts for a specific user*

Summary

This chapter explained how we can manage our team members and their permissions. It is pretty straightforward, but please carefully consider which permissions you grant.

We have also explained how we can configure different alerts that will notify us when status changes occur. These status changes could be every time a build completes or when a changeset is checked in, just to mention a few.

The next chapter will explain how TF Service can help us plan and execute our sprint.

■ ■ ■

CHAPTER 7

InitialS printP lanning

This chapter starts right where we left Fiona at the end of Chapter 5. Fiona had done everything to build an initial product backlog and create the team. At this point she does not have any input as to how long the project will take or how much it will cost. In order to get this information so she can show it to the stakeholders, there are a few steps she needs to take. Let's take a look at these because this will also involve planning the first sprint.

Initial Velocity

Fiona needed a few more things before she would arrive at the time estimates for the project. She needed to know the initial velocity of the team. The *velocity* is nothing more than the speed of the team. How much work (user stories) can they take on in a given sprint? She also needed to know how many hours they actually have for work in the sprints.

AvailableT ime

To calculate the available time for the team Fiona used the following method:

- *How long is the sprint?* In this case two weeks.

- *How many working days are available in the sprint?* Fiona would have ten working days.

- *How many days does each team member work during the sprint?* She needs to know planned vacation or other days off, planned meetings, and so on. She looked at each team member's schedule and filled in the numbers in TF Service.

Fiona deducted the time for sprint planning, review, and retrospective meetings, which would be eight hours per person for this sprint. The TF Service calculated the result of this. What we get is the capacity before drag. *Drag* is wasted time or unknown activities. Because the team was new and Fiona had not worked much with any of them, she used a standard 25 percent for the drag as she knew this could be a good landmark. Included in this is 10 percent backlog grooming. This usually results in six hours capacity per day (Figure 7-1).

Sprint 1

contents **capacity**

Team Member	Capacity Per Day	Activity	Days Off
Jakob Ehn	6	▼	2 days
jamie.cool@microsoft.com	2	▼	0 days ➕
Joachim Rossberg	6	▼	2 days
markpowers@apress.com	0	▼	0 days ➕
Mathias Olausson	6	▼	0 days ➕
Mattias Sköld	6	▼	0 days ➕
ravishan@live.com	2	▼	0 days ➕
Will Smythe (MSA)	2	▼	0 days ➕
		Team Days Off	0 days ➕

***Figure 7-1.** Entering capacity into TF Service*

Now Fiona had the available number of hours in the sprint: 290.

Capacity Planning in TF Service

TF Service is excellent to use for capacity planning. In the backlog section, in the current sprint, click the Capacity tab (Figure 7-1). Here you can set capacity, activities, and days out of office for vacations and holidays. As you set capacity, activity, and days off, graphical information about hours and capacity is automatically generated in the pane on the right.

In Figure 7-2, we can see that in the current sprint (Sprint 1) we have two tabs: one for contents and one for capacity. The capacity is also shown in the Contents tab in the far right and can be switched on or off.

***Figure 7-2.** Viewing team capacity in sprint planing*

The sprint planning features in TF Service offer three ways for the team to determine whether they have enough capacity: by person, by activity, or at the whole team level. This is very useful information for the product owner. We can see these figures in the right panel in Figure 7-2 at the top under "Team," which shows the collective work hours for the team. Below that we see "Work By: Activity" showing the work that has been done so far in the "Development" and "Documentation" activities. We can also see "Work By: Assigned To" showing how much of each team member's capacity is assigned to tasks.

Initial Sprint Planning

To calculate the initial velocity of the team, Fiona usually did an initial sprint planning. This is exactly the same as any sprint planning except that it is performed before the actual sprint starts. Fiona had in previous projects used this sprint planning in the first sprint because the two sprint planning meetings would be very similar and it would be unnecessary to perform it again.

During this meeting, the team estimates the tasks in hours so they can plan the sprint and decide on how many user stories they can take on in their sprint. This is the way the Fabrikam team performed this:

- Estimate the first user story in detail
- Break down what the team needs to do to deliver the story
- Estimate hours for each activity and summarize
- Deduct the summary from the available time the team has in the sprint
- Is there still time left?
    - Take a new user story and repeat the process until no available time is left
- Summarize the number of story points from the stories that were included in the sprint. Now we have a theoretical velocity.

The first (highest prioritized) user story on the backlog was:

As a sales person I want to manage expense reports so I can be more efficient.

The number of story points for this was five in the planning poker session. This was broken down into smaller tasks:

- Createe xpenser eport
- Delete expense report
- Modifye xpenser eport
- Send expense report for approval
- Logontoe xpenser eports ystem

Together with the team, Fiona prioritized these so they had a beginning for the sprint backlog. The sprint backlog looked like this after prioritization:

- Create expenser eport
- Send expense report for approval
- Modifye xpenser eport
- Delete expense report
- Logon toe xpenser eportsy stem

They continued breaking each of these down into smaller pieces and estimated them in hours. For creating the expense report, they came up with the following tasks:

- Create the graphical user interface (GUI)
- Createb usinessl ogic
- FulfillD oDr equirement
- Writeu serm anual

The estimated number of hours for this user story was 137. With an available time of 290 hours, they still had 153 left in the sprint. This meant that they still had room for more work, so they continued with the next user story on the backlog. This was:

As a controller I want to be able to manage the users in the system so I have full control over the users.

This was worth three story points.

After breaking this down they had 95.5 hours left so they continued with another user story worth two story points. When this planning was done there remained 23.5 hours of available time, but Fiona and the team chose not to take on anything more in the sprint. The team was new and if there were problems, they wanted some space. It's better to finish the tasks than to reach the end of the sprint and not be able to finish some of the tasks. If the team had time left in the sprint, they could take on more tasks, but they left that to decide later.

The total amount of story points for the sprint was now ten. This is the team's initial velocity. The sprint backlog now looked like this:

- Createe xpenser eport
- Send expense report for approval
- Modifye xpenser eport
- Delete expense report
- Log on to expense report system
- Createu ser
- Modifyu ser
- Deleteu ser
- Createc ustomer
- Modifyc ustomer
- Deletecustom er

Each of these had tasks associated with them that are part of the complete sprint backlog.

Updating Backlog and PBI

Throughout the sprint planning, Fiona updated the sprint backlog and inserted the new tasks into the TF Service. She associated them with the first sprint using the dropdown control (Figure 7-3). She also added the date when the first sprint would start under Manage schedule and iterations so that TF Service was updated with this information.

New Task 1*: **Create Expense Report GUI**

💾 ✕ 🔄 ⤺ ⤻ 🗗   Copy template URL

Tags Add...

Create Expense Report GUI

Iteration Book\Release 1\Sprint 1

STATUS		**DETAILS**	
Assigned To		Remaining Work	
State	To Do	Backlog Priority	
Reason	New task	Activity	
Blocked		Area	Book

DESCRIPTION	**HISTORY** LINKS ATTACHMENTS
B I U ⚏ ✕ ☰☰ ⤵⤴ ▨	B I U ⚏ ✕ ☰☰ ⤵⤴ ▨

Figure 7-3. *Associating tasks with the sprint*

One thing worth considering here is what to do with the epic user stories in the backlog after they have been broken down. Are they still valid in the backlog at that point? In our opinion, we can safely remove these backlog items (by setting the status to Removed) as long as we are certain that the content is covered in the broken-down tasks. But this is a matter of how you want to work. Some people want to keep the epics, some don't. Microsoft says the Removed state is used "when the team will not implement the backlog item because product requirements or other work conditions have changed." But as stated earlier, this is a matter of how you want to work. Fiona removed the epics and got fine granularity of the backlog items at the top of the backlog and larger epics the farther down the list she came. At this point Fiona had a groomed backlog as well as a first sprint backlog.

■ **Note** An *epic* is a large user story that is so big it is impossible to estimate how much effort it would take to develop it. It can also be a user story that is too large to fit into a single sprint, so it needs to be broken down. You can compare an epic to this user story:

As a human I would like to have world peace so that we humans will not kill one another anymore.

Although this example is farfetched, so are many epic user stories—at least until they are broken down into smaller, more manageable, user stories.

Forecasti nT FS ervice

There is a nice feature in TF Service that will let you create a forecast on how much work you can have in each sprint. It requires that you fill in the effort estimate on each work item. In the example in Figure 7-4, we have story points estimated in effort. We can also see that forecasting is based on the velocity of five story points and TF Service automatically draws the sprints and the work items that will fit into each sprint. The forecast can be switched off as well if we do not want to see it, simply by toggling on or off in the right top of the page.

Product Backlog

Forecast	Order	Title	State	Effort	Iteration Path
	1	Create Expense Report	Approved	2	Expense Reporting\Release 1\Spr...
	2	Modify Expense Report	New	3	Expense Reporting\Release 1\Spr...
Sprint 2	3	Delete Expense Report	New	1	Expense Reporting\Release 1\Spr...
	4	Send Expense Report For Approval	New	5	Expense Reporting\Release 1\Spr...
	5	Logon to Expense Report	New	6	Expense Reporting\Release 1\Spr...
Sprint 3	6	Create User	New	3	Expense Reporting\Release 1\Spr...
	7	Modify user	New	2	Expense Reporting\Release 1\Spr...
	8	Delete User	New	2	Expense Reporting\Release 1\Spr...

Forecasting based on velocity of **10**

Product Backlog — Current — Sprint 1 — Future — Sprint 2 — Sprint 3 — Sprint 4 — Sprint 5 — Sprint 6 — contents — forecast on — add items off

Figure 7-4. *Forecast in TF Service*

We can use the Velocity report in the upper-right corner of the product backlog to look at the historical velocity numbers, and, based on that, figure out a good velocity forecast number (Figure 7-5).

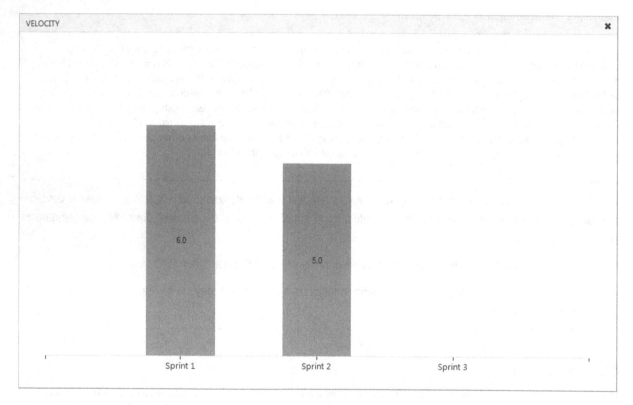

Figure 7-5. *Velocity report in web access*

You can also base a forecast on hours instead of story points, just change the values as you want.

Release Planning

Based on the information she knew now, Fiona could start planning the releases of the project. She knew the management team would like to know how many releases were planned, and she wanted to give them this information as soon as she could. The first thing she did was look for themes (see Chapter 2 for more detail) in the user stories so she could come up with a release plan.

Themes

Fiona looked at the backlog and came up with several themes:

- Expense report management
- Searchf unctionality
- Userm anagement
- Customerm anagement
- Projectm anagement
- Smartphonea vailability

She quickly saw that three themes were going to be part of the first sprint. According to the initial sprint planning, expense report management, user management, and customer management were all part of the first sprint.

Considering that there were many chores in the first sprint, she knew that it would not be possible to finish all three at the same time. She aimed on getting only the expense report management theme done in the first sprint. The other themes would come in the following sprints.

Fiona also knew the initial theoretical velocity (ten story points), which she used as an input for how much work she could expect in each sprint. With 44 story points total, the project would take 4.4 sprints to complete. She rounded this up to five sprints.

■ **Note** A *chore* is just something a team needs to do. It could be setting up a build server, fixing the team room, fixing white boards, installing necessary software, and so on. Chores are never estimated. In the beginning, the first sprints are probably filled with chores just to get started. This means that the velocity in the first sprints will be lower than in the coming sprints when most chores are complete. There is just not as much room left for estimated work in the first sprints.

So, a rough overview would give the following release plan for the themes:

- Expense report management will be delivered in Sprint 1
- User management, customer management will be delivered in Sprint 2
- Project management, search management will be delivered in Sprint 3
- Smartphone availability will be delivered in Sprints 4 and 5, depending on smartphone type

EstimatedT imeP lan

Fiona then used Excel to create a simple time plan for the project. She knew this was going to be temporary and could change depending on what happened during the project, so she would only show it to the stakeholders and not let themk eepa c opyo fi t.

Creating the Sprints in TF Service

Now Fiona went to the Control Panel in Team Web Access. She navigated to the Iterations tab (Figure 7-6) and clicked the Set dates link for the first sprint.

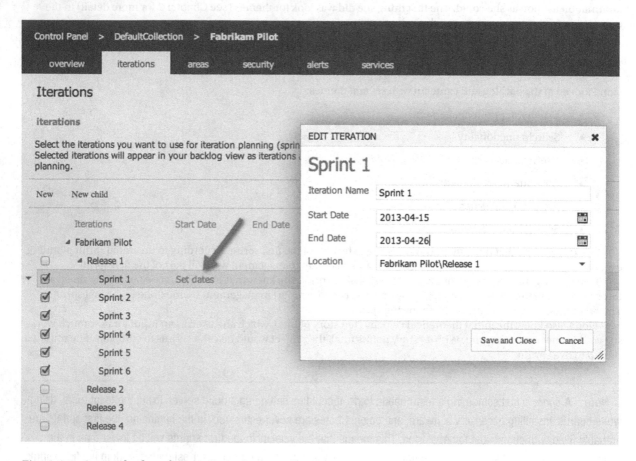

Figure 7-6. *Setting the dates for a sprint in the Control Panel*

Then Fiona continued adding the dates for her sprints and releases (Figure 7-7) until all her estimated planning was entered. A nice feature of TF Service is that it uses the values of the first sprint to suggest values for the next sprint. Both start and end dates are suggested when you click the date control.

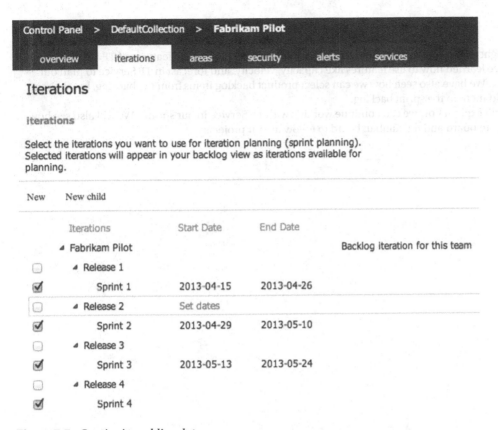

Figure 7-7. Continuing adding dates

Estimated Project Cost

After this was completed, Fiona could come up with an initial estimate of the project cost. She knew how many weeks the project would take based on initial estimation, which was ten weeks. With the help of the administrative department, she could calculate the weekly cost of each of the team members. She then multiplied the weekly cost by the number of weeks and came up with a cost estimate. On top of this she added the hardware, software, and other costs she knew would appear. She arrived at an estimated project cost, which she used as input for the management meeting, where she would present the time plan and project budget. Luckily the management team approved the project and she was good to go.

Fiona was now ready to start the project. She began by looking at the start-up dates, confirmed again with all managers of the team, and then sent out the invitation for the sprint planning meeting that would kick off Sprint 1. In the sprint planning meeting of Sprint 1, the team would use the initial sprint planning as explained in this chapter and see if anything had changed. If there had been changes, they might have to break down new user stories or change other aspects of the sprint. Hopefully, the initial sprint planning will remain the same as the actual Sprint 1 planning.

Summary

This chapter takes off right where Chapter 5 ended. We have seen how a PO can use the features of TF Service to plan the (first) sprint. We have learned how to use features like capacity, velocity, and forecast in TF Service to plan our releases during a project. We have also seen how we can select product backlog items from the backlog, break them down into tasks, and add them to the sprint backlog.

The next chapter will explain how we can continue working with TF Service in our sprints. We will also see how we can use both the Scrum board and the Kanban board to follow up our projects.

CHAPTER 8

■ ■ ■

Running theS print

In Chapter 7 we followed Fiona, the product owner, as she prepared the backlog for the first sprint. Fiona and the team have also done an initial sprint backlog planning to estimate an initial velocity. The team is now ready to jump into the first sprint. We will now leave Fiona and the team and talk more in general terms about how you can use TF Service during your sprints, based on the Scrum process template.

Before we take a look at how TF Service can help you run your sprints, let's take a brief look at the different meetings that take place during a sprint, as a refresher of the material covered in Chapter 2. This chapter uses the Microsoft Scrum template for all of the examples. If you use any other process template, you will see some differences.

Scrum Meetings During the Sprint

During the sprint we have several meetings that are included in the Scrum process:

- *Sprint planning meeting*: At this meeting the development team, together with the product owner, selects user stories from the top of the backlog, breaks them down into tasks, and then estimatest het asksi nh ours.

- *Daily standup*: During the daily standup, which takes place at the same time every working day, the team members report what they have done since the last meeting, what they plan to do until the next meeting, and if they have any impediments.

- *Sprint review*: During the sprint review the team demonstrates the software they have built for the stakeholders and product owner. The results of the feedback from the participants can lead to new user stories, changes to user stories, or perhaps removal of user stories.

- *Sprint retrospective*: During the sprint retrospective, the team discusses what they have done well during the sprint, what was not so good, and what they can do to improve their process.

- *Backlog grooming*: Although not an official scrum meeting, the backlog grooming is important. During this session the product owner and the team look at user stories for coming sprints (usually one or two sprints ahead) and estimate the stories in story points. The estimation occurs after the PO has explained what each story contains.

TF Service can help support these meetings in various ways during the sprint, so let's start by looking at the sprint planning.

Sprint Planning

Most of the work at the sprint planning meeting will be to break down user stories into tasks and estimate the time for each task. The team starts with the top story from the product backlog, breaks it down, and places it on the sprint backlog. They continue doing this until the amount of available time for the sprint is full.

In TF Service, we can add tasks to a user story in a couple of different ways. From inside a user story we can go to the Tasks tab and click the Add linked work item icon, as shown in Figure 8-1.

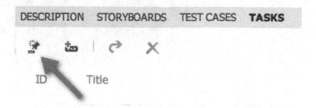

Figure 8-1. *Adding a new task from inside a user story*

This will open the form shown in Figure 8-2. Once the form is opened, you can add some basic information, such as a title and comments. When you are done with this, click OK to create the Task.

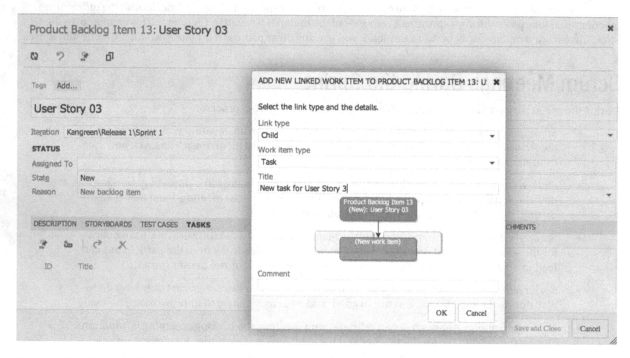

Figure 8-2. *Add new task form*

Note that you cannot add any other work item this way. To link a user story (or other work item) to another work item type you need to follow another workflow, which we will explain below. Clicking OK will open the Task for more detailed editing, as shown in Figure 8-3.

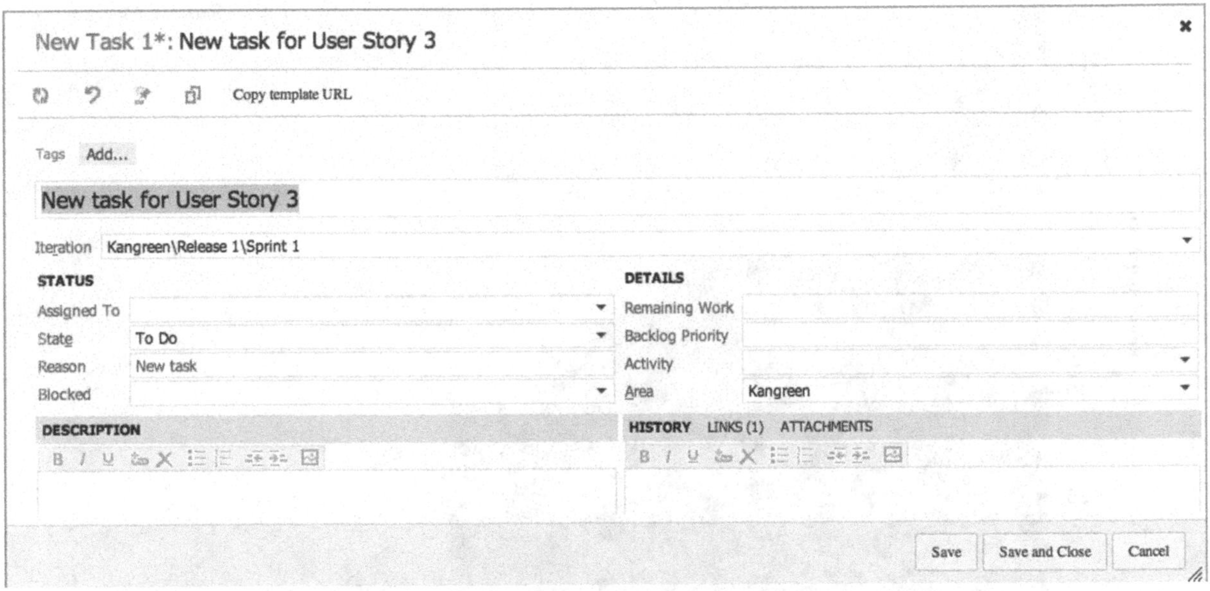

Figure 8-3. Filling in additional information on a task

During sprint planning, you can choose to assign the tasks right away or you can wait until all tasks for the sprint have been estimated. This depends entirely on how you want to work.

You can also fill in the description of what the task means, which is something you should not forget to do. We have seen many tasks without a good description, which causes confusion once work starts on the task. A good suggestion is to let the team decide on what information they want in a task to minimize waste of time.

One thing that we would say is mandatory is the field Remaining Work, which you will find in the Details section. It is important to register remaining work on a project and a common suggestion is to update this field at the end of every working day. This field is the only field you can use in the process template for following up and estimating hours on a task. The burndown chart (Figure 8-4) uses this information to display how much total work time there is left for all tasks in the sprint. This will help you see a trend of when you can expect to be done with all of the tasks. You would have had to list all of the team members' capacity for the sprint in order for this to be correct.

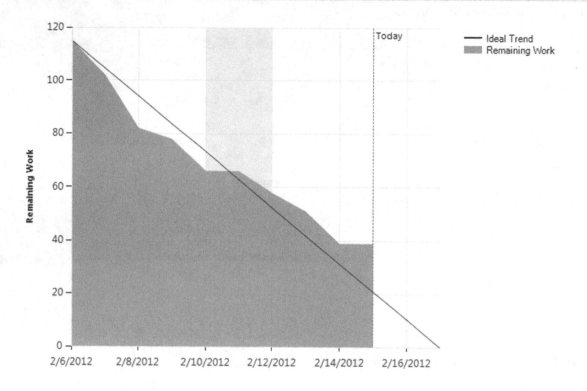

Figure 8-4. The burndown chart uses the remaining work field to calculate when the tasks in a sprint will be done

You can also add information about what activity the task is connected to. Here you can define these activities yourself from the Control Panel, so this can be tailored to your own needs. The same goes for the Field area. *Activity* is often the field used for defining what part of the process a task belongs to, and the *Area* is the field often used for functional or component breakdown, but you can use them as you see fit. This gives flexibility in how you can search and find tasks and other work items when you need to.

A new feature added in Visual Studio 2012 update 1 was tagging, which lets you tag a work item with one or more tags and then later filter the backlog using these tags. A *tag* is just a short text and you can define as many as you want to.

As shown in Figure 8-5, we have created a tag on this backlog item that indicates that the work being done is related to integration.

Figure 8-5. Adding tags to a work item

Now we can use tags on the product backlog to quickly find only items that are related to integration. Click the little filter icon on the very right of the product backlog to see the list of available tags for this backlog, as shown inF igure 8-6.

Figure 8-6. *Tag filter*

Note that each tag also shows the number of work items on the current backlog that have this tag. You can click a tag to filter the backlog to only show the items with the corresponding tag.

As with any other work item you can also add attachments and links to a task. Attachments (Figure 8-7) could be of any kind: documents, figures, and what have you.

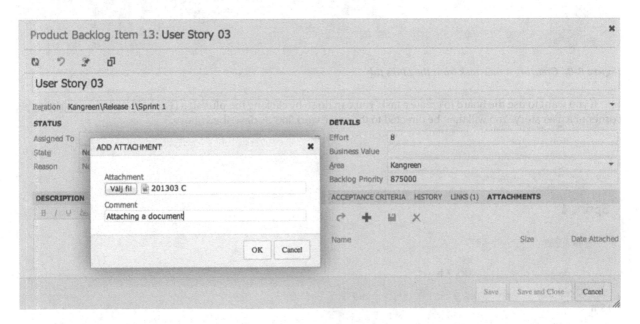

Figure 8-7. *Adding attachments to a work item*

Using links you can link one work item to another work item type. The difference from adding a task from the Tasks tab is that you can choose any type of work item and link to that. Figure 8-8 shows how you can choose to create a new task and link to that task. You can, if you want, link to an existing task (or other work item) as well by referencing the work item ID. Once the Add new linked work item dialog box is opened, you would follow the same steps as describeda bove.

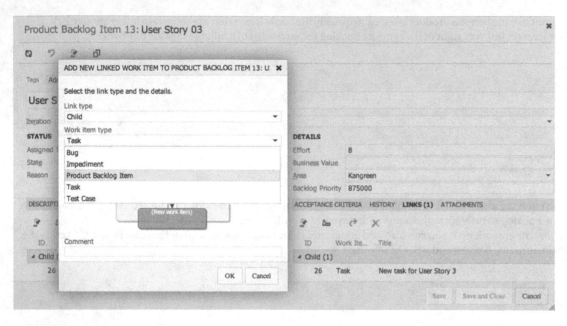

Figure 8-8. *Creating a new task from the Links tab*

If you want to use the board to create a task, you can do so by clicking the plus sign (Figure 8-9) at the top right corner of a user story. You will then be directed to the same workflow as described above.

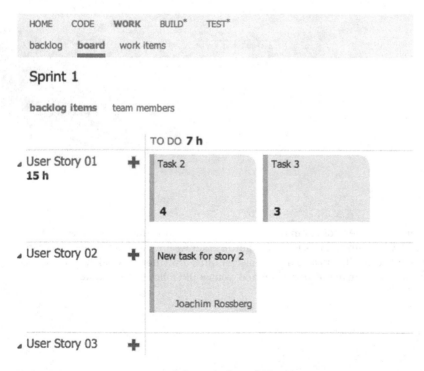

Figure 8-9. *Creating a new task from the board view*

All of these possibilities to break down backlog items into tasks, link to attachments, other work items in conjunction with the tags field, area, activity, remaining work, and so on are essential to have during sprint planning. During this meeting you can find new user stories that need to be added or impediments you need to create.

Because test cases are included in the things you can create and link to tasks and user stories, testers can also benefit from the TF Service features during sprint planning. Depending on how testers want to work, they can create test cases and link them directly to a product backlog item. In one recent project, our tester used the acceptance criteria in the product backlog item to create test cases, linking them directly to our product backlog item.

DailyS tandup

During the daily standup, the team reports what they have done since the last standup and what they will do until the next. During this meeting it is common to use the sprint board and group it by team members (Figure 8-10).

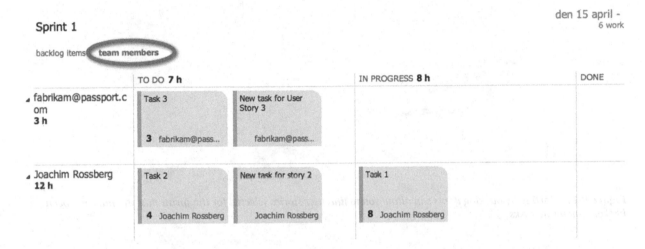

Figure 8-10. *When using the board at daily standup, you can sort the board on team members and then each team member can easily discuss the things he or she is working on*

Then each team member can easily discuss the things they are working on and update the status of each task. You can update the remaining work by clicking the number in the lower left of the task. The team can also choose to display the board based on backlog items if they want (Figure 8-11).

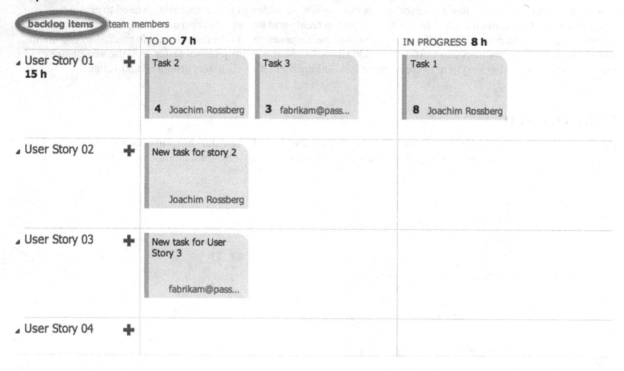

Figure 8-11. *Sorting by backlog items can allow you to find user stories selected for the sprint that still have not been broken down into tasks*

This view will better allow the team to notice any stories that have been selected for the sprint but still do not have any tasks assigned to them. In Figure 8-11 User Story 4 has not been assigned any tasks yet, and this is a reminder not to forget to break it down. This situation should not happen in the best of worlds, because all user stories should have been broken down during sprint planning, but it can happen from time to time.

Using drag and drop, the team can move a task between the different columns and, for instance, move a task to done when it is ready as defined in the definition of done. This feature also allows you to quickly move a task between team members so you do not have to open the task and select a new assignee—really useful in our opinion!

■ **Note** The board is based on tasks only. We do not show user stories in the columns. If you want a board for user stories, you can use the Kanban board, which is described in Chapter 9.

At the daily standup the team also discusses any impediments they might have. Using the linking features described above, you can create and link an impediment (Figure 8-12) to a task or user story and assign the impediment to the correct person. You can also select a priority (between 1 and 4) if you want.

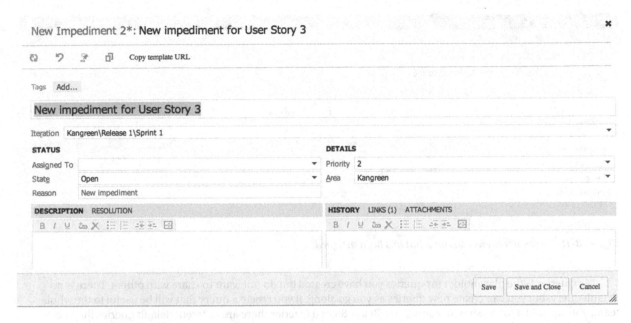

Figure 8-12. Impediments work item type form

Retrieving Data from TF Service

If we navigate to the Work items tab on the Team Web access we have some options of getting information from TF Service that can be useful during the sprints.

■ **Note** Please note that with TF Service we don't have all the options that we have with an on-premises TFS when it comes to reports. The burndown chart, velocity, and the cumulative flow chart are basically the only reports we have. We need to write queries to retrieve most of the other information we might need.

The Work items tab by default shows all work items that have been assigned to an individual (Figure 8-13). If you take a look at the left menu, you see queries that will give more information about the status of our projects. You can see that we can add queries to My favorites, which will be useful if we quickly want to find a specific query. You can also see that we have some Team favorites where we can add queries that will be accessible for the whole team.

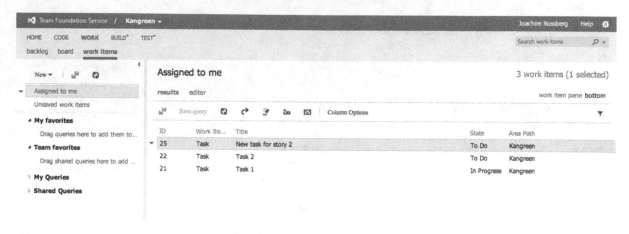

Figure 8-13. *Work items view shows what has been assigned*

My Queries is the placeholder for queries you have created but do not want to share with others. There is no default query, but you can create new queries as you go along. If you create a query that will be useful to the whole team, you can add it to the Shared Queries list. Below Shared Queries there are different default queries that are available automatically (Figure 8-14).

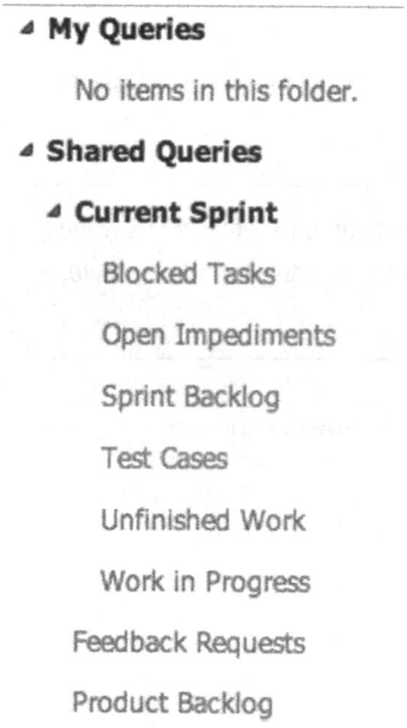

▲ My Queries

No items in this folder.

▲ Shared Queries

▲ Current Sprint

Blocked Tasks

Open Impediments

Sprint Backlog

Test Cases

Unfinished Work

Work in Progress

Feedback Requests

Product Backlog

Figure 8-14. *My Queries and Shared Queries*

Running a query results in a list with the work items affected by the query. Figure 8-15 shows the results from the Product Backlog query.

Product Backlog   10 work items (10 top level, 0 linked and 1 selected)

results   editor   work item pane **bottom**

Save query   Column Options

ID	Work Item Type	Backlog ...	Title	A: State	Effort	Busin...	Iteration Path
11	Product Backlog Item	500000	User Story 01	New	5		Kangreen\Release 1\Sprint 1
12	Product Backlog Item	750000	User Story 02	New	3		Kangreen\Release 1\Sprint 1
13	Product Backlog Item	875000	User Story 03	New	8		Kangreen\Release 1\Sprint 1
14	Product Backlog Item	937500	User Story 04	New	7		Kangreen\Release 1\Sprint 1
15	Product Backlog Item	968750	User Story 05	New	3		Kangreen\Release 1\Sprint 2
16	Product Backlog Item	984375	User Story 06	New	6		Kangreen
17	Product Backlog Item	992188	User Story 07	New	2		Kangreen

Figure 8-15. *Query result from the Product Backlog query*

If you want to go into a query and edit it, you can do so by clicking the Editor link, as we saw in Chapter 5. That way you can modify the query or create a new one.

These shared queries are very useful to many team members. The PO can retrieve status information from TF Service regarding the project and the project health. The team members can quickly find work items that are connected to them so they can keep track of what work is at hand.

BacklogG rooming

As we explained in Chapter 5, during the sprint the PO needs to groom the backlog so it is in good shape. This means that the backlog should be ordered and that the top backlog items should be broken down into smaller, more manageable pieces. The team helps the PO with this, and we estimate roughly 10 percent of available time for the team for this task.

The PO updates the TF Service backlog so it reflects reality. There might be new user stories that must be added, modifications to others, and so on. You can easily drag and drop items on the backlog to change the order, which is a nice feature.

Backlog grooming follows the guidelines already discussed in Chapter 5, so you can refer to that chapter for more in-depthinf ormation.

SprintR eview

The sprint review is the meeting where the team shows the PO and any other stakeholder(s) what they have built during the sprint. Any working software should be demoed so that the PO can sign off on the user stories that have been delivered. Nothing of what is shown should be a surprise to the PO. He or she should have been a continual part of the sprint so there should be no surprises here.

In the sprint review meeting the team can look at the sprint backlog to verify that all backlog items that were worked on and marked as complete are covered in the review.

SprintR etrospective

During the retrospective, we look at what was good and what was bad during the sprint. This is by far the most important meeting in scrum. Why? Because this is where you can learn how to improve. Constant retrospective and adaptation is essential for the team if they are to deliver quality software and business value.

This meeting will help you discover what needs to change in the way you run your meetings, for example. You can also determine whether there is a problem with communication with the PO or another part of the organization. This input is valuable so that you can change the way your teams work in order to achieve even better results for the next sprint.

We usually execute the sprint retrospective by using a white piece of paper and dividing it with a marker pen. The left side is what was good (marked by a +) and the right side is what was not good (marked by a -). The team then calls out what their opinions are and the scrum master documents this on the paper. Sometimes some very hands-on issues such as writing better comments during check in are listed, but there can also be softer issues such as "improve communications in the team."

Another way to run this meeting is to answer three questions:

- Whats houldw es topd oing?

- What should we start doing?

- Whats houldw ec ontinued oing?

The answers to these questions will give great input to your continuous improvement process. Both of the described methods work very well. Use a method that works for your team, the importance is that you perform the meeting and take the opportunity to adapt from the results.

Based on this retrospective, the scrum master and the team select a few issues from the bad side and commit to improve these. Issues that need to be taken care of are documented as tasks or impediments in TF Service so that you can follow up on them and assign them to the correct person.

Summary

This chapter walked through the features related to working in a sprint in TF Service. We have shown that we can benefit from using TF Service in most scrum meetings and that in our opinion the TF Service Scrum process template is a good implementation of Scrum.

The next chapter will dive into Kanban, another agile process that also has great support in TF Service.

CHAPTER 9

■ ■ ■

Kanban

Although our preferred project management method for development projects is Scrum, we realized that Scrum is not perfect in every situation. Scrum can be somewhat scary in the sense that it could require major changes in the way we work in our organizations. The drawback of this can be that it is hard to implement Scrum fully because we as humans seem to have some inherent resistance to change. Wouldn't it be great if we could find a process that is agile but made it possible for us to make the changes gradually? We'll look at just such a process in this chapter.

The Kanban Method

There is another process we would like to present that is usually mentioned with the agile frameworks and that actually can be implemented without changing your current process. Kanban, as it is called, has been very popular in many organizations and is used by several of our customers today.

We have also found some operations are hard to perform using Scrum. Think about this situation for a moment. Let's assume we have three-week sprints for our operations team. One week into a sprint we suddenly realize there is a service outage in the system that has had an impact on our production. This outage needs to be fixed very soon, so we write a backlog item and present it to the product owner. Now we have a situation where we would bring this into the next sprint planning, two weeks from now. Then it would take three weeks for the outage to be fixed because we have three-week sprints. In worst case we would have to wait five weeks before the fix would be available for deployment.

Of course this is a very rare situation. There are obviously ways to handle this better using Scrum. We could, for instance, always have a PBI of 10 percent of our available time set aside for bug fixes, outages, and other unplanned things and have this PBI at the top of our sprint backlog, allowing us to work on bugs as they are discovered. But still I do not think Scrum is optimal for operations work. This is why I started to look at Kanban.

The name Kanban comes from the Japanese word for signboard. Kanban goes back to the early days of the Toyota production system. Taiichi Onho, between 1940 and 1950, developed *kanbans* to control production between processes and to implement just-in-time (JIT) manufacturing at Toyota plants in Japan. The *Kanban method* was developed by David J. Anderson (*Agile Management for Software Engineering: Applying the Theory of Constraints for Business Results*, Prentice Hall, 2003 and *Kanban*, Blue Hole Press, 2010) and is intended to create an incremental, evolutionary process as well as help with systems' change for organizations. By using a work-in-progress (WIP) limited pull system as the core mechanism, the Kanban method exposes system operation (or process) problems. It also stimulates collaboration to continuously improve the system because optimization of the flow is a core component of Kanban. The Kanban system is one example of such a pull system, and the Kanban method was named after this popular form of a WIP limited pull system. This chapter will explain this in more detail.

> ■ **Note** A pull system is quite simply a system where a new task is pulled into work when a previous task is moved to the next step. Let's say that we have three phases in a workflow: new, in progress, and done. As long as there is free space in the in progress phase, we can pull tasks from the new phase into it. When the in progress phase is full (i.e., its work in progress limit is full), we must wait until a task is pulled to the done phase before we can pull a new one into the in progress phase.

There are three basic principles in the Kanban method, which are described in the sections that follow.

Start with What You Do Now

There are no specific roles or process steps in Kanban. It is not even a project management process in itself. The Kanban method starts with the roles and processes you already have and stimulates continuous, incremental, and evolutionary changes to your system. This is the thing we like the best about Kanban. It allows us to continue using what we have invested in; the biggest difference is that we can implement big improvements to the existing process without causing our employees to worry.

Agree to Pursue Incremental, Evolutionary Change

An organization or a team that implements Kanban must be aware of and support the idea that continuous, incremental, and evolutionary change is the way to make system improvements and ensure these improvements stick. Overwhelming changes may seem more effective but often fail because of resistance and fear in the organization in most cases. Using the Kanban method, we can implement continuous incremental (maybe even evolutionary) changest oo uro rganization.

Respect the Current Process, Roles, Responsibilities, and Titles

Most organizations have parts of their processes that work fine as they are and can be preserved. In order to implement change, we need to remove the fear of change, and we can do this by respecting current roles, responsibilities, and job titles. In the end, this will help us get more support for our Kanban initiative. We could do this in many ways. One way would be to present Kanban and a more revolutionary approach that would change titles, roles, and responsibilities so that we take the edge off the initial fear of changing to the Kanban method. That way we could more easily convince people to try the new method.

The Five Core Properties

In *Kanban: Successful Evolutionary Change for Your Technology Business*, David J. Anderson identified five core properties that were part of each successful implementation of the Kanban method. These are outlined in the sections that follow.

Visualizet heW orkflow

In order to understand how work works, so to speak, it is important to visualize the flow of work. The right changes are harder to perform if we don't understand the workflow. One common way to visualize the workflow is by using a card wall with cards and columns, called a Kanban board. The columns on the card wall represent the different states or steps in the workflow, and the cards represent the feature, story, task, or result of the workflow, usually referred to as worki tems.

What is great is that we use the steps of our existing workflow and we don't need to enforce a new way of working that dramatically changes the current way. We sort of place the Kanban process on top of what we have and visualize this flow. This often feels more comfortable to coworkers and keeps them more positive to the small changes we impose on them.

Figure 9-1 shows a sample Kanban board used to visualize the work flow.

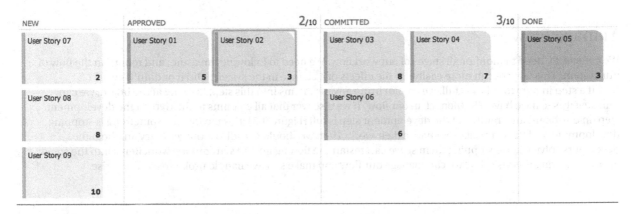

Figure 9-1. *A Kanban board*

But wait, some might say, isn't this just like a Scrum board (Figure 9-2)? They are very similar, but there is one significant difference if you compare Figure 9-1 to Figure 9-2 closely. Above the Approved and Committed columns to the right in Figure 9-1 there is a number that identifies the WIP limit.

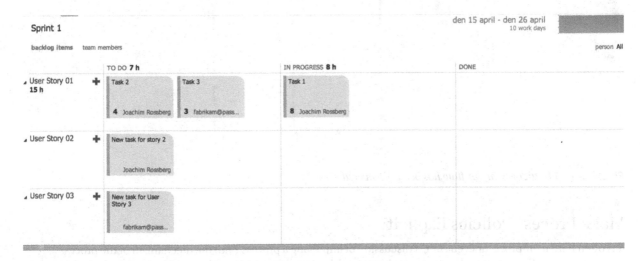

Figure 9-2. *A Scrum board*

Work-in-ProcessL imit

The WIP limit is important and tells us how many work items we can have in each of our steps (columns on the Kanban board). When the limit is reached, we cannot pull any new items into this step until another work item leaves this step. This pull system will act as an important stimulus for continuous, incremental, and evolutionary changes to your system because one of the main points is to continuously optimize the process to let more items pass through the system. It is important, not to say critical, that WIP at each state in the workflow is limited.

Manage Flow

We constantly need to monitor all stages of our workflow. We need to follow up, measure, and report on the flow of our system. This way we can more easily see the effects of a change in the system. Did it or didn't it work?

If a step in our workflow is full, we cannot bring any new items into this step. Looking at the board, we can quite easily see if we have a bottleneck in our flow. If we discover that all columns to the right of the development step on our board are empty, but the development step is full (Figure 9-3), this means that something is stopping development and the team cannot finalize their work. Then we should use idle resources to try and help the developers solve what is stopping them so we can restart the flow again and start pulling work items into the steps again. By having this visibility, we can manage our flow and make sure we handle problems as they arise.

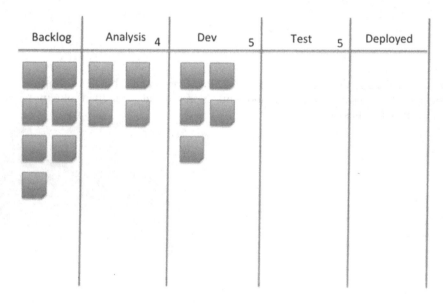

Figure 9-3. A bottleneck in our flow has been discovered

Make Process Policies Explicit

It is often hard to improve, or even start, a discussion of improving a process until the mechanism of the process is made explicit. We need to understand how things work in our workflow and understand how we perform our work. This way we can more easily reach a consensus around the improvements we suggest. If we do not have an understanding of these things, we often end up in very subjective or emotional discussions.

ImproveC ollaboratively

As we explained earlier, Kanban supports small continuous, incremental, and evolutionary changes that should stick to our organization. Small steps are easier to overcome than revolutionary changes, something that David Anderson soon discovered. If the small steps also have a great payback, change is even easier to implement. Anderson stresses that teams that have a shared understanding of theories about work, workflow, process, and risk are more likely to be able to build a common understanding of a problem. This makes it easier to reach an agreement on the improvement steps that are necessary. The Kanban method suggests that we use a scientific approach in order to implement our changes. It does not, however, say exactly what scientific method we should use.

Common Models Used to Understand Work in Kanban

There are some common models that are often used with Kanban to understand how work actually works. We will not go into these in detail here, but we include a short summary of each for reference.

- *Theory of Constraints* (the study of bottlenecks): This is a management view that says there is at least one constraint (bottleneck) in a system that limits the possibility to achieve the goals of the system. In this theory we focus on identifying the bottleneck and restructuring the organizationa roundt hec onstraint.

- *System of Profound Knowledge* (a study of variation and how it affects processes): W. Edwards Deming, the founder of this model, stated that in order to transform an organization or management style we must view it from the outside almost like looking through a lens. This outside view is what he calls the system of profound knowledge.

Kanban in Team Foundation Service

If we open up the Team Web Access in TF Service and navigate to the Backlog tab, we can actually see that we have two boards available to us (Figure 9-4). Just by looking at them from this viewpoint you could easily be misled that they point to the same thing.

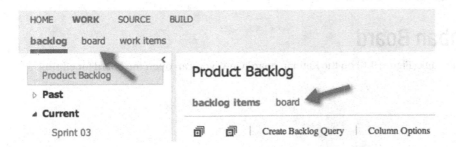

Figure 9-4. *There are two boards in Team Foundation Services, which can be confusing*

This layout can be quite confusing at first because it directs the user to two different boards. The top one sends you to the Scrum board we worked with previously in the book. The lower one sends you to the Kanban board (Figure 9-5), which is a relatively new addition to the Team Web Access. Keep in mind that the Scrum board displays tasks from the sprint backlog, and the Kanban board displays product items from the backlog. This is an important difference, and once you have an understanding of this, the differences and similarities of the two boards make this lessc onfusing.

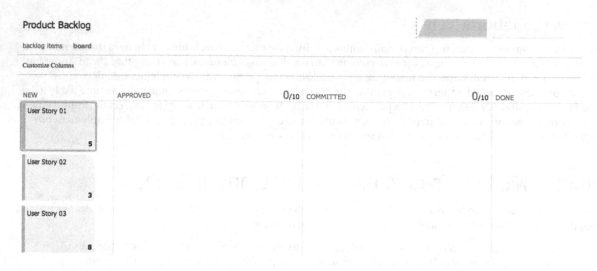

Figure 9-5. *Kanban board*

By default we get four different columns in TF Service using the Scrum process template:

- New

- Approved

- Committed

- Done

For the CMMI process template, the defaults are Proposed, Active, Resolved, and Closed, and for agile, it's New, Active, Resolved, and Closed.

This will probably not work for many Kanban projects, as the whole point of Kanban is to tailor the board in order to visualize the process. We need a way to create and modify the columns for most projects. Fortunately, Microsoft has enabled us to make changes to the board in an easy way.

Setting Up the Kanban Board

By clicking the Customize Columns link (Figure 9-6) on the Kanban board view, you can open the board for editing.

Product Backlog

backlog items   **board**

Customize Columns

NEW	APPROVED
User Story 01	

Figure 9-6. *Customizing the Kanban board is possible from Team Web Access*

This dialog box (Figure 9-7) allows you to easily add, remove, and modify the Kanban board columns. Clicking the plus sign between the columns inserts a column at that place. Using the arrows in the lower corners of the columns, you can move that column right or left so you can reorder your columns easily. From the Kanban editor you can also change the WIP value for your columns. Remember that the WIP limit indicates the maximum number of items that can be in a specific state. The board itself displays up to 20 items per column, but you can have more than 20 items in that specific state.

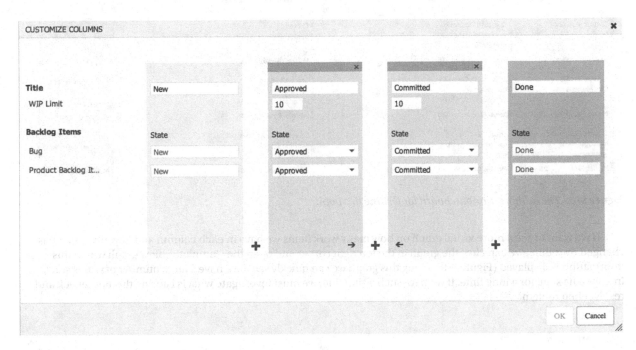

Figure 9-7. *Kanban board editor*

■ **Note**   You must map every state of each work item type to the corresponding Kanban column. This is what makes the Kanban board work for all your process templates.

How to Use the Board

Now that you have an understanding of the Kanban board, you are ready to use it. The whole point of the board is to visualize workflow and find bottlenecks. During team meetings you can drag and drop items between the columns just like with the Scrum board. This is an easy way to change the state of a user story. You can, of course, also let your team members update as they go along. Having a new modern whiteboard connected to a PC, you can have actual drag and drop using your hands, which is a really cool way to replace actual sticky notes on a wall.

By keeping the board visible to the team, you can easily see if there are any bottlenecks in your workflow. This way you can quickly start working on removing the bottleneck and get the flow back again.

Figure 9-8 shows how we customized the Kanban board for our own book-writing project. We have added some columns and we have changed the WIP limit.

Product Backlog

backlog items | **board**

Customize Columns

NEW	IN PROGRESS 3/10	READY FOR REVIEW 0/5	SENT TO APRESS 14/25	TR FEEDBACK 0/25	DONE
Chapter 9: Kanban Joachim Rossberg **10**	Chapter 8: Sprinting, working with the task board Joachim Rossberg **15**		Chapter 0: Introduction Mathias Olausson **5**		Chapter 15: Configuring Build Services Jakob Ehn **10**
Chapter 12: Git fundamentals Mattias Sköld **10**	Chapter 10: Engaging the customer Jakob Ehn **10**		Chapter 1: What is ALM and why is it important? Joachim Rossberg **5**		Find reviewers for the book Mathias Olausson
Chapter 14: Coding in heterogeneous environments Mattias Sköld **25**	Chapter 20: Test management (working with MTM) Mathias Olausson **25**		Chapter 2: About agile planning, development and Joachim Rossberg **5**		Lägg in dokumentmallar i TFS Mathias Olausson

Figure 9-8. *The authors' Kanban board for writing this book*

If we want to see a more visual graph on how many work items we have in each column and how this value has changed over time, we can click the graph in the top right corner and open the Cumulative flow graph where this information is displayed (Figure 9-9). Using this graph we can quickly see if we have a large number of issues stuck in a specific state for a long time. If we have such a situation, we must investigate what is causing this bottleneck and resolvet hep roblem.

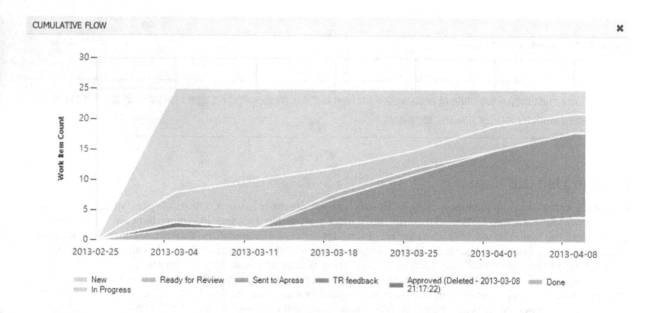

Figure 9-9. *Cumulative flow graph*

Summary

This chapter explained what Kanban is and how you can use it to streamline your workflow. We have also explained how you can use TFS to visualize your workflow using a Kanban board. In TF Service you can customize the board so that it matches your workflow, and you can then use it to follow up and find any bottlenecks in the flow.

The next chapter will focus on how you can use TF Service to engage the customers in your software deliveryp rojects.

CHAPTER 10

■ ■ ■

Engagingt heC ustomer

One could argue that the most important person or role in a software development project is the customer. The customer is ultimately who decides when a project or a feature is finished and when the quality is acceptable. Yet historically, involving customers in projects has proven to be problematic for various reasons. Often it is hard to get the customer to allocate enough time to actually participate in meetings and sprint demos. And when customers are included in the process, they often start participating too late, usually when it is time to start doing the acceptance testing. By that time all the decisions have already been made and changing the underlying requirements at this point often costs a lot of time and money.

The earlier you can involve the customer and other stakeholders in the process the better, and any feedback or changes in requirements will be less time consuming to implement. This is a fundament of all agile software development processes, as we have discussed at length in Chapters 1 and 2. Using short iterations and involving stakeholders for early feedback is crucial for succeeding with delivering the right software within the budget.

This chapter will discuss two different tools available in Visual Studio 2012 and Team Foundation Service that will enable you to involve your customers and get feedback from them early on:

- PowerPoint Storyboarding allows you to quickly show your proposed solution of a feature or application in the form of mockups, usually simple UI sketches that show the stakeholders what the software will look like without having to build the software or the underlying functionality.

- Microsoft Feedback Client enables you to request feedback from the customers once you have something the customer can access. The feedback response will be sent back and stored in Team Foundation Service and linked to the original feedback request, giving full traceability.

Creating Application Mockups

Using mockups is a common technique to show customers and end users what the application will look like without writing a line of code. Visual Studio 2012 provides a tool that lets you storyboard your ideas. The tool, PowerPoint Storyboarding, comes as an add-in to Microsoft PowerPoint and is installed when you install Visual Studio 2012 Premium or Ultimate on a computer that has Microsoft PowerPoint installed.

■ **Note**   Microsoft selected PowerPoint as the foundation for their storyboarding tool because of its presence in the industry; most people already know how to use PowerPoint, so no extra learning is necessary. Also, PowerPoint supports animation (Microsoft Visio, for example, doesn't), which can be very valuable when creating a storyboard.

Storyboarding a User Story

Let's create a storyboard for a new user story that we have in the backlog called "Service rep can delete customers," which is shown in Figure 10-1.

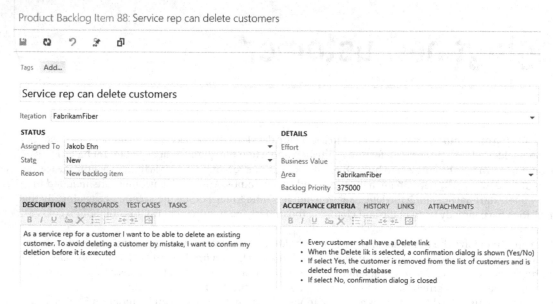

Figure 10-1. *Delete customer user story*

1. Select the Storyboards tab. This tab shows all storyboards that are linked to the current user story. For this new user story, we have no storyboards yet, so click the Start storyboarding button, as shown in Figure 10-2. This button starts PowerPoint and passes it information about the TFS connection and work item ID of the user story.

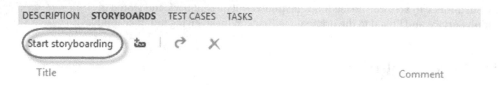

Figure 10-2. *Start storyboarding*

2. Once PowerPoint has started up, select the Storyboarding ribbon. Here you have tools for adding screenshots, pictures, and standard PowerPoint shapes, but the most important tool here is Storyboard Shapes. This shows all of the Storyboard shapes you have installed on your computer, as shown in Figure 10-3.

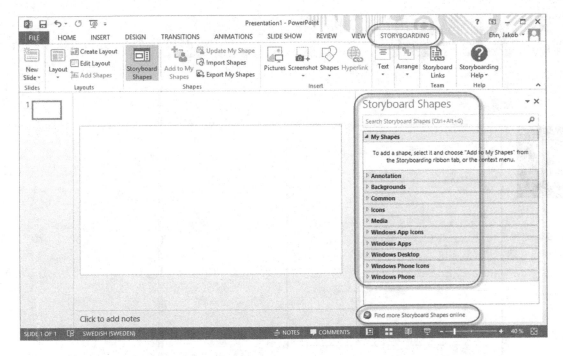

Figure 10-3. *Storyboarding in Microsoft PowerPoint*

3. Browse through the different shapes that are available, most of them are related to Windows development, but the Common section contains useful shapes for web applications.

■ **Note**   Notice the link at the bottom right, *Find more Storyboard Shapes online*. This link will take you to the Visual Studio Gallery from where you can browse and import both extra storyboard shapes from Microsoft and other third-party shapes as well. For example, you can download shapes for mocking iOS applications and shapes for touch gesture interfaces. Make sure you check back regularly for new content here.

---

4. Now we can create the mockup for the Delete UI. We want to show the profile of the selected customer together with a Delete button and a back link for canceling the operation. We use the shapes from the Common section of the Storyboard Shapes, together with the Web Browse background shape from the Backgrounds section, all of whicha res howni nF igure 10-4.

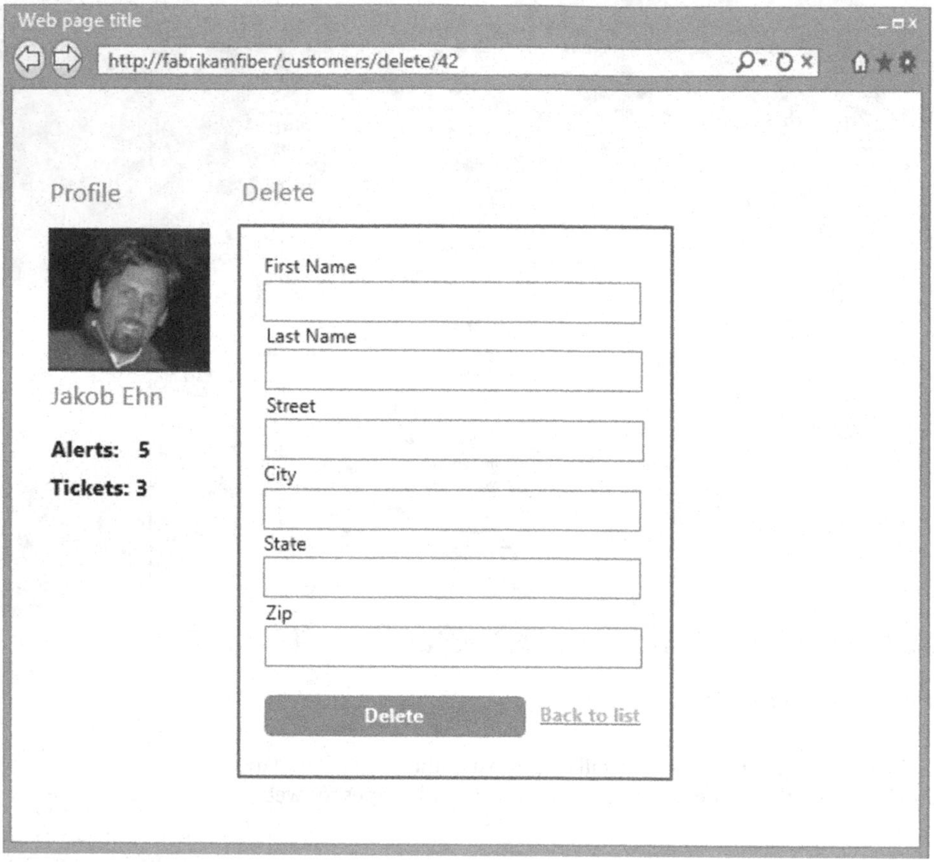

Figure 10-4. *Delete customer mockup*

■ **Note** Because this is a standard PowerPoint presentation slide, we can use any of the existing features and techniques that we already know. We don't have to learn a new tool for this, so we can present our mockups just like any other PowerPoint presentation. Also because PowerPoint use is so widespread, it is usually no problem to send a link to the original document and let the stakeholders view and edit it directly.

When mocking new applications or features that have no existing UI, it often makes sense not to invest too much time in making it look like the finished product. It can prevent the brainstorming that is a part of the requirement-gathering process. For this purpose, there are several "sketchy" shapes available on the gallery. Using these shapes instead, the example could look something like the one shown in Figure 10-5.

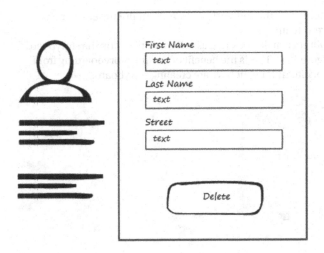

Figure 10-5. *Delete customer sketchy mockup*

SharingY ourS toryboards

So we are satisfied with the mockup for the new functionality. Now we want to save this storyboard and link it to the user story requirement we started this exercise from. Linking a storyboard to the requirements in TFS is done using the Storyboard Links tool (the button to start it is shown in Figure 10-6).

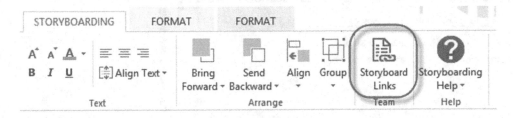

Figure 10-6. *Linking storyboard to requirements*

If you save the presentation on your local computer and then click the Storyboard Links button, you will get the message shown in Figure 10-7.

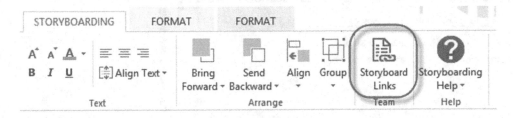

Figure 10-7. *Linking requirements*

A shared location here means, for example, a shared folder on the network, a SharePoint document library, or on SkyDrive, basically any place that is accessible to all your team.

Now, if we instead save the document on SkyDrive, we will get a dialog box that asks if we want to link the storyboard to the requirement work item we started from, as shown in Figure 10-8. This is the benefit of starting Storyboarding from the user story work item: PowerPoint already knows which work items for which we are creating storyboards.

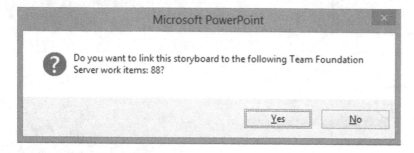

Figure 10-8. Automatic requirement linking

If we hadn't done this, or if we select No, we can manually link the storyboard to one or more requirements. We do this by selecting the Storyboard Links button again and find the work item(s) we want to link to, as shown in Figure 10-9.

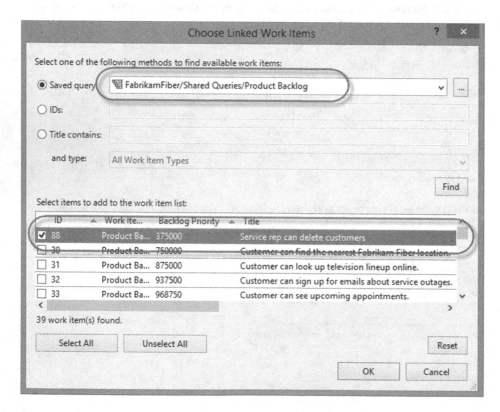

Figure 10-9. Linking requirement

In both cases the result will be the same, the user story work item is now linked to the storyboard by its URL, ass howni nF igure 10-10.

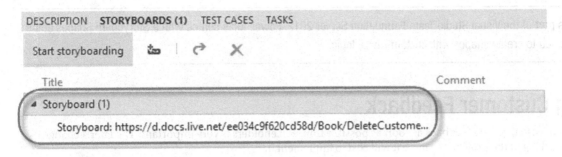

Figure 10-10. *Storyboard links*

CreatingR eusableS toryboardS hapes

We mentioned previously that there is a public Storyboard shapes gallery hosted by Microsoft. You can download these shapes and import them into your mockups. But you can also create your own reusable shapes for later use.

Let's say we have created a button that will be used for reporting errors. We want to use this button on several different mockups. To do this, select the button and click Add to My Shapes. This will save the shape and show it in the My Shapes section, as shown in Figure 10-11.

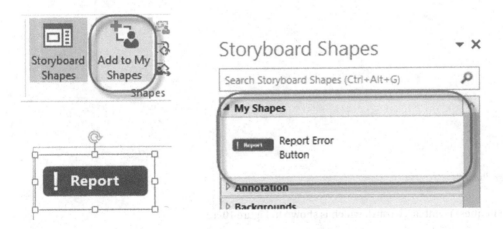

Figure 10-11. *Add custom shape to My Shapes*

To share this shape, you select Export My Shapes from the Storyboarding ribbon and save it as an .sbsx file (Storyboard Shapes File). This file can then be place anywhere your team members can access it and import it.

■ **Note**   As part of the Visual Studio Team Foundation Server 2012, Power Tools comes with a Storyboard Shapes editor that enables you to create shapes with custom resize logic.

Getting Customer Feedback

As mentioned earlier, getting feedback as soon as possible from stakeholders is very important. The later a change gets on the backlog of the project, the more it will cost to implement it.

Getting feedback means showing your solution to the customer and then in some way recording all the feedback from the customer while they are using the system. Often this communication is done using e-mail and phone calls, where it can be hard to aggregate the feedback and trace it to the original requirements.

This is where the new Microsoft Feedback Client tool comes in. It is a smart client application that is publicly available; details of the download are provided when a feedback request is sent to a stakeholder. This is discussed later in the chapter.

Sending a Feedback Request

When a new version is deployed to a staging or test environment that the stakeholders can access, you can request feedback from them. This is done from the home page of Team Web Access in the Activities section (Figure 10-12).

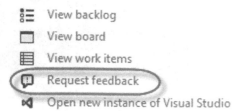

Figure 10-12. Request feedback

This will launch the Request Feedback wizard, which is shown in Figure 10-13.

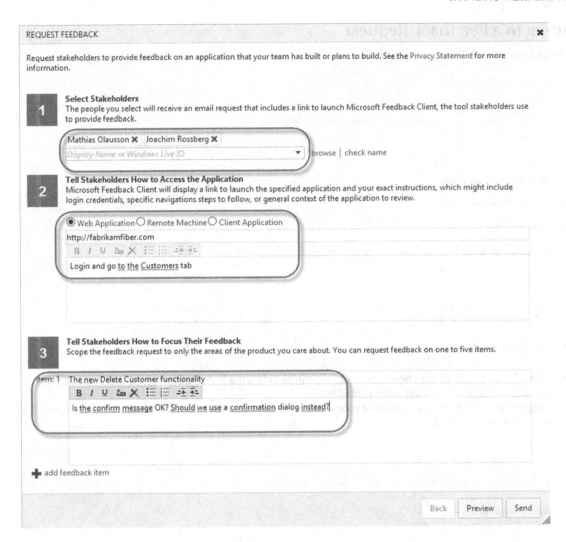

Figure 10-13. *Request Feedback wizard*

In the first section you add one or more stakeholders who should receive the feedback request e-mail. Note that you can either select members from the current team here or you can enter an e-mail address.

■ **Note**   Although you can send a feedback request to anyone using e-mail addresses, the person who should send the feedback must have a valid login on the corresponding TFS project. However, they do not need a Client Access License (CAL).

In the second section you specify how the stakeholder should access the application, typically a URL for a web solution or a path to an executable. Also you should enter any information necessary in order to get started with the feedback session, for example, login credentials.

Lastly you create one or more feedback items, each with a description of what you want the customer to focus on. Every feedback item you add will create a separate feedback request.

Responding to a Feedback Request

Every stakeholder listed in the feedback request will receive an e-mail that looks like the one shown in Figure 10-14.

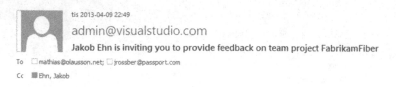

tis 2013-04-09 22:49
admin@visualstudio.com
Jakob Ehn is inviting you to provide feedback on team project FabrikamFiber

To ☐ mathias@olausson.net; ☐ jrossber@passport.com

Cc ■ Ehn, Jakob

We want your feedback for the following items:

1. The new Delete Customer functionality

Start your feedback session

If the feedback tool is not already installed on your machine, install the feedback tool.

Thanks,
Jakob Ehn

If clicking the "Start your feedback session" link fails to launch the feedback session, copy the following URL (mfbclients://pro-tfs.visualstudio.com/DefaultCollection/p:FabrikamFiber?rid=89) and paste it into a browser address bar to start the session.

Figure 10-14. *Feedback request e-mail*

If the user already has the feedback client installed, they can just click the link Start your feedback session. If not, there is a separate link to install it included in the e-mail text.

When starting the tool, it will dock to the left of your screen and show the information about how to access the application, as shown in Figure 10-15.

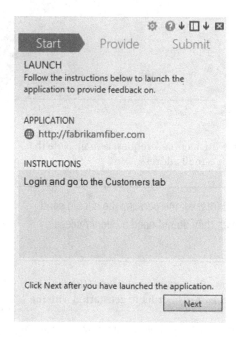

Figure 10-15. *Start feedback session*

Clicking Next starts the feedback session. You can now provide feedback for each item that was entered in the original feedback request, as shown in Figure 10-16. Using the tool you can comment on what you see, add screenshots, and attach files. You can also turn on screen or voice recording while you are running the application. At the bottom you can also give an overall rating of the feature that was tested.

Figure 10-16. Providing feedback

Once you are done, clicking Next will summarize the feedback (see Figure 10-17) before you submit it to TFS with the Submit and Close button.

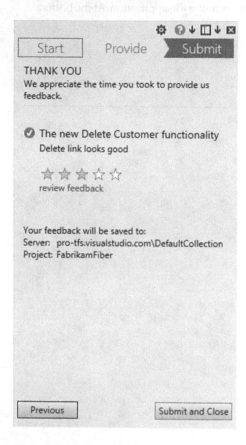

Figure 10-17. *Submitting feedback*

Following Up on Feedback Responses

Both feedback requests and feedback responses are stored as work items in TFS. So the best way to keep track of them is to create work item queries for them. There is a default work item query called Feedback that returns all active feedback response work items, as shown in Figure 10-18.

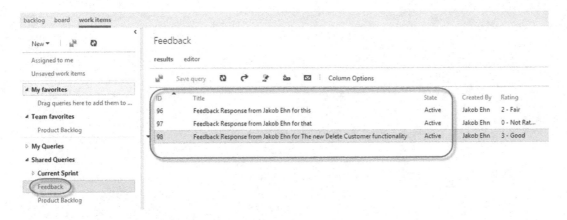

Figure 10-18. *Viewing feedback responses*

The feedback response is automatically linked to the feedback request it originated from, together with links to any recordings and files that were added during the feedback session. This is shown in Figure 10-19.

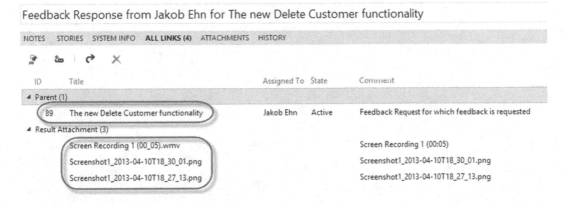

Figure 10-19. *Feedback response links*

■ **Note**   You need to decide how to handle the feedback responses you get back. Because these are work items in TFS, a common thing to do is to create new work items and link them to the feedback response. Depending on the response, it can, for example, result in a bug or a new product backlog item. Linking the work items gives traceability back to the stakeholder response.

Summary

Throughout this chapter we have looked at different ways of engaging customers and stakeholders in the software development process using the tools for storyboarding in Visual Studio 2012 and getting feedback using TFS and the Microsoft Feedback Client.

The next chapter will start looking at the source control features in TFS.

■ ■ ■

CHAPTER 11

Choosing Source Control Options

In TF Service you can choose which source control system to use on a team project level. You have the choice between:

- Team Foundation Version Control (TFVC), a central source control system developed for the enterprise
- Git, a distributed version control system developed for loosely coupled open-source projects

Microsoft is working on lowering the bar for teams to adopt Git by providing a first-class integrated user experience for using Git with Visual Studio.

This chapter will explain the capabilities for TFVC and Git to help you choose which option to use for your team project.

■ **Note** Microsoft's Git integration in Visual Studio is still a work in progress, and the goal is to provide full support in the next major release of Visual Studio. During development Microsoft continuously releases previews of the Git support for Visual Studio 2012, but they are not feature complete yet.

Overview of Team Foundation Version Control

TFVC is a centralized version control system developed for enterprises. All operations are performed against a single central master repository. It is possible to work disconnected against a local snapshot and commit the changes to the central repository later. TFVC has full integration with Active Directory and an advanced fine grained security system that lets you control permissions down to individual files and users.

TFVC is integrated into Visual Studio and Eclipse and has command line tools for working on non-Windows environments, such as Linux (and other Unix systems) and Mac OS X.

Below is a list of the major and most important capabilities of TFVC; we'll cover each in more detail in the following sections:

- Atomicc heck-in
- Check-inp olices
- Shelving
- Teamvisib ility
- Locks
- Labeling

- Branching

- Branchv isualizationa ndt racking

- Cross-platforms upport

- Disconnectedw ork

AtomicC heck-In

Each check-in within TFVC is an atomic transaction that keeps all changed files, associated work items, comments, and check-in notes together.

Check-In Policies

TFVC can add validation rules to validate and prohibit check-ins that don't pass the required policies. Here are some examples of check-in policies:

- *Comment policy* that requires each check-in to have a comment.

- *Work item policy* that requires each check-in to be associated with a work item.

- *Builds policy* that stops you from committing code to the central repository if your continuous integrationb uildsi sf ailing.

Check-in polices execute on the client as part of the check-in process. There are some check-in policies built in to the out-of-the box product, and more check-in policies are shipped in the Microsoft Visual Studio Team Foundation Server 2012 Power Tools and available from the community. You can also create your own check-in policies.

■ **Note** For more information about available check-in policies and how to write your own polices, refer to http://www.teamsystempro.com/go/checkinpolicies.aspx.

Shelving

Shelving is the capability to store or back up your current work to the server, without checking it into the code base. This is useful for a number of scenarios, such as backing up your work, saving your work to solve another problem, or sharing the code you're working on with a colleague. In fact many of the new collaboration features of Visual Studio are based on shelving.

TeamV isibility

TFVC has the capability to know what every user is doing in the source control system and to display that information to other users, such as if a file is checked out by another user.

Locks

TFVC is a central repository that has the capability to let users lock files for access. This can be very useful for teams who want to avoid merging files.

Labeling

A *label* in TFVC is a collection of files and their version. Labels are editable, provided you have the right permission, and the labels themselves are not versioned.

Labels are often used to tag files you would like to later fetch or access as one unit. If you need to, you can get (fetch) a label and you will receive the files for the version at which they were labeled. You can also create a branch based on a label.

One example of how labels are used is the build system. Each build will label the source code used in the build unless you turn it off in the build definition. Once the code is labeled, you can fetch the label to get the exact code that was in the build.

■ **Caution**   Labels are not undisputable and traceable records, because they can be altered without leaving any trace in the source control history. If you think labels are too weak to rely on, you should consider converting your labels to branches.

Branching

Branching is the capability to isolate code bases and enable parallel work on the different isolated code bases. In TFVC, branching is a lightweight server side operation. This means that when you're creating a branch, you're not copying all files. Instead you create a reference to the versions used in the branch. A very efficient operation in regards to time and space is needed.

■ **Note**   For guidance about branching and merging with TFVC, please refer to the Visual Studio TFS Branching and Merging Guide `http://tfsbranchingguideiii.codeplex.com`.

BranchV isualizationa ndT racking

With the use of branches, it becomes important to know how the branches are organized and if a specific change has been implemented in a branch. To solve this, TFVC offers capabilities like:

- *Branch Hierarchy*, visualizing the hierarchy and relation between branches
- *Tracking Changeset*, visualizing the flow of changesets across branches and time
- *Tracking Work Items*, visualizing how the work item has been implemented across branches andtim e

One example of the Tracking Work Item capability is shown in Figure 11-1.

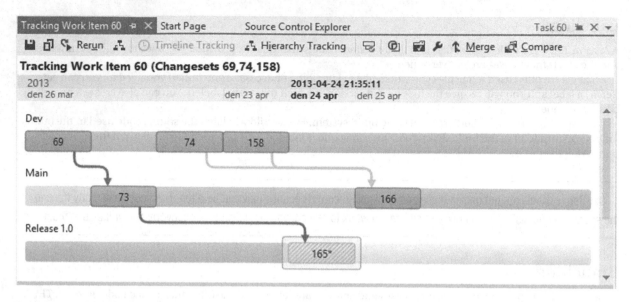

Figure 11-1. *The Track Work Item window in timeline mode showing how all changesets related to a work item have flowed through the branch structure*

One key advantage of Track Work Item is that you can initialize branching operations like creating or merging branches directly from these graphical visualizations.

Cross-PlatformS upport

As one might suspect, Microsoft provides a full and integrated solution for working with TFVC from within Visual Studio. But for most enterprises it's important to offer good tooling on platforms other than Windows and .Net. For that reason Microsoft provides Team Explorer Everywhere. All versions come with both a full feature Eclipse integration and a command line utility for most Linux/Unix versions including Mac OS X.

Disconnected Work

With the introduction of Local Workspaces, TFVC enables you to work when disconnected from the central repository. If you use a Local Workspace, all files are editable so you can edit "checked-out" files without communicating with the central repository. To keep track of changes, the local workspace keeps a copy of the last downloaded file in a hidden $tf folder.

Overview of Git

Git is a distributed version control system developed for disconnected open-source development over the Internet. In Git, there is no central repository, as every user has a complete copy of the repository and all operations are performed against the local repository. Changes can then be synchronized among different repositories. From a technical point of view, there is no central master repository, all copies are equal. But in reality, one repository is viewed as the central repository.

Git has become a very popular and widespread solution for version control, with clients for most platforms like Windows, Linux, and Mac OS X. However, Git is most commonly managed through a command line interface; Microsoft has announced Git support with first-class user experience in the coming version of Visual Studio.

■ **Note** Microsoft is focusing on delivering a first-class experience for Git inside Visual Studio, whether or not it's a TF Service-hosted Git repository.

Here are the major and most important capabilities of Git; as we did for TFVC, we'll cover each in more detail in the following sections:

- Disconnectedw ork
- Distributedd evelopment
- Rewritingh istory
- Workflows
- Tagging
- Rebasing
- Branching
- Branchv isualization
- Cross-platformc lients

Disconnected Work

Because the local Git repository you have on your machine is a complete version control server, you can do every Git operation disconnected from the network.

DistributedDe velopment

Git supports flowing and integrating changes from different repositories into branches that can be merged in the same way as locally developed branches.

Rewriting History

Git has the option to rewrite the history of a repository. You can actually change the history and even remove commits. You would do this to clean up the repository's history before sharing your repository with others.

Workflows

Git supports advanced workflows for nonlinear development. Thanks to the distributed nature of Git, repositories can serve as integration points, and code changes can flow through a structure of different repositories. An example of this iss howni nF igure 11-2.

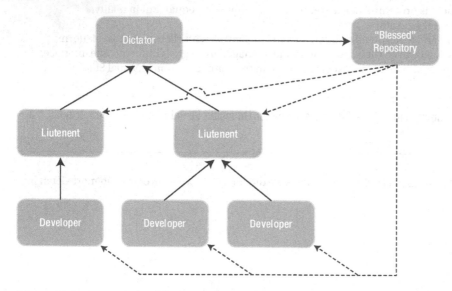

Figure 11-2. *An example of the hierarchical Dictator and Liutenent workflow useable for large projects*

Tagging

A tag in Git is used like a label in TFVC. Git supports both lightweight tags and annotated tags.

- *Lightweight tags*a rep ointerst oa s pecificc ommit.

- *Annotated tags* are check summed and can be signed with private or public keys to protect and validate the content of the tag

Rebasing

Rebasing in Git is another way of merging branches to get a cleaner history. Instead of showing the development as parallel, rebasing will add the commits to the end of the target branch. This can be used to provide a cleaner and more readable history than just merging code from a local experimental branch to the repository.

Branching

Branching is the capability to isolate code bases and enable parallel work on the different isolated code bases. In Git, branching is very lightweight and only points to a commit. Git uses published and unpublished branches, so you can create a temporary local branch for your work without affecting others. A branch always affects the complete system.

BranchV isualization

There is some textual visualization and tracking available with the Git command line utilities and a lot of other tools and services for visualizing Git branches.

Microsoft has implemented some branch visualizations, as shown in Figure 11-3.

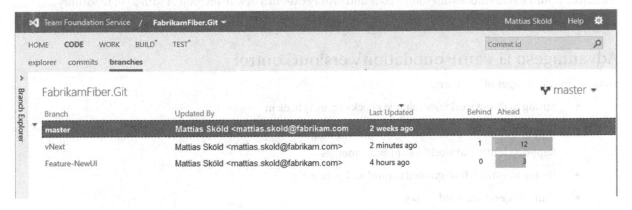

Figure 11-3. *The Branch view showing all server repository branches and how far ahead or behind a branch is compared with the selected branch*

But so far Microsoft hasn't implemented any of the branch visualization capabilities found in TFVC, such as branch hierarchy view, changeset tracking, and work item tracking.

Cross-PlatformC lients

Git has become a very popular and widespread solution for version control, with clients, both command lines and graphical user interfaces, for a wide variety of platforms, including Windows, Linux, and Mac OS X. Git can also be ported to other languages.

Git-TF: A Third Option

If your project is leaning toward (or using) TFVC but would like to have the capabilities of Git for some situations, there is a solution for you. Microsoft has released Git-TF, a cross-platform command line tool that can act as a bridge between TFVC and Git. This makes it possible to have a team project with TFVC as the source control system and still create and work with a local Git repository.

Git-TFc an:

- Clone a TFVC repository to a Git repository
- Fetch changes from the TFVC repository to the local Git repository
- Pull changes from the TFVC repository to the local Git repository
- Push changes from the local Git repository to TFVC repository

We cover Git-TF in detail in Chapter 14.

Choice of Source Control System

The choice of source control system is offered when you create your team project in TF Service, as we saw in Chapter 4. Once you have created your team project, you cannot change your choice of source control system. And there is no conversion available to convert between TFVC and Git. You could, however, use the Git-TF tool to create a Git repository from TFVC to move your source code and history over to a new team project with a Git repository.

It's therefore important to think about your team's needs and which source control system matches those needs best.

Advantageso fT eamF oundationV ersionC ontrol

Some of the advantages of TFVC are:

- Strong in direct workflows, simple check out and check in
- Supports visibility to other team members
- Supports looks and workflows to avoid merges
- Strong in central fine-grained control and policies
- Handlesv eryl argec odebases
- Supportsd isconnectedw ork
- Fulls upporti nsideV isualS tudioa ndE clipse

Advantageso fG it

Some of the advantages of Git are:

- Designedf ordist ributedde velopment
- Lightweightpe rsonalb ranching
- No need for network access
- Advancedc odep romotionw orkflows
- Provides a flexible work style for teams and individuals
- Populara ndf astg rowings ourcec ontrols ystem

Summary

This chapter explained the source control systems available in TF Service. We have looked at the capabilities of both TFVC and Git and pointed out the advantages of each system.

We have also introduced the Git-TF tool that lets you create a local Git repository from a team project with TFVC source control.

The next two chapters will dive deeper into using TFVC and Git in Visual Studio 2012.

CHAPTER12

■ ■ ■

Working with Team Foundation VersionC ontroli n Visual Studio

Team Foundation Version Control (TFVC) is a centralized version control system designed and built for enterprises. Microsoft provides first-class integration and user experience in both Visual Studio and Eclipse and provides command line interfaces and other integration points for other environments. This chapter will explain how to work with Visual Studio 2012 against a TFVC repository.

To get a basic understanding of TFVC and how to choose a source control system in TF Service, please refer to Chapter 11.

Team Explorer

Team Explorer is the central place where most TF Service–related operations start. The Team Explorer view is built up with sections and pages and is dynamically built based on the installed capabilities of your Visual Studio, TF Service, and team project capabilities.

For example, the Team Explorer window connected to a team project with TFVC as the source control system, as shown in Figure 12-1, looks different compared with a team project with Git as the source control system.

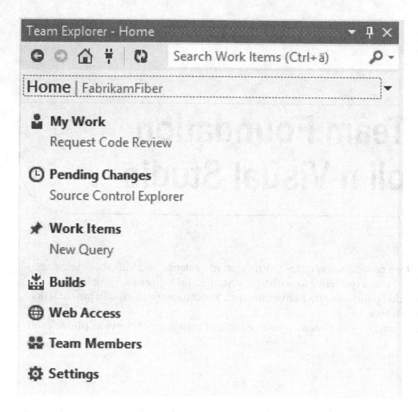

Figure 12-1. *Team Explorer Home page for a TFVC team project*

Each section, or hub as they are sometimes called, is clickable and opens a page for that specific topic. Each page can then contain sections or direct links to other pages.

If you're connected to a TF Service team project with a TFVC repository, you will have the following sections available on the first page:

- *My Work*: The new center for your daily activities, covered later in this chapter. A link takes you directly to the page for requesting a new code review.

- *Pending Changes*: The center for your current changes, shelvesets, and check ins, also covered later in this chapter. The direct link opens up Source Control Explorer in a new window.

- *Work Items*: In the Work Items hub you can access the available work item queries in your project, and you can create new Work Items by clicking the New Work Item link.

- *Builds*: In the Builds hub, you can view and create builds. More about this hub is covered in Chapter 16.

- *Team Members*: An area for interacting with team members, an add on described in the nexts ection.

- *Web Access*: This section is basically just a link that opens Team Web Access in a new browserw indow.

- *Settings*: In the Settings hub, you can access settings for the team project such as areas and iterations, source control settings, projects alerts, and security settings.

TeamM embersE xtension

The Team Members hub is actually an add on and a part of the Microsoft Visual Studio Team Foundation Server Power Tools, released by Microsoft. The Team Members hub is the place where you can communicate with your team members on Lynch or other Instant Messaging systems. You can also view and modify some of the team information, such as team queries, and use it to distribute Shared Custom Components, such as check-in policies, across the team.

■ **Note**   You can find the Microsoft Visual Studio Team Foundation Server Power Tools on Visual Studio Gallery at `http://visualstudiogallery.msdn.microsoft.com/b1ef7eb2-e084-4cb8-9bc7-06c3bad9148f`.

Connecting to a Team Project

One of the first things you might need to do is to select a team project. This is done by clicking the team project name and dropping down the menu, as shown in Figure 12-2.

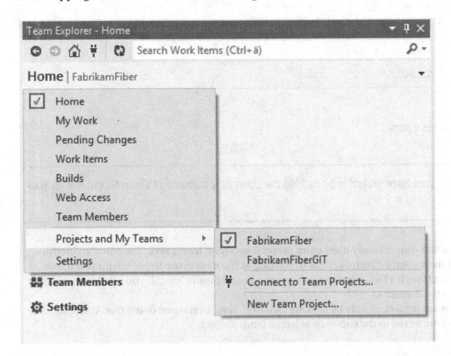

Figure 12-2. *Connecting to a team project*

If you have previously connected to a team project on the current server, it will appear in the list and you can select it directly. If you haven't connected to a TF Service server or if you need to connect to team projects on another server, click the Connect to Team Projects menu. That will take you to the Connect page, as shown in Figure 12-3.

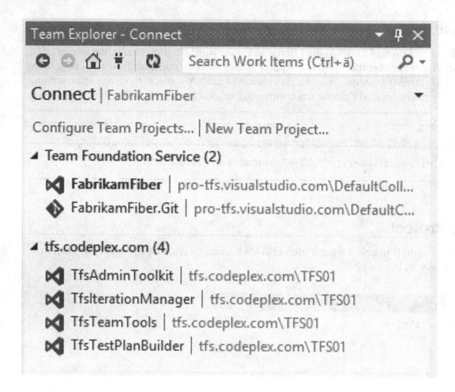

Figure 12-3. *The Team Explorer Connect page*

■ **Tip** A quick way of connecting to your team project is by clicking the Open new instance of Visual Studio link on your team home page in TF Service.

On the Connect page, you can see your recently used team projects grouped by servers. You can also identify which team projects have TFVC as their source control system by looking at the icon to the left of the project name, as shown in Figure 12-3. Team projects with TFVC repositories have the Visual Studio icon. If you need to connect to a new server or project, please refer to Chapter 4.

You can now connect to your team project, simply by clicking its name. Note that when doing this, Visual Studio will close any open solution that is connected to the currently selected team project.

Source Control Operations

Once you have connected to a team project, it's time to take a look at the basic source control operations. Most source control operations are done from the Source Control Explorer. To open the Source Control Explorer window, click the Source Control Explorer link on the Home tab, as shown in Figure 12-4.

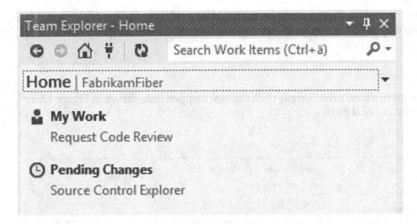

Figure 12-4. *The Team Explorer Home page with link to Source Control Explorer*

Using Source Control Explorer

The Source Control Explorer, as shown in Figure 12-5, is the central window for most TFVC tasks. From Source Control Explorer you can execute most source control–related activities and browse the entire version control repository.

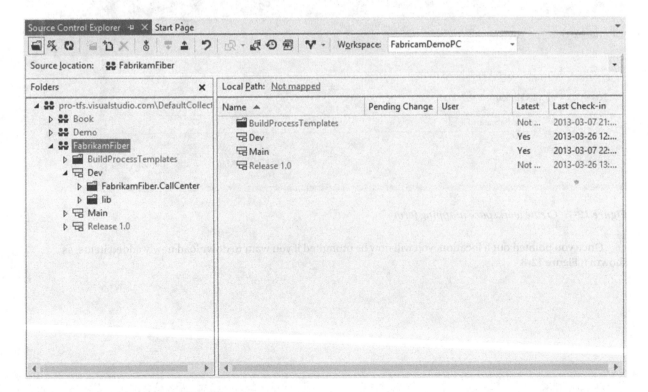

Figure 12-5. *The Source Control Explorer window*

Most of the activities regarding source control are done on your local sandbox, or workspace. One of the first actions you need to do is create a workspace by mapping a location in the central repository to a path on a drive.

MappingW orkspaces

To create a workspace and map a server path to a local drive, simply click the Not mapped link, shown in Figure 12-6, in the top of the Source Control Explorer under Local Path.

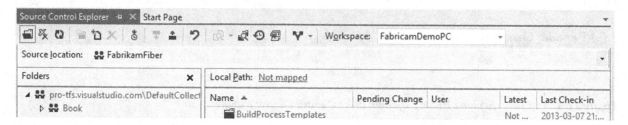

Figure 12-6. *Source Control Explorer with a folder not mapped in a workspace*

It will display the form shown in Figure 12-7 where you can specify the path where you want to store your local fileson .

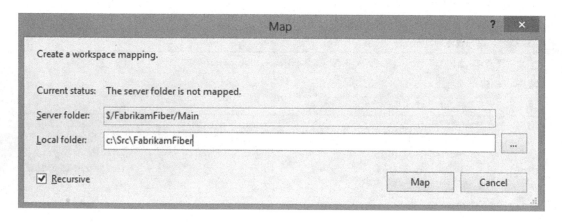

Figure 12-7. *Create workspace mapping form*

Once you pointed out a location, you will now be prompted if you want to download newly added items, as showni n Figure 12-8.

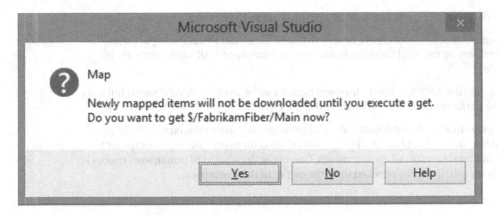

***Figure 12-8.** Prompt from the Source Control Explorer asking if you want to get the newly mapped part of source control*

After this operation is complete, you can perform all activities on your workspace. The right pane of the Source Control Explorer now also represents your workspace, which is your local sandbox.

■ **Note** It's a good practice to try to map as deep down as possible in the source control, such as the current branch you're working on. By doing so you will avoid unnecessary file downloads and use of disc space. Deep mapping will also help in situations where the 260-character limitation of Windows applies. TFVC supports paths with more than 260 characters, so in cases of long paths it might lead to problems and errors. By mapping $/FabricamFiber/FabricamFiber Releases/FabricamFiber Release 1.0/ServicePack to c:\Src\Fabricam you save a lot of characters.

Different Kinds of Workspaces

TFVC offers two kinds of workspaces:

- *Server workspace*: In a server workspace, all operations and states are handled in communications with the TF Service server. This offers several advantages if you're in an always connected environment or if you're handling large repositories. The central repository always knows if someone is editing a file, enabling it to accurately show the current status of all files and whether there is work in progress in some files. With server workspace you can also enable locks on files and prevent checkouts.

- *Local workspace*: In a local workspace, all operations and states are kept on the client side. The biggest advantage of a local workspace is that it enables you to work in a disconnected environment without network communication to the TF Service server. It can also improve the performance when working on a slow network connection. On the other hand, many of the advantages of server workspaces are not possible, because it's not possible to know or prevent a disconnected client from starting work with a file.

■ **Note** For a new project in TF Service, local workspace is the default. You can change the default workspace type for your team project under Team Project Settings ➤ Source Control ➤ Workspace settings. You can always override the project default and then create your own workspace.

Apart from the types of workspaces, you can also control the access of a workspace to three different levels:

- *Private workspace*: A private workspace is only visible to the owner of the workspace and reserves the folders on the local machine to that user or namespace. All workspaces are by defaultp rivate.

- *Public workspace (limited)*: A public limited workspace can be used by all valid users, but only the owner can perform check-ins and manage the workspace.

- *Public workspace*: In a public workspace, all valid users can use the workspace, including check-in and administration of the workspace. This is good for teams sharing a computer or wanting to collaborate on shared environments. One of the drawbacks of public workspaces is that all check-ins will display as checked in by the owner of the workspace.

■ **Note**   If you're starting a new project, that's the time to think about your branching strategy. You should at a minimum prepare for future branching needs by creating a main folder to use as your solution's root folder. For guidance about branching and merging with TFVC, please refer to the Visual Studio TFS Branching and Merging Guide `http://tfsbranchingguideiii.codeplex.com`. It's written by the ALM Rangers, a community of people from Microsoft personnel, partners, MVPs, and other community thought leaders. The ALM Rangers deliver out-of-bounds guidance and tooling to remove adoption blockers in real-world scenarios.

CheckO ut

Once your solution is loaded and under source control, it's time to get started working on your tasks. You can simply open your source files and start editing; Visual Studio will automatically check out the file for you. You can also right-click a file in Source Control Explorer and select Check Out for Edit.

ViewH istory

If you want to view the history of a file or a folder, right-click the file and select View History and the History window, as shown in Figure 12-9, which will list all changes for your file or folder.

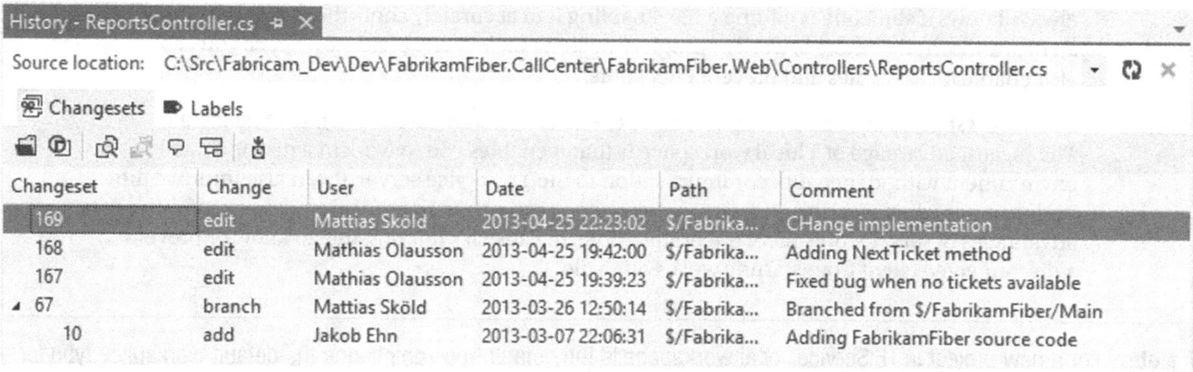

Figure 12-9. History window

You can compare the selected version of the file to your local file in your workspace by selecting the Compare tool in the toolbar. You can also select two versions of the file or folder and compare them to each other.

CompareF ileV ersions

You can use the Compare feature to compare different versions of your file, including your current edited local file. This is done by right-clicking a file and selecting Compare. This will bring up the form shown in Figure 12-10, which lets you select which versions you want to compare.

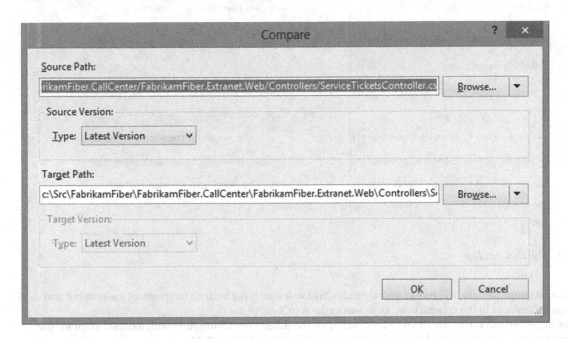

Figure 12-10. *The file Compare version selection form*

Once you've selected the version you want to compare to, the Diff windows, as shown in Figure 12-11, appear and show you the differences between the selected versions.

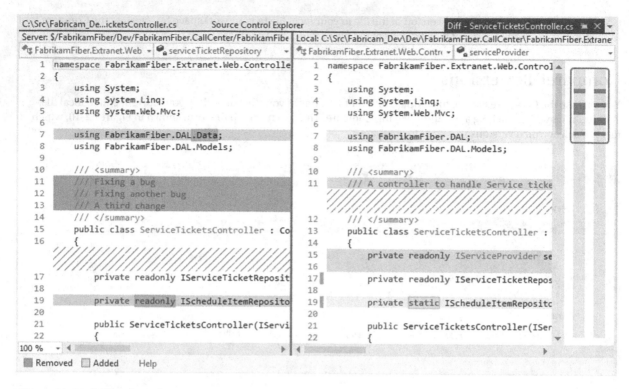

Figure 12-11. *Diff tool window*

Microsoft has improved the Diff tool in Visual Studio 2012 so it now gives both an overview of the number and location of the differences in the comparison, as shown in the scrollbars to the right.

Another improvement is that the Diff tool now highlights the differences within rows with a darker color for the actual changed parts, as shown in the first and last marked differences in Figure 12-11.

■ **Tip**   Even if the Diff tool in Visual Studio 2012 is improved, you might want to use your own favorite. This can be done by selecting Tools ➤ Options ➤ Source Control ➤ Visual Studio Team Foundation and clicking the Configure User Tools button.

Annotate

Annotate is another way to view the history of a file, and it can be done from within the source file, Source Control Explorer, or Solution Explorer. Annotate brings up a new source code window with annotations in it, as shown in Figure 12-12. In the Annotated window, information about who changed the code is shown in the right margin of the source code window.

```
ReportsController.cs;C169 (Annotated)  □  ×
168  Mathias Olausson  2013-04-25     }

10   Jakob Ehn        2013-03-07     public ActionResult Employees()
                                     {
                                         var employees = this.employeeRepository.All.Select(e => new Empl
                                         foreach (var summary in employees)
                                         {
169  Mattias Sköld     2013-04-25         var tickets = this.serviceTicketRepository.AllIncluding(t =>
                                             summary.AssignedTickets = tickets;
10   Jakob Ehn        2013-03-07             summary.AssignedTicketsCnt = tickets.Count();

                                             var firstTicket = tickets.FirstOrDefault();
                                             summary.CurrentCustomer = firstTicket == null ? null : first
                                         }

                                         return View(new EmployeeReportViewModel { Employees = employees
                                     }

                                     public ActionResult Tickets()
                                     {
167  Mathias Olausson  2013-04-25         if (this.serviceTicketRepository != null)
                                         {
10   Jakob Ehn        2013-03-07             var report = this.serviceTicketRepository.AllForReport(
                                                 serviceticket => serviceticket.Customer,
                                                 serviceticket => serviceticket.CreatedBy,
                                                 serviceticket => serviceticket.AssignedTo);
167  Mathias Olausson  2013-04-25         }
10   Jakob Ehn        2013-03-07             return View();
                                     }
                                 }
                             }
```

Figure 12-12. *Example of an annotated source file*

You can also annotate a previous version of the file by viewing the history of the file and selecting Annotate for a specificv ersion.

ViewP endingC hanges

The Pending Changes page in Team Explorer, as shown in Figure 12-13, is the place where you can keep track of your current work. It's also the place where you can shelve your code or perform the actual check in. You can navigate to the Pending changes window either by right-clicking a file and selecting Check In or by going to the Home tab of Team Explorer and selecting Pending Changes.

Figure 12-13. *Pending Changes window*

The Pending Changes page consists of four different sections:

- *Comment*: In this section you can submit a comment describing the change you have made.

- *Related work items*: In this section you can add work items to the check in, either by dragging them from a query to this section or by entering the ID. You can also select if you want to only associate a work item or if you want to perform a state transition upon check in.

- *Included changes*: This section lists all of the files to be included in the check in. You can drag files to the Excluded Changes section if you don't want them to be a part of the current check in. To assist you, Visual Studio will help by filtering what gets added based on extensions and the scope of the selected solution.

- *Excluded changes*: This section lists all of the files to be excluded in the check in. You can drag files to the Included section to include them in the current check in or click the Include All link to include all files to the current check in.

Once you're happy with everything, you click the Check In button to commit your check in to the central repository. Before anything gets committed, the check-in policies get evaluated, and if one or more policies does not meet the standard, a Policy Warnings section will appear, as shown in Figure 12-14. This section will show all failing polices that you need to satisfy before checking in the code.

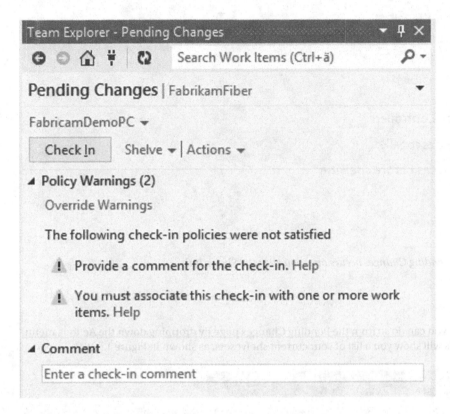

Figure 12-14. *Pending Changes window with two Policy Warnings*

You can always check in the code by choosing to override the policies and provide a policy override comment to motivate overriding the policies.

From the Pending Changes page you can also perform other actions such as shelving your code, retrieving a shelveset, or undoing all changes.

Shelving

Shelving is the capability to store your current changes to the server, without checking it into the code base. Shelving is done through the Pending Changes page by clicking the Shelve link.

This will show the Shelve section, as shown in Figure 12-15, where you can enter a name for your shelveset and select if you want to preserve your pending changes. You can also perform the same validation for your shelveset as the check-in procedure will apply.

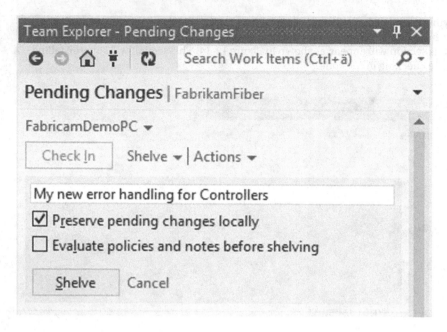

Figure 12-15. Shelving section of Pending Changes occurs once you click the Shelve link

RetrievingS helvesets

If you want to retrieve a shelveset, you can do so from the Pending Changes page by dropping down the Actions menu and selecting Find Shelvesets. This will show you a list of your current shelvesets, as shown in Figure 12-16.

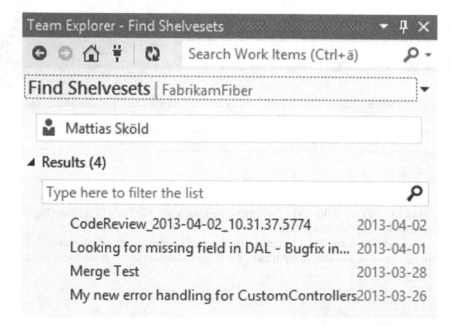

Figure 12-16. Find Shelvesets page where you can view your own and other users' shelvesets

You can search for other users' shelvesets by replacing your name with the other user's name. You can also view the details of a shelveset by either double-click it or right-clicking and selecting View Details. It will show the Shelveset Details page, as shown in Figure 12-17.

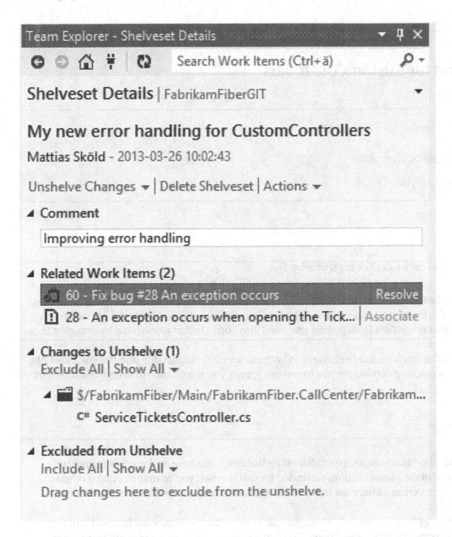

Figure 12-17. *Shelveset Details page*

You can retrieve the shelveset by click the Unshelve Changes link, which will open up the Unshelve section, as shown in Figure 12-18.

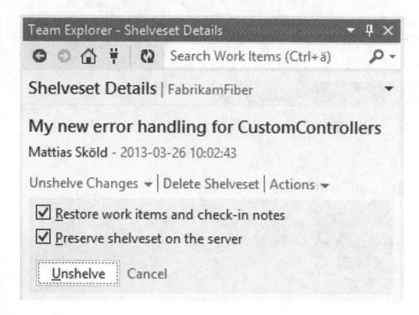

Figure 12-18. *Unshelve section occurs once you click the Unshelve link*

In this section you can select whether you want to restore the associated work items or check notes. You can also select to preserve the shelveset on the server or if you want to delete it after it's unshelved. Before you unshelve you can also select if you want to exclude certain files from getting retrieved into your current workspace by dragging them to the Excluded from Unshelve section.

When unshelving a shelveset after you have made changes to both the local workspace file and the shelveset file, the unshelve operation will trigger a pending conflict for you to resolve, giving you the chance to merge the different versions with the Merge tool.

Branching

Branching is the solution for teams who need to work in parallel on an isolated code base and want to minimize the risk of affecting one another. One of the most common scenarios for this is when you're maintaining a release in production and developing the next version. There are many other and more complicated scenarios that can be relevant for your situation and needs.

When forming a branching strategy for your project, it's important to keep the requirements in mind and not create an overcomplicated strategy to meet any potential need. To keep it simple and useful, there are three rules to follow:

- Only branch when you need to.

- Think about how your code should be merged and organize your branch structure accordingly.

- Brancha tt her ootl evelo fy ours olution.

■ **Tip**   Remember that you can consult the Visual Studio TFS Branching and Merging Guide (http://tfsbranchingguideiii.codeplex.com) for guidance about branching.

Creating a B ranch

Once you have decided on a branching strategy, you will probably need to create a branch at some point of time depending on your strategy.

To create a branch, right-click the folder you want to branch from, and select Branching and Merging ➤ Branch. This will show the form as shown in Figure 12-19.

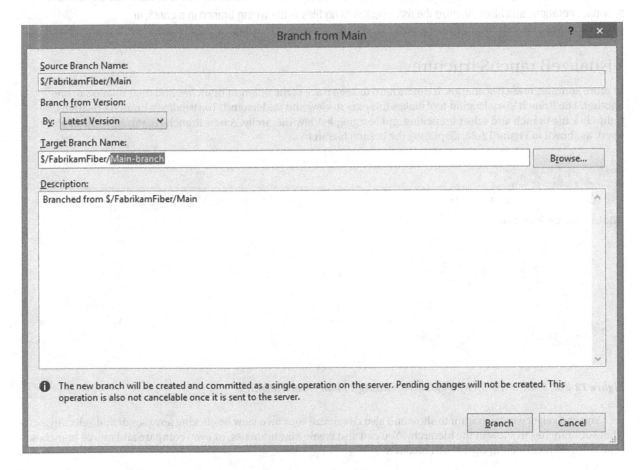

Figure 12-19. *Branch from Main form*

Make sure you change the Target branch to something appropriate such as Release 1.0 or Dev. You can select to create your branch from different versions. The options you have are:

- *Latest Version*: Branches after the latest check-in in source control
- *Changeset*: Branches after the specified changeset
- *Date*: Branches after the specified point in time
- *Label*: Branches from a specified label, useful for creating branches from a successful build
- *Workspace version*: Creates a branch from the versions of the selected workspace

By clicking the Branch button, you will start the branch operation, which will create your new branch for you. Once the branch is created, you can start working on your new branch and check in code in the new branch without affecting the other branches.

___

■ **Note**   It can be a good idea to create different workspaces for different branches. This is to minimize the size and network operations and also minimize the risk of committing files in the wrong branch in a check in.

___

VisualizeB ranchS tructure

In more complex branch scenarios, it can be hard to keep track of the different branches and their relation to one another. The Branch Visualization tool makes this easy to view and understand. To visualize a branch's relations, right-click the branch and select Branching and Merging ➤ View Hierarchy. A new Branch Hierarchy window will open, as shown in Figure 12-20, displaying the branch hierarchy.

Figure 12-20. Branch Hierarchy window visualizing a main branch hierarchy

You can select what you want to show and also customize your own view by clicking any parent and selecting what subbranches to show in the hierarchy. You can also create new branches, or even compare and merge branches, from this graphical view of the branch hierarchy.

Merging

Merging is the process of combining the work or changes done in a branch into another code base. If a file has been edited in both branches, you will have a conflict; if the change in the different branches is done in different parts of the file, TFVC can autoresolve the conflict. If the conflict can't be resolved, you will have to resolve the conflict manually.
TF Service manages TFCV merging in three steps:

1.   TF Service merges the code bases to your workspace.

2.   The result of the merge may contain conflicts you have to resolve manually in your workspace.

3.   You have to validate and check in the merged files to complete the merge.

Performing a Merge Between Branches

To merge changes from one source branch into a target branch, select the source branch in Source Control Explorer, right-click and select Branching and Merging ➤ Merge and the Merge wizard will show the form as shown inF igure 12-21.

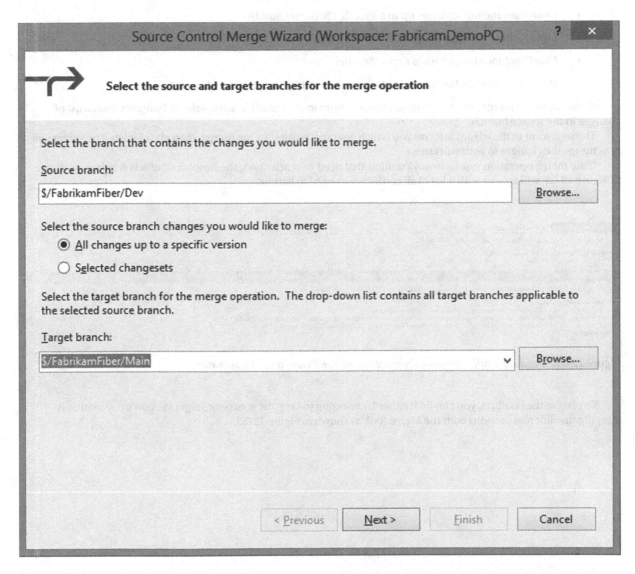

Figure 12-21. First page of the Merge wizard

Make sure the source and target branches are correct and select if you want to merge all changes or just a selected changeset.

If you want to merge all selected changes, the next form in the wizard will ask you if you want to include all changes up to a specific version, and you can select the following limitations:

- *Latest version*: Include all changes

- *Changeset*: Include changes up to a specific changeset number

- *Date*: Include changes up to the specified point in time

- *Label*: Include changes up to a specific label

- *Workspace version*: Include changes up to the versions of the selected workspace

If you choose to merge selected changes, the next form in the wizard lets you select Changeset from a list of changes in the source branch.

The next form in the wizard informs you which operations will start the merge, then click Finish. The server will now merge the changes to your workspace.

If the merge operation results in any conflicts that need your attention, the Resolve Conflicts window, as shown in Figure 12-22, will appear with a list of all conflicts you need to handle.

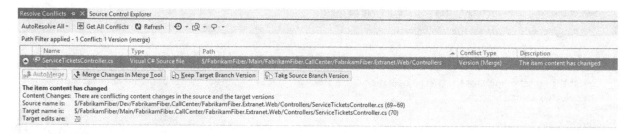

Figure 12-22. *Pending conflict window showing you all conflicts of a merge operation*

To resolve the conflicts, you can do it either by selecting to keep the source or target version or by manually merging the different versions with the Merge tool, as shown in Figure 12-23.

Figure 12-23. *Merge tool window*

In the Merge tool you're shown the source and the target file, with all changes marked out and with a check box to the left of the change. By marking the check box you can select to use this change in the resulting file. It you choose to include both changes, they will be placed in order in the file. It's also possible for you to edit the results before continuing.

Once all conflicts have been resolved, you can accept the merge. It's now up to you to verify that the merge was successful and hasn't introduced any new defects before you go to the Pending changes page to complete the merge by checking in the merged files. Merged files will have a [merge] comment, as shown in Figure 12-24.

Figure 12-24. Pending Changes page showing the pending merge operation you are about to check in

The merge operation is not completed until you perform the check in. If you undo all changes, you can restart the merge process from the beginning.

Forward and Reverse Integration

As mentioned earlier, branching is done to minimize the risk of parallel changes, causing problems in a code base. But merging code back to the parent branch introduces this risk, and the more change you merge in, the greater the risk.

To reduce the risk, it's a common pattern to start with merging all changes from the parent branch into the child branch. This is called *forward integration* (FI). FI should be performed as often as possible to expose potential problems in the child branch as early as possible.

Merging code back from the child branch to the parent branch is called *reverse integration*(R I).R Iis c ommonly performed once the code is complete. Before initializing an RI, it's a good practice to perform an FI and validate the system. An example of FI and RI is shown in Figure 12-25.

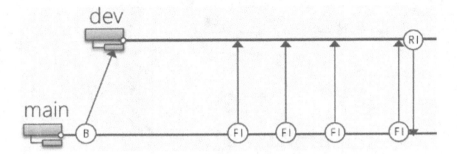

Figure 12-25. *Illustration of a typical branch strategy with the different types of merge*

Branch Visualization and Tracking

If you have done some work on the branch and want to know how that change has flowed into the other branches, Microsoft has developed a set of branch visualization and tracking capabilities, outlined in the sections that follow.

TrackC hangeset

One of the visualization and tracking features is the Track Changeset feature. Anywhere you have a changeset, such as in the History window or at the Links tab of a work item, you can choose to track it across your branch hierarchy by right-clicking it and selecting Track Changeset. This will show the Select Branches form as shown in Figure 12-26.

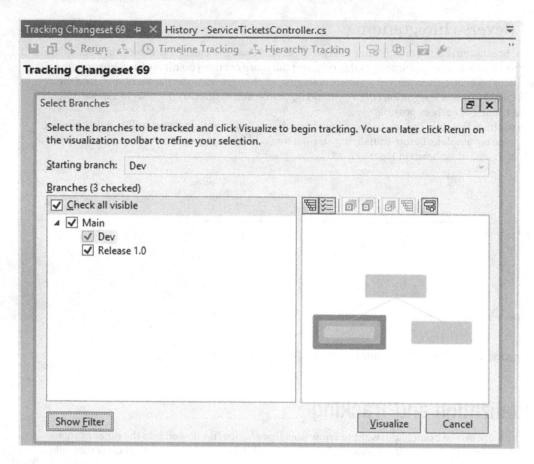

Figure 12-26. *Select Branches page of the Track Changeset window*

Select which branches you are interested in tracking the changeset for and click Visualize. This will bring up the Track Changeset window. It has two modes: Timeline tracking and Hierarchy tracking. In both modes, branches are colored in green for all branches that have received the tracked changeset, as shown in Figure 12-27.

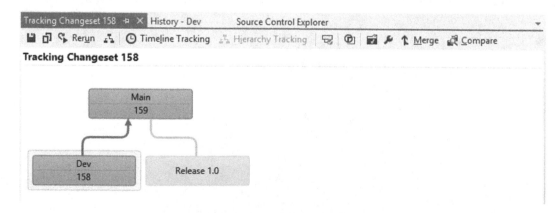

Figure 12-27. *Track Changeset window in Hierarchy tracking mode*

In the Hierarchy tracking mode, it shows the branching hierarchy and which branch has received the changes and the path the changes have taken, including the changeset number. In the Timeline tracking mode, it shows how the change is flowing from branch to branch along a timeline, as shown in Figure 12-28.

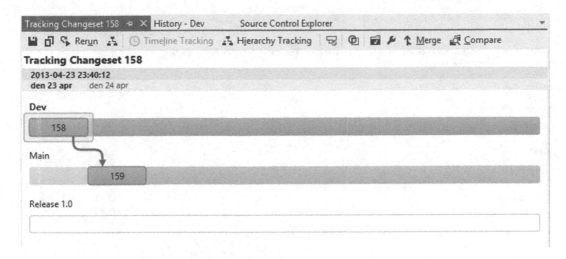

Figure 12-28. *Track Changeset window in Timeline tracking mode*

___

■ **Tip** It's also possible to drag and drop a changeset between branches to initialize a merge operation. If you do so, the merge wizard is prepopulated with the branches and changeset number.

___

TrackW orkI tem

Tracking changesets could be a very useful feature, but most of the time we're working with work items such as stories, bugs and tasks. There are many situations where you want to make sure all code changes required to resolve a bug have been integrated across your branch structure.

By using the Work Item tracking feature, you can track the related work to any work item across your branches. It offers the same capabilities as the Track Changeset feature, but because a work item can be related to several changesets, a work item can be only partially merged into a branch. The work item tracking feature can help ensure that all code changes related to a work item have been implemented into the branch structure.

To activate the Track Work Item feature, open a work item, right-click it and select Tracking Work Item. This will show the Select branches form as shown in Figure 12-29.

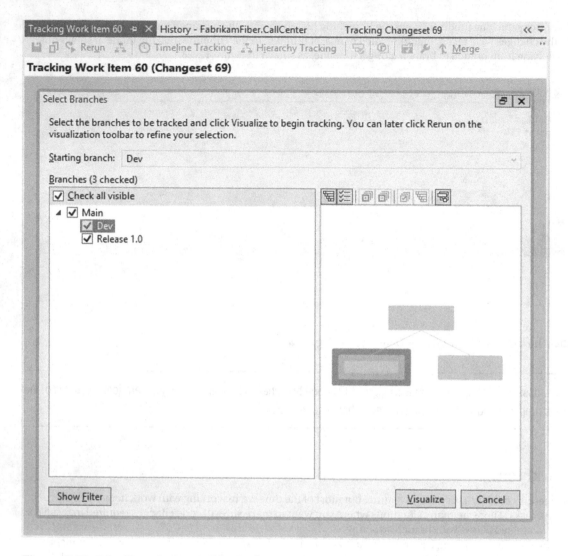

Figure 12-29. *Select Branches page of the Tracking Work Item window*

Select which branches you are interested in tracking the work item for and click Visualize. This will bring up the Tracking Work Item window.

Like the Track Changeset window, the Tracking Work Item window has two modes: Timeline tracking and Hierarchy tracking. In both modes, branches are colored in green for all branches that have received all related changesets to a work item; if a branch has received some but not all changes, it's colored in a yellow and green striped color, as shown in Figure 12-30.

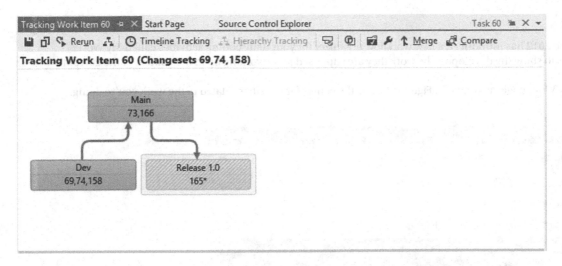

Figure 12-30. *Tracking Work Item window in Hierarchy tracking mode displaying a partial merge to the Release branch*

In the Hierarchy tracking mode, it shows the branching hierarchy and which branch has received the changes and the path the changes have taken, including the changeset number.

In the Timeline tracking mode, it shows how the change has flowed from branch to branch along a timeline, as shown in Figure 12-31. In this case, we can see that an additional check in occurred after the merge operation and that the last two changesets (74,158) of the work item have been merged down to Main, but currently have not been merged to the Release branch.

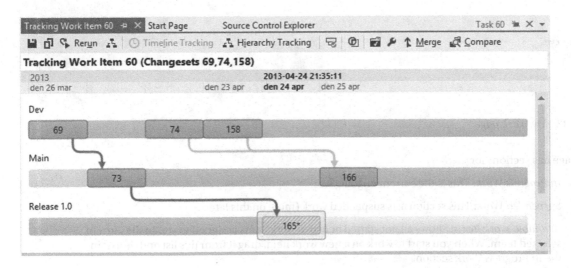

Figure 12-31. *Tracking Work Item window in Timeline tracking mode displaying a partial merge to the Release branch*

MyW ork

Visual Studio 2012 has introduced a new workflow organizer for your daily coding activities called My Work. The intent is to show the developers the work they are supposed to be working on in the context of the currently selected team.

The My Work page, as shown in Figure 12-32, is the center for activities related to the work you're doing.

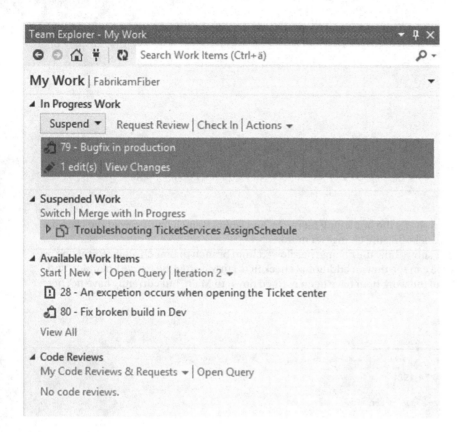

Figure 12-32. *My Work page*

The page has sections for

- *In Progress Work*: This is the current ongoing work.

- *Suspended Work*: This section lists suspended work (more on this later).

- *Available Work Items*: Shows all not started or active work items assigned to you in the current selected team. When you start to work on a new work item, drag it from this list and drop it in the In Progress Work section.

- *Code Reviews*: This section shows all my Code Reviews and Requests (more on this later).

StartingN ewW ork

When you start working on something, you can simply pick a work item or drag it to the In Progress Work section. By doing so, you're changing the state of the work item to "in progress." But you're also creating a useful context for your current work. The My Work feature of Visual Studio will collect all aspects of the work you're doing and relate it to the current context. All that information is later used when you check in or suspending your work.

SuspendingY ourC urrentW ork

Even if context switching generally is an expensive operation that should be kept to a minimum, it does tend to happen in the real world. Visual Studio 2012 tries to minimize the context switching cost by allowing you to easily suspend your current work and later on resume it.

By suspending your work, you're saving the current state of visual studio, including things like:

- Pendingc hanges
- Relatedw orki tems
- Openw indows
- Activeb reakpoints
- Watchw indowsv ariables

You suspend the current work by clicking the Suspend button, and a new area where you can provide a description for the work you're about to suspend shows up, as shown in Figure 12-33. If you have associated a work item to your work, the default description will be the title of that work item.

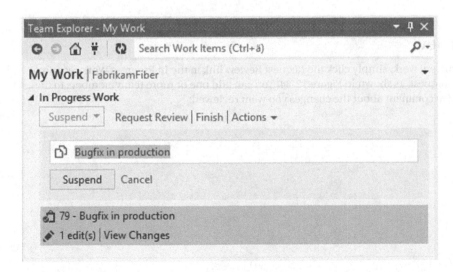

Figure 12-33. *Suspending the current work*

By clicking the Suspend button, your work gets suspended. Visual Studio will reset your development environment to a fresh working state, ready to begin work on the urgent stuff, for example, a bug fix in a production branch. You can have multiple works suspended and switch back and forth among these.

ResumingY ourS uspendedW ork

Once you are ready to resume work on the previously suspended work, you have three options. You can:

- *Resume*: If you have finished the current work in progress you can resume a previously suspendedw ork.

- *Switch*: Switch the in progress work with the one you want to resume.

- *Merge with In Progress*: The suspended work and Visual Studio settings will be merged into the currentV isualS tudioe nvironment.

Once resumed, all source code, windows, breakpoints, and other suspended settings will be restored to the state active before the suspended operation. This is what minimizes the cost of context switching—you are right back to where you were when you suspended what you were doing at the time.

Code Reviews

Code reviews are very important in a software development process. They are also a key factor in improving the quality of the code that is begin written. It is also a very good way to increase learning and spread knowledge across the team. With TF Service, code reviews are fully integrated into Team Explorer, so you don't have to leave Visual Studio.

Requesting a Code Review

To request a code review of your current work, simply click the Request Review link in the In Progress Work section. This will open a new Code Review request, as shown in Figure 12-34. You can add one or more team members to the request, as well as write a descriptive comment about the changes you want reviewed.

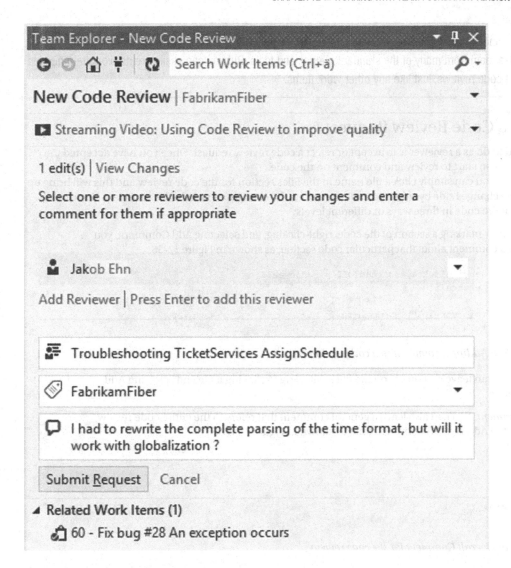

Figure 12-34. New Code Review request page

When you submit a Code Review request, all reviewers are notified by e-mail, and the Code Review request will turn up in their My Work page, under the Code Reviews section, as shown in Figure 12-35.

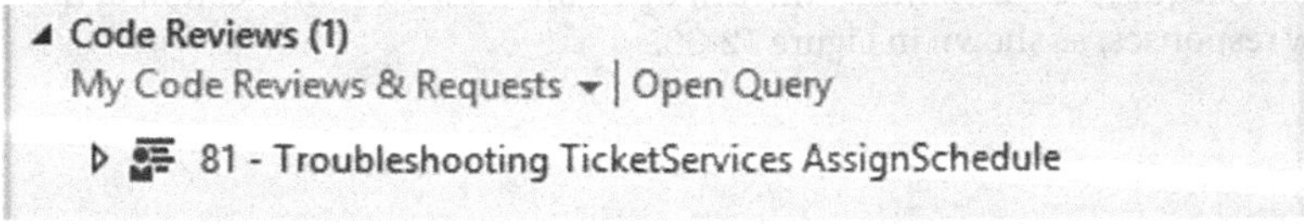

Figure 12-35. Code Review request shown in the Code Reviews section for all reviewers

■ **Note**   Code review requests and responses are implemented as work items. They are, however, marked as hidden, which by default excludes them from many of the standard queries and tools. But you can easily create work item queries to find information about code reviews, just like any other work items.

Responding to a Code Review Request

The first thing you need to do as a reviewer is to accept or reject a code review request. Once you have accepted the code review request, you can start to review and comment on the code.

To view the changes, you can simply click a file name in the Files section for the code review and this will bring up the Diff tool showing the changes side by side. You can now review the changes or switch files to review. You can also submit comments about the code in three ways or different levels:

- *Code section*: By marking a section of the code, right-clicking, and selecting Add Comment, you can submit a comment about that particular code section, as shown in Figure 12-36.

Figure 12-36. Adding a comment to a code section

- *File level*: You can leave comments on the file level by right-clicking a file and selecting Add FileC omment.

- *Overall comment*: You can also leave a general comment that refers to the entire code review by clicking the Add Overall Comment link, as shown in Figure 12-37.

◢ Comments (4)
▷ Overall (2)
  Add Overall Comment

Figure 12-37. Adding an Overall Comment for the code review

Once you are done commenting, you can submit your comments by clicking the Send Comments button. By doing so, you publish your comments so the other reviewers and the requester can view them.

Viewinga ndR espondingt oa R eview

When someone responds to your Code Review Request, the responses will turn up in the Code Reviews section of the My Work page with an arrow indicating new responses, as shown in Figure 12-38.

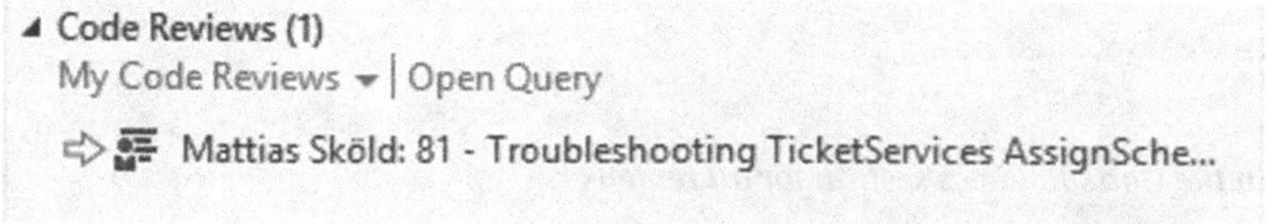

◢ Code Reviews (1)
  My Code Reviews ▾ | Open Query
  ⇨ ▦ Mattias Sköld: 81 - Troubleshooting TicketServices AssignSche...

Figure 12-38. Code review responses are indicated with an arrow on the My Code Reviews section

To view the response, double-click Code Review Request and it will open the Code Review page where you can view all comments made by the reviewers. You can also leave comments to the code reviewers comments or have a discussion about the changes, as shown in Figure 12-39.

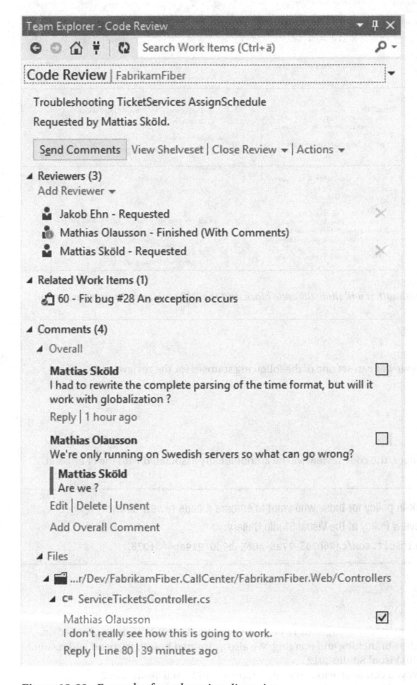

Figure 12-39. Example of a code review discussion

If a comment is related to a code block, it will show the code block inside the Diff tool, as shown in Figure 12-40.

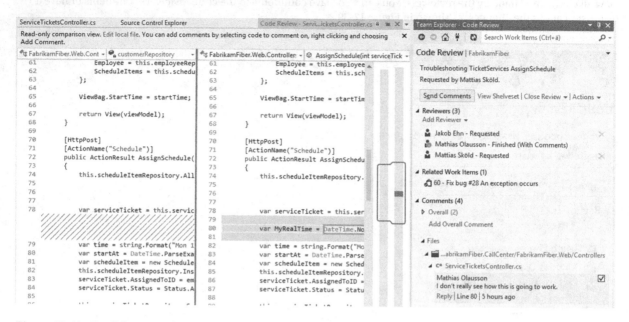

Figure 12-40. *By clicking a code block comment, it will show the code block and the Diff tool from the prevous version*

Finalizinga C odeR eview

Once the code review is complete, each reviewer can set one of the following statuses for the review:

- LooksG ood

- WithC omments

- NeedsW ork

When you check in the pending changes, the code review will be automatically associated with the changeset.

■ **Note**   There is no out-of-the-box check-in policy for those who want to enforce a code review for every check in. However, there is a free Code Review Policy at the Visual Studio Gallery: http://visualstudiogallery.msdn.microsoft.com/c476b708-77a8-4065-b9d0-919ab688f078.

Summary

This chapter explained the most common tasks of working with TFVC and Visual Studio 2012. We have touched on the basic source control operations as well as branching and merging. We also examined how to suspend and resume your work and how to do code reviews with Visual Studio 2012.

The next chapter will go through how you can work with Git source control and Visual Studio 2012.

■ ■ ■

Working withG it in Visual Studio

Git is a distributed version control system that has become very popular in the past few years. Microsoft has chosen to support Git to offer a distributed version control solution and is committed to provide a first-class, integrated user experience inside Visual Studio when working with Git.

As noted in Chapter 11, Microsoft's goal is to provide full Git support in the next major release of Visual Studio. As a part of Microsoft's walking their agile talk, they are continuously releasing previews of the new Git tools for Visual Studio 2012 to enable them to gather and respond to feedback.

This chapter will explain how to work with Visual Studio 2012 against a TF Service Git repository. To get a basic understanding of Git and how to choose a source control system in TF Service, please refer to Chapter 11.

■ **Note** Microsoft is committed to follow and support the Git community and to offer a first-class experience for Git inside Visual Studio for all Git repositories, whether it's a Microsoft TF Service repository or a third-party Git repository.

■ **Caution** The Visual Studio 2012 Git tools extension is a preview and not feature complete. For some operations you will still have to rely on the Git command line utilities and other third-party tools.

Installing Git Extensions to Visual Studio 2012

The first thing you need to do is install the latest Git extensions for Visual Studio 2012. Then when you start Visual Studio 2012, it will prompt you if you want to download the extension from Visual Studio Gallery with a direct link.

Microsoft Git extensions don't require you to download and install any Git command line utilities, but once you have cloned your first Git repository, you will be prompted to install third-party Git command prompts tools. It would be a good idea to do so to get the full power of Git.

■ **Note** Another good starting point to find and download other Git tools is http://git-scm.com/downloads.

Using Team Explorer

Team Explorer is the place where most TF Service–related operations start. The Team Explorer view is built up with sections and pages and is built dynamically based on the installed capabilities of your Visual Studio, TF Service, and team project capabilities.

For example, the Team Explorer window looks different for a team project with Git as the source control system (shown in Figure 13-1) compared with a team project with TFVC as the source control system.

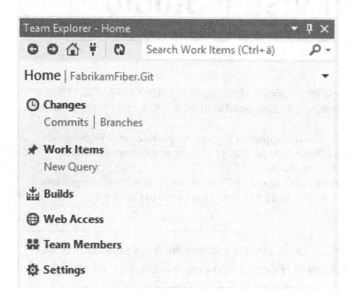

Figure 13-1. *Team Explorer for a Git team project*

Each section, or hub as they are sometimes called, is clickable and opens a page for that specific topic. Each page then contains sections or direct links to other pages.

If you're connected to a TF Service team project with Git as the source control system, you will see the following sections on the first page:

- *Changes*: The center for your current changes and commits. The direct links for commits and branches take you directly to those pages.

- *Work Items*: Here you can access the available work item queries in your project, and you can also create new work items by clicking the New Work Item link.

- *Builds*: Here you can view and create builds. More about this hub is covered in Chapter 16.

- *Web Access*: This section is basically just a link that opens Team Web Access in a new browser window.

- *Team Members*: An area for interacting with team members, an add on described in the nexts ection.

- *Settings*: Here you can access settings for the team project such as areas and iterations, projects alerts, and security settings. You can also find your Git settings such as username and e-mail, `.gitignore`,a ndo therr epository-levels ettings.

TeamM embersE xtension

The Team Members hub is actually an add on and part of the Visual Studio 2012 TFS Power Tools released by Microsoft. The Team Members hub is a place where you can communicate with your team members on Lync or other Instant Messaging systems. You can also view and modify some of the team information such as team queries and use it to distribute shared custom components across the team.

■ **Note**   You can find the TFS Power Tools on Visual Studio Gallery at
`http://visualstudiogallery.msdn.microsoft.com/b1ef7eb2-e084-4cb8-9bc7-06c3bad9148f`.

Connecting to a Team Project

One of the first things you might need to do is select a team project. This is done by clicking the team project name and dropping down the menu, as shown in Figure 13-2.

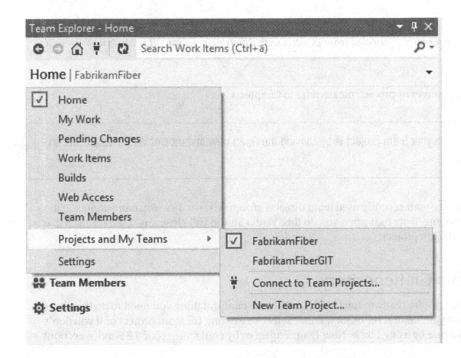

Figure 13-2. *Connecting to a team project through Team Explorer*

If you have previously connected to a team project on the current server, this will appear in the list and you can select it directly. You can also identify which team projects have Git as their source control system by looking at the icon to the left of the project name, as shown in Figure 13-3. Team projects with TFVC repositories have the Visual Studio icon, and team projects with Git repositories have the Git icon, seen preceding FabrikamFiber.Git in Figure 13-3.

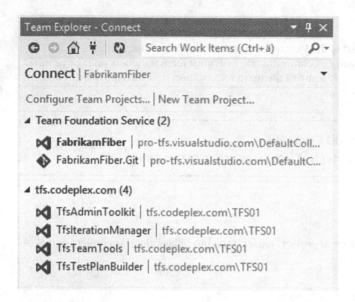

Figure 13-3. *Connect page showing recently connected team projects with different icons for Git projects and TFVC projects*

If you need to connect to a new server or project, please refer to Chapter 4.

■ **Note** A quick way of connecting to your team project is by clicking the Open new instance of Visual Studio link on your team home page in TF Service.

On the Connect page, you can see your recently used team projects grouped by servers. You can connect to a team project simply by clicking its name. Note that when you do this, Visual Studio will close any open solution that is connected to the currently selected team project.

Connecting to a Remote Git Repository

Once you have the Git tools in place, you're ready to start working. The most natural thing you need to do then is to make sure you have a server to host your central repository. Either select an existing Git team project or if you don't have a team project, you can create one by using File ➤ New Team Project or by contacting your TF Service account administrator.

You can also start by creating a local empty repository and later push your local repository to a remote Git server.

■ **Tip** You can also host your Git repository at any Git hoster such as GitHub, CodePlex, Bitbucket, or any other third-party Git hoster. It's also possible to start by creating your own Git repository locally and later finding a Git hoster.

Once you have selected a team project, Team Explorer will show the options available for a Git project, and you will be prompted to Clone the project's Git repo to your local machine, as shown in Figure 13-4.

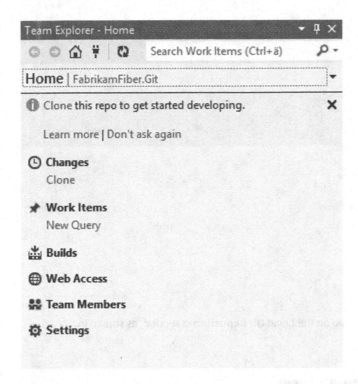

Figure 13-4. Team Explorer prompting you to clone the server repository

Cloning the central repository will download a complete copy of the server Git repo to your local machine, including all of its history.

Clicking the Clone link will take you to the Connect page of the Local Git Repositories section, as shown in Figure 13-5, with the options prefilled to clone the team project's Git repo to a local clone on your computer.

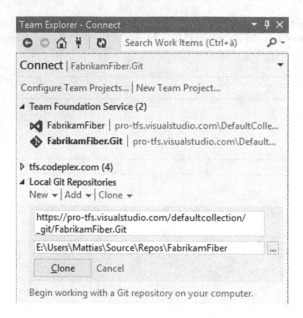

Figure 13-5. *Cloning a server repository*

Once completed, you will find the newly cloned repo on the Local Git Repositories section, as shown in Figure 13-6.

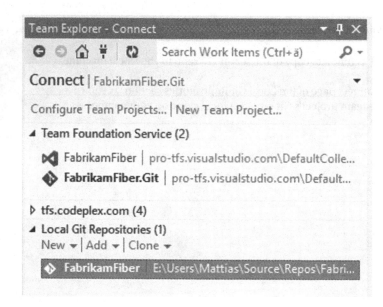

Figure 13-6. *Connect page with a local repository*

Browsingt heS ourceC ode

Because all operations on Git are made on your local repo and Git is file based, there is no Git Source Control Explorer inside Visual Studio, as shown in Figure 13-7.

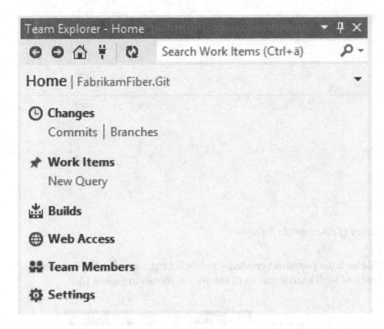

Figure 13-7. Git projects don't have a Source Control Explorer

You can, however, view the local files of the repository by navigating to the folder in an ordinary file explorer. A quick way is to select the Branches link to navigate to the Branches page and then select Action ➤ Open In File Explorer.

You can also view the server repository by clicking the Web Access link and then clicking the Code tab. There will be more about viewing the central repository in web access later in the chapter.

ViewH istory

If you right-click a file name in Solution Explorer and select the History menu, you can view the history of that file; Figure 13-8 shows the Git History window.

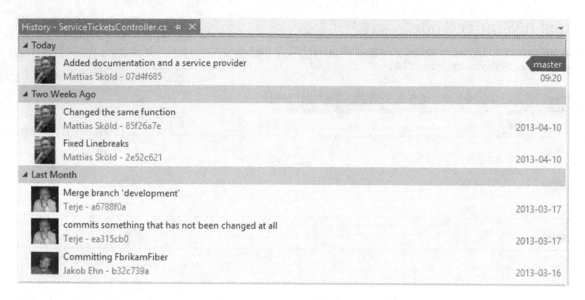

Figure 13-8. *Git History windows showing the history of all commits for a file*

You can compare the selected version of the file with the previous version by right-clicking and selecting Compare with Previous in the menu. It will show you the Diff tool with both versions of the file, as shown in Figure 13-9.

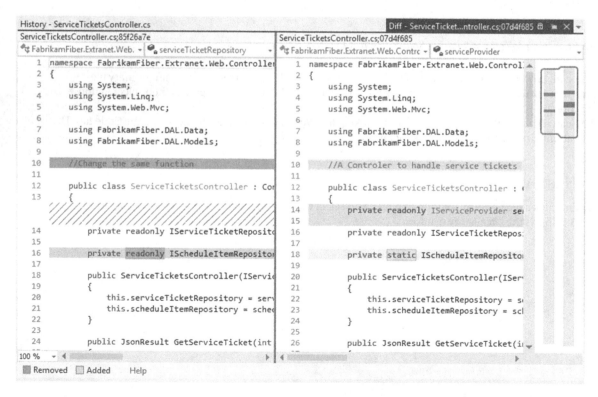

Figure 13-9. *Diff tool showing the differences between different versions of a file*

Microsoft has improved the Diff tool in Visual Studio 2012 so it now gives both an overview of the number and the location of the differences in the comparison, as shown in the scrollbars to the right.

Another improvement is that the Diff tool now highlights the differences within rows with a darker color for the actual changed parts, as shown in the first and last marked differences in Figure 13-9.

Committing Changes toY ourL ocalR epository

The Changes page in Team Explorer is the place where you can keep track of your current work. It's also the place where you perform the actual commit to your local repository.

You can navigate to the Changes window, as shown in Figure 13-10, either by right-clicking a file name and selecting Commit or by going to the Home tab of Team Explorer and selecting Changes.

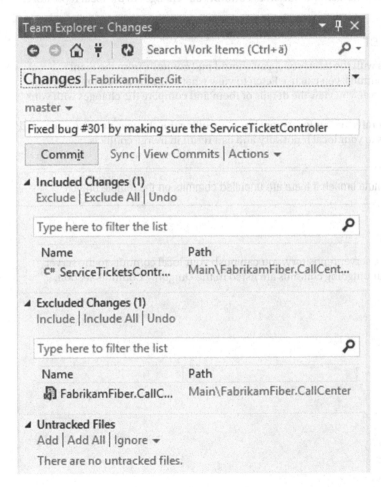

Figure 13-10. Changes page showing a change ready for commit

■ **Tip** In Git you're working and committing (checking in) changes to your own local repository. In order to share your commits with other team members, you need to push them to the server repository.

The Changes page consists of different sections:

- *Comment*: On the top of the page, you can supply a comment for the commit. To associate a work item to the commit, type a hash tag (#) followed by the work item number.

- *Included Changes*: This sections list all files to be included in the commit. You can drag files to the Excluded Changes section if you don't want them to be part of the current commit.

- *Excluded Changes*: This section lists all files to be excluded in the commit. You can drag files to the Included section to include them in the current commit or click the Include All link to include all files to the current commit.

- *Untracked Files*: This section lists all files not being tracked.

Once you're happy with everything, you click the Commit button to commit your changes to the local repository.

Pulling Changes from the Server

In order to ensure that the code you have works with the latest code, you should pull commits from the team repository on a regular basis. Before you pull commits, you can use Fetch to view what commits are on the server. After you have fetched the commits from the server, you view the details of them and compare the changes with your local repository.

Then you want to integrate the remote commits to your local repository by pulling the changes down to your local repository. This will merge the remote commits to your local repository and can result in merge conflicts.

■ **Note**   You cannot push your changes to a remote branch if there are unpulled commits on the remote branch.

PushingC hangest ot heS erver

Once your code works with the latest code in the server repository, you can push your local commits to the server. This is done from the Commits page, where your outgoing commits are listed in the Outgoing Commits section, ass howni nF igure 13-11.

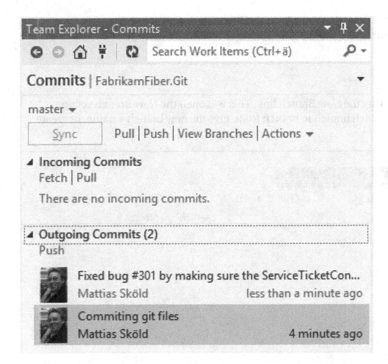

Figure 13-11.   Commits page showing Outgoing Commits waiting to be pushed to the server

Branching

You can easily view and select which branch you work on by navigating to the Branches page, as shown in Figure 13-12, from the Home page.

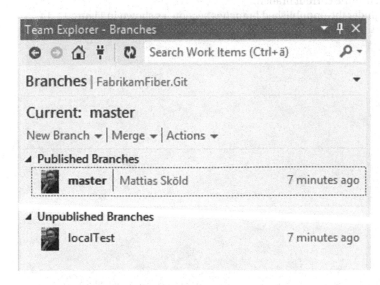

Figure 13-12.   Branches page showing both published and unpublished branches

The Branches page consist of two sections: one section is for Published Branches, available for remote repositories, and the other is for your local Unpublished Branches, available only in your own repository.

Create a New Local Branch

You can easily create a new local branch by clicking the New Branch link. This will open the New Branch section, as shown in Figure 13-13, where you can select which branch to branch from, give the new branch a name, or create ab ranch.

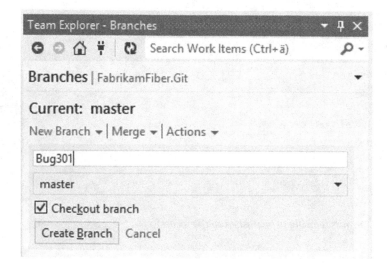

Figure 13-13. *Team Explorer Branches page options*

This will create a new unpublished branch in your local repository; if you check mark the Checkout branch option, it will automatically select the new branch as the current branch.

Once the branch is created, it will show up under the unpublished branches section, as shown in Figure 13-14.

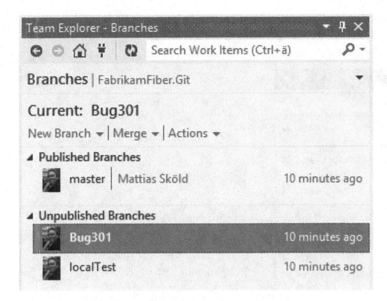

Figure 13-14. *Branches page with the newly created branch*

SwitchingB ranches

If you're done working on one branch and want to work on another branch, you can simply right-click the other branch and select the Switch option. This will set the selected branch as the current branch.

Merging Branches

If you're done working on a branch and want to merge it to any other branch, you can do so by clicking the Merge link on the Branches page. This will open the Merge section where you can select source and target branches, as shown in Figure 13-15.

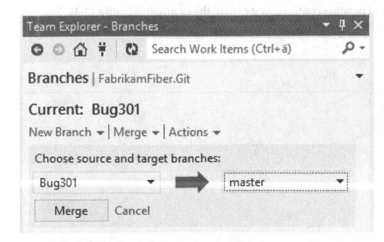

Figure 13-15. *Merging two branches on the Branches page*

When you merge the branches, it will try to merge the content, and sometimes the branches can't be automatically merged. You will then be prompted to resolve one or more merge conflicts, as shown in Figure 13-16.

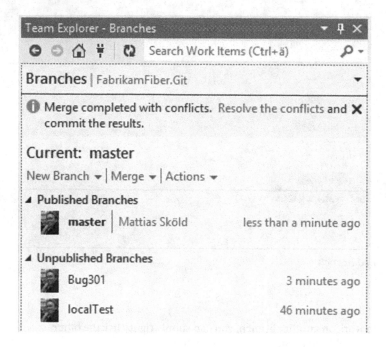

Figure 13-16. *Merge resulted in conflicts*

In order to complete the merge, you need to resolve those conflicts and commit to the repository. The easiest way is to click the Resolve the conflicts link.

ResolveC onflicts

On the Resolve Conflicts page, you will see a list of pending conflicts, as shown in the example in Figure 13-17. You can select each conflict and choose which action you want to perform.

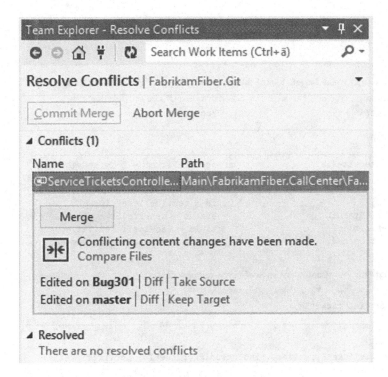

Figure 13-17. *Resolve Conflicts page with a conflict selected*

You can choose to either take the source version, keep the target version, or merge the files with the Merge tool. If you choose to merge the files, the Merge tool window will open with the files preloaded, as shown in Figure 13-18.

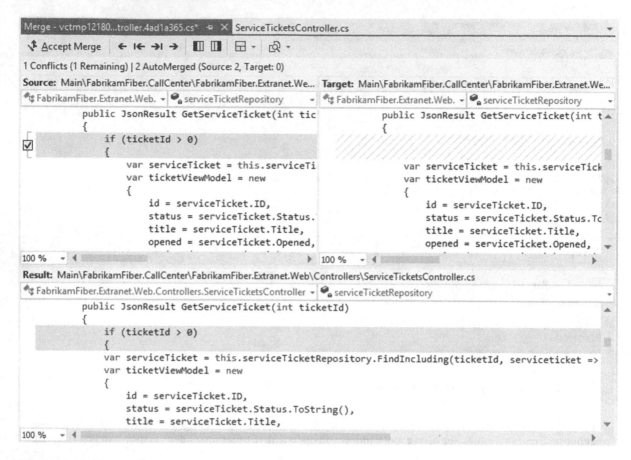

Figure 13-18. *Merge tool merging two versions to a local file*

In the Merge tool, you're shown the source and the target file, with all changes marked out and with a check box to the left of the change. By marking the check box you can select to use this change in the resulting file. It you choose to include both changes, they will be placed in order in the file. It's also possible for you to edit the results before continuing.

Once all conflicts have been resolved, the Changes window will look like Figure 13-19. You can commit the merge to your local repository. This is done by using the ordinary Commit page.

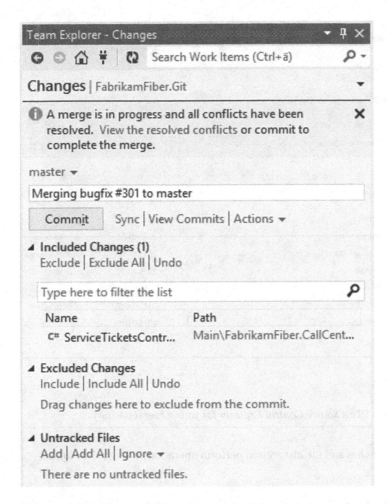

Figure 13-19. Changes page ready to commit the merge to your local repository

It's now up to you to verify that the merge was successful and hasn't introduced any new defects before you push your changes up to the server.

Publishing a Branch to the Server

If you want to share a branch with the team, you can publish a branch to the server by right-clicking it and selecting the Publish option. Once the branch is published to the server repository, you can view it under the Code tab of Team WebA ccess.

Viewing the Server Repository

If you want to view the central repository, you can do so by navigating to Team Web Access and selecting the Code tab. There you will find an Explorer-like interface, as shown in Figure 13-20, where you can view the code in the server repository.

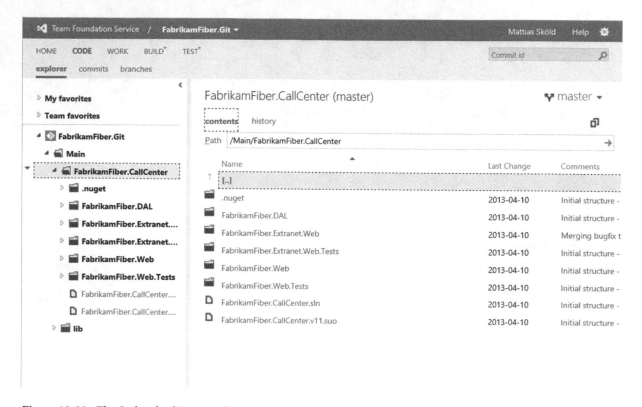

Figure 13-20. *The Code tab of Team Web Access is like a Source Control Explorer for your server repository*

From the web you can view the different branches and the history and perform operations such as showing the differences for a file across different versions.

Using Non-Microsoft Git Tools

To use non-Microsoft Git tools against a central TF Service Git repository, you need two things:

- Thec loneU RL
- Credentialstothe T FS ervice

To get the clone URL, simply browse the server repository and click the clone icon at the right of the repository. This will bring up the repository's URL to use when cloning the repository in other tools, as shown in Figure 13-21.

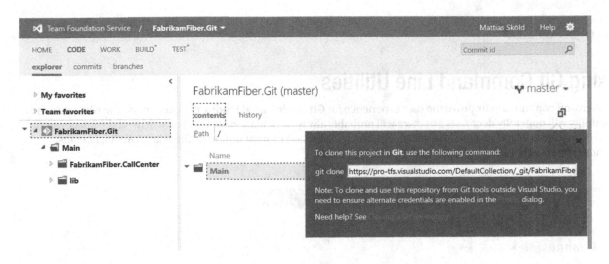

Figure 13-21. Clicking the Clone icon will give you the Clone URL to use with other tools

To get the credentials to connect to your repository outside of Visual Studio, you need to activate an alternate authentication. This can be done by clicking the link in the form or by editing your User Profile by selecting the Credentials tab, as shown in Figure 13-22.

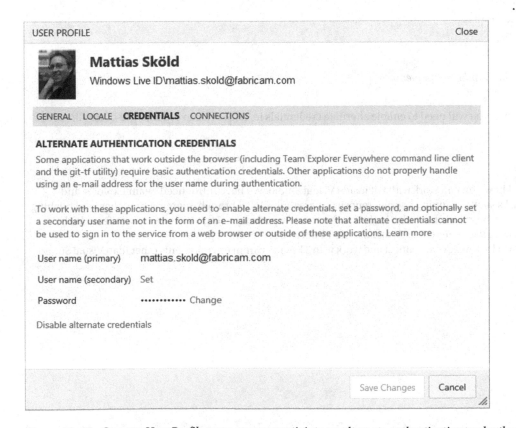

Figure 13-22. On your User Profile page, you can activiate an alternate authentication under the Credentials tab

By setting a password (and if needed an alternate username), you can use this credential when connecting with your favorite Git tools.

Using Git Command Line Utilities

As Microsoft continues to improve the user experience for Git inside Visual Studio, the need to use the Git command line utility will hopefully decrease. But there will probably always be situations where you will need the full power of the Git command line; therefore, you will find an Open Command Prompt option in Git-related Actions menus, as shown in Figure 13-23.

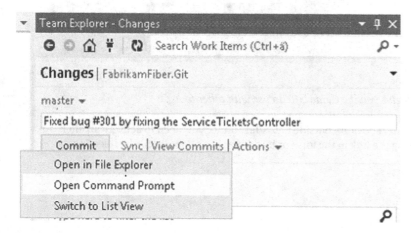

Figure 13-23. *Open Command Prompt menu*

As mentioned before, you will need to enable alternate credentials in TF Service in order to use other Git tools.

Summary

This chapter explained how you can work with Git inside Visual Studio. We have introduced Team Explorer and covered the normal tasks such as cloning a server repository, creating a local branch, merging branches, and pushing changes to the server repository. We have also looked at the server repository using the Code view of Team Web Access and covered how to use other Git tools against the TF Service server Git repository.

The next chapter will look at how to connect and work with TF Service from environments other than Visual Studio.

CHAPTER 14

■ ■ ■

Working in Heterogeneous Environments

This chapter will look at different ways to get to TF Service information when you're not working on a Windows format or using Visual Studio. We can of course always use the Team Web Access to manage work items, look at code changes, work with testing, and manage builds, but sometimes it's desirable to have the integration with TF Service right inside the development environment.

We will focus on three different solutions. First, the Team Explorer Everywhere plug-in for Eclipse, which offers Visual Studio–like functionality for Java developers. Second, by using Git in TF Service, we get native source code support in Xcode for iOS developers. And, finally, we look at Git-TF, a Java command-line client to integrate a local Git repository with a central TFVC repository.

Working with Eclipse

Back in the early versions of Team Foundation Server, cross-platform support for TFS in Eclipse was built by a company called Teamprise. In November 2009 Microsoft bought Teamprise and renamed the product Team Explorer Everywhere. Through this move, Microsoft started its ongoing efforts to support clients running on non-Windows platforms to work against Team Foundation Server and use its ALM features.

The integration in Eclipse, which is installed as a plug-in, is very rich and works very much the same way as Team Explorer in Visual Studio 2012 does. Figure 14-1 shows how Team Explorer Everywhere looks in Eclipse, connected to the same Fabrikam Fiber team project in TF Service.

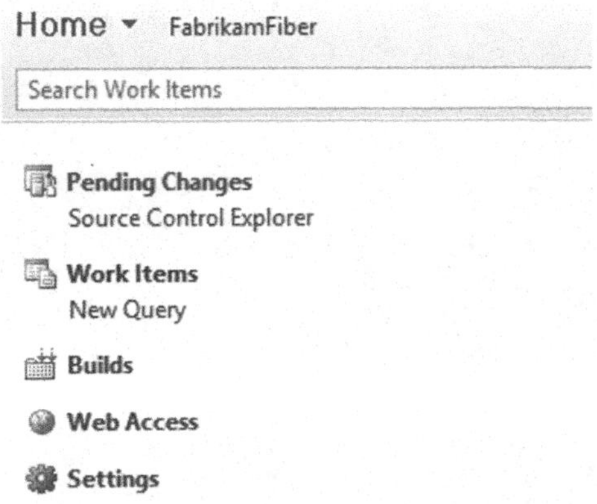

Figure 14-1. Team Explorer Everywhere

This section will walk through how to install Team Explorer Everywhere, add a project to source control, and integrate with work items.

■ **Note** If you are new to Eclipse, you can learn more about it at `http://www.eclipse.org/home/newcomers.php`.

InstallingT eamE xplorerE verywhere

As mentioned in the previous section, Team Explorer Everywhere is a plug-in to Eclipse and is therefore installed just like any other plug-in in Eclipse.

Let's walk though how to install Team Explorer Everywhere and connect to your TF Service account.

■ **Note** Team Explorer Everywhere supports all Eclipse versions from version 3.5 and above. In this walkthrough we are using version 4.2.2, but the steps should be very similar in previous versions as well.

---

1. In Eclipse, select Install New Software from the Help menu, as shown in Figure 14-2.

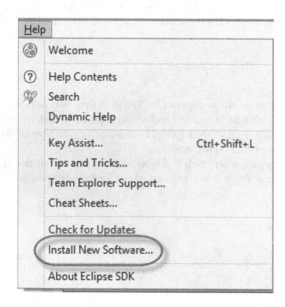

Figure 14-2. *Install New Software option*

2. Click the Add button, which will show the Add Repository dialog box, as shown in Figure 14-3. Enter the following values:

   Name: Team Explorer Everywhere

   Location: http://dl.microsoft.com/eclipse/tfs

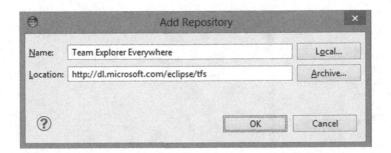

Figure 14-3. *Installing the Team Explorer Everywhere plug-in*

3. In the next dialog box, mark the Team Foundation Server Plug-in for Eclipse check box, as shown in Figure 14-4.

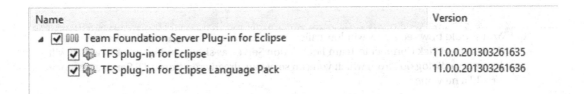

Figure 14-4. *Installing Team Foundation Server Plug-in for Eclipse*

4. Run through the wizard with the default settings, and accept the agreements to complete thei nstallation.

5. To view Team Explorer, select Windows ➤ Show View ➤ Other and select Team Explorer, ass howni nF igure 14-5.

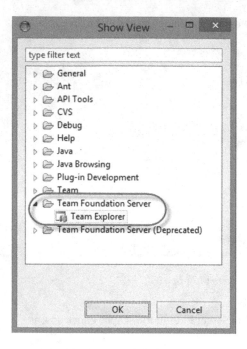

Figure 14-5. *Accessing Team Explorer*

6. You should now see a new window called Team Explorer. From here you can connect to TF Service. Click Connect to Team Foundation Server, as shown in Figure 14-6, which will bring up a dialog box from which you can select an already registered TF Service instance or add a new one.

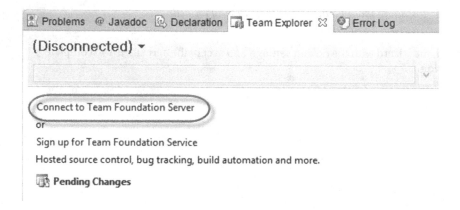

Figure 14-6. *Connecting to Team Foundation Server*

7. Once you have selected a TF Service instance, you can select a project collection and one or more team projects, just like in Visual Studio, as shown in Figure 14-7.

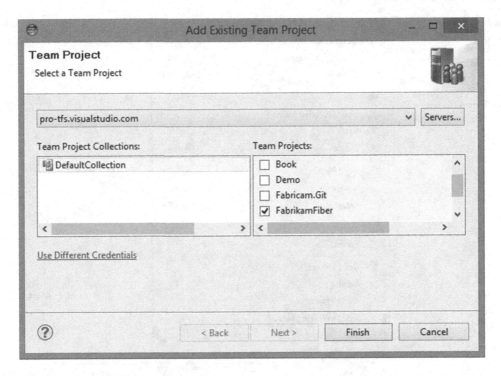

Figure 14-7. Adding a Team Project

8. ClickF inishtoconne cttoT FS ervice.

Adding an Eclipse Project to Source Control

Once you have connected to TF Service, you can add new or existing projects to source control. The key thing that needs to be done is to map the Eclipse workspace to the TF Service workspace. This is done by *sharing* the project in Eclipse.

Here we have created a new application for the Fabrikam Fiber solution that will handle notifications sent to customers.

To add the project to TFVC, right-click the root package in Package Explorer and select Team ➤ Share Project, as shown in Figure 14-8.

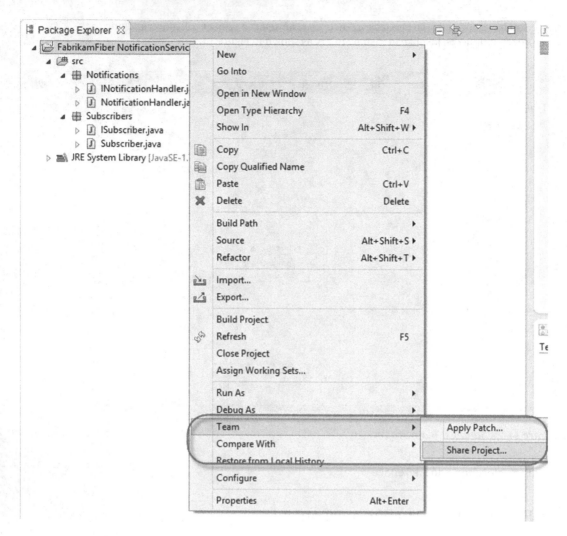

Figure 14-8. *Sharing a project*

Next up, select Team Foundation Server as the repository plug-in and then select your TF Service workspace, as showni nF igure 14-9.

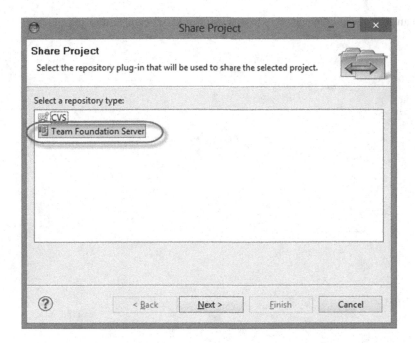

Figure 14-9. Selecting the repository type

Finally, browse to the source control folder in TFVC where you want to add your project. As shown in Figure 14-10, we put our application below the Main branch of FabrikamFiber.

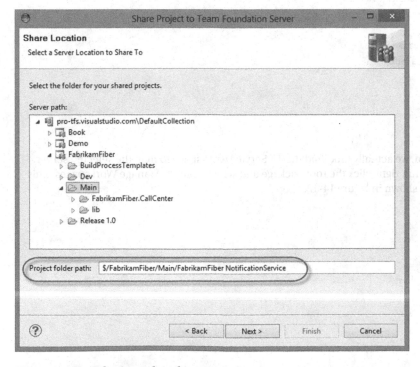

Figure 14-10. Selecting a share location

After confirming the operation, you can see your pending changes just as you would in Visual Studio Team Explorer, ass howni nF igure 14-11.

Figure 14-11. *Pending changes*

When we selected a share location, we actually modified the TF Service workspace to map the selected server path to the Eclipse workspace. To see this, right-click the root package and select Team ➤ Manage Workspaces. This will show the workspace mappings, as shown in Figure 14-12.

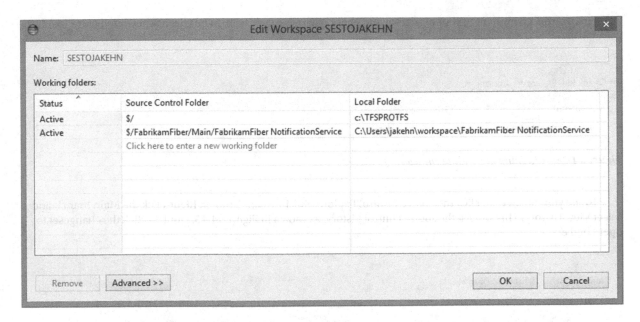

Figure 14-12. Workspace mappings

As you can see, we mapped our Eclipse workspace path (which defaults to `c:\users\<user>\workspace`) to the server path we browsed to in TFVC.

To associate our check-in with a work item, we follow the same procedure as in Visual Studio Team Explorer. We can either enter the Work Item ID directly or use a query from which we can add work items to the current pending changes, a ss hown inF igure 14-13.

ID	Work Ite...	Backlog P...	Title	Assigned To	State	Effort	Busin...	Iteration Path
110	Product B...	187500	Cross platform service for handling notifications	Jakob Ehn				
88	Product B...	375000	Service rep can delete customers	Jakob Ehn				
30	Product B...	750000	Customer can find the nearest Fabrikam Fiber location.					
31	Product B...	875000	Customer can look up television lineup online.					
32	Product B...	937500	Customer can sign up for emails about service outages.					
33	Product B...	968750	Customer can see upcoming appointments.					
34	Product B...	984375	Customer can sign in using Facebook account.					

Figure 14-13. Associated work item to pending changes

Finally, add a comment to your changeset and check it in using the Check In button, as shown in Figure 14-14.

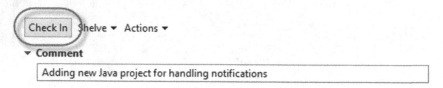

Figure 14-14. *Checking in pending changes*

To see your changeset, click the Source Control Explorer link in Team Explorer. Right-click the Main branch and select View History. This will list the source control history, as shown in Figure 14-15. Double-click the changeset to opent hed etails.

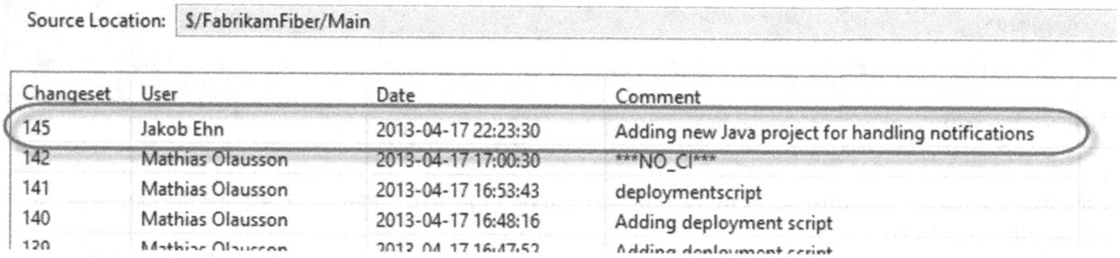

Source Location: $/FabrikamFiber/Main

Changeset	User	Date	Comment
145	Jakob Ehn	2013-04-17 22:23:30	Adding new Java project for handling notifications
142	Mathias Olausson	2013-04-17 17:00:30	***NO_CI***
141	Mathias Olausson	2013-04-17 16:53:43	deploymentscript
140	Mathias Olausson	2013-04-17 16:48:16	Adding deployment script
139	Mathias Olausson	2013-04-17 16:47:52	Adding deployment script

Figure 14-15. *Viewing the source control history*

UsingW orkI tems

Navigating around Team Explorer Everywhere is in many aspects identical to its counterpart in Visual Studio. The Work Items node is pretty much the same and should be familiar to any user of Visual Studio. As you can see in Figure 14-16, you can manage and run work item queries, search work items, and define favorite queries just as you would in Visual Studio.

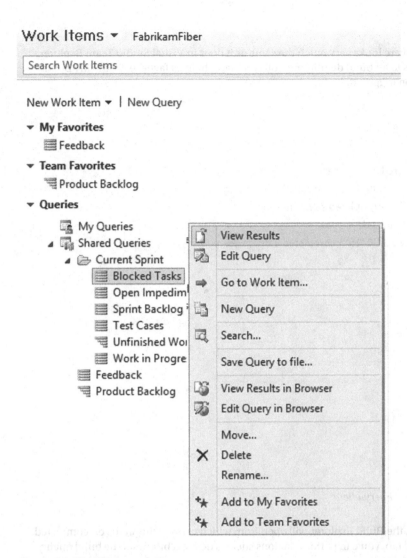

Figure 14-16. *Using work items*

You manage favorite team queries the same way you would in Visual Studio. If you run a work item query and then open a work item, you will see a work item form from which you can edit the work item. This is new in Team Explorer Everywhere 2012 (previously Eclipse opened an external browser that pointed to Team Web Access). Now you get a much better integrated experience when editing work items in Eclipse.

■ **Note**   The My Work feature that we mentioned in Chapter 13 is not yet available in Team Explorer Everywhere.

UsingB uilds

The builds page in Team Explorer Everywhere looks very much the same as it does in Visual Studio Team Explorer. As shown in Figure 14-17, you have access to all build definitions, you can mark them as favorites in the My Builds section, and you see the last five builds you triggered.

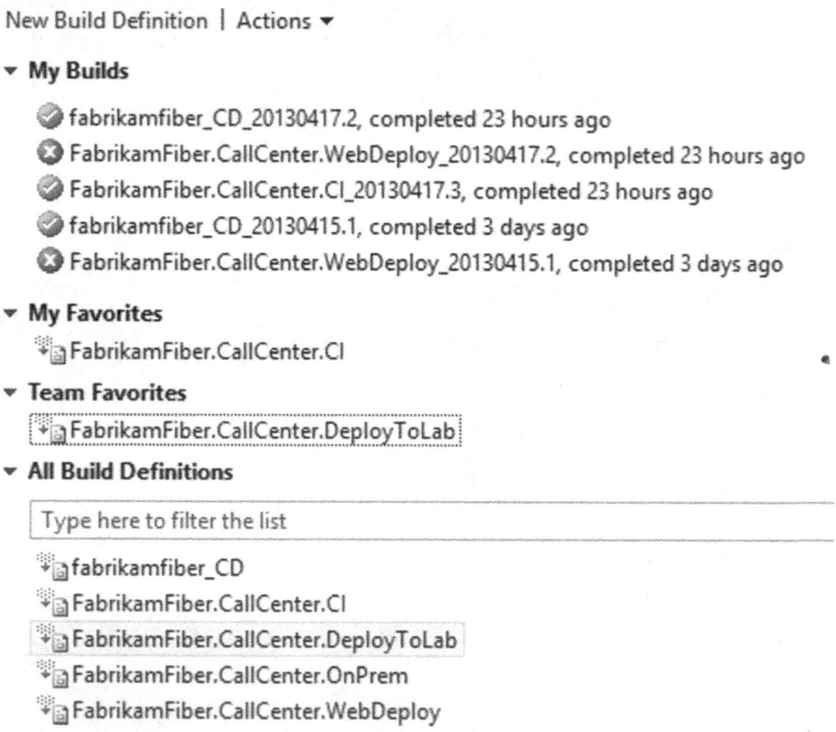

New Build Definition | Actions ▼

▼ **My Builds**

- fabrikamfiber_CD_20130417.2, completed 23 hours ago
- FabrikamFiber.CallCenter.WebDeploy_20130417.2, completed 23 hours ago
- FabrikamFiber.CallCenter.CI_20130417.3, completed 23 hours ago
- fabrikamfiber_CD_20130415.1, completed 3 days ago
- FabrikamFiber.CallCenter.WebDeploy_20130415.1, completed 3 days ago

▼ **My Favorites**

- FabrikamFiber.CallCenter.CI

▼ **Team Favorites**

- FabrikamFiber.CallCenter.DeployToLab

▼ **All Build Definitions**

Type here to filter the list

- fabrikamfiber_CD
- FabrikamFiber.CallCenter.CI
- FabrikamFiber.CallCenter.DeployToLab
- FabrikamFiber.CallCenter.OnPrem
- FabrikamFiber.CallCenter.WebDeploy

Figure 14-17. Builds page in Team Explorer Everywhere

If you double-click a build definition, the Build Explorer will open from which can see the status on completed and running builds. Under the Completed tab, you can perform actions such as delete a build, set the build quality, access the drop location, or open the build details.

■ **Note** When you open the build details, Eclipse will still open an embedded browser that points to the build page in Team Web Access.

You can also create new build definitions. Team Explorer Everywhere supports creating build definitions for Java, Ant, or Maven with Team Foundation Build. It does not support creating or modifying Windows Workflow builds. You can read more about working with Team Foundation Build in Chapter 16.

■ **Note**   TF Service does not currently support running Java, Ant, or Maven builds. To do this you must install a separate build server on the premises and register it with your TF Service account. This is explained in detail in Chapter 15.

The following additional software must be installed on the build server, after installing the Team Foundation Build Service:

- *Team Foundation Build Extensions Power Tool*: This is a part of the TFS 2012 Power Tools and can be downloaded from `http://visualstudiogallery.msdn.microsoft.com/2d7c8577-54b8-47ce-82a5-8649f579dcb6/`.

- *Java Development Kit* (JDK): Can be downloaded from `http://www.oracle.com/technetwork/java/index.html`.

- *Ant*: Ant is to Java what MSBuild is to .NET. Download it from `http://ant.apache.org/`.

- *Maven*: If you want to run Maven builds, download it from `http://maven.apache.org/`.

■ **Note**   Creating Ant or Maven builds are outside the scope of this book. For more information about building applications with Team Explorer Everywhere, see `http://msdn.microsoft.com/en-us/library/gg490754(v=vs.100).aspx`.

Working with Xcode

Another commonly used development environment would be to use Xcode for iOS development. Currently, Xcode has no extensibility model to allow third-party source code repositories to integrate with the Xcode development environments, which means there is no way to get the rich experience from Visual Studio Team Explorer or from Team Explorer Everywhere. But with the support for Git in TF Service, we can create a team project using Git as the source code repository and use the native Git integration in Xcode.

■ **Note**   In order to use the Xcode Git client with TF Service, you need to configure your TF Service account with alternate authentication credential. This was described in Chapter 13.

Cloninga T FS erviceR epository

To get started using TF Service in Xcode, we need to connect to TF Service and clone a local repository. The following steps will walk you through the process:

1. First, we need the clone URL for the TF Service Git repository. We can get this URL from Team Web Access: go to the Code, Explorer view, and click the Clone icon in the top right-handc orner(Figure 14-18).

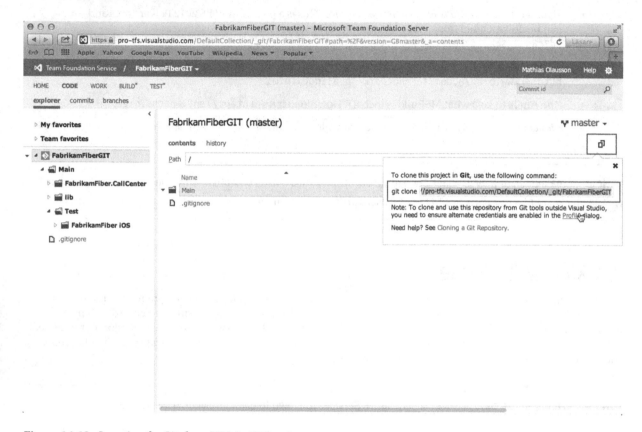

Figure 14-18. Locating the Git clone URL in TF Service

2. Connectt ot heT FS ervicer epository(Figure 14-19).

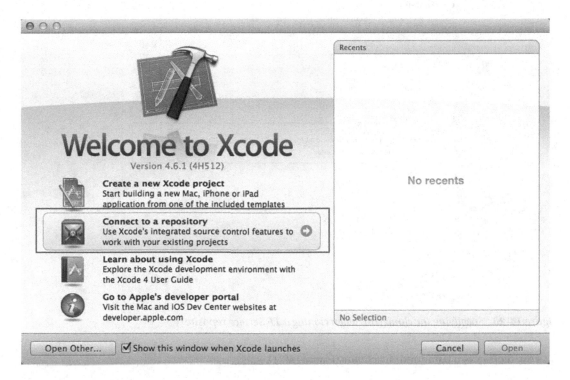

Figure 14-19. *Connecting to a TF Service Git repository in Xcode*

3. Configure your TF Service account with the alternate authentication credential. This was described in Chapter 13.

4. Specify the clone URL for the remote repository (Figure 14-20).

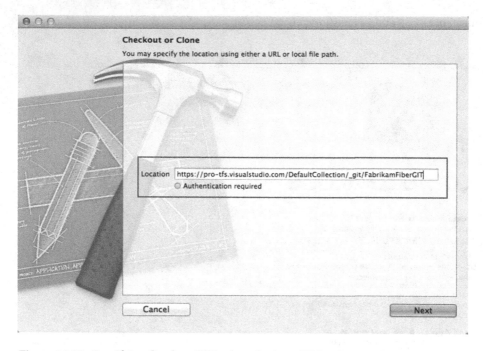

Figure 14-20. *Specifying the clone URL when cloning a TF Service repository*

5. Give the repository a name and click Clone (Figure 14-21).

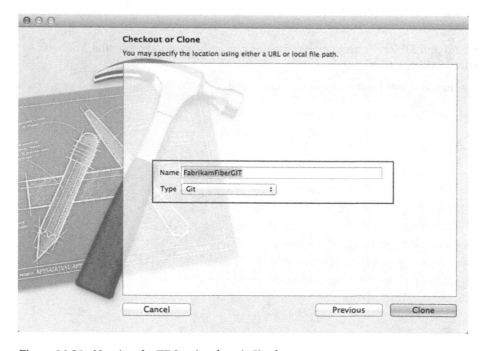

Figure 14-21. *Naming the TF Service clone in Xcode*

6. Pick a directory to clone your TF Service repository in to (Figure 14-22) and click Clone.

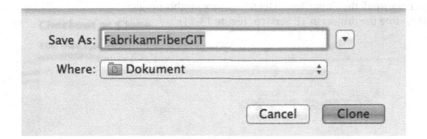

Figure 14-22. *Select location for TF Service clone*

7. Ther epositoryisno wclone da ndr eadyf orus e.

Adding an Xcode project to Source Control

Once the Git repository from TF Service has been cloned, we can start adding code to the local repository and check in changes to TF Service. The steps below show how to add a new project to source control and check it in to TF Service.

1. Start Xcode and create a new project (Figure 14-23).

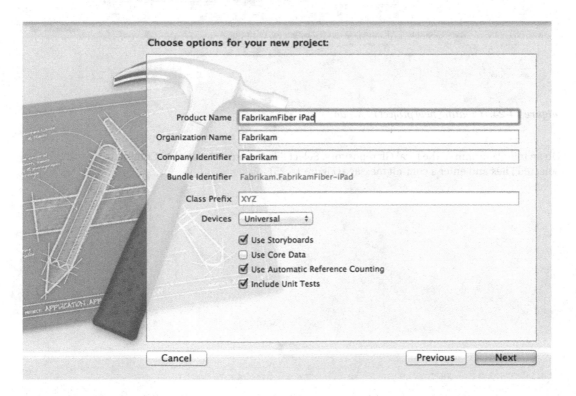

Figure 14-23. *Options for creating a new Xcode project*

2. Save the project in a location under the local Git repository created in the previous section. This will map the new project to the local Git repository to get the source control integration to work. Do not check mark the Create local Get repository for this project check box because we want to store the project in TF Service (Figure 14-24).

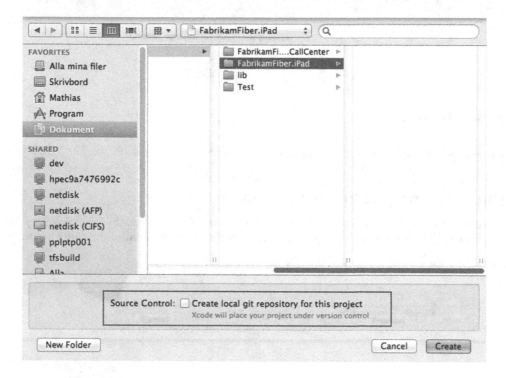

Figure 14-24. *Creating new project in Xcode*

3. Do an initial commit to the local Git repository. Select File ➤ Source Control ➤ Commit Selected Files and enter a commit message (Figure 14-25).

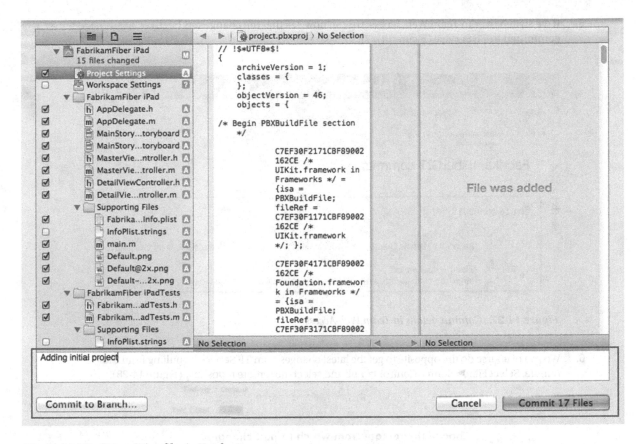

Figure 14-25. *Committing files in Xcode*

4. Push the changes to TF Service. Select File ➤ Source Control ➤ Push and select the remote repository, as shown in Figure 14-26.

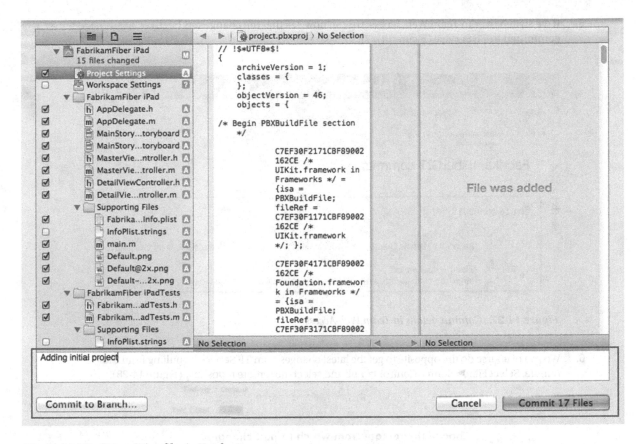

Figure 14-26. *Pushing to remote in Xcode*

5. If we switch over to Team Web Access, we can now see that the change has been committed to TF Service (Figure 14-27).

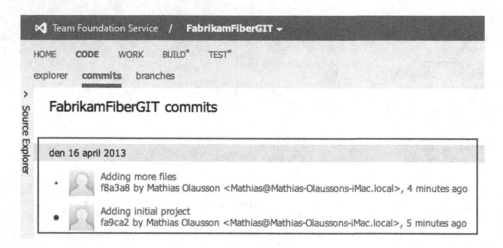

Figure 14-27. Commit details in Team Web Access

6. We can of course do the opposite to get the latest changes from TF Service by pulling from the remote. Select File ➤ Source Control ➤ Pull and select the remote repository (Figure 14-28).

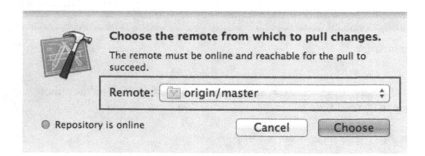

Figure 14-28. Pulling from remote in Xcode

Working with Git-TF

We've seen that when working with Xcode we can only use Git as the source code repository. In many cases we have a mixed development environment, where some will use TF Service from Visual Studio, some from Xcode or Eclipse, or we may want to use the TFVC repository instead of Git. To solve this we can use a local Git repository and sync it with the TF Service using a tool called Git-TF. Git-TF will also enable clients such as Xcode to use the native source code support in the IDE with TFVC. Git-TF is implemented on top of the TFS Java software development kit, which means it can be used virtually everywhere Java can be run, including Mac OS, Linux, and other Unix systems.

Git-TF is maintained as an open-source project on CodePlex and can be downloaded from
`https://gittf.codeplex.com/`.

Setting Up Git-TF

Getting started with Git-TF is quite simple; except for the prerequisites—Java runtime and Git tools—we only need to download and extract the Git-TF archive:

1. Download and install a suitable Java runtime (http://www.java.com).

2. Downloada ndi nstallG it(http://git-scm.com/downloads).

3. Download the latest version of Git-TF from http://www.microsoft.com/en-us/download/details.aspx?id=30474.

4. Extract the content of the Git-TF .zip file to a folder on the local machine (i.e., /user/git-tf onM ac/Linux).

5. Add the path where you extracted Git-TF (i.e., C:\git-tf) to your PATH environment variable.

6. Configure your TF Service account with alternate authentication credential. This was describedi nC hapter1 3.

■ **Note** If you don't want to be prompted for username and password when connecting to TF Service, you can store your default settings using the following commands:

```
git config git-tf.server.username your_username
```

```
git config git-tf.server.password your_password
```

Cloninga T FS erviceR epository

The following scenario shows how to clone an existing TFVC repository, make a change, and check in the changes to TF Service.

■ **Note** Type git tf /help to get a list of available commands and git tf <command> /help for more information about each command.

1. Create a clone from the TFVC repository with the following line of code, as shown in Figure 14-29:

    ```
    git tf clone https://pro-tfs.visualstudio.com/DefaultCollection $/
    FabrikamFiber/Main
    ```

```
C:\tfs\Git-Tf>git tf clone https://pro-tfs.visualstudio.com/DefaultCollection $/
FabrikamFiber/Main
Connecting to TFS...
Username: slaw0000m
Password:
Cloning $/FabrikamFiber/Main into C:\tfs\Git-Tf\Main: 100%, done.
Cloned changeset 145 as 0abf950
```

Figure 14-29. *Creating a repository clone using Git-TF*

2. Make local changes with the following line of code and commit:

```
git commit -a -m "adding readme file"
```

3. Get the latest changes from TFVC with the following line of code:

```
git tf pull --rebase
```

4. Check in changes to TFVC with the following line of code. There are many options to the check-in command, for instance we can check in and associate the changeset with a work item(Figure 14-30).

```
git tf checkin --resolve=118
```

```
C:\tfs\Git-Tf\Main\FabrikamFiber.CallCenter>git tf checkin --resolve=118
Connecting to TFS...
Username: olaussonm
Password:
Checking in to $/FabrikamFiber/Main: 100%, done.
Checked commit bbe83a1 in as changeset 152
```

Figure 14-30. *Checking in to TF Service using Git-TF*

The results are shown in Figure 14-31.

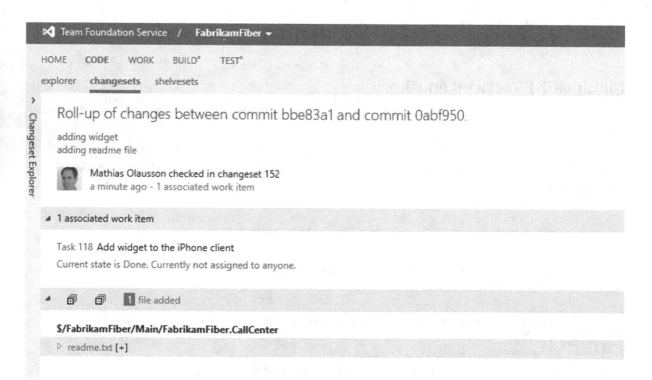

Figure 14-31. *Changeset checked in from Git using Git-TF*

Summary

This chapter looked at various ways to work with the TF Service from non-Microsoft environments. Eclipse with the Team Explorer Everywhere plug-in gives a rich developer experience very similar to the Visual Studio Team Explorer. Other development environments may get nice source code integration when using a Git repository, and for the other scenarios we have the option to use the command-line tools and sync a local Git repository with the TF Service using the Git-TF tool. Of course, we can also use the Team Web Access to access TF Service data such as work items, tests, and builds.

This completes the chapters on source code control, where we have looked at how the TF Service can be used to host source code independent of if we are using Visual Studio or a different IDE or if we are running on Windows, a java platform or Mac OSX. In the coming chapter s we will look at automated build and deployment using the TF Service. First we'll cover the fundamentals of TFS build followed by a chapter on build customization and extensibility. Having covered the build system we will then look at how to use it in practice to implement a continuous deployments olution.

CHAPTER 15

■ ■ ■

ConfiguringB uild Services

Next to source control, many consider the most important part of running software projects successfully is usage of build automation. It is considered to be the heartbeat of the software development process, continuously compiling, testing, and analyzing projects as developers keep checking in changes to the codebase. If the project build succeeds, it is an indication that the project is healthy and can be built and tested on any computer. If the build fails, you will soon find out and be much more likely to fix the problem quickly. It is also an absolute necessity if you want to increase your release cadence and be able to deploy new versions to production more often. There is no or minimal room for manual processes when the release cadence increases.

This chapter will discuss build automation in general and you will learn about the hosted build server, the build automation engine in TFS, in particular. You will learn how to configure it, understand the capabilities of it, and in which scenarios you will need to extend your build system to your build servers.

About Build Automation

When we talk about build automation, we usually refer to *end-to-end* builds. These builds do not just involve compiling the source code, and they typically perform at least the following tasks:

- Create a clean workspace and get the latest version of the code
- Labelt hec ode
- Compile
- Analyze the code, for example, by using static code analysis (FxCop)
- Test the code using different unit test frameworks
- Producei nstallersa ndp ackages
- Generateb uildr eports
- Notifyu serso ft heb uildo utcome

The main reasons for using build automation are:

- *Continuous integration*: By continuously running compilation, testing, and analyzing every check in, you will catch any errors as soon as possible. The developers will usually be able to fix code that fails much faster if they get a notification five minutes after they submitted the change as opposed to when an error is caught a week later when someone tries to integrate and run the project.

- *Never releasing from a development machine*: By using a separate build server, you can be confident that you are always building and releasing the latest version that is checked into source control. If you produce the release from a local machine, you run the risk of both including new, not yet finished, changes that haven't been checked in, as well as not building the latest version.

201

- *Automating repetitive tasks*: Almost all release processes include additional steps that need to be performed every time for every new release, things like versioning, signing, packaging, producing documentation, and so forth. All these are things that should be done automatically to reduce the risk of forgetting to do one or more of the steps.

- *Avoiding the "magic machine syndrome:"* A common phenomenon when not using build servers is that when the project has been running for a while, there are a lot of dependencies that have been installed and referenced in different ways on the developer's machines. In the end, no one knows all the steps that need to be done to actually build and test the project, so it becomes very hard to, for example, introduce a new developer into the team with a new clean PC. By using a build server with a minimum amount of software installed on it, you can be confident that you can build the project on any machine.

- *Enforcing traceability*: Many build automation engines will automatically include a list of which changes were built in a particular build. Team Foundation Build will automatically link all changesets and the work items associated with these changesets to the build. This means that for a given build you can trace which changes went into it, who made these changes, and why they were made (work items).

Team Foundation Build

Team Foundation Build contains a powerful scalable build system that lets you easily set up continuous integration builds that run on every check in, and execute the builds on a pool of build agents that can be distributed on any machine in the network.

■ **Note** This book is about Team Foundation Service and the hosted build service, but most of the features and capabilities are the same as when running Team Foundation Server on premises. In this book, the term Team Foundation Build refers to both situations.

The build infrastructure consists of build controllers and build agents. The main task of the build controller is to maintain a pool of build agents and, when a new build is queued, select an available build agent that matches any criteria that have been defined for the build. A build controller can only belong to one team project collection; however, a team project collection can have multiple build controllers.

The build agents are often installed on another machine, and they perform the actual work of compiling, testing, and analyzing the project. This part is very CPU intensive and they should not be installed on the same machine where TFS is running. The build controller can be installed on the TFS app tier, because it does not use a lot of CPU resources.

The build orchestration engine is built on top of Windows Workflow, but uses MSBuild internally to actually compile the project. A build workflow consists of a set of workflow activities that perform the different tasks of getting source code, labeling, compiling, and so forth. There are plenty of workflow activities available out of the box, but it is also possible to develop your own custom activities. There is also a growing community focused on creating reusable workflow activities that can be used for free in your build processes.

Configuring Hosted Build Server

When using the hosted build server, things couldn't be easier when it comes to getting started. There is no set up at all! TFS automatically provides the infrastructure for running automated builds.

Team Foundation Hosted Build consists of a hosted build controller, one per team project collection, which is responsible for provisioning a temporary build agent that will run the build.

Figure 15-1s howst hel ogicala rchitectureo ft heh ostedb uilds ervice.

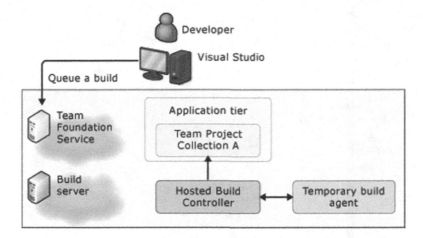

Figure 15-1. *Hosted build service architecture*

In some scenarios, which are discussed later in this chapter, the capabilities of the hosted build server is not enough. In these situations you can register additional build servers that run on premises, inside your company firewall.

To manage the build controller and build agent, go to the Builds hub in Team Explorer and select Manage Build Controllersf romt heA ctionsm enu,a ss howni nF igure 15-2.

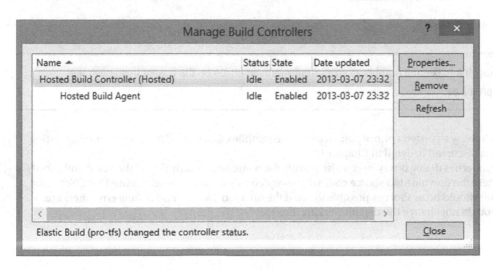

Figure 15-2. *Managing the hosted build controller*

Selecting Properties for the hosted build controller lets you manage the build controller. In the resultant Build Controller Properties window, you can change the name and description of the build controller and enable or disable it, as shown in Figure 15-3.

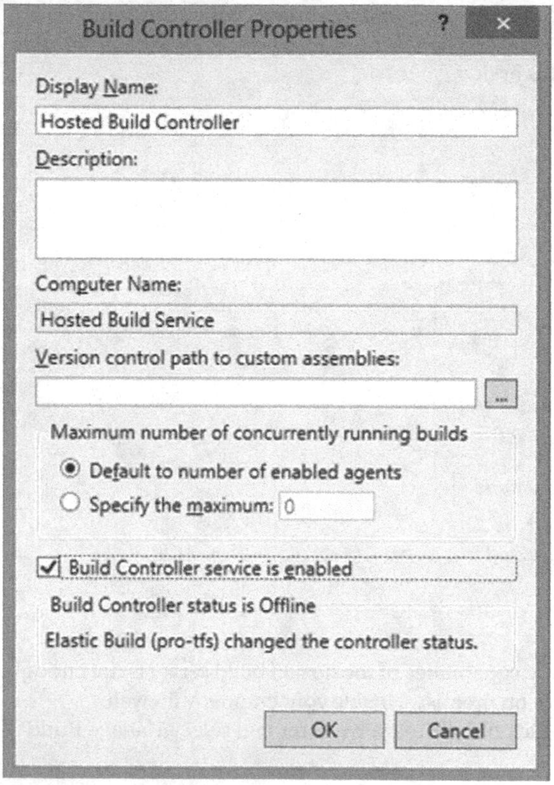

Figure 15-3. *Build Controller Properties*

■ **Note**   You cannot modify the maximum number of concurrently running builds on the hosted build controller, this can only be done on premises.

In addition, you can specify a version control path to custom assemblies that is used for custom build activities and test adapters, which is discussed in detail in Chapter 16.

In the Build Agent Properties dialog box, you can also modify the name and description of the agent and specify the working directory where the downloaded source code will be copied as part of the build (Figure 15-4). Note that the working directory path should be as short as possible to avoid the dreaded *The path is too long* error message. We recommended that you do not change the default working directory.

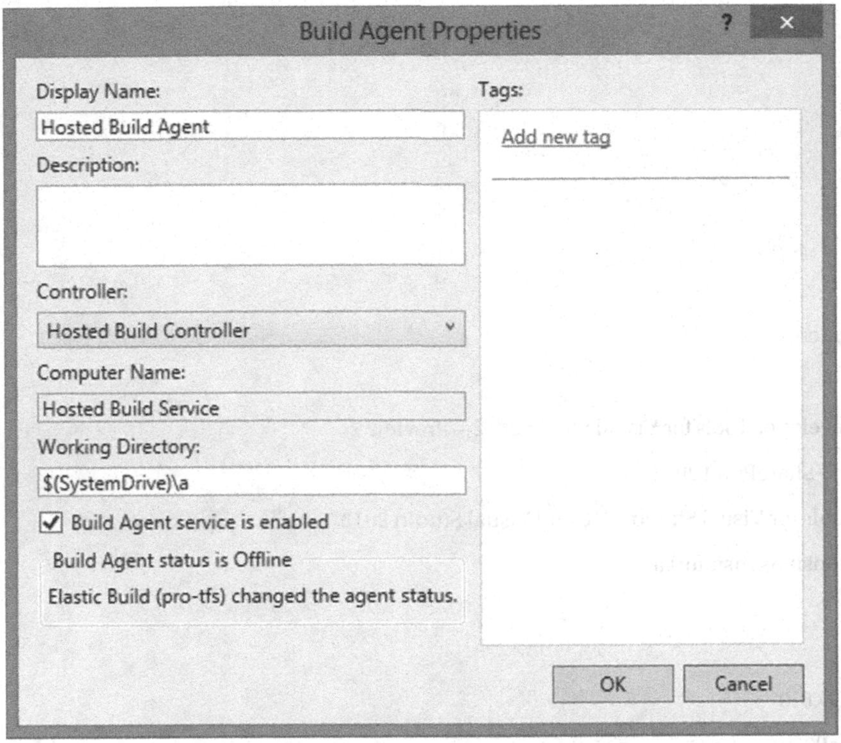

Figure 15-4. Build Agent Properties

Tags are used to control where a build is executed. If you have several build agents running on different machines, you might have different software on different machines. Tags let you specify that a build definition will be executed on a build agent with a matching tag. When it comes to the hosted build service, you only have one build agent, so tags are not useful unless you decide to scale out by adding on to the premises' build servers.

Software on the Hosted Build Server

The machine that your hosted builds will run on is provisioned each time on the fly in Windows Azure. The machine itself is a standard Hyper-V virtual machine (VM), which is identical to those used for hosted builds. The configuration of the machine is continuously changing, and you will need to go online for an up-to-date version of the specification (https://tfs.visualstudio.com/en-us/learn/build/hosted-build-controller-in-vs#software).

At the time of writing, the TFS resources state that the hosted build server is deployed with the following software:

- Windows Server 2008 R2 (64-bit environment)

- Team Foundation Build (Team Foundation Server 2012)

- VisualS tudio

  - VisualS tudio2 012U ltimateR TM

  - Visual Studio SDK 2012 RTM

  - VisualS tudio2 010S P1

- The. NETF ramework
  - .NET4 .5
  - .NET3 .5S P1
- WindowsA zure
  - SDK1 .8
  - SDK1 .7
  - SDK1 .6
  - IntegrationC omponents1 .6
- Otherc omponents
  - Microsoft Office Developer Tools for Visual Studio 2012—Preview 2
  - SharePoint 2010 and SharePoint 2013
  - SQL Server Data Tools for Visual Studio 2010 and Visual Studio 2012
  - TFS2 012_BuildExtensions.msi(forJ ava)
  - TypeScript0 .8.2
  - WebD eploy3 .0
  - WindowsP honeS DK8 .0
  - WindowsP owerShell3 .0

Hosted Build Server Limitations

The obvious upside with the hosted build service is that it requires no set up and is fully managed and updated by Microsoft. You will never need to upgrade or patch it, and it will never be offline or unavailable. There are some limitations, however, that should be considered. All of these limitations can be mitigated against by adding build servers that run on premises, which is discussed later in this chapter. The limitations are:

- *No control or access*: Because the build agent is provisioned on the fly, you have no access to it and can't install any additional software you might need on it. All dependencies must be either checked into source control or downloaded as part of the build (more on this later).

- *Only one build agent per account*: Currently it is only possible to have one build agent on the hosted build controller. As the number of projects grow in your collection, and the number of build definitions increases, the single build agent will become a bottleneck.

- *Can't build Windows 8 Store apps*: Windows 8 Store apps must be built on a Windows 8 machine, which means that it currently cannot be built using the hosted build service, since Windows Azure does not yet support Windows 8.

- *No interactive build agent*: The hosted build service runs as a Windows service, which means that it cannot interact with the desktop. This means that you will not be able to run coded user interface tests as part of your hosted builds.

- *Administrative tasks*: Hosted build cannot perform any tasks that require administrative privileges on the build agent.

- *Maximum execution time and storage*: The maximum agent execution time on the hosted build service is limited to one hour. Also, a build on the hosted service cannot use more than 1GB of total storage. These two options might be limiting factors for companies building large complex products, but should not be a problem for most companies.

Managing Dependencies

As mentioned earlier, you have no control over the machines where your builds will be executed. This means that you need to make sure that everything your projects depend on to build must be either checked in to source control or must be downloaded as part of the build. This section covers both options.

Keeping all dependencies in source control is generally a best practice, as it means that it is easy for any build system or person to build the projects.

UsingS ourceC ontrol

The first option is very simple—just create a folder in source control where you can add all the dependencies your project needs. This folder must be included in the workspace for the build definition, so make sure it is located somewhere below the root folder for the corresponding project, typically where the solution file(s) is located.

Using NuGet Restore Packages

The other option, downloading files as part of the build, is easiest done using NuGet. NuGet is a Visual Studio extension, part of the default installation, that makes it easy to install and update third-party libraries and tools in Visual Studio. NuGet is built around packages that contain all the binaries and necessary configuration that needs to be done, and also dependencies on other packages. The packages are store in a NuGet repository, from which they can easily be downloaded.

A feature of NuGet is that packages can be restored at build time. This means that developers do not need to check in all the binaries to source control, only a NuGet package configuration file is necessary. Then, during the compilation, NuGet will automatically download the package from the NuGet repository and resolve the references. You can specify in the configuration file if you want a specific version of a package or if you want the latest version every time.

There are two things you need to start using Package Restore. First, you must enable it on all the development machines. Go to Tools ➤ Options and select the Package Manager tab, as shown in Figure 15-5.

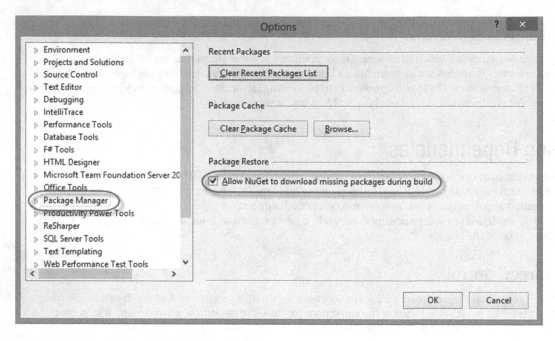

Figure 15-5. *Configuring NuGet Package Restore*

If this setting is not changed, the compilation will fail with a message stating that this option needs to be turned on to enable NuGet package restore for your solution. Right-click the solution and select Enable NuGet Package Restore, as shown in Figure 15-6.

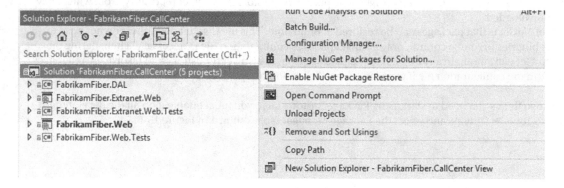

Figure 15-6. *Enable NuGet Package Restore in Solution Explorer*

This will add some new files to your solution beneath a .nuget folder, as shown in Figure 15-7.

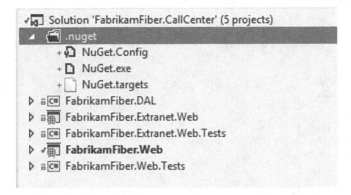

Figure 15-7. *Solution structure with NuGet package restore*

All the project files have now been modified to include the `NuGet.targets` file, which implements the package download as part of the compilation.

If you compile the solution now, you will see that it will automatically populate the packages folder with all the referenced NuGet packages. Check in the solution and make sure you do not include the content in the packages folder in the changeset.

If you build it now on your hosted build service, it should complete successfully. Looking into the MSBuild log will reveal that all the packages were actually downloaded during the build, as shown in Figure 15-8.

```
Project C:\a\src\MvcApplication1.sln (1) is building C:\a\src\MvcApplication1\MvcApplication1.csproj (2) on node 1 (default targets).
RestorePackages:
  "C:\a\src\.nuget\nuget.exe" install "C:\a\src\MvcApplication1\packages.config" -source ""  -RequireConsent -solutionDir "C:\a\src\ "
  Successfully installed 'knockoutjs 2.1.0'.
  Successfully installed 'Microsoft.AspNet.Razor 2.0.20710.0'.
  Successfully installed 'Microsoft.AspNet.Web.Optimization 1.0.0'.
  Successfully installed 'DotNetOpenAuth.OAuth.Core 4.0.3.12153'.
  Successfully installed 'DotNetOpenAuth.Core 4.0.3.12153'.
  Successfully installed 'EntityFramework 5.0.0'.
  Successfully installed 'jQuery 1.7.1.1'.
  Successfully installed 'Microsoft.AspNet.WebApi 4.0.20710.0'.
  Successfully installed 'Microsoft.AspNet.WebPages.OAuth 2.0.20710.0'.
  Successfully installed 'DotNetOpenAuth.OpenId.Core 4.0.3.12153'.
  Successfully installed 'DotNetOpenAuth.AspNet 4.0.3.12153'.
  Successfully installed 'DotNetOpenAuth.OpenId.RelyingParty 4.0.3.12153'.
  Successfully installed 'jQuery.Validation 1.9.0.1'.
  Successfully installed 'Microsoft.AspNet.WebApi.Client 4.0.20710.0'.
  Successfully installed 'Microsoft.AspNet.Mvc 4.0.20710.0'.
  Successfully installed 'Microsoft.AspNet.WebPages.Data 2.0.20710.0'.
  Successfully installed 'Microsoft.Net.Http 2.0.20710.0'
```

Figure 15-8. *NuGet Package Restore build output*

OtherO ptions

If you cannot use NuGet to download the dependencies (not all dependencies are available as NuGet packages), the other option is to customize the build process to explicitly download the dependencies. We will cover how to customize the build process in Chapter 16, which should give you an idea of how to implement this.

Adding On Premises Build Servers

Some of the limitations with the hosted build server mentioned previously might trigger the need for you to add your own local build servers to the build resource pool. This feature makes it possible to handle the common scenarios with the hosted build service and then add local build servers for the builds that need specific functionality such as custom software. As shown in Figure 15-9, these servers run on premises and are registered with the team project collection in TFS.

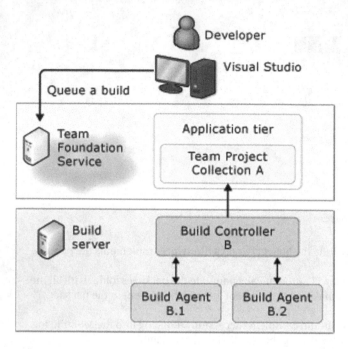

Figure 15-9. *On Premises build servers*

You can install Team Foundation Build services anywhere you want to; as long as it has an Internet connection, it can be used as a build service. Note that there is no communication from the hosted build service to the build servers, instead the local build service polls the hosted build service continuously to retrieve the status of running builds and queue requests. This is what makes it possible to put build servers on premises behind firewalls and still be able to use them on the hosted build service.

The following operation systems are supported:

- 64-bit version of Windows Server 2008 with Service Pack 2 (Standard or Enterprise Edition)

- 64-bit version of Windows Server 2008 R2 with Service Pack 1 (Standard or Enterprise Edition)

- 64-bit version of Windows Server 2012

- 32- and 64-bit versions of Windows 7 with Service Pack 1 (Home Premium, Professional, Enterprise, or Ultimate Edition)

- 32- and 64-bit versions of Windows 8

■ **Note**   An instance of Team Foundation Build service can only be connected to one team project collection. This means you cannot use a build server for multiple TFS accounts, and you will need at least one build server for each account.

So, how do we add a local build server to our hosted build service? The following steps will guide you:

1. Start by installing the TFS 2012 build service components using the standard installer media. You can download the media from http://www.microsoft.com/visualstudio/eng/downloads.

2. In the Configuration Center, select the Configure Team Foundation Build Service wizard.

3. Then you need to browse to the project collection on the hosted service, as shown in Figure 15-10. You might need to provide valid Live ID credentials to perform this.

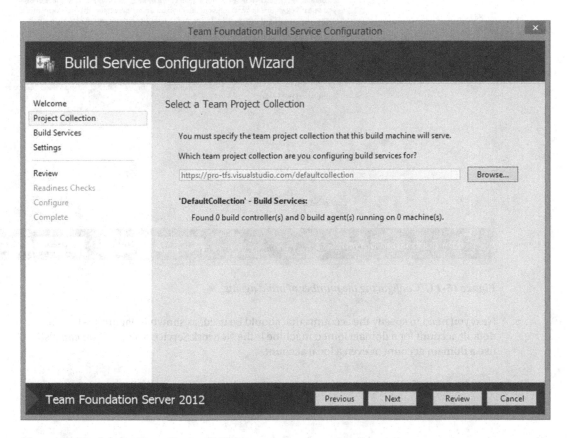

Figure 15-10. Select a Team Project Collection

■ **Note** The hosted build controller is not discovered here, because you can't add new build agents to the hosted build controller.

---

4. Configure how many build agents you want to run on the machine, as shown in Figure 15-11. The default value is the number of CPUs. Select this if the machine is to be used only as a build server, otherwise you might want to select a lower number here. The number of agents equals the number of builds that can be executed in parallel.

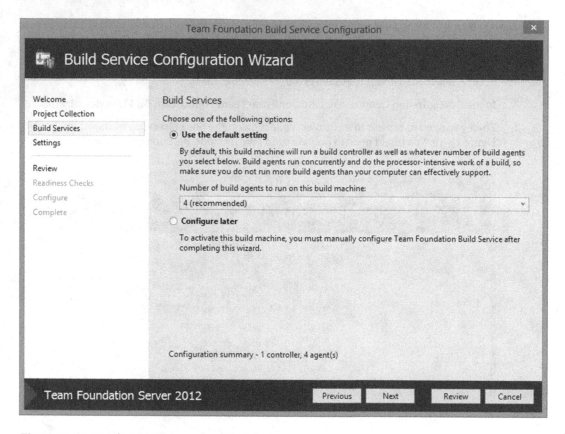

Figure 15-11. Configuring the number of build agents

5. Next you need to specify the accounts that should be used, as shown in Figure 15-12. The default account for a domain joined machine is the Network Service account. You can also use a domain account or even a local account.

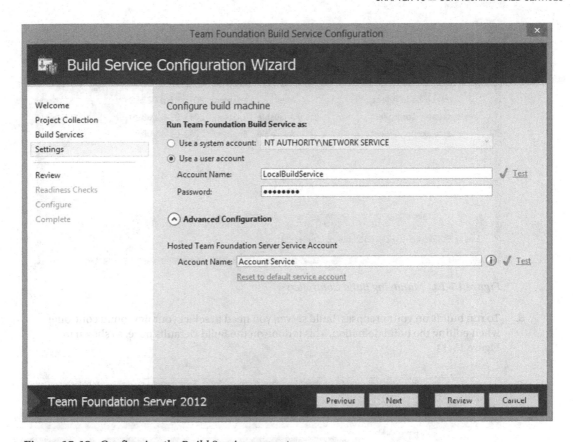

Figure 15-12. Configuring the Build Service accounts

6. The second set of credentials that are involved here is the Hosted Team Foundation
    Server Service Account. This default to Account Service is an account that is automatically
    created on your hosted service. Usually you don't need to change this account, but if you
    want to, you need to go to the administration page of the hosted service collection and
    create a new service account there that is part of the Project Collection Build
    Service Accounts group. The administration page can be found at
    `https://youraccountname.visualstudio.com/DefaultCollection/_admin/_security`.

7. Click Next to verify the settings and then Configure to perform the configuration. If all goes
    well, you now have a new build controller and one or more build agents connected to your
    hosted build service.

8. To verify this, open the Manage Build Controllers dialog box again and verify that it shows
    the new build controller and build agents, next to the hosted build controller, as shown in
    Figure 15-13.

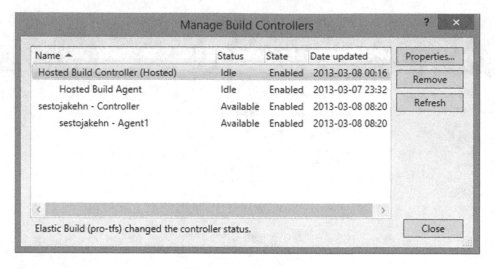

Figure 15-13. Managing Build Controllers

9. To run builds on your premises' build server, you need to select your new build controller when editing the build definition. This is done on the Build Defaults page, as shown in Figure 15-14.

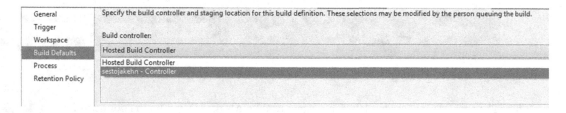

Figure 15-14. Assigning Build Controller to your build

We will cover all the details on how to create build definitions in Chapter 16.

Summary

This chapter discussed the architecture of the hosted build service and how to configure it. As with every solution, there are advantages and drawbacks. The possibility of adding extra build servers on premises is very powerful, but it can cause several drawbacks, as mentioned.

The next chapter will dive into how to use build automation, how to create new builds, and how to customize the underlyingb uildt emplates.

■ ■ ■

Working withB uilds

As mentioned in Chapter 15, using build automation is a very important part of the ALM process as it allows you to continuously integrate your software on every check in and also automate otherwise manual tasks. This will by itself raise the quality of your process and you will find that you spend less time on release software and more time on development and testing.

This chapter will walk you through setting up and running automated builds in Team Foundation Service, when you have the source code in both Team Foundation Version Control and in Git repositories.

Build Artifacts

There are three main artifacts that are important to understand when it comes to automated builds in TF Service:

- *Build definitions*: When you want to set up a new automated build for a project, you create a build definition. A build definition contains a large set of properties that can be used to customize many portions of the build process. When creating a build definition, you select which projects to build, the details of logging, which agent to use, and a lot of other things. Build definitions are stored in the TF Service database and they are connected to a team project.

- *Build process templates*: A Windows Workflow file (.xaml) that dictates the entire build process. It contains activities that download source code, create labels, compiles, and many others. There are several default templates that are included out of the box that handle most of the common build scenarios. However, if you need functionality that is not included in the default template, you will need to customize it. Build process templates are located in source control and can be shared across team projects within the same team project collection.

- *Builds*: This is the actual build that is started by queuing a build definition. Every build will get an ID and a Uniform Resource Identifier (URI) that is unique across the team project collection.

Creating a Build Definition

Let's walk through how to set up a new build definition for our sample application, Fabrikam Fiber Call Center. We will create a CI build that will run every time anything is changed. The build will perform get latest, compile, and run unit tests and report all the results back to TF Service where the team members will be able to see the build results.

1   Verify that you have the source code checked in to TF Service. In our example, the code is located below $/FabrikamFiber/Main/(Figure 16-1).

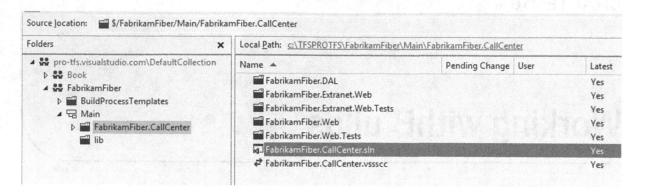

Figure 16-1. *Sample project in source control*

2. Open Team Explorer and go to the Builds hub.

3. SelectN ewB uildD efinition(F igure 16-2).

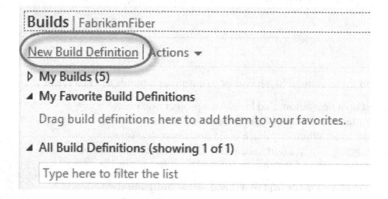

Figure 16-2. *New Build Definition*

4. Enter a suitable name for the build definition. We recommend you use a naming convention for your builds, for example, <Project>.<Branch>.<BuildType>, where BuildType is the kind of build you are creating. Often <Branch> is left out when you are in the Main (Trunk) branch, as shown in Figure 16-3. In this example, we name it FabrikamFiber.CallCenter.CI because we are creating a CI build (e.g., a build that will beq ueueda ftere veryche ckin).

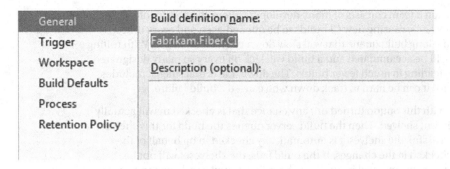

Figure 16-3. *Build definition name*

■ **Note**   Using a naming convention will make it easier to locate build definitions. A large team project can often contain 100 or more build definitions. Also the intent of the build (CI, Release, QA) becomes very clear when using a convention.

5.   Ont heT riggert ab,s electh owt hisb uilds houldb et riggered(Figure 16-4).

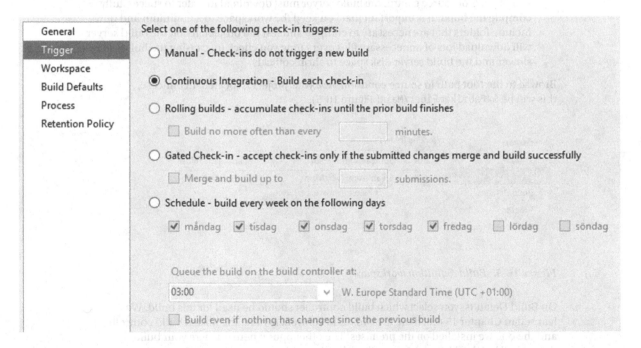

Figure 16-4. *Build definition trigger*

The options are:

- *Manual*: Build is queued manually. Often used for release builds that are built on demand.

- *Continuous Integration*: This option will trigger a new build every time anything is checked in inside the workspace of the build definition (see next step).

- *Rolling builds*: When a team consists of many developers, there can be a lot of simultaneous check ins, causing new CI builds to be queued each and every time. This can result in a long build queue that will slow down the feedback loop. With rolling builds, changes will be accumulated and a build will kick off every so many designated minutes instead, leading to much fewer builds. The downside is that since it includes several changesets, it can be hard to track down who caused a build failure.

- *Gated Check-in*: With this option turned on, any change that is checked in will actually not be checked in but shelved. Then the build server queues the build for this shelveset. If the build is successful, the shelveset is automatically checked in on behalf of the developer who checked in the changes. If the build fails, the shelveset will not be checked in, and the developer will be notified about this. Gated check ins can be very effective when there is a problem with keeping the build successful (e.g., due to lack of communication). For global teams working in different time zones, communication is often a problem, and gated check-in builds can help keep the builds green. The trade-off of course is that check ins are prevented, and even if developer A fixes their issue the build can still fail because of another issue from developer B.

- *Schedule*: Here you can specify that the build would be queued at a certain time every day. This is usually used for running larger QA builds or release builds during the night. For this scenario, select Continuous Integration. On the Workspace tab we need to specify which parts of source control the build server must download in order to successfully compile the build. It is important that you keep the workspace to a minimum and only include folders that are necessary to compile and test the project. If not, the build server will download lots of unnecessary files every time you check in, causing the builds to run slower and the build server disk space to shrink quickly.

Browse to the root path in source control where your project is located. In our case, this will be $/FabrikamFiber/Main(Figure 16-5).

Figure 16-5. *Build definition workspace*

6. On Build Defaults, you select which build controller should be used for this build. We learned in Chapter 15 that there are two build controllers here: the hosted build controller and the one we installed on the premises. The other option here is where your build output will be placed, and you have the following options:

- *This build does not copy output files to a drop folder*: The build will not produce any output. This can be suitable for CI builds that are only used for verifying what was checked in.

- *Copy build output to the following drop folder*: Can currently only be used on premises. Because we are using a hosted TF Service, there is no publicly available share. If you select this option, the build will fail with the error message *The network name cannot be found*.

- *Copy build output to the following Source Control folder*: Places the build output into source control. This was initially the default option on TF Service and the only way of actually accessing the build output. The downside with this solution is that it creates new revisions in the source control, causing unwanted notification, and also can increase the database size considerably. One must also make sure to cloak the selected path to avoid including it in the build.

- *Copy build output to the server*: This option was introduced in Visual Studio 2012 update 1 and is now the default and best option. With this option selected, the build output will be placed on the hosted build server and will be available from the build summary page, as you will see later.

The Process tab is where you select what to build and how to build it. The first thing you need to select is which build process template to use. To see the available templates, click the Show details button, and then expand the drop-down list (Figure 16-6).

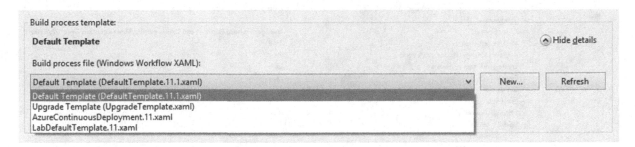

Figure 16-6. *Build definition's Build process template*

Remember that build process templates are Windows Workflow files, checked into source control. For every team project, there is a folder called `BuildProcessTemplates` located at the root that will contain the templates shown above when it is created. You can add your own build process templates here if you want, but consider adding them together with your project source code. The current templates available are:

- `DefaultTemplate.11.1.xaml` is the standard build template you will use most often. If you need to customize and extend your build process, this is the file you will base your changes on.

- `UpgradeTemplate.xaml` is used for legacy builds, pre-Team Foundation Server 2010 that used MSBuild instead of Windows Workflow as the build orchestration language.

- `AzureContinuousDeployment.11.xaml` is used for setting up builds that will be automatically deployed to a Windows Azure web site or web role. This template is discussed in detail in Chapter 18.

- `LabDefaultTemplate.11.xaml` is part of the Lab Management feature in Team Foundation Server. Although Lab Management is currently not supported in TF Service, you can still use the template to deploy a build to an available machine, typically in Windows Azure, and run coded UI tests for verification. This is also discussed in Chapter 21.

If you currently have the solution open in Visual Studio, the server path to the solution file will be automatically filled out in the Items to Build parameter. This is actually the only parameter that is required in the Default Template, but there are plenty of customization options here (Figure 16-7).

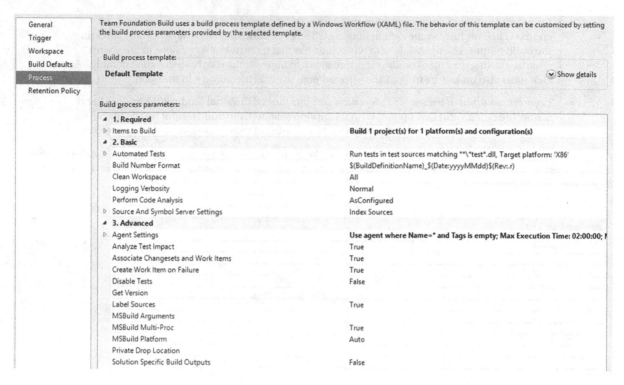

Figure 16-7. Build definition process parameters

The process parameters are divided into three sections: Required, Basic, and Advanced. We will not discuss all of the parameters here, but Table 16-1 lists the most important ones.

Table 16-1. Default Build Process Parameters

Section	Parameter	Description
Required	Items to Build	Specifies which solutions or projects to build and which configuration and platform to build. Note that you can build multiple solutions or configurations in the same build.
Basic	Automated Tests	Configures which test to run as part of the build. This is discussed in detail later.
	Clean Workspace	Controls if the build should be a full rebuild (default) or if it should be incremental (e.g., only perform get latest and build the changes). Consider changing this for builds that take a long time to complete.
Advanced	Agent Settings	Defines tag and name filters that allow you to control on which agent(s) this build definition should be queued. You could, for example, define a tag called SharePoint, which would mean that this build must be executed on a build agent that has the same tag. This way you can make sure the build runs on a build agent with the necessary prerequisites installed.

(continued)

Table 16-1. (*continued*)

Section	Parameter	Description
	Analyze Test Impact	This is a very powerful feature that analyzes the changes that have been made compared with the last successful build, and from this it generates a list of all tests that are impacted by these changes. This is mainly used for manual tests and those exposed in the Microsoft Test Manager, which gives testers valuable information on which tests they need to retest for a new build.
	Associated Changesets and Work Items	When set to true, the build will list all the changesets and the work items that were associated with those changesets as part of the build summary. This is the foundation for release notes and allows you to audit which changes actually made it into the build.
	MSBuild Arguments	Used for specifying MSBuild arguments that will be passed into the MSBuild activity that compiles the projects. This is useful for several things, for example, to enable automatic deployment of your web applications using Web Deploy, which is implemented using MSBuild. (You will see several examples of how to use this parameter in Chapter 17.)

Keep the default values for all parameters for now.

7. On the Retention Policy tab, you can select how many builds should be kept per build outcome. The default setting is ten for each type, exception for stopped builds where only the latest build is retained. For on-premises installations, these settings are crucial to avoid the amount of disk space on the build server to grow out of control.

8. You ared one,s avet hen ewb uildd efinition.

Running a Build

To queue the build you just created, you have two options: either manually queue it using Team Explorer or make a change to the source code and check it in. Since this is a CI build, it will automatically start a new build. Here we will queue the build manually, as shown in Figure 16-8.

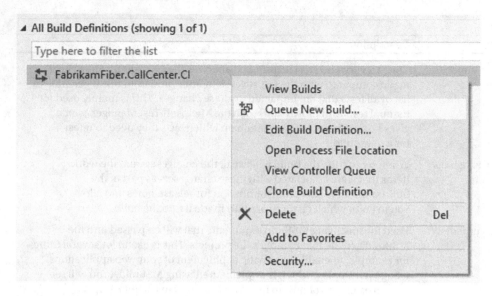

Figure 16-8. *Queue a new build*

The build will be queued and is available beneath the My Builds section in Team Explorer. Double-click it to see the build Activity Log for the running build. On this screen, shown in Figure 16-9, you can see detailed information about the running build, such as who triggered it and for which changeset, how long it has been running, and so forth.

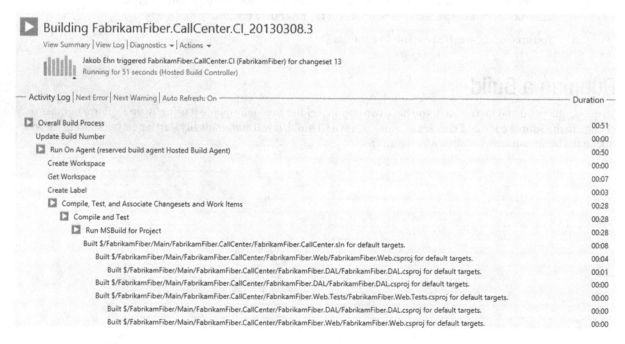

Figure 16-9. *Build log*

Once the build completes, you will see the build Summary screen, as shown in Figure 16-10.

 FabrikamFiber.CallCenter.CI_20130308.3 - Build succeeded

View Summary | View Log ‑ Open Drop Folder | Diagnostics ▾ | <No Quality Assigned> ▾ | Actions ▾

 Jakob Ehn triggered FabrikamFiber.CallCenter.CI (FabrikamFiber) for changeset 13
Ran for 84 seconds (Hosted Build Controller), completed 12 seconds ago

Latest Activity

Build last modified by Elastic Build (pro-tfs) 12 seconds ago.

Request Summary

Request 8, requested by Jakob Ehn 2,1 minutes ago, Completed

Summary

Debug | Any CPU

0 error(s), 0 warning(s)

◢ $/FabrikamFiber/Main/FabrikamFiber.CallCenter/FabrikamFiber.CallCenter.sln compiled

$/FabrikamFiber/Main/FabrikamFiber.CallCenter/FabrikamFiber.CallCenter.sln - 0 error(s), 0 warning(s), View Log File

◢ 1 test run completed - 100% pass rate

buildguest@WIN-BK3RDSTIKSE 2013-03-08 21:19:26_Any CPU_Debug, 4 of 4 test(s) passed

No Code Coverage Results

Impacted Tests

No tests were impacted

Figure 16-10. *Build summary*

You can see that it lists the solutions that were built, with links to the MSBuild logs, and also the test result summary. Click the Test result link to view the full details of the tests that were executed.

■ **Note** When talking about build logs, there are two separate logs: one from the Windows Workflow build process, which is the same that is shown in the build log screen, and one from MSBuild, which contains the output from the compilation. This is the same information you get when compiling in Visual Studio. Both log files are available from the build summary page.

The build and test results are grouped by configuration and platform. In this case, we selected Debug and Any CPU, but as mentioned earlier, it is possible to build multiple solutions or multiple configurations. The build summary page will list each combination beneath the summary with the corresponding build and test results.

The Impacted Tests section shows any tests that were impacted by the changes, if you have enabled Test Impact Analysis.

On the top menu, you can access the build logs and drop folder. For this build definition, we selected "Copy build output to the server," which will let us access the build output from the build summary directly. Clicking the Drop folder link opens the build summary page on TF Service, from which you can download the output as a .zip file, as showni nF igure 16-11.

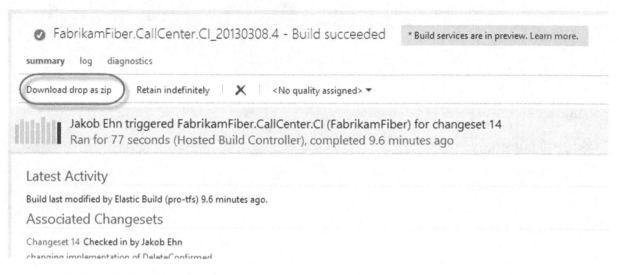

Figure 16-11. *Download build output*

An important feature of automated builds in TF Service is that it will keep track of the changes that were included in a specific build. This gives you the ability to audit things and is the basis for producing release notes, which can be sent to the testers or customers. Let's see how this works:

1. Create a new Bug work item in the Fabrikam Fiber team project (Figure 16-12).

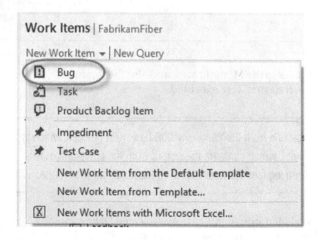

Figure 16-12. *Create a new bug*

2. Make a change in the FabrikamFiber.CallCenters olution.

3. Check in the changes, and make sure you associate the change with the Bug work item you just created. You can use the Work Item ID to quickly associate the changeset.

4. This will kick off a new build; wait for it to finish, and open the build summary.

5. Now you will see two new sections at the bottom of the summary that lists associated changesets and their associated work items, as shown in Figure 16-13.

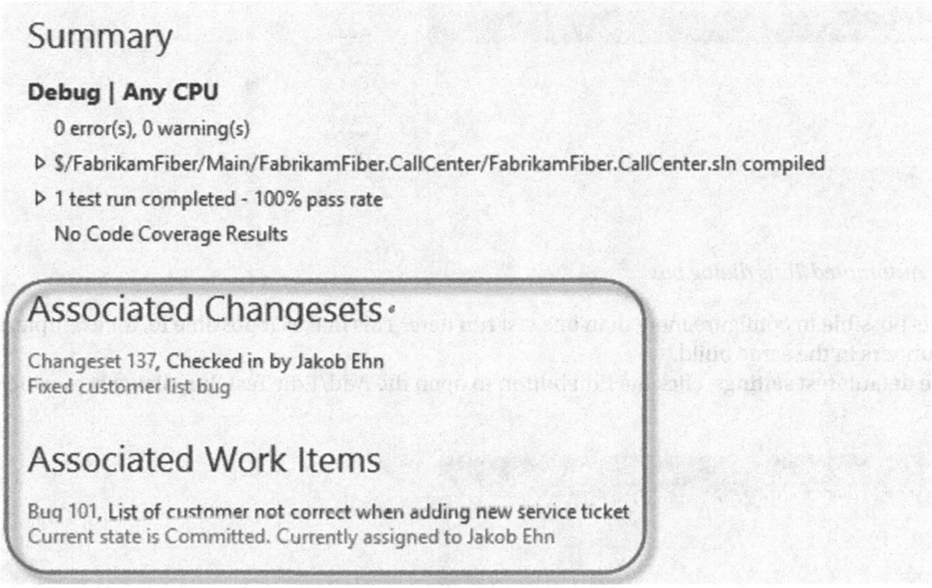

Summary

Debug | Any CPU

0 error(s), 0 warning(s)

▷ $/FabrikamFiber/Main/FabrikamFiber.CallCenter/FabrikamFiber.CallCenter.sln compiled

▷ 1 test run completed - 100% pass rate

No Code Coverage Results

Associated Changesets

Changeset 137, Checked in by Jakob Ehn
Fixed customer list bug

Associated Work Items

Bug 101, List of customer not correct when adding new service ticket
Current state is Committed. Currently assigned to Jakob Ehn

Figure 16-13. Associated changesets and work items

A build will list all changes that have been made since the last successful build. So if you check in a change that breaks the build, the next build will include both that changeset and the new one with the fix.

■ **Note** Because of the logic mentioned here, there must be at least one successful build before the summary page will list the associated changes. Make it a habit to always create a build definition for your projects at the very start and make sure that it succeeds before proceeding with the implementation.

Executing Tests

In Visual Studio 2012, the unit test runner was completely rewritten. The main reason for this was to be able to support multiple test frameworks, not only MSTest. The new test runner is also available during automated builds, which will also let you run tests for any supported test framework in your builds. Since there have been some changes in how the settings are defined with the new test runner, the old MSTest runner is still available for automated builds, as you will see in this chapter.

This section will walk you through how to configure unit tests for automated builds and how to enable different test adapters.

Configuring Unit Tests for Automated Builds

As mentioned earlier, test settings for a build definition are configured using the Test Settings process parameter that is located in the Basic section on the Process tab. To edit the settings, click the Browse button, which will bring up the Automated Tests dialog box, as shown in Figure 16-14.

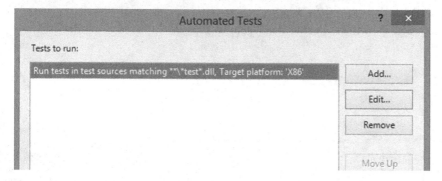

Figure 16-14. *Automated Tests dialog box*

Note that is possible to configure more than one test run here. This makes it possible to, for example, use several different test runners in the same build.

To edit the default test settings, click the Edit button to open the Add/Edit Test Run dialog box, which is shown in Figure 16-15.

Figure 16-15. *Configure Add/Edit Test Run dialog box*

Test settings specifies which test runner you want to use (see below), which tests should be run, and additional options, such as whether code coverage should be enabled. Which test runner you choose impacts how you configure these options.

The following test runners are available:

- *Visual Studio Test Runner*: The new default test runner that supports multiple frameworks. It has also been optimized and runs tests much faster than the previous test runner.

- *MSTest.exe Runner*: The test runner that existed in Visual Studio 2010. It can still be used in cases where builds are dependent on existing settings file or for legacy build templates that have not yet been upgraded to support the new test runner. This test runner uses .testsettings files for test run options, such as enabling code coverage and collecting other diagnostic information. We will not cover this file here, but for detailed information about this file and in which cases you should use it, go to http://msdn.microsoft.com/en-us/library/vstudio/ee256991.aspx.

- *MSTest Test Metadata File*: Used for running tests that are denied in Test metadata files (.vsmdi). These files are deprecated and no longer supported in Visual Studio 2012, but they are still supported in Team Foundation Build for legacy builds.

SpecifyingT estF ilters

There are several ways to specify which tests to run. First, you select which assemblies should be searched for tests by using the Test assembly file specification field, as shown in Figure 16-15. The default is ***test*.dll, which means that any assembly that contains the word test will be scanned for tests.

To specify a more fine-grained filter, go to the Criteria tab. Here it is possible to create a test case filter expression that evaluates attributes on the unit tests to determine which tests to run, as shown in Figure 16-16.

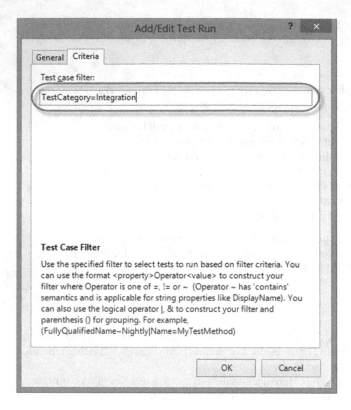

Figure 16-16. *Test case filter*

Test case filters are quite powerful and can be combined to produce more complex expressions. Here are some examples:

- `TestCategory=Performance | Priority=1`: Run all tests with `TestCategory = Performance` *or* where `Prioritye quals1`.

- `Owner=Jakob & TestCategory != UI`: Run all test where the owner attribute is Jakob *and* the TestCategory is set to UI.

The properties that can be used are currently limited to:

- `Name=<TestMethodDisplayNameName>`

- `FullyQualifiedName=<FullyQualifiedTestMethodName>`

- `Priority=<PriorityAttributeValue>`

- `TestCategory=<TestCategoryAttributeValue>`

- `ClassName=<ClassName>` (Valid only for unit tests for Windows Store apps, currently not availablef orc lassicM STest)

The operators that are currently supported are:

- `=`(equals)

- `!=`(note quals)

- ~ (contains or substring, only valid for string values)
- &(a nd)
- |(or)
- () (grouping)

As you can see, it is possible to combine these into quite advanced expressions.

Enabling Different Test Adapters

To be able to use any test adapter other than MSTest on the hosted build server (and on premises), you must deploy the test adapters to it. By default, only MSTest tests will be executed on the build server, other framework tests will simply be ignored.

■ **Note** For an updated list of supported test adapters, go to `http://blogs.msdn.com/b/visualstudioalm/archive/2012/03/02/visual-studio-11-beta-unit-testing-plugins-list.aspx`.

Deployment is done by adding the assemblies to source control and configuring the build controller with the path. Here is how you would go about installing the xUnit test adapter.

1. Start by creating a folder in source control where the test adapter assemblies can be checked in. Locate the `BuildProcessTemplates` folder at the root of the team project and create a subfolder called `CustomActivities`. Make sure you check in the new folder.

2. On the Builds page in Team Explorer, select Action > Manage Build Controller.

3. Select the Hosted Build Controller and click the Properties button.

4. In the Version control path to custom assemblies property, browse to the new folder in source control(Figure 16-17).

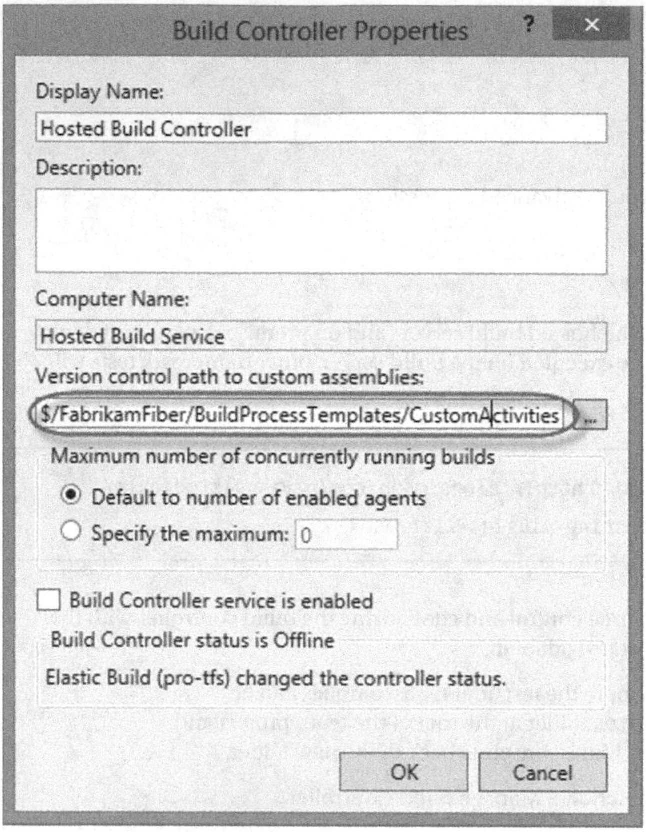

Figure 16-17. *Configure build controller to enable custom test adapters*

5. To be able to run xUnit tests locally, download the latest version of the test adapter from the Visual Studio Gallery. You can do this by going to Tools > Extensions and Updates and searching for xUnit in the online gallery (Figure 16-18).

Figure 16-18. *Installing the xUnit.net runner*

6. After restarting Visual Studio, verify that you can run xUnit tests using the test runner (Figure 16-19).

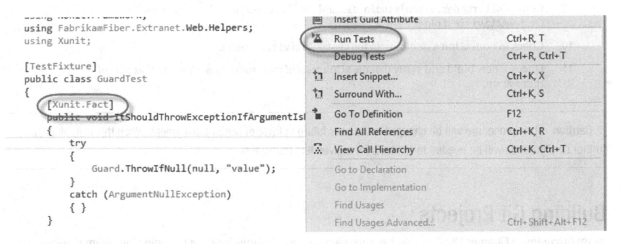

Figure 16-19. *Running xUnit tests in Visual Studio*

7. To be able to use the test adapter in Team Foundation Build, you need to extract the assemblies from the test adapter installer. The easiest way to do this is to download the .vsix file to your local machine and extract it (a .vsix file is just a renamed .zip file). Go back to the Extension Manager, locate the xUnit adapter in the Installed section, and click the More Information link (Figure 16-20).

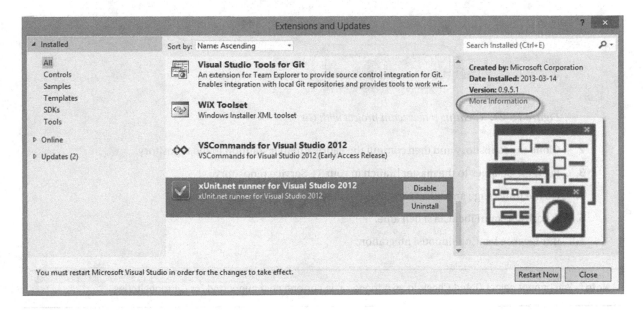

Figure 16-20. *Getting the xUnit assemblies*

8. Downloadt he `.vsix` file from the web page, rename it using the `.zip` file format, and extract it somewhere onto your local machine.

9. Copy `xunit.runner.visualstudio.dll` and `xunit.runner.utility.dll` to the `CustomActivities`f older.

10. Check in both xUnit assemblies in the `CustomActivities`f older.

11. Queue a new build and verify that the xUnit tests of your solution are executed as part of thet estr un.

■ **Caution**   This procedure will be changed in the near future in favor of NuGet deployment. When this is in place, no further configuration will be needed to run tests for a given test framework.

Building Git Projects

As we discussed in Chapter 12, when you have installed the Visual Studio Tools for Git extension, Team Explorer becomes a full-fidelity Git client that can work against any Git repository, not just against TF Service. It is also possible to run automated builds for your Git projects, which we will explain in this section. As the functionality is still in an early phase, expect it to evolve over time.

The process of creating a build definition in a Git Team project is very similar to what you saw previously, but there are some differences you will notice:

1. Create a new Team Project and make sure you select Git as version control (Figure 16-21).

Figure 16-21. *Creating a new team project with Git*

2. Clone the repository and then commit the FabrikamFiber solution to the repository.

3. Push the changes to the master branch in your TF Service repository.

4. Go the Build page and select New Build Definition.

5. EnterF abrikamFiber.CIa st hen ame.

6. Intr igger,se lectCon tinuousI ntegration.

■ **Note**   You cannot select Gated Check-in as a trigger; it is currently not supported for Git repositories.

---

7. In the Source Settings, add the branches you want to build to the Monitored branches list. Here you only have a master branch, so add this. Note that you must provide the full Git path to each branch (Figure 16-22).

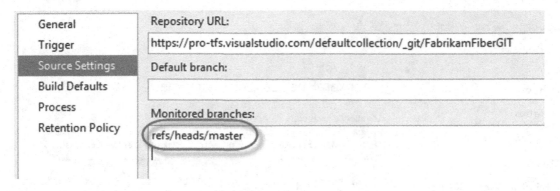

Figure 16-22. *Selecting which Git branches to build*

8. On Build Defaults, select Hosted Build Controller and keep the default staging location.

9. On Process, note first the build template that is selected by default. It is called
GitTemplate.xamla ndi st heo nlyc hoiceb yd efault(Figure 16-23).

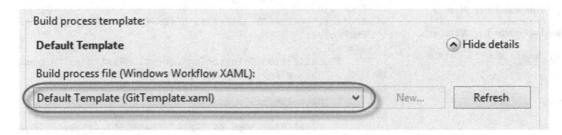

Figure 16-23. *Select GitTemplate.xaml*

■ **Note** It is currently not possible to change this template, it is the only choice. The build process template is not even stored in source control. The reason for this is that Microsoft wants to be able to update this frequently with new functionality, and letting users customize it would block automatic upgrades. So expect this to change.

---

10. Under Solution to build you need to enter the full path to the solution. The easiest way to determine this path is to go to the web access and browse to the solution in the Code tab. When you select it, the full path is shown at the top (Figure 16-24).

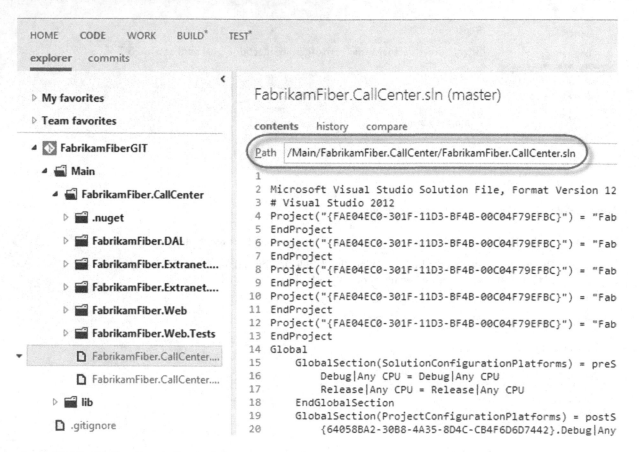

Figure 16-24. *Finding the solution path in source control*

11. Enter Configuration and Platform for the build (Figure 16-25). Although it is not required, you should always do this.

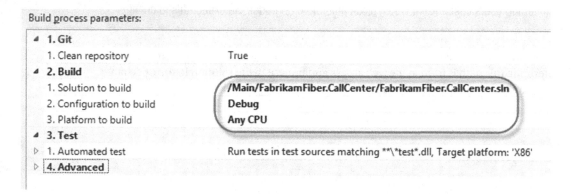

Figure 16-25. *Specify configuration and platform*

12.   Save the build definition, and push a new commit to the server in the master branch. This will automatically queue a new build that should finish successfully. Note that the buildr eferst ow hichb ranchw asb uilt(Figure 16-26).

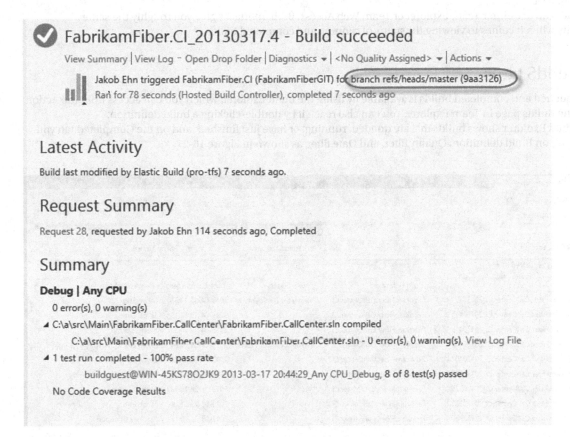

Figure 16-26. Build summary page for a Git build

■ **Note**   Currently, the `GitTemplate.xaml` build process template does not support associating changesets and work items with the build. Although you can associate a work item with a changeset by adding a #<WorkItemId> in the commit comment, it will not show up in the build summary. This and other missing features, such as support for gated checkins, is currently under development and will likely be released later this year.

Tracking Build Status

If you are responsible for automated builds on a team project, you need to be able to view build results over time to be able to track down problems or get an overview of the build status for different projects. You also want to be notified when different events occur, such as when builds are queued or fail.

As mentioned earlier, there is currently no underlying data warehouse available in TF Service, and there is no integration with Microsoft SQL Reporting Services, as there is for an on-premises installation. Hence, there are no build reports that let you view build status and outcome over a longer period of time. Hopefully, this will be enabled in a future release.

Instead, you use either Team Explorer or Team Web Access. Both interfaces give you roughly the same functionality when it comes to viewing the status of running and completed builds.

ViewB uildS tatus

Access to queued and completed builds is available by using the Build Explorer, which you can access from the Action menu on the Builds page in Team Explorer. You can also reach it by double-clicking a build definition.

The Build Explorer shows builds that are queued, running, or have just finished, and on the Completed tab you can filter both on Build definition, Quality filter, and Date filter, as shown in Figure 16-27.

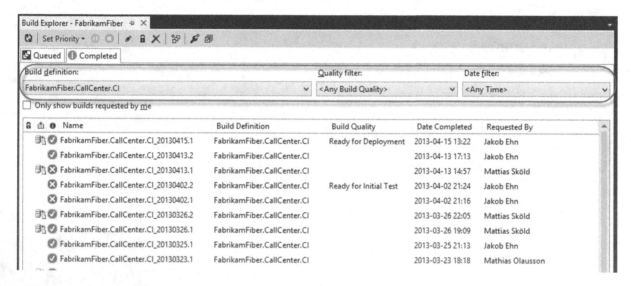

Figure 16-27. *Build Explorer*

■ **Note**   Remember that builds are deleted according to the retention policies configuration for the corresponding build definition.

By right-clicking a completed build, you can perform several actions, such as delete, retry, or edit the build, as showni nF igure 16-28.

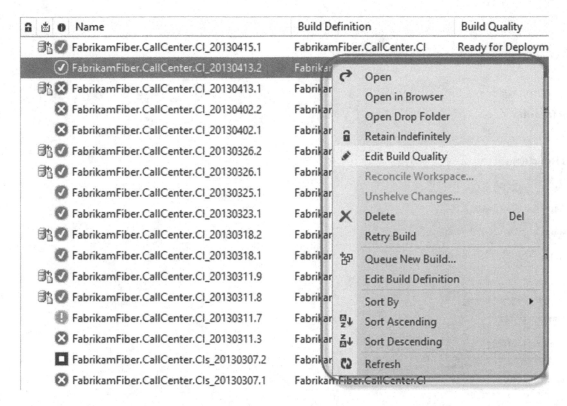

Figure 16-28. *Completed build actions*

■ **Note**   The Build Explorer only works at the team project level (e.g., it only shows running and completed builds
for the currently selected team project). For working with builds and build definitions across multiple team projects,
you can try the Community TFS Build Manager, which is available from the Visual Studio Gallery:
`http://visualstudiogallery.msdn.microsoft.com/cfdb84b4-285e-4eeb-9fa9-dad9bfe2cd10`.

Build Favorites

Some builds are more interesting than others, especially during specific parts of a project. At the beginning of a
project, you often find yourself checking the status of the CI builds. When you are starting to roll out deployments to a
staging environment, you want to monitor the status of this build more often.

This is what Build Favorites is for. You can mark one or more build definitions as favorites. This will cause the
build definition to show up in different places for easy access in Team Explorer and Team Web Access. An extra benefit
is that the status of the last and previous ten builds is shown together with the build definition name, as shown in
Figure 16-29. This lets you quickly see the status without having to open the build.

Figure 16-29. *Add Favorite Build definition*

Build definitions can either be Personal or Team favorites. You can mark a build definition as a personal favorite from both Team Explorer and from Team Web Access.

Personal favorites will show up in the My Favorites section in Team Explorer and Team Web Access. This makes it quick and easy, for example, to queue a new build or access the queue for that build definition. Remember that the list of build definitions can become very long, and although you can filter it, the filter is not persisted.

Adding a build as a Team Favorite can only be done from Team Web Access. Doing this will expose the build definition as a tile on the team home page in Team Web Access, as shown in Figure 16-30.

TEAM FAVORITES

Figure 16-30. *Team Favorites tile*

The tile shows information about the latest build but also the outcome and relative total time of the previous ten builds. Clicking it takes you right to the Build Explorer for this build definition.

Build Alerts

In the previous section, you saw how to use the Team Web Access to visualize the status of the build definitions you are most interested in. But most of the time, you will not be sitting around watching the builds execute or logging in to see if the builds were successful. If there is a problem with your build, you want to be notified.

This is where Build Alerts comes in to play. You learned how to configure personal and team alerts in Chapter 6. Figure 16-31 shows the existing predefined templates you can use for creating build alerts.

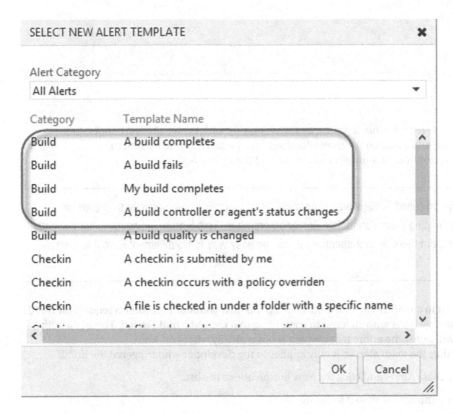

Figure 16-31. *Build Alert templates*

Let's create an alert that will notify you anytime a developer queues a private build.

Select the A build completes template from the list shown in Figure 16-31. In the alerts editor, click the Add new clause link and select the field Build Reason and the value Private (Figure 16-32).

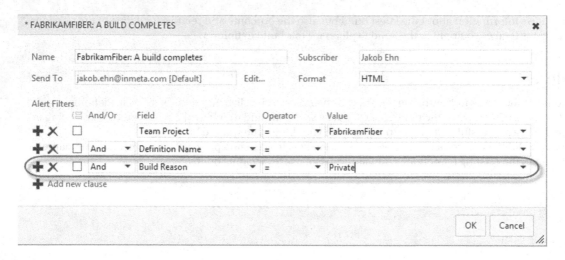

Figure 16-32. *Build Alert editor*

In the Subscriber field, you can selected either a person or a team that should receive the alert notification e-mails. In the Send To field, you can add additional e-mail addresses that the alert should be sent to.

The Format field controls if the notification e-mail should be in HTML or plain text.

■ **Note** There is a third format option called SOAP, which is normally used for calling web services to implement integration scenarios when you are hosting Team Foundation Server on premises. This feature, however, is not currently supported on TF Service. It will work, but there is no authentication and no easy way to troubleshoot it, so it is currently advised not to use this feature.

There are times when you want to create alerts for the entire team, not just yourself. A common request for Build Alerts is to automatically notify the developer who checked in something that caused a build to fail. There is a built-in alert for builds that fails, but this will notify the entire team, which is not typically what you want.

Instead, it is better to personalize the team alert so it only applies to the developer who triggered the build.

1. Select Fabrikam Fiber Team Alerts and click the New button above the list.

2. Select the A build fails template, as shown in Figure 16-33.

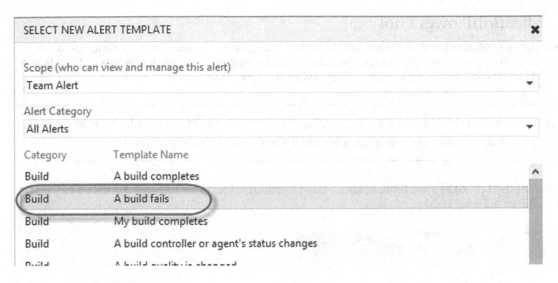

Figure 16-33. *New Build Team Alert*

3. Add a n ewc lause,a ss howni nF igure 16-34.

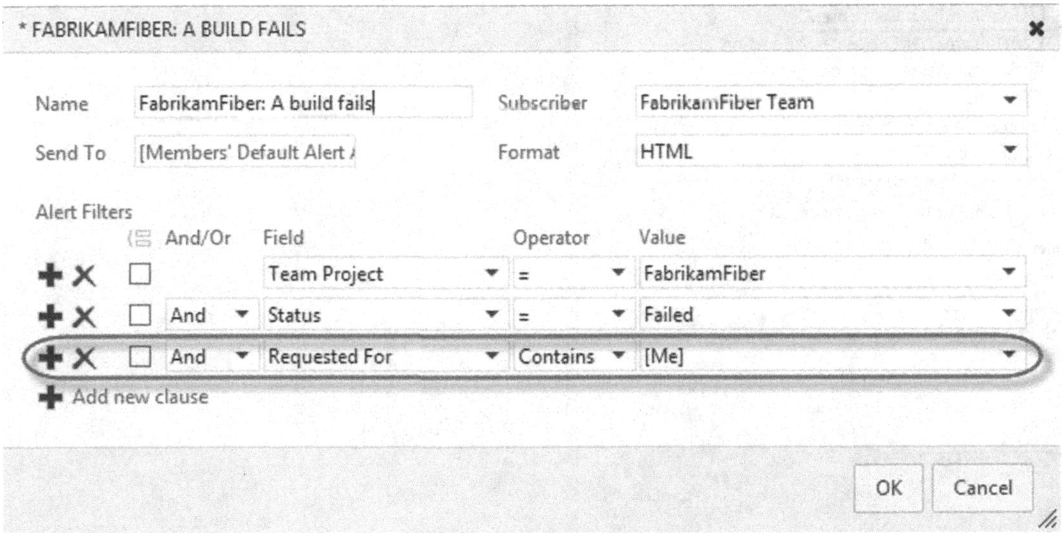

* FABRIKAMFIBER: A BUILD FAILS ✖

Name	FabrikamFiber: A build fails|	Subscriber	FabrikamFiber Team
Send To	[Members' Default Alert /	Format	HTML

Alert Filters

	And/Or	Field	Operator	Value
✚✖ ☐		Team Project ▼	= ▼	FabrikamFiber ▼
✚✖ ☐	And ▼	Status ▼	= ▼	Failed ▼
✚✖ ☐	And ▼	Requested For ▼	Contains ▼	[Me] ▼
✚ Add new clause				

OK   Cancel

Figure 16-34. *Team Build Alert*

As you can see, Subscriber is now set to the FabrikamFiber Team, which will cause this alert to apply to all team members, but it will only trigger for the person who requested the build that failed.

Build NotificationP owerT ool

Another way of being notified of build events is to use the Build Notification Power Tool that comes with the Team Foundation Server 2012 Power Tools. This is a tray application you can configure to monitor specific or all builds and notify you of different events by showing a small pop-up window at the tray area.

■ **Note**   The current version of the Microsoft Visual Studio Team Foundation Server 2012 Power Tools can be found at `http://visualstudiogallery.msdn.microsoft.com/b1ef7eb2-e084-4cb8-9bc7-06c3bad9148f`.

After installing the TFS 2012 Power Tools, locate the Build Notification tool in the tray area and click it to configure it, as shown in Figure 16-35.

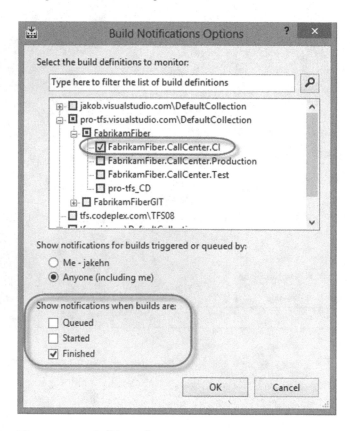

Figure 16-35. *Build Notification Power Tool*

By configuring it like this, you will be notified anytime a build of `FabrikamFiber.CallCenter.CIc`ompletes, as shown in Figure 16-36.

Figure 16-36. *Build Notification dialog box*

■ **Note** A powerful feature of this power tool is that it supports multiple project collections (e.g., you can monitor builds across different TF Service accounts or on-premises installations of Team Foundation Server).

Summary

This chapter showed you how to create and run build definitions, including how to configure and run tests as part of the build using the new Visual Studio test runner. We also looked briefly at how to set up an automated build for Git projects.

In addition, we showed different ways to track the build status of your projects, both current and historically. We can use alerts and the Build Notification Power Tool to be notified instantly when builds are queued and completed.

The next chapter will take a look at how to customize builds, adding your own functionality to perform different tasks during the build.

CHAPTER17

■ ■ ■

CustomizingB uilds

Chapter 16 discussed how to create new build definitions and how to run and track the status of your builds. After you start using automated builds, you will soon find that you want to do more than what is included in the default build process templates.

There are two levels of customization. The first level is to modify the existing process parameters of the build definition, as we explained in Chapter 16. You can, for example, control the level of logging, if the build should produce output, and so on. This doesn't require any changes to the template. The second level is when you need to add new functionality that does not exist in the template, where you need to customize the template itself. These changes will then, when you have checked them in to the source control, affect all build definitions that are using the build process template.

This chapter will show how to customize build process templates and add new functionality to them. Since build process templates are built on top of Windows Workflow Foundation, you must first know a little bit about this framework.

About Windows Workflow Foundation

As mentioned before, build process templates are defined using Windows Workflow Foundation 4.0, which is a framework from Microsoft used for creating workflows that considerably build time by using these techniques. Windows Workflow Foundation solves a lot of problems that could not be solved using MSBuild, which was the orchestration language used by Team Foundation Build before Team Foundation Server 2010. It makes it easy to execute tasks in parallel and it is possible to distribute tasks on remote computers. Windows Workflow Foundation also comes with a designer where developers can add new activities by dragging them from the toolbox and then configure them using a standard property window.

There are three main components of Windows Workflow Foundation:

- *Activities*: The building blocks of a workflow, they perform the actual tasks such as copying a file or building a project. Activities are often composed within other activities to create more complex workflows. For example, the Sequence activity is used for running a set of activities in a specified order, and these activities are composed within the activity. The top level activity is what defines a workflow.

- *Variables*: Stores data during the workflow. Variables can be of any .NET type, and they are scoped much like variables in C#. For example, a variable defined in a Sequence activity is visible only inside this activity and for all composed activities.

- *Arguments*: Used for sending data into activities and for returning data from activities. This is what ties together the activities and allows data to flow between the activities and the workflow. The input arguments of the top-level activity are what define the process parameters for the corresponding build definition. So, for example, on the top level activity in the `DefaultTemplate.11.1.xaml` there is an argument called `RunCodeAnalysis` of type `Boolean`. This argument is displayed as a process parameter in the build definition editor, which was explained in the previous section.

■ **Tip**   For a good introduction to Windows Workflow Foundation 4.0, see
http://msdn.microsoft.com/en-us/library/ee342461.aspx.

Figure 17-1 shows a collapsed view of the DefaultTemplate.11.1.xaml.

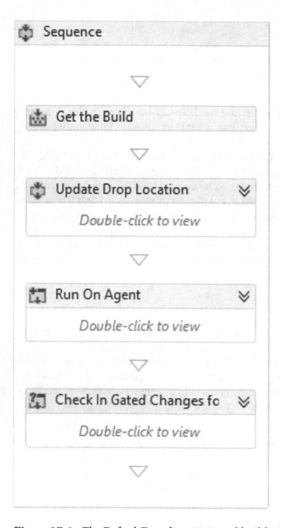

Figure 17-1.   *The DefaultTemplate.11.1xaml build process template*

The Sequence activity on the top is where the workflow starts and all activities inside are executed sequentially. The start of the workflow (Get the Build, Update Drop Location) is executed on the build controller, but the major part of the workflow is inside the Run On Agent activity, which is actually executed on the build agent. The build agent is often running on a machine separate from the build controller, which means that everything within the Run On Agent activityise xecutedr emotely.

Customizing Build Process Templates

Let's walk through how to customize the build process template. The goal with the customization is to add a custom summary section to the build summary page that will include some deployment information.

Modify the Build Process Template

This section will present an example where we add a new activity to the workflow, which will add a new summary section on the build summary page. For this, we use one of the activities that came out of the box with Team Explorer 2012.

■ **Note** You should never modify the build process templates that come out of the box. We recommend that you branch or at least copy these templates and perform your modifications there instead.

---

1. Locatet he `FabrikamFiber.CallCenter.CI` build definition that we created previously and selectE ditB uildD efinition,a ss howni nF igure 17-2.

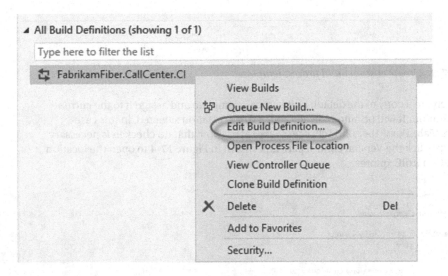

Figure 17-2. Edit Build Definition

2. In the Process tab, expand the Show Details section and click the New button. Enter `CustomBuildProcessTemplate.xaml`a st hen ewf ilen ame,a ss howni nF igure 17-3.

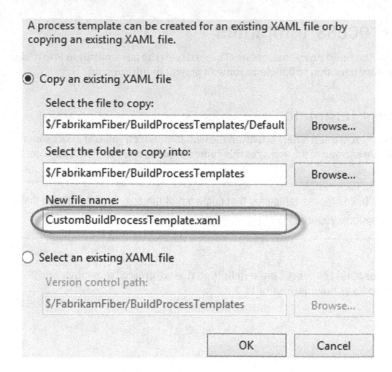

Figure 17-3. *Create custom build process template*

3. This will create a copy of the default build process template and assign it to the current
    build definition. It will be automatically added to the location selected, in this case
    beneath $/FabrikamFiber/BuildProcessTemplates. Note that no check in is necessary
    in this step. Click the Version control path link shown in Figure 17-4 to open the location
    inS ourceCon trolE xplorer.

Figure 17-4. *Assign new build process template*

4. Note that the new file will be grayed out since you haven't yet downloaded it to
    your workspace. To do this, right-click CustomBuildProcessTemplate.xaml and select
    GetL atest.

5. Double-click the file to open it in the Workflow designer. Click the Collapse All link at the
    topr ight.

6. Now open the toolbox, which should be visible as a collapsed tab to the left. If you can't
    see it, open it by using the View ➤ Toolbar menu item.

7. The toolbox, shown in Figure 17-5, will show all the standard activities that come with
    Windows Workflow and also two sections that are specific to Team Foundation Build.
    Locate the WriteCustomSummaryInfo activity at the bottom of the Team Foundation Build
    Activitiess ection.

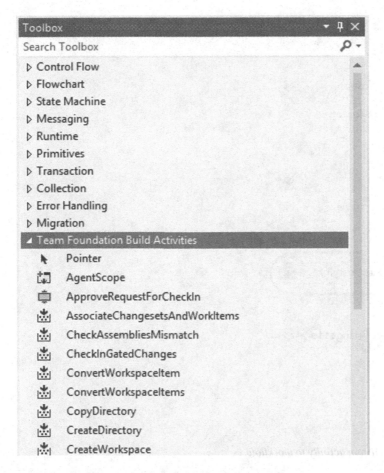

Figure 17-5. *Team Foundation Build Activities toolbox*

■ **Tip** For documentation on the Team Foundation Build activities, see
`http://msdn.microsoft.com/en-us/library/vstudio/gg265783.aspx`.

---

8. Now, drag this activity onto the workflow designer and drop it after the RunOnAgent
    activity, as shown in Figure 17-6. To find the RunOnAgent activity, collapse the workflow
    byc lickingt heC ollapseA lll inka tt het opr ight.

Figure 17-6. *Adding custom activity to workflow*

■ **Note**   You will get a warning symbol on the activity, this is because we need to fill out all the required arguments of this activity.

---

9. Right-click the WriteCustomSummaryInfo activity in the designer and select Properties. In the Properties window, enter the values shown in Figure 17-7. Note the syntax for specifying URLs:

   • Message is the string that is displayed inside the section.

   • SectionDisplayName specifies the name to display on the Build Details View.

   • SectionKey specifies a unique identifier for the section.

   • SectionPrioritys pecifiest her elativep riorityo ft hiss ection.

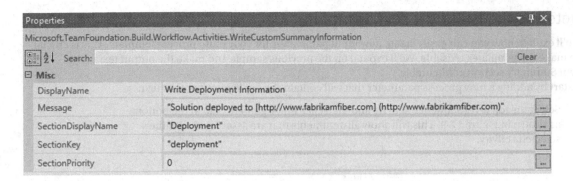

Figure 17-7. *Custom activity properties*

10. Save the build process template and then check it in. Note that the build process templates was automatically checked out when you started to edit it before.

■ **Tip**   A common mistake is to forget to check in the modified build process template. Unlike the build definition, which is stored in the TFS database, the build process template is a source-controlled file that must be checked in.

---

11. To test the new build process template, queue a new build from Team Explorer and wait for it to finish.

12. When the build has finished, open the build summary page and you should see the new section at the top of the page, as shown in Figure 17-8.

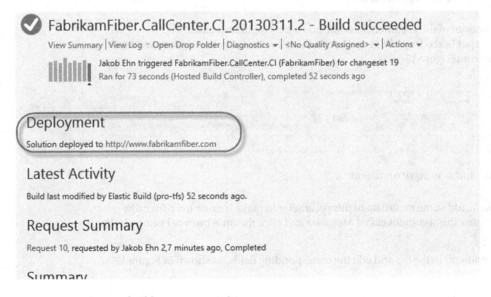

Figure 17-8. *Custom build summary section*

Parameterize the Build Process Template

Next up we'll explain how you can easily create new input parameters for your build process template. This is crucial in order to make the templates reusable. We'll expand on the previous sample and make the output text in the Deployment Summary section configurable.

Let's start by adding a new process parameter that will contain the deployment output text:

1. Select the top level Sequence activity and then click the Arguments tab at the bottom, as shown in Figure 17-9. This will show all arguments that are associated with the selecteda ctivity.

Figure 17-9. *Locting the arguments tab*

2. Scroll to the bottom of the arguments list and add a new argument called DeploymentOutputTexto ft ype `String`. Enter a default value for it, the same as we used before,a ssho wninF igure 17-10.

Figure 17-10. *Add new input argument*

3. In addition we'll add some metadata to this parameter to make it more user-friendly. To do this, located the argument called Metadata and click the little browse button on the veryr ight.

4. Add a new parameter in the list and edit the corresponding fields, as shown in Figure 17-11.

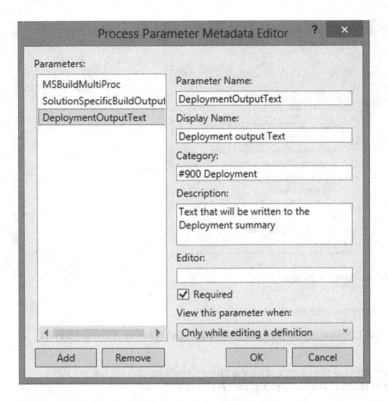

Figure 17-11. *Process Parameter Metadata Editor*

Here we've added metadata for the DeploymentOutputText parameter and given it a friendly name, description, and a category, which will affect where this parameter is displayed, as we'll see later. We've also specified this parameter as Required, which means that the user must supply a value when using this build template. Note that the Parameter Name must be identical to the name of the corresponding argument.

5.   Click OK to close the dialog box.

6.   Now we'll add a change to the template so that it uses the new parameter, instead of the hardcodeds tring.

7.   Locate the WriteCustomSummary activity and go to the Properties window. Delete the hardcoded string in the Message property and type DeploymentOutputText. Note that IntelliSense will have picked up your new parameter, as shown in Figure 17-12.

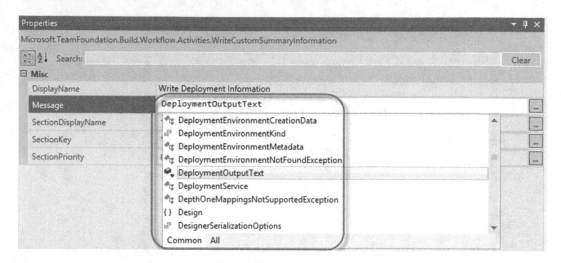

Figure 17-12. *Using new argument in workflow*

8. Save the build process template and check it in.

9. Now, go back to Edit Build Definition for the `FabrikamFiber.CallCenter.CIb uild.S` elect the Process tab.

10. If you can't see the new process parameter, click the Show details button on the top right and then on the Refresh button, as shown in Figure 17-13.

Figure 17-13. *Refresh build definition*

This will reload the build process template from source control, and you should now see a new section called Deployment with your new parameter, as shown in Figure 17-14.

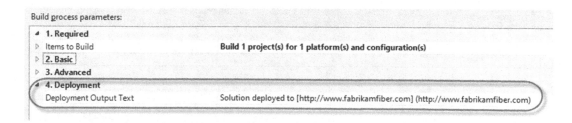

Figure 17-14. *Use new parameter in build definition*

Note that if you try to clear the value, you will get a warning symbol. This is because we set the parameter to be required.

11. Save the build definition and queue a new build. The result should be just like before, but now the template is suddenly reusable for different build definitions.

■ **Note**   Process parameters can be complex, containing lots of different data, and use custom editors for editing the corresponding values. Jason Prickett has a nice series of posts that talks about custom process parameters in depth: `http://blogs.msdn.com/b/jpricket/archive/2009/12/23/tfs-2010-custom-process-parameters-part-1.aspx`.

Using External Custom Activities

As you have seen, Team Foundation Build comes with a number of custom activities out of the box. Pretty soon, however, you'll need to extend your build workflows with functionality that is not part of the default activities. One option is to develop your own custom activities, which we'll explain in the next section. But before choosing this route, make sure that such an activity doesn't already exist. There are a lot of third-party custom activities available in the community, and that list is growing.

The CodePlex project Community TFS Build Extensions (`http://tfsbuildextensions.codeplex.com`)is the largest community site for custom activities. At the time of this writing, there are around 100 different custom activities available, and they span several different areas such as Azure, IIS, Amazon Web Services, Lab Management, XML authoring, and so forth.

This section will show you how to use one of the activities from this library. We'll use the AssemblyInfo custom activity, which is used for adding versioning to a TFS build. Unfortunately, the process of working with custom activities is somewhat complex, because of how Windows Workflow works under the hood when it locates custom activities.

■ **Note**   This series of steps only needs to be done once to get the activities into the workflow toolbox.

GettingC ustomA ctivitiesi ntoV isualS tudio

Let's get started:

1. Download and unzip the latest version of the TFS Community Build Extensions package.

2. Create a new C# class library. Make sure that the target framework is set to .NET 4.5. Name it `CustomActivities`. For this walkthrough, it does not matter where you store the project, but for production you should make sure to check in this project to have it source controlled.

3. Delete `Class1.cs` from the project.

4. Right-click the project and select Add Existing Item. Browse to the `CustomBuildProcessTemplate.xaml`, select it, and click the Add As Link button, as shown inF igure 17-15.

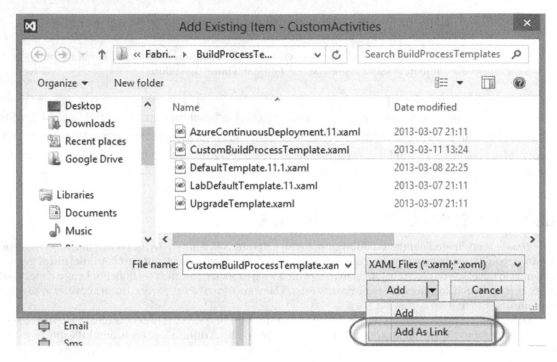

Figure 17-15. *Add build process template to project*

5. Now you need to add references to the custom activity assemblies you want to use. In this case, we need to use an activity that is located inside the TfsBuildExtensions.Activities.dll, so add a reference to this file from the project.

6. The project should now look like Figure 17-16.

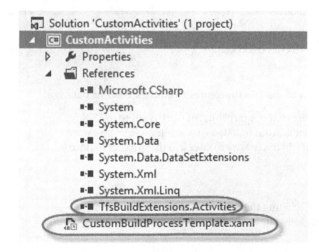

Figure 17-16. *Custom Activities solution*

7. Note the special symbol on the CustomBuildProcessTemplate.xaml file, which indicates that it has been added as a link.

8. The last thing you need to do is add the custom activity assembly to the toolbox to be able to drop activities onto the workflow designer surface.

9. Opent he CustomBuildProcessTemplate.xaml in the designer and then open the toolbox. Right-click inside the toolbox and select Add Tab and name it TFS Build Extensions.

10. Right-click inside the new tab and select Choose Items. Browse to the TfsBuildExtensions.Activities.dll and click OK.

11. You should now see all the custom activities in the toolbox, as shown in Figure 17-17.

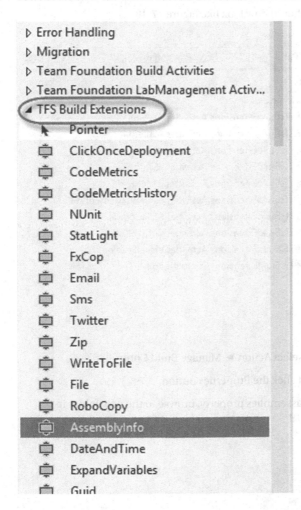

Figure 17-17. Viewing external activities in toolbox

12. Verify that you can drag a custom activity from the toolbox and drop it anywhere on the designer surface.

Deploying Custom Activities to the Hosted Build Server

We also need to make sure that the hosted build server will find the custom build activities. Team Foundation Build uses source control as the deployment mechanism, and each build controller has a (configurable) path in source control where it will look for custom build activities. The build controller will then automatically deploy these into each of the build agents that is registered with the controller.

1. Locate the `CustomActivities` folder that you created previously beneath the `BuildProcessTemplates` folder at the root of your team project.

2. Copy all assemblies (`*.dll`) from the VS2012 folder of the Community TFS Build Extensions package.

3. Check in all files to source control. It should now look like Figure 17-18.

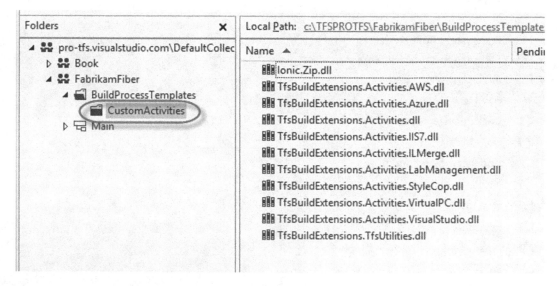

Figure 17-18. *Custom Activities in source control*

4. On the Builds page in Team Explorer, select Action ➤ Manage Build Controller.

5. Select the Hosted Build Controller and click the Properties button.

6. In the Version control path to custom assemblies property, browse to the new folder in source control, as shown in Figure 17-19.

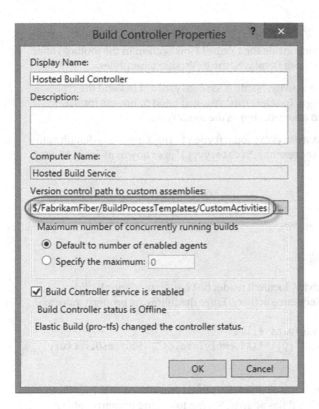

Figure 17-19. Build controller custom assembly path

Adding Custom Activities to the Build Process Template

Now you're ready to use the custom activities to implement versioning in your build. We want to use the AssemblyInfo activity to version all our projects that are being built. To do this we need to add this activity after the build has downloaded the source files but before it starts the compile phase.

1.   In the workflow designer, expand the RunOnAgent activity. We want to place our modification after the Initialize Workspace activity.

2. Make the following changes to the template:

   a. Drop a Sequence activity (located inside the Control Flow section in the toolbox) after the Initialize Workspace activity. Set DisplayName to Version assemblies.

   b. Add a variable to the Sequence activity. Name it `AssemblyInfoFiles` and the type should be `IEnumerable<string>`. To select this type, you need to browse for the `IEnumerable<T>` type and then select `string` as the inner type.

   c. Add another variable called `AssemblyVersion`, of type `string`. Give it the default value `"$(current).$(current).$(increment).$(date:yyyy)"`, as shown in Figure 17-20.

Name	Variable type	Scope	Default
AssemblyInfoFiles	IEnumerable<String>	Version Assemblies	Enter a VB expression
AssemblyVersion	String	Version Assemblies	"$(current).$(current).$(increment).$(date:yyyy)"

Figure 17-20. Variables for Assembly versioning

   d. Drop a FindMatchingFiles activity (located inside the Team Foundation Build Activities section) inside the Sequence activity. Enter the following property values:

```
DisplayName: Find AssemblyInfo.cs files
MatchPattern: String.Format("{0}\**\AssemblyInfo.cs", SourcesDirectory)
Result: AssemblyInfoFiles
```

   e. Drag the AssemblyInfo activity (located inside TFS Build Extensions in the toolbox) and drop it after the FindMatchingFiles activity. Set the following property values:

```
Files = AssemblyInfoFiles
AssemblyFileVersion = AssemblyVersion
AssemblyVersion = AssemblyVersion
```

   This activity has a lot of properties. For this walkthrough you can ignore the rest of them. You should now have the workflow shown in Figure 17-21.

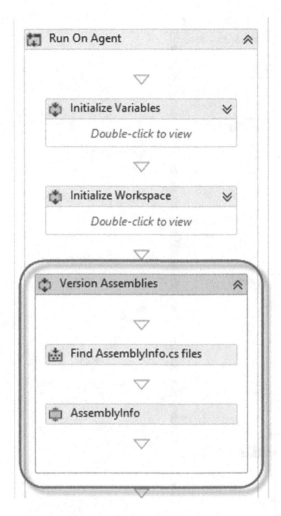

Figure 17-21. *Finished workflow*

3. Save the template and check it in.

4. Queue a new build and wait for it to finish.

5. When finished, click the Open Drop Folder link and download the drop as a .zip file.

6. Extract the .zip file and select one of the assemblies and select Properties. You should see that both the File version and the Product version properties have been set with a version format that matches the pattern we specified before, as shown in Figure 17-22.

Figure 17-22. *Version assemblies*

Creating Custom Activities

You've now seen how you can reuse third-party custom activities to extend your build workflows. But sometimes you need to do something specific that none of the available activities can do for you, and in these cases you need to develop your own custom activities.

Custom activities can be written in two ways:

- In XAML, by reusing existing custom activities

- Inc ode(C#/VB.NET)

Using XAML is the best way if possible; this results in the highest degree of reuse. You will then be able to create new activities that are based on existing ones. The limitation is, of course, that you can only use what is already in the toolbox. This limitation makes developing custom activities using code far more common. It requires a little more work, but then you have the full power to do just about anything as part of your activity.

■ **Note** When developing custom activities, always aim to make them as generic as possible. This way you will be able to reuse them across different workflows and also create larger composite custom activities that are used in your smaller ones. Also separate the build logic from the custom activity code so you can use the same code for other purposes than just during builds.

The next section will show you how to create and deploy a new custom activity using C#. We'll write a very simple activity, called Sleep, which just sleeps a configurable amount of milliseconds before returning.

Solution for Developing Custom Activities

To get started we need to set up a solution in Visual Studio that will make it as easy as possible to develop custom activities. Just like before, this only needs to be done once. To be able to work with custom activities efficiently, you need to create a solution that contains two projects:

- One activity library project that contains your custom activities.

- One project that contains the build process template(s) you want to extend using those activities. This project must reference the custom activity project.

By following this approach, the custom activities will automatically show up in the toolbox when you open the build process template in the designer.

1. Close any open solution and select New Project and then go to the Visual C# ➤ Workflow templatef older.

2. SelectA ctivityL ibrary.

3. Namet hep roject `FabrikamFiber.CustomActivities`.

4. Check the Create directory for solution check box and name the solution `FabrikamFiber.CustomActivities`a sw ell.

5. Select the location where Fabrikam Fiber is mapped locally and click OK.

6. Deletet he `Activity1.xaml` file from the project.

7. Add the following references to the project:

   - `Microsoft.TeamFoundation.Build.Client`(version1 1.0.0.0)

   - `Microsoft.TeamFoundation.Build.Workflow`(version1 1.0.0.0)

8. Right-click the solution and select Add new project.

9. SelectV isualC# ➤ Class Library.

10. Namet hep roject `FabrikamFiber.BuildProcessTemplates` and click OK.

11. Delete the `Class1.cs` class from the project.

12. Add a project reference from the `FabrikamFiber.BuildProcessTemplates` project to the `FabrikamFiber.CustomActivities`p roject.

13. Add a reference to `Microsoft.TeamFoundation.Build.Client` from the `BuildProcessTemplates`p roject.

14. Add the `CustomBuildProcessTemplate.xaml` file you worked with before to the `FabrikamFilber.BuildProcessTemplates` project. Again, select Add existing item and browse to the template file and select Add As Link.

15. Selectt he `CustomBuildProcessTemplate.xaml` file in the project and look at the properties window. Locate the Build Action property and select the value None.

Yours olutions houldl ookl ikeF igure 17-23.

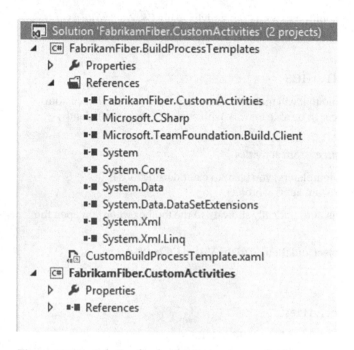

Figure 17-23. *Solution for developing custom activities*

Developing a Custom Activity

Now that the infrastructure is in place, let's add our new custom build activity.

1. Right-clickt he `FabrikamFiber.CustomActivities` project and select Add New Item.

2. SelectW orkflow ➤ Code Activity.

3. Namet hea ctivity `Sleep.cs`.

4. Replacethe g eneratedcode w iththe f ollowingc ode:

```
namespace FabrikamFiber.CustomActivities
{
    using System;
    using System.Activities;
    using System.Threading;
    using Microsoft.TeamFoundation.Build.Workflow.Activities;
    using Microsoft.TeamFoundation.Build.Client;
```

```
/// <summary>
/// Sleep a thread for the specified number of milliseconds
/// </summary>
[BuildActivity(HostEnvironmentOption.All)]
public sealed class Sleep : CodeActivity
{
    /// <summary>
    /// Sepecifies the number of milliseconds to sleep for
    /// </summary>
    [RequiredArgument]
    public InArgument<int> NumberOfMilliseconds { get; set; }

    protected override void Execute(CodeActivityContext context)
    {
        try
        {
            int numberOfMillisecs = this.NumberOfMilliseconds.Get(context);
            context.TrackBuildMessage(
                string.Format("Sleeping for {0} milliseconds", numberOfMillisecs),
                                            BuildMessageImportance.High);
            Thread.Sleep(numberOfMillisecs);
        }
        catch(Exception ex)
        {
            context.TrackBuildError(ex.ToString());
        }
    }
}
}
```

Note several things here:

- The class is attributed with the [BuildActivity] attribute. This is required for all custom build activities, and Team Foundation Build only loads classes that have this attribute.

- The custom activity has one input argument: NumberOfMilliseconds. It is of type int,a nd it is attributed with the [RequiredArgument], which will require input from the user when using it in a workflow.

- It overrides the Execute method, where everything happens once the custom activity has been instantiated and has been populated with the values of the input arguments.

When reading from or writing to parameters in custom activities, you must always do this using the instance of the CodeActivityContext that is passed into the Executem ethod. The CodeActivityContext class also has methods for logging informational messages and errors, as you can see in the code above.

5. Save the class and make sure it compiles.

6. Opent he CustomBuildProcessTemplate.xaml again. You should now see your custom activity in the toolbox, as shown in Figure 17-24.

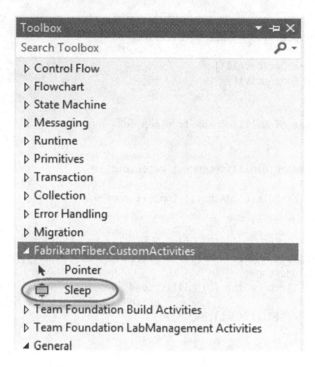

Figure 17-24. *Custom activity in toolbox*

7. Drag the activity to the workflow designer and drop it right before the Run On Agent activity, as shown in Figure 17-25.

Figure 17-25. Adding custom activity to workflow

8. In the Properties window, set the NumberOfMilliseconds property to 2000.

9. Save the template and check it in from Source Control Explorer (since we haven't added this solution to source control, which you would normally do).

10. To deploy the new custom activity, remember that the binary assembly must be checked in to source control. Copy the resulting assembly to the local path that corresponds to $/FabrikamFiber/BuildProcessTemplates/CustomActivities.

11. Add the assembly to source control and check it in, as shown in Figure 17-26.

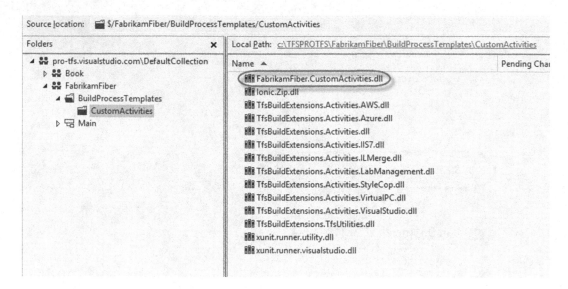

Figure 17-26. *Adding custom activity assembly to source control*

12. Queue a new build of the FabrikamFiber.CallCenter.CI build definition. Once finished, click the View Log link at the top of the Build Summary page. At the very start of the log, you should see the output from the custom activity, as shown in Figure 17-27. You should also see that the duration was 2 seconds, as expected.

Activity Log	Next Error	Next Warning	Duration
Overall Build Process	01:19
Update Build Number	00:00
Run On Agent (reserved build agent Hosted Build Agent)	01:18
Sleep	00:02
Sleeping for 2000 milliseconds	
Create Workspace	00:00
Get Workspace	00:08

Figure 17-27. *Running custom activity*

A COMMON ERROR

Deploying custom activities can be a source of frustration, a common error message when trying to use a build template that references custom activities is:

TF215097: An error occurred while initializing a build for build definition \TeamProject\MyBuildDefinition: Cannot create unknown type '{clr-namespace:[namespace];assembly=[assembly]}Activity.'

There are several things that can cause this problem, the error just says that for some reason it could not find or load the custom activity. This blog post can help you troubleshoot this error: http://geekswithblogs.net/ jakob/archive/2011/12/08/tfs-2010-build---troubleshooting-the-tf215097-error.aspx.

Summary

This chapter discussed customizing build process templates as well as using and developing custom activities. This is a huge topic with a lot of details and we recommend you download and study the ALM Rangers' Team Foundation Build Customization Guide, which contains tons of good information about build customization. You can find this at http://vsarbuildguide.codeplex.com/.

The next chapter will take a look at how to implement continuous deployment with Team Foundation Services.

■ ■ ■

ContinuousD eployment

Having automated builds is the most important part of the continuous integration process that we have discussed in other chapters. Being able to build, test, and integrate your software on every check in makes your software development process very effective with less time spent on fixing integration bugs.

But in order to be able to test a new version, you must deploy it where your customers and testers can access it. And you want to be able to do this as fast as possible and without any manual steps that could introduce errors.

There are many advantages of being able to release new versions of your software daily, or even after every change. During development you will be able to get feedback from testers and pilot customers as early as possible. In production you will be able to deploy bug fixes as fast as possible. Also, more focus can be spent on development and less on how to deploy the applications.

This chapter will cover different techniques for automating deployments of web and Cloud applications and SQL databases using the hosted build services. Deployment is a vast topic with plenty of details that are very specific to what you are deploying and to where you are deploying it. All these details are outside the scope of this book, but by touching on these different areas you will see how you can leverage Team Foundation Service to enable continuous deployment of your software.

Automatic Deployment to Windows Azure

Since the early days of Team Foundation Service, it has been possible to automatically build and deploy your projects to Windows Azure web sites or Cloud services. The integration between Team Foundation Service and Windows Azure is very tight, making this scenario really smooth to set up. It does not solve all scenarios but can often work as a quick start to get your application up and running on Windows Azure. As you will see later, you can customize this integration by modifying the underlying build process template.

Setting It Up

Let's walk through the steps to enable automatic deployment for our Fabrikam Fiber web solution, including the database that is built with Entity Framework Code First. We will start with creating a Windows Azure web site with an SQL database for the Fabrikam Fiber solution.

■ **Note** To follow this exercise, you will need both an active Windows Azure subscription and either Visual Studio 2012 or Visual Studio 2010 SP1 with the Compatibility GDR installed. To build a Windows Azure project, such as a Cloud service, you will also need the Windows Azure SDK.

---

1. In the Windows Azure Management Portal, click the Web Sites tab and then New.

2. SelectC ompute ➤ Web Site ➤ Custom Create (as shown in Figure 18-1). This will let us create a web site together with a database.

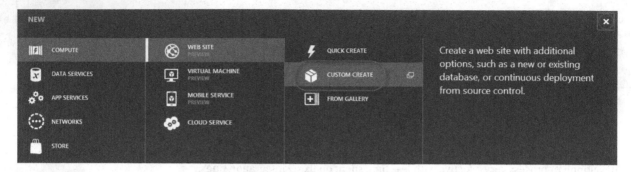

Figure 18-1. Create a Windows Azure web site

3. Enter a unique name for your Windows Azure web site and a name for the database connection string. This is the key that is used in the web.config files of your solution.

4. Make sure you check the Publish from source control check box, as shown in Figure 18-2.

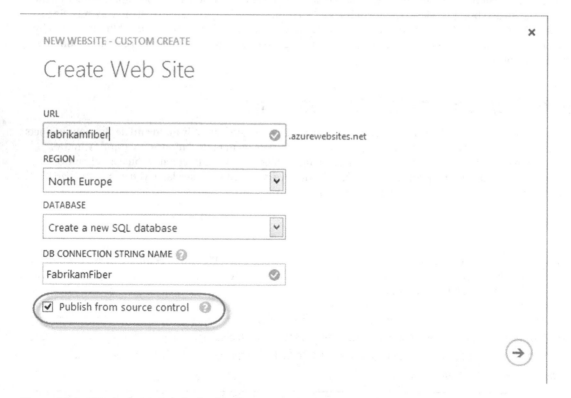

Figure 18-2. Windows Azure web site details

5. On the New SQL Database page shown in Figure 18-3, enter a name for the database and select the SQL database server and credentials that will be used for connecting to the database.

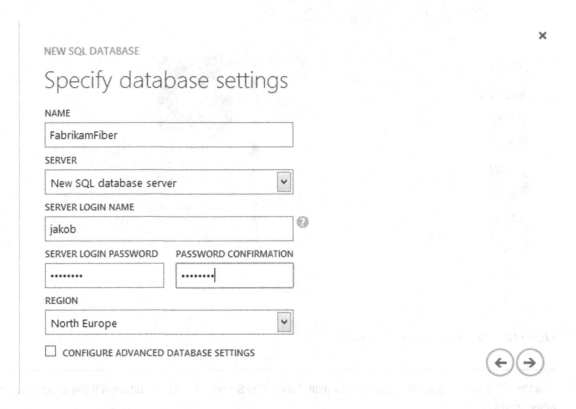

Figure 18-3. *Windows Azure SQL database settings*

6. Next up you select which source control provider you are using, as shown in Figure 18-4. Note that you can set up automatic deployment if you have your source code in Team Foundation Service, but it also works for CodePlex, GitHub, or even if you have your sourcec odeo nD ropbox.

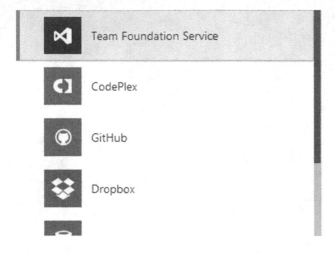

Figure 18-4. *Select source control provider*

■ **Note** The following steps are specific to Team Foundation Service, and will be different if you choose any of the other providers.

---

7. Enter the name of the Team Foundation Service account and click Authorize Now, as shown in Figure 18-5. You will need to enter your Microsoft account credentials to perform thisa uthorization.

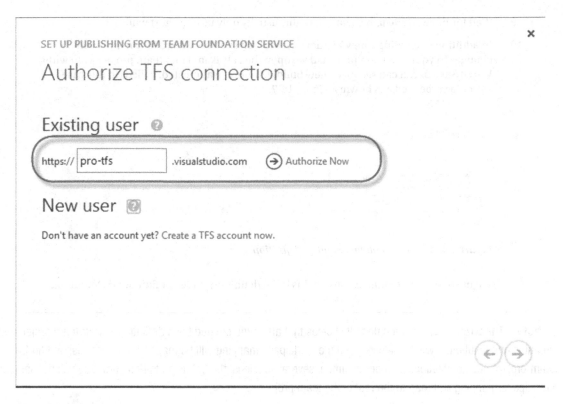

Figure 18-5. Authorize TFS connection

8.   Click Accept on the following screen. The last step is to select which team project to connect to, as shown in Figure 18-6.

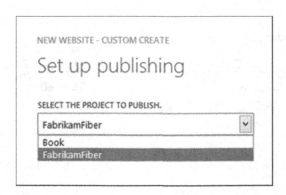

Figure 18-6. Selecting the team project

9. Wait for the web site to be connected, this usually only takes a short while.

10. In addition to creating a new Windows Azure web site, this wizard also made some changes in your TFS team project. If we open the Fabrikam Fiber team project from within Visual Studio, you can see that a new build definition was created, called (in this case) fabrikamfiber_cd, as shown in Figure 18-7.

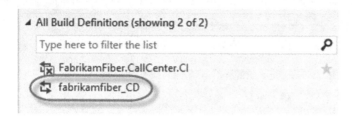

Figure 18-7. Azure deployment build definition

11. We need to change some details on this build definition, so select Edit Build Definition.

■ **Note** The wizard makes some default choices that affect the created build definition. If your team project only contains one solution, it will be selected and the workspace mapping will be mapped to the corresponding folder. If your team project has no solutions or, more common, several solutions, the Solutions to Build property will be blank and the workspace mapping will map to the root of the team project.

---

12. If the build definitions is disabled, change it to Enabled.

13. On the Source Settings tab shown in Figure 18-8, modify the workspace so it only includes the necessary path.

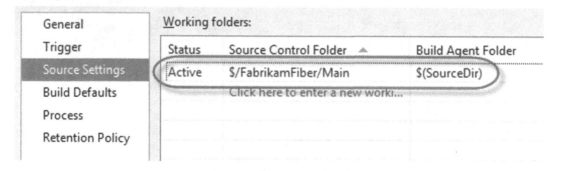

Figure 18-8. Source settings

14. In the Process tab, select the Solution To Build, as shown in Figure 18-9.

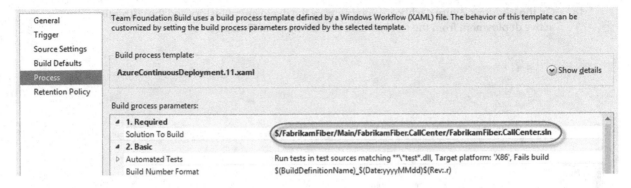

Figure 18-9. *Solution to build*

15. Savet heb uildd efinition.

16. Make a change to the project and check it in. This will trigger the continuous deployment build you just created.

17. When the build has finished, you will see a link to your Windows Azure web site in the Deployment Summary section, as shown in Figure 18-10.

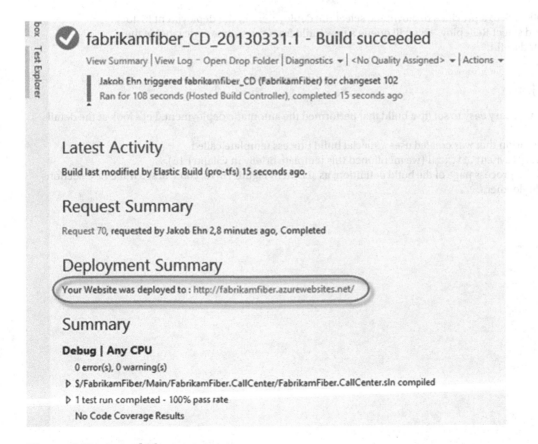

Figure 18-10. *Azure deployment summary*

18. On the Windows Azure dashboard you can view the deployment history and the currently active deployment from the Deployments tab, as shown in Figure 18-11.

Figure 18-11. Windows Azure web site deployment history

19. To roll back to a previous deployment, select the deployment in the deployment history list and select Redeploy. This will queue a new build from the source code label of the selected build.

HowI tW orks

As you just saw, it was very easy to set up a build that performed the automatic deployment. Let's look at the details behind this magic.

The build definition that was created uses a special build process template called AzureContinuousDeployment.11.xaml (we mentioned this template briefly in Chapter 16).

If you look at the process page of the build definition, as shown in Figure 18-12, you will see three new sections related to Azure deployment.

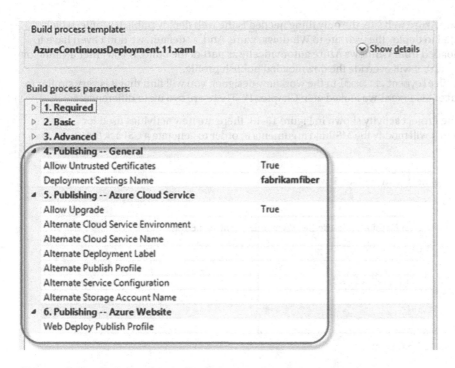

Build process template:

AzureContinuousDeployment.11.xaml   ⊙ Show details

Build process parameters:

▷ 1. Required
▷ 2. Basic
▷ 3. Advanced
◢ 4. Publishing -- General
   Allow Untrusted Certificates   True
   Deployment Settings Name   **fabrikamfiber**
◢ 5. Publishing -- Azure Cloud Service
   Allow Upgrade   True
   Alternate Cloud Service Environment
   Alternate Cloud Service Name
   Alternate Deployment Label
   Alternate Publish Profile
   Alternate Service Configuration
   Alternate Storage Account Name
◢ 6. Publishing -- Azure Website
   Web Deploy Publish Profile

Figure 18-12. *AzureContinuousDeployment.11.xaml process parameters*

The most important parameter here is the Deployment Settings Name. The name is a bit misleading, it actually refers to the name of the corresponding Windows Azure web site or Cloud service. This setting is used to, among other things, download the publishing profile.

Table 18-1 describes the rest of the parameters.

Table 18-1. *Azure Publishing Process Parameters*

Property	Description	Defaultvalu e
Allow Untrusted Certificates	True will allow nonrooted certificates during deployment	True
Allow Upgrade	Specify whether upgrade is allowed on deployment	True
Alternate Cloud Service Environment	Specifies Cloud service environment, can be either production or staging	Staging
Alternate Cloud Service Name	Alternate Cloud service name	The name of the service you are connected to
Alternate Deployment Label	Alternate deployment label	The same as the service name
Alternate Service Configuration	Alternate service configuration	ServiceConfiguration.Cloud.cscfg
Alternate Storage Account Name	Name of an alternate storage account	Blank, which means try to find a storage account.
Alternate Publish Profile	Source control path to an alternate publish profile	The .azurePubxml file; if you check in one, you can choose it here
Web Deploy Publish Profile	Source control path to a web deploy publish profile	If blank, it will be downloaded from Windows Azure

When deploying to a Windows Azure web site, the only thing needed is the web deploy publish profile, which contains all the information needed to deploy the web site to Windows Azure. And by default, we don't even have to specify this since it will be downloaded from Windows Azure automatically as part of the build. If you enter a value for this parameter (a source control path), it will override the downloaded publish profile.

If you open AzureContinuousDeployment.11.xaml in the workflow designer, you will find that it is very similar to the DefaultBuildProcessTemplate.11.1.xaml we looked at in Chapter 17. There are two main differences:

- Inside the Compile the Project activity shown in Figure 18-13, there are new activities used for Azure Cloud services that will modify the MSBuild arguments in order to generate a CSPack file.

Figure 18-13. *Build workflow details*

- The actual deployment is carried out at the end of the Compile and Test activity, in the Deploy Output sequence (shown in Figure 18-14). For Azure web sites, MSDeploy is used to deploy the web site. For Azure Cloud services, the deployment is done by a custom activity called DeployAzureCloudApp.

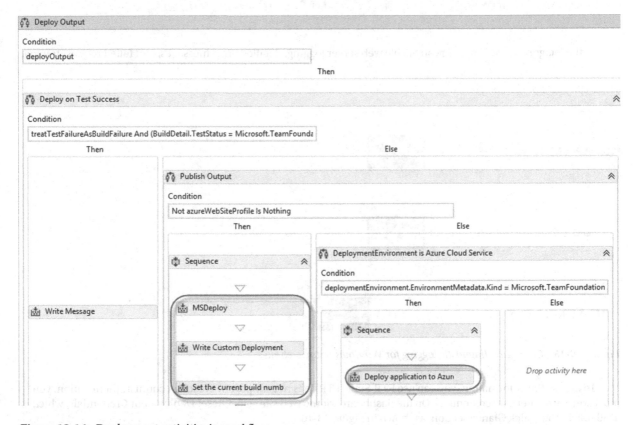

Figure 18-14. *Deployment activities in workflow*

■ **Tip** As you have seen, the deployment is done by a regular build process template, so go ahead and modify it and add functionality to it as needed, just like we did in Chapter 17. The build process template is not meant to cover all possible deployment scenarios to Windows Azure, so consider it as a starting point that covers all the basics and build upon it.

TroubleshootingA zureD eployments

Although the process of setting up the deployment to Windows Azure is easy, things will eventually go wrong, such as invalid connection strings, missing files, and so on. By default it is much harder to troubleshoot deployment errors in Windows Azure because you can't log in to the server and analyze the state of the deployment. You can, however, enable diagnostics for a Windows Azure web site or Cloud service.

To do this, go to the Configure tab on the Start page for the Fabrikam web site, as shown in Figure 18-15.

In the Diagnostics section you can enable web server logging, detailed error messages, and failed request tracing.

diagnostics

WEB SERVER LOGGING — ON / OFF

DETAILED ERROR MESSAGES — ON / OFF

FAILED REQUEST TRACING — ON / OFF

Figure 18-15. *Configure diagnostic logging for Windows Azure web sites*

To access this information, you can use FTP. Since FTP does not support Microsoft account authentication, you must configure alternate credentials. On the dashboard for the web site select Reset Deployment Credentials, which is available in the Quick Glance section, as shown in Figure 18-16.

quick glance

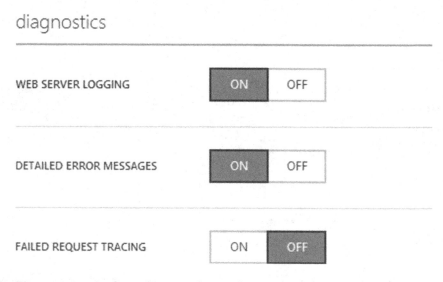

ⓘ View connection strings.

⤓ Download publish profile

⟳ Reset deployment credentials

⟳ Reset publish profile credentials

⟲ Disconnect from TFS

⟳ Renew TFS certificate

Figure 18-16. *Reset deployment credentials*

In the dialog box that appears, enter the user name and password. Now you can connect and download the logs using any FTP application. You can find all the URLs on the dashboard page, as shown in Figure 18-17.

FTP HOSTNAME

ftp://waws-prod-db3-
001.ftp.azurewebsites.windows.net

FTPS HOSTNAME

ftps://waws-prod-db3-
001.ftp.azurewebsites.windows.net

DEPLOYMENT / FTP USER

fabrikamfiber\jakob

FTP DIAGNOSTIC LOGS

ftp://waws-prod-db3-
001.ftp.azurewebsites.windows.net/LogFiles

FTPS DIAGNOSTIC LOGS

ftps://waws-prod-db3-
001.ftp.azurewebsites.windows.net/LogFiles

Figure 18-17. Diagnostic logs

Deploy On Premises Using Web Deploy

In the previous section, we showed how to automatically deploy web sites to Windows Azure using a custom-build process template. As far as the deployment is concerned, the build template relies on Web Deploy to push the changes from the hosted build server to the Windows Azure web site or Cloud service.

Web Deploy is a framework that can synchronize basically any data between two locations. This sound very generic, and it is. Web Deploy uses a provider model that lets each provider handle the details of the particular source and destination location. The most common providers are related to the Internet Information Server (IIS), but there are also providers for SQL databases, MySQL, GAC assemblies, the Windows registry, and many more.

■ **Tip**　For a full list of Web Deploy providers, see the following TechNet article:
http://technet.microsoft.com/en-us/library/dd569040(WS.10).aspx.

This means that we can use Web Deploy to deploy our web applications to any web server that is available from the hosted build service, not just Windows Azure web sites or Cloud services. As you will see later, Web Deploy by default listens to port 80, which makes it easier from a security perspective to access it from outside.

The next section will walk you through installing Web Deploy and how to set up automated deployment for the Fabrikam Fiber build definition.

InstallingW ebD eploy

Web Deploy can be installed for both administrator and nonadministrator deployments. The latter means that you must set up delegation to be able to deploy remotely using Web Deploy. Often this is required in shared hosting environments where you will not be allowed to get administrative access. This section will show you how to set up Web Deploy for administrator deployments, because this does not require as many steps (Figure 18-18).

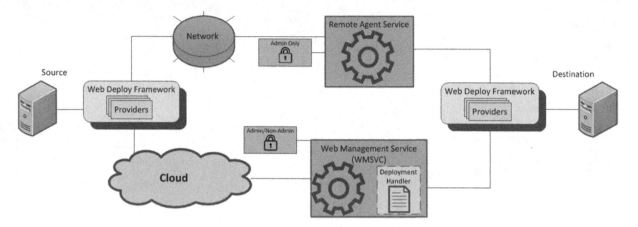

Figure 18-18. *Web Deploy overview*

■ **Note**   For more information on Web Deploy, please see `http://www.iis.net/downloads/microsoft/web-deploy`.

To set up Web Deploy for administrative deployment:

1. Download and run the Web Platform Installer from `http://www.microsoft.com/web/downloads/platform.aspx`.

2. Search for Recommended Server Configuration for Web Hosting Providers, as shown inF igure 18-19.

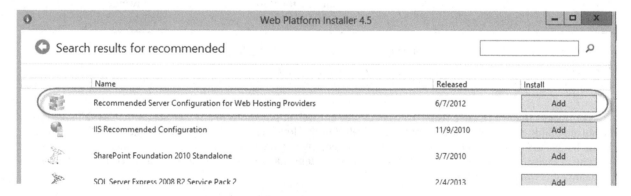

Figure 18-19. *Installing Recommended Server Configuration*

3. SelectA dda ndthe nI nstall.

4. If you won't be needing some of the additional components, such as MySQL and PHP, you can deselect them.

5. Search for Web Deploy, as shown in Figure 18-20.

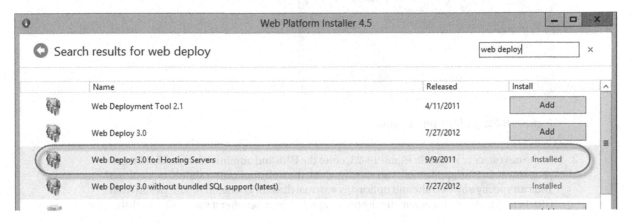

Figure 18-20. *Install Web Deploy*

6. If Web Deploy 3.0 for Hosting Servers is not already installed, select Add and click Install.

7. You will now have the Web Deployment Agent Service installed and running. This is a Windows service that will listen to requests and perform the deployments. As you can see in Figure 18-21, it runs as the Network Service account by default.

Name ▲	Description	Status	Startup Type	Log On As
Visual Studio Test Controller	Provides Distributed Test Engine controller services	Running	Automatic	.\administrator
Volume Shadow Copy	Manages and implements Volume Shadow Copies used for ba...		Manual	Local System
Web Deployment Agent Service	Remote agent service for the Microsoft Web Deploy 3.0.	Running	Automatic	Network Service
Web Management Service	The Web Management Service enables remote and delegated ...	Running	Automatic	Local Service
Windows All-User Install Agent	Install AppX Packages for all authorized users		Manual (Trig...	Local System
Windows Audio	Manages audio for Windows-based programs. If this service is		Manual	Local Service

Figure 18-21. *Web Deployment Agent Service*

For administrative deployments, this is all that is needed. The Web Deployment Agent Service listens on port 80 for a specific URL (`http://[server]/MsDeployAgentService/`), so normally it should not be a problem to access the servicer emotely.

Creatinga P ublishP rofile

Now that Web Deploy is running on the server, it is time to set up automatic deployment for our Fabrikam Fiber solution. When using Web Deploy, all information about how it is deployed is contained in a publish profile. This is an XML file that is stored in source control and, therefore, shared across the team. A publish profile typically maps to a specific target environment (dev, test, production, etc.) and contains settings specific to these machines.

1. Selectt he `FabrikamFiber.Web` project and select Publish from the Context menu.

2. Select New in the drop-down list and enter `FabrikamFiber.Production` as the name, ass howni nF igure 18-22.

Figure 18-22. *Publish profile name*

3. In the next screen, shown in Figure 18-23, enter the URL and administrator credentials to your server. In Site/application, you specify where the web application should be deployed. You can specify any web site and optionally a virtual directory beneath it. The Destination URL field is just used for automatically opening a web browser after a successful publish.

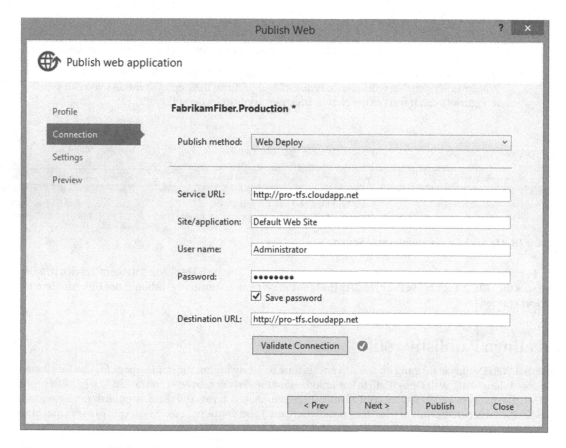

Figure 18-23. *Publish profile connection*

4. Click the Validate Connection button to test your settings. If everything is correct, you will see a green icon.

5. Click Next. In the dialog box that appears, shown in Figure 18-24, select which configuration you want to publish and enter a valid database connection string to where the Fabrikam Fiber database will be located.

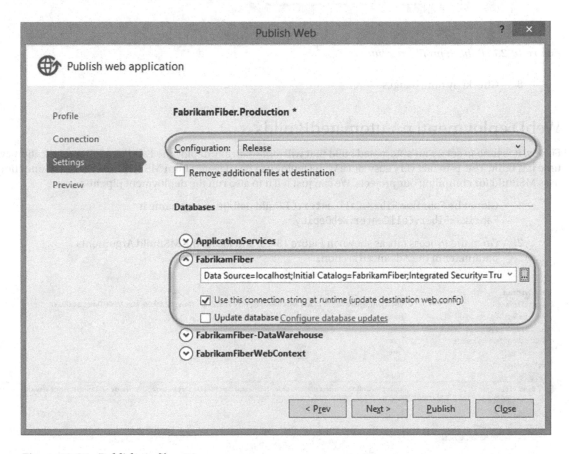

Figure 18-24. Publish profile settings

In this example, we are running a local SQL server to the connection string that uses a local host. Also, since the Fabrikam Fiber application uses Entity Framework Code First, the database will be automatically created the first time it is accessed.

■ **Note** Notice that Windows Integrated Security is used in the example. If you use this, make sure that the Application Pool account running the Fabrikam Fiber web site has sufficient permission to create a database on the designated server.

6. Click Next ➤ Start Preview. It will show you a preview of the deployment.

7. Click Close (NOT Publish) to save the new publish profile. It should appear in your solution, as shown in Figure 18-25.

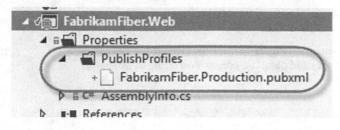

Figure 18-25. *Publish profile in solution*

8. Checki ny ourc hanges.

WebD eploymenti nA utomatedB uilds

Finally, it is time to set up an automated build that will automatically deploy the Fabrikam Fiber application every time it is built. This is in fact very easy since Web Deploy can be triggered from MSBuild, and Team Foundation Build uses MSBuild for compiling our projects. We can just tell it to also run the deployment pipeline.

1. Clonet he `FabrikamFiber.CallCenter.CI` build definition and name it `FabrikamFiber.CallCenter.WebDeploy`.

2. Go to the Process tab, as shown in Figure 18-26, and locate the MSBuild Arguments parameter in the Advanced section.

3. Advanced	
▷ Agent Settings	**Use agent where Name=* and Tags is empty; Max Execution Time: 02:00:00; Max Wait Time: 04:00:00**
Analyze Test Impact	True
Associate Changesets and Work Items	True
Create Work Item on Failure	True
Disable Tests	False
Get Version	
Label Sources	True
MSBuild Arguments	**/p:DeployOnBuild=true;PublishProfile=FabrikamFiber.WebDeploy.pubxml;UserName=Administrator;Password=\<PASSWORD\>**
MSBuild Multi-Proc	True
MSBuild Platform	Auto
Private Drop Location	
Solution Specific Build Outputs	False

Figure 18-26. *Using Web Deploy in the build definition*

3. Enter the following string:

```
/p:DeployOnBuild=true;PublishProfile=FabrikamFiber.Production.pubxml;
UserName=Administrator;Password=<PASSWORD>
```

4. Save the build definition and queue a new build.

5. When the build has finished, you should see that the web site has been deployed to your webse rver.

■ **Note** If you have multiple web projects in the same solution, you will get an error when running Web Deploy like this. The reason is that the MSBuild arguments are passed in as global MSBuild properties and apply to all projects that are processed. When the Web Deploy targets cannot find a publish profile for any of the other web projects, it will raise an error. For a solution to this problem, see http://sedodream.com/2013/03/06/HowToPublishOneWebProjectFromASolution.aspx.

Deploying SSDT Database Projects

The last type of deployment we will look at is how to automatically deploy SQL Server Data Tools (SSDT) database projects using Team Foundation Service build.

The SSDT database projects are very powerful and let you source control your schemas, run schema compare operations to generate upgrade scripts, perform refactoring and run unit tests for your stored procedures, to name just a few of the features.

■ **Note** SSDT ships with Visual Studio 2012 Professional and higher. The SSDT team regularly ships updates, so make sure you have the latest version. It is also available for Visual Studio 2010 SP1, but it needs to be installed separately.

The deployment model of SSDT is similar to Web Deploy in that it uses publish profiles for storing information about the deployment. The publish profile can then be passed into the build using the MSBuild arguments.

Creatinga S SDTP ublishP rofile

For this scenario, we have created a new SSDT database project called FabrikamFiber.Database.sqlproja nd imported the existing database to create the files for tables and other SQL database artifacts.

Publish profiles are created by selecting Publish on the database project. In the dialog box that appears, as shown in Figure 18-27, enter the connection string for your target database and save the publish profile with a name that reflects the target environment. In this case, we save it as Production.publish.xml.

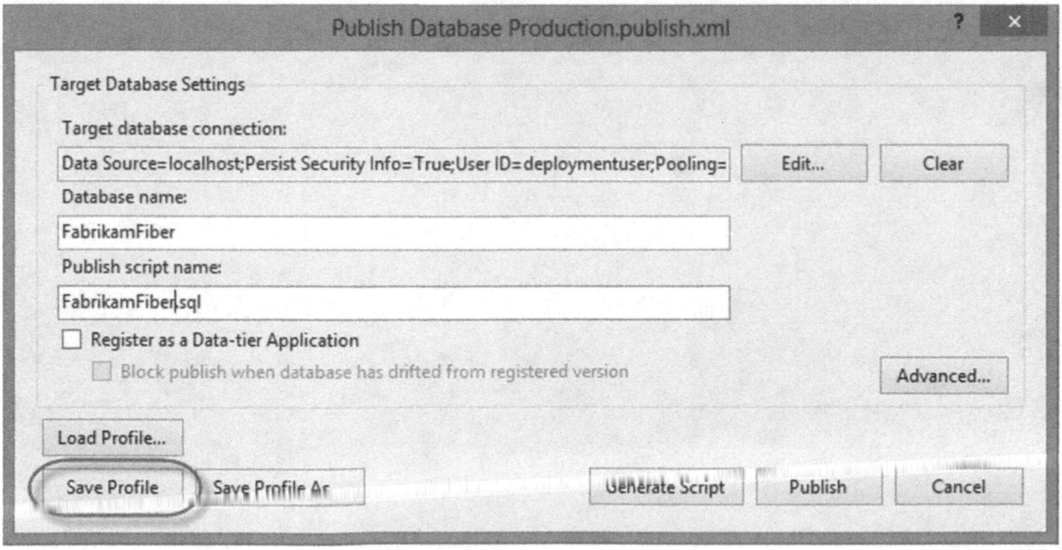

Figure 18-27. *Publish profile connection string*

■ **Note** The naming convention for SSDT profiles is `*.publish.xml`.

Since Windows Azure SQL databases currently only support SQL authentication, you must edit the generated publish profile and add the password for the account that will be used. Right-click the publish profile in Solution Explorer and select Open With then select XML Editor, and add the password to the `TargetConnectionString` element, as shown in Figure 18-28.

```
<Project ToolsVersion="4.0" xmlns="http://schemas.microsoft.com/developer/msbuild/2003">
  <PropertyGroup>
    <IncludeCompositeObjects>True</IncludeCompositeObjects>
    <TargetDatabaseName>FabrikamFiber</TargetDatabaseName>
    <DeployScriptFileName>FabrikamFiber.sql</DeployScriptFileName>
    <TargetConnectionString>Data Source=localhost;Persist Security Info=True;User ID=deploymentuser;Password=xxxx;Pooling=False</TargetConnectionString>
    <ProfileVersionNumber>1</ProfileVersionNumber>
  </PropertyGroup>
</Project>
```

Figure 18-28. Publish profile target connection password

■ **Note** Typically you create one publish profile for each environment you intend to deploy your database to. Make sure you give it a name that reflects which target environment it is intended for, such as `Production.publish.xml`. Each profile can have settings specific to the environment, for example, on a dev server you might want to redeploy the database every time, but on a staging or production environment, you will want to perform an upgrade.

DeployS SDTP rojectsi nA utomatedB uilds

Just like with Web Deploy, we use MSBuild arguments to hook into the build process and trigger functionality in SSDT. We need to make sure that the publish target is called and also give the name of the publish profile we want to use for deployments, as shown in Figure 18-29.

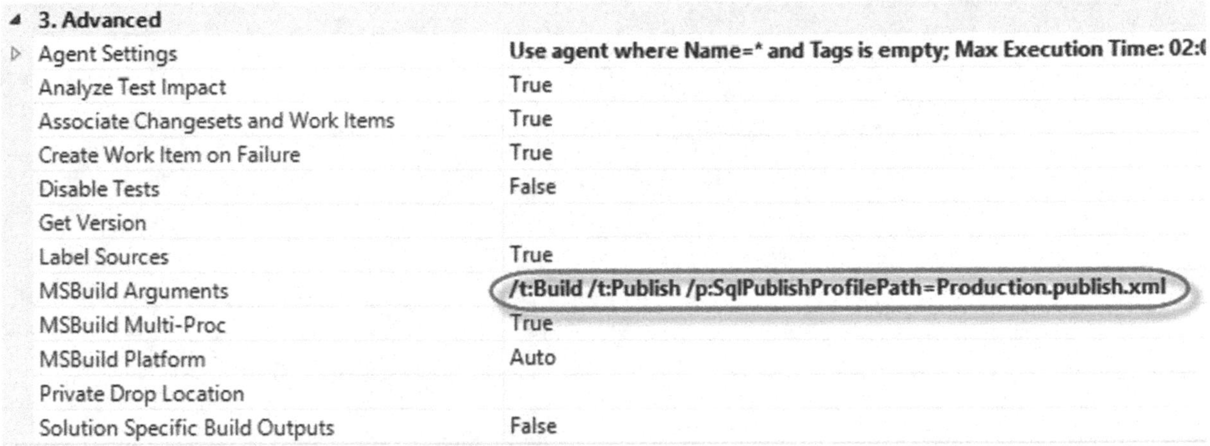

⊿ 3. Advanced	
▷ Agent Settings	**Use agent where Name=* and Tags is empty; Max Execution Time: 02:0**
Analyze Test Impact	True
Associate Changesets and Work Items	True
Create Work Item on Failure	True
Disable Tests	False
Get Version	
Label Sources	True
MSBuild Arguments	/t:Build /t:Publish /p:SqlPublishProfilePath=Production.publish.xml
MSBuild Multi-Proc	True
MSBuild Platform	Auto
Private Drop Location	
Solution Specific Build Outputs	False

Figure 18-29. *Publish SSDT projects from build definition*

This setting will trigger the publishing of any database projects in the solution. You need to make sure the account you specified in the connection string previously has proper permissions to be able to create the database on the target SQL server.

Summary

This chapter looked at continuous deployments and how we can use this with Team Foundation Service. We have covered deploying to Windows Azure, to on-premise servers using Web Deploy, and deploying SSDT database projects as part of your hosted builds.

The next chapter will move on to testing, looking at the tools available for specifying and running manual tests.

AgileT esting

Agile projects are challenging. With a common mindset in which we embrace change and want to work incrementally and iteratively, we have good conditions to deliver what our customers ask for on time.

To get testing to work in an agile environment, we need to rethink the testing approach we use. Working with incremental development typically means we need to do lots of regression testing to make sure the features we have developed and tested still continue to work as the product evolves. Iterative development with short cycles often means we must have an efficient test process or else we will spend a lot of time in the cycle preparing for testing rather than actually running the tests.

We can solve these problems by carefully designing our tests to cover the core user scenarios; this helps us maintain only the tests that actually give value to the product. As the product evolves through increments, so too should the tests, and we can choose to add only relevant tests to our regression test suite. To make the testing more efficient, we should automate the tests and include them in our continuous integration scheme to get the most value from the tests.

This chapter will show you how to get started with agile testing. We will look at creating a test plan, creating test cases, and running tests. We will also look at exploratory testing, which is an interesting technique to get started with testing early in the process.

But before we get going with testing, let's look first at how a tester gets the knowledge of what to test. Traditionally we write requirements documents and product backlog items to describe how functionality works. In agile development, it has also become popular to use acceptance criteria.

Acceptance Criteria

Acceptance criteria are to testing what user stories are to product owners. Acceptance criteria sharpen the definition of a user story or requirement. We can use acceptance criteria to define what needs to be fulfilled for a product owner to approve a user story.

■ **Note** The acceptance criteria are part of the user stories and are owned or defined by the product owner. Testers can use the acceptance criteria to raise questions or generate test cases or scenarios, but they do not make changes to the acceptance criteria.

In Chapter 5 we looked at the agile planning process and how product management can use user stories to define the product. With acceptance criteria, we have yet another technique to help us refine the stories.

A user story can be stated as simply as this:

- As a service repair I want to be able to view ticket details from the dashboard so that the tickets are easy to access when we're with our customers.

The conversation around this statement between the product owner and the development team can raise questions such as:

- How should the service representative view the tickets? Search? Filter?

- In what way will the service representative access the tickets? Over the web? Phone?

- Is the ticket read-only or can the service representative work with it? Assign to someone else?

We use this information to formulate acceptance criteria. Take, for example, the question "How should the service representative view the tickets?" From this we can formulate acceptance criteria such as the following:

- A service representative should be able to:

  - Click the service ticket number in the list on the dashboard and see the details

  - Search by customer, geography, and time

  - Filtert her esultst o geta b ettero verview

This exercise then leads to more questions to the product owner, for example, should a service representative only be able to change open tickets? So having this type of conversation not only helps us know what to test but also helps us define the product.

When working with TF Service, we can capture all important pieces of information from this process in the product backlog work item. The PBIs give good traceability to follow the user story (requirement) to its acceptance criteria. Figure 19-1 shows an example of how the Visual Studio Scrum template shows this information side by side.

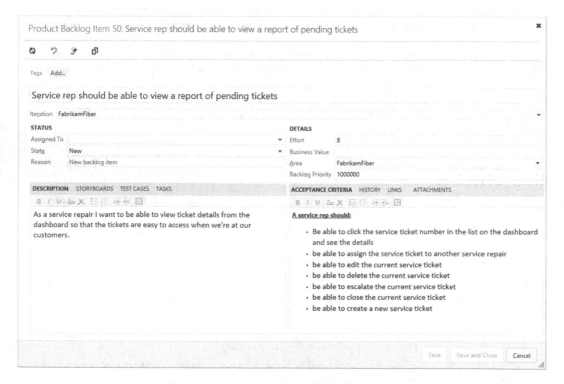

Figure 19-1. *Documenting acceptance criteria as part of a PBI*

Evolving Tests

As a part of the agile process, we need to deal with the incremental and iterative development of test assets. As the product goes through the specification-design-implementation-release cycle, the test cases also need to adapt to this flow. Initially we know very little about a new feature, and we typically need to run tests against all acceptance criteria defined for the requirement. When a feature has been completed, we should be confident it has been tested according to the test cases and that it works as expected. After that we only need to run tests to validate changes in the requirement, which means we must have a process for how we know which tests to run.

Another side of the agile story is to look at how to speed up the testing process to keep up with short iterations. If we follow the ideas presented in this section, we will have techniques to learn more about which tests to run. But running all tests manually will probably not be feasible, so we need to rethink how we design these test cases.

One way to think about how we can structure our test base is to think of it as a pyramid. Figure 19-2 shows how the types of tests from the testing quadrant can be put in proportion in our specific case.

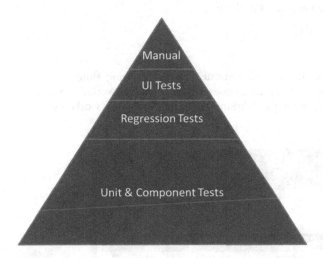

Figure 19-2. *Proportions of types of tests*

Typically we would focus on the big part of unit and component tests (tests authored by developers using a unit test framework) because these are the least expensive to implement and maintain. But these tests do not test the system as a whole, so we need to add regression tests (manual or API-level tests, which can also be implemented using a unit test framework) to run end-to-end tests. Some of the regression tests can be implemented as user-interface (UI) tests (using a UI test framework) to really simulate how an end user would use the system, but UI tests are more complex to design and maintain and it is often not practical to have more than a small set of these tests unless you have a proper organization for managing the tests. All of these types of tests can and should be automated to give us an efficient way to keep up with the changes in the product.

Clients for Managing Tests

We'll consider two options for managing tests: the desktop application Microsoft Test Manager and the web-based Microsoft Web Test Manager.

MicrosoftT estM anager

The Microsoft Test Manager (MTM) is a stand-alone desktop application added to the product family when Visual Studio and Team Foundation Server 2010 were released. It can be thought of as the Visual Studio for testers, the one-stop shop for the entire test process. A tester can do all the testing activities within a single application (not entirely true, but pretty close actually).

At a high level MTM provides functionality for:

- Test planning
- Suitem anagement
- Testd esign
- Test runner and test run analysis
- Rich bug reporting with data collection from the machines under test
- Work item tracking (including bug tracking, of course)
- Labe nvironmentm anagement

We will start exploring some of these capabilities in this chapter and continue with test planning, suite management, and other powerful testing features in Chapter 20. Chapter 21 goes into the details of working with lab management, ranging from manual testing to automated testing and automated build-deploy-test workflows. Figure 19-3 shows the MTM client application.

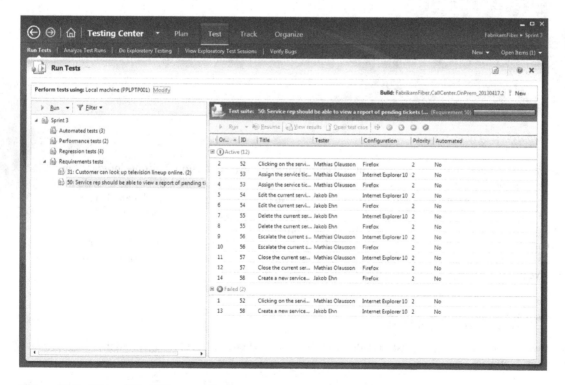

Figure 19-3. *Microsoft Test Manager client*

MTM comes with Visual Studio 2012 ALM Premium and Ultimate or Microsoft Test Professional 2012.

MicrosoftW ebT estM anager

The second client for working with test cases is the Microsoft Web Test Manager (WTM) or the Test Hub (Figure 19-4). WTM is a lightweight solution for when you want the integrated testing experience with TFS but don't want to (or cannot) install the MTM client. Currently WTM offers a subset of functionality and will also require someone in the team to work with MTM to manage part of the testing configuration. The scenarios WTM enables are:

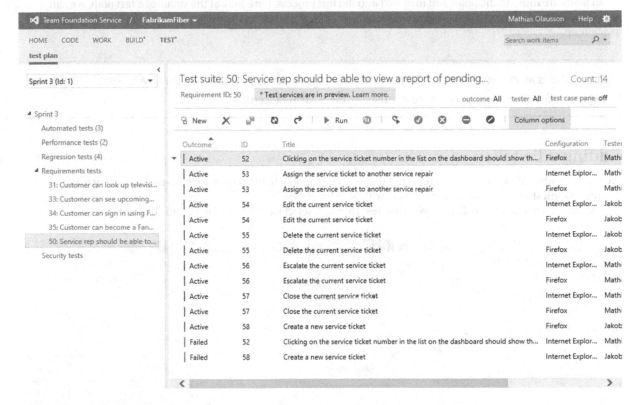

Figure 19-4. *Microsoft Web Test Manager client*

- Basict estp lanc reation
- Suitem anagement
- Testd esign
- Testr unner
- Basicb ugr eporting
- Work item tracking (part of the Team Web Access)

To use the WTM you need to have a valid license for MTM.

Getting Started

To start testing we must create a test plan to organize our tests. A team project can contain multiple test plans, but a test plan can't contain other test plans. Depending on how you organize your team project, a test plan will typically be associated with an application, a release, or a specific sprint or iteration.

We recommend keeping test plans small; we prefer one test plan per sprint over one for the entire the release. Small plans are more to the point and map well into the test process. If we look at the status of a test plan, we can grasp what it means. If the plan covers the entire project, it is much harder to understand whether we are progressing as planned.

■ **Note**   This is an involved subject, so for more details we recommend taking a look at the ALM Rangers' Test Release Management Guidance at `http://vsartestreleaseguide.codeplex.com/`.

Adding a Test Plan

We can use either MTM or WTM to create test plans. This chapter will focus on the web-based experience, but Chapter 20 will show examples of how to work with MTM as well.

To create a test plan in WTM, we go to the Test Hub and select Create test plan (Figure 19-5).

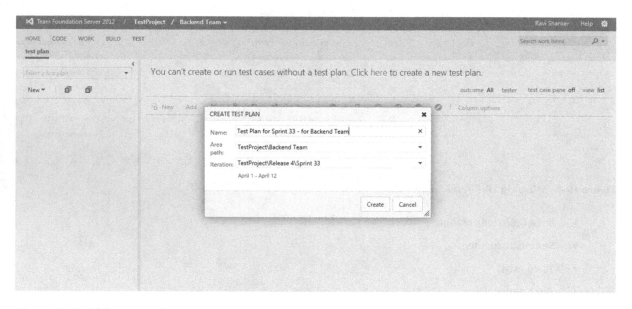

Figure 19-5. *Adding a test plan*

We give the test plan a logical name, and if we want to we can also associate the test plan with an area and an iteration. Doing so will relate work we do in the test plan with work items with the same classification. We will look more at the test plan properties in Chapter 20.

Creating a Test Case with WTM

This section will explain how to add test cases to a test plan using the WTM. You can do the same with MTM, and in Chapter 20 we will look at some of the more advanced features available when working with test cases in MTM.

A test case represents the test instruction for a tester. It is implemented as a TFS work item, which means we can use the regular work item management tools to manage them, relate them to other work items, and so on to capture all the context a tester needs to complete the test run. The test case can be viewed and changed in any TFS client except for the test steps, which can only be edited in MTM and from the TFS Web Client.

To create a test case you will:

1. Create a test plan from the Test Hub (or select an existing one).

2. Add a new test to the test plan (Figure 19-6).

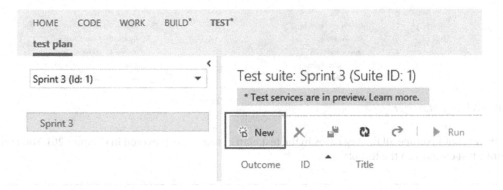

Figure 19-6. *Creating a new test case*

3. Give the test case a title. Add steps and other test case details (Figure 19-7).

Figure 19-7. *Adding test case step to create a complete test case*

4. Save and close.

Working with WTM

Getting started with testing using the Test Hub in Team Web Access is very straightforward. The WTM lets you select a testp lant ow orki n,a ss howni nF igure 19-8.

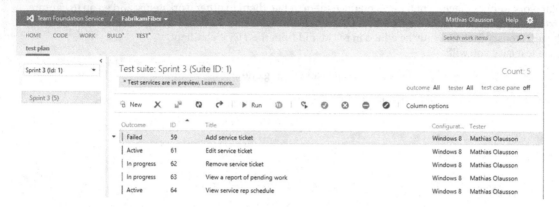

Figure 19-8. *Web Test Manager*

From the test plan you see all the test cases in the test plan or test suites (covered in Chapter 20). You can add, edit, or remove test cases from the test plan.

■ **Note**   Removing a test case in this view will not remove the test case from TF Service, only from this test plan, so if you remove it accidentally it can be found again.

You can set the status of a test in the test plan without actually starting the test run, in particular you have the ability to pass or fail a test without starting the Test Runner. You can also mark a test case as blocked (something is preventing you from running this test) or not applicable (out of scope in this test plan).

There are options to customize which fields to display in the test case view and you can also filter the test case list by outcome or tester. You can also use the test case pane to view a test case without having to open it, something that can really save time when browsing through a list of test cases.

Running a Test Case with WTM

With the test plan in place and test cases created we're ready to start running some tests. We have three ways of starting a test run: selecting a single test, selecting multiple tests, or selecting a test suite to run all tests in that suite.

1. Go to the Test Hub in the TF Service web client.

2. Select the test cases to run and click the Run button (Figure 19-9).

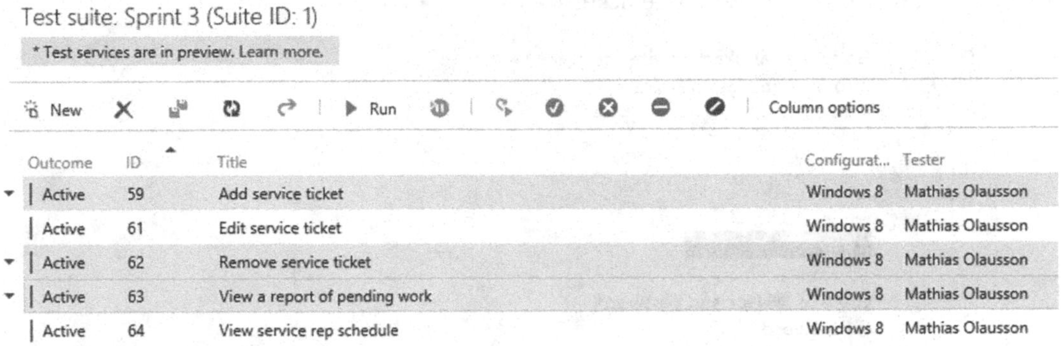

Figure 19-9. *Selecting tests to run*

3. The web Test Runner opens and lets you look at the test steps and walk through the test case. As you complete a test step, you just pass or fail the test. You can also bulk select all the steps and mark them pass or fail in one shot. If you have started multiple test runs, you navigate between them with the Next/Prev buttons. It's also possible to add comments and attachments to the test run by pressing the + button. Also note how image attachments are shown inline with the test step (Figure 19-10).

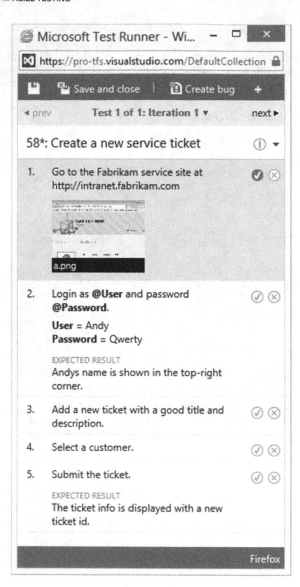

Figure 19-10. *Running a test case*

4. You can also pass or fail the whole test case if you want from the topmost status icon. It is also possible to set other states, including pausing the test (which then can be resumed later by you or another tester from WTM or MTM). Figure 19-11 shows the status options in WTM.

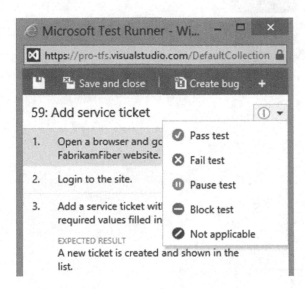

Figure 19-11. Setting the test run status.

5. Using the Test Runner, you can also edit the test cases inline during execution (Figure 19-12).

Figure 19-12. Editing test cases inline during a test run

6. If a problem is discovered, you can easily report a bug by clicking the Create bug button. The details from the test run are copied over to the bug report, as shown in Figure 19-13.

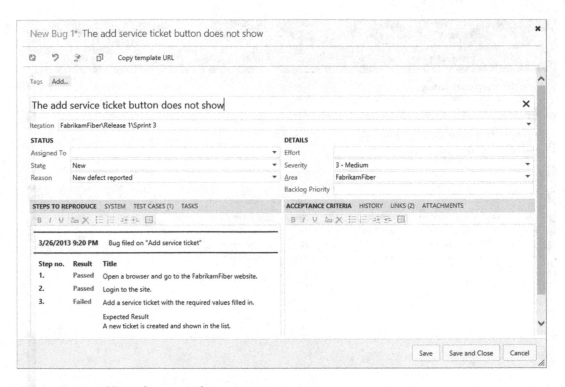

Figure 19-13. Adding a bug report from a test run

7. The new bug will automatically get linked to the test case being tested, adding transparency without extra effort.

We're just scratching the surface of what can be done when it comes to effective bug tracking with the testing tools, and we will look at that in more depth in Chapter 20.

Exploratory Testing

Exploratory testing is a form of software testing in which the individual tester can design and run tests in more free form. Instead of following detailed test scripts, the tester explores the system under test based on the user stories. As the tester learns how the system behaves, the tester can optimize the testing work and focus more on testing than documenting the test process.

To do exploratory testing you start MTM and go to the Test Hub in the Do Exploratory Testing view. From this view you can quickly start exploring by clicking the Explore button, as shown in Figure 19-14.

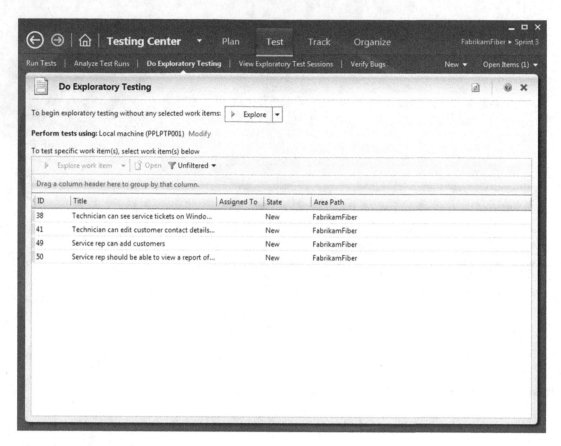

Figure 19-14. *Starting an exploratory test setting*

From the Test Runner you can now start exploring the application, taking notes as you go along (Figure 19-15). If you want to log how the application appears, just click the Add screenshot button and the screen clip gets added to the test session.

Figure 19-15. Working with the Test Runner

If you find a bug, you can easily add a bug report by clicking the Create bug button, and all details from the test session are copied over to the bug report, including the UI actions. This is a really nice feature that helps developers quickly understand how the tester ran the application to get to the point where the problem occurred (Figure 19-16).

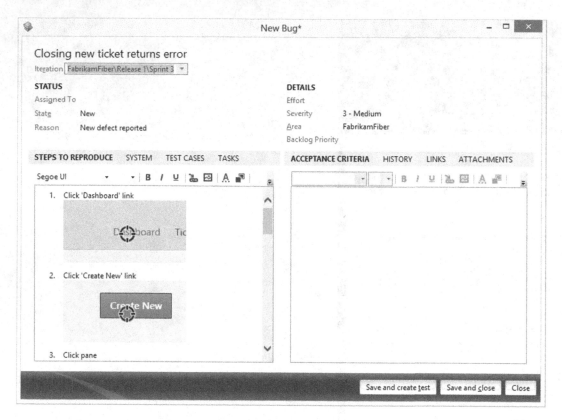

Figure 19-16. *Creating a bug report from an exploratory test*

Creating a Test Case from an Exploratory Test

Exploratory testing can be seen as simultaneous test design and test execution. To achieve this, you can use the capability of the Create Test Case feature from the Test Runner or pressing the "Save and create test" button t from the Create Bug dialog box. This is an easy way to get started with test cases when you have used exploratory testing to learn what needs to be kept for regression testing. Creating a new test case this way will automatically add the sequence from the exploratory test session as test steps in the test case (Figure 19-17).

Figure 19-17. *Creating a test case from an exploratory test*

If you are testing backlog items for the sprint or release, you can take advantage of the capability of exploratory testing a specific work item. You can also select multiple test cases and rung a series of exploratory tests on them, asF igure 19-18s hows.

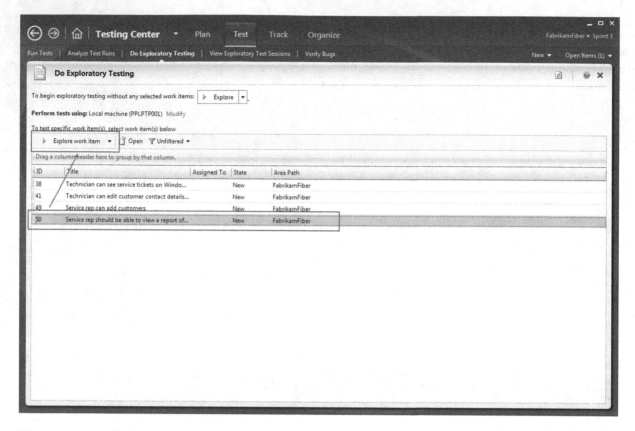

Figure 19-18. *Exploratory testing a work item*

You start the session by clicking the Explore work item button. The only difference from the previous mode is that the work item (backlog item) is shown at the top of the Test Runner. Clicking the work item will show a little pop-up window with the acceptance criteria, which really adds value to documenting the testing requirements this way (Figure 19-19). Now you can follow the acceptance criteria much like a scripted test but you don't have to take the effort of writing a test case before you're actually sure you want the test as a test case. Can testing be any more agile than this?

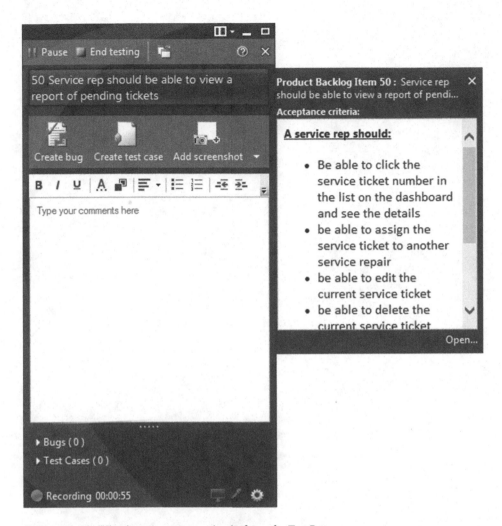

Figure 19-19. Viewing acceptance criteria from the Test Runner

You will see more features such as data collection and bug tracking covered in Chapter 20.

Summary

This chapter showed you how you can practice agile testing by using a lightweight and evolutionary approach to the way you validate your applications. By consciously designing test plans, we make sure we get the most testing done without writing lots of test documentation. During development we rarely know exactly how a feature will turn out. At this point it may make sense to work with acceptance criteria and do exploratory testing to validate the acceptance criteria. As the feature evolves, we also learn more about how to test it and we can create more formal test cases in order to do regression testing in a repeatable way. With the new web-based testing tools, we can get started with testing very easily, and as our skills and requirements grow, we can extend our test design with the tools in the Microsoft Test Manager.

The next chapter will look at advanced testing practices, such as test plan design, data collection, and bug tracking.

TestMan agement

In Chapter 19 we looked at testing using the TF Service and the Web Test Manager. Intentionally we wanted to show how to get started with testing in an agile, lightweight way. This chapter will explain how we can evolve our testing process into more structured testing, meaning we will create test plans for various purposes, use test suites to organize the test cases, and design test cases with all of the details needed for easy use by any tester.

With test plans and test cases in place, we will run tests and use the different tools to capture rich data from the test sessions, something that will be of huge help when we follow up our test runs, not to mention when bugs are reported and in later fixing them. Apart from the structured testing, we can also use the same test infrastructure to get rich test diagnostics from exploratory testing, which was also introduced in Chapter 19.

Planning the Tests

This first section will discuss how to use the planning features in the testing tools to create a plan for our testing. We can use either the Web Test Manager (WTM) from the Team Web Access Test Hub or the Microsoft Test Manager (MTM) desktop application (Chapter 19 gave a comparison of these tools). We will use the WTM as the default application in the examples and show MTM for the features currently only available in the desktop client.

What Is a Test Plan?

A *test plan* holds the details about the tests we plan to run, which environments we run the tests in, which test settings apply by default, and so forth. But primarily it is the container for the set of tests to run. Of course a test plan is not the only thing the testers (and the team) will use for testing. We can also use Tasks to track the testing work and bugs to follow up any errors we find during testing.

We recommend keeping test plans small; we prefer one test plan per sprint over one for the entire release. A small plan is more to the point and maps well into the test process. If we look at the status of a test plan, we can grasp what it means. If the plan covers the entire project, it is much harder to understand whether we are progressing as planned.

Chapter 19 showed how to create a test plan. Now we will add more structure to the test plan by adding test suites and test cases to it.

TestS uites

Test suites group together the tests we want to run and track in a plan. We can choose from three types of suites:

- *Static suite*: The contents of this suite are manually added test cases.

- *Query-based suite*: A query-based suite lists all test cases matching a given work item filter.

- *Requirements-based suite*: This suite shows the test cases associated with a selected TF Service requirement.

A static suite is likely what you would start with. The static suite is mainly used to create a folder structure in the test plan with a static set of test cases.

The query-based suite is great for any situation where you want to make sure you have an up-to-date list of tests based on some criteria. Typical uses are suites of tests for a specific application area or all automated tests. Figure 20-1 shows how to create a query-based suite from the WTM.

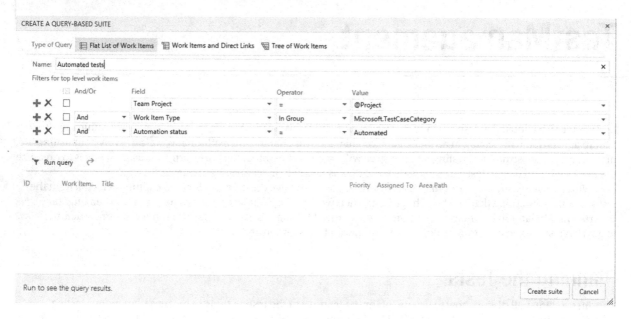

Figure 20-1. *Query-based suite for all automated test cases*

The requirement suite is a little different. Here we use a work item category that maps to the configured work item type(s) representing a requirement. In our scenario using Scrum, this would map to a product backlog item and bug.

We would typically add all requirements in the sprint to the test plan to associate the acceptance tests with the corresponding requirement. Figure 20-2 shows how we use a work item query matching the requirement category to find the requirements we now can add to our plan.

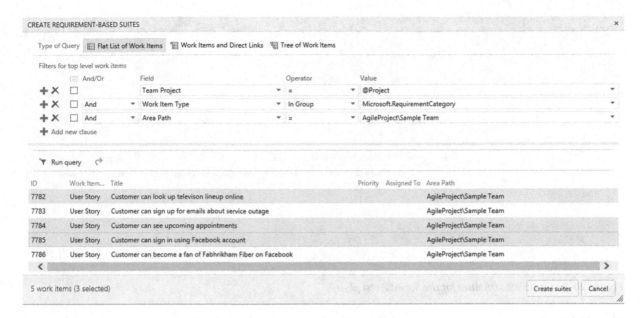

Figure 20-2. *Adding requirements to our test plan*

■ **Note**   Removing a test case from a requirement deletes the link to the requirement and therefore affects other plans using the same test case or requirement association. Adding a test case has a similar effect—the test case will be added to all existing test plans where the requirement is used. This will affect the test statistics for the test plans, so make sure to think through how this behavior affects your testing so you don't have any unwanted surprises. If you are only interested in marking certain tests to not be run for a particular requirements within a test plan, you can use the Not Applicable option to mark them appropriately instead of deleting or removing them from the requirement suite.

The complete structure for the Sprint 2 test plan is shown in Figure 20-3 with suites for requirements tests, regression tests, and automated tests.

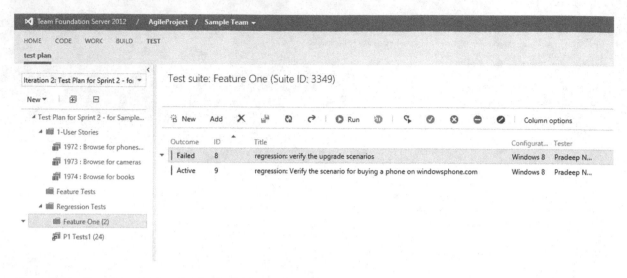

Figure 20-3. *Complete structure for the Sprint 2 test plan*

TestP lanP roperties

Currently, we must use MTM to manage the test plan properties, as shown in Figure 20-4. The test plan contains general information about the test plan, details on how test runs are set up, as well as links to documents and other resources. The links are useful when we want to add more context to the plan, for instance, we can reference a test document containing all details about the testing for the release we are working on. We will cover more of the test plan properties, such as configurations and data collection profiles, later in this chapter.

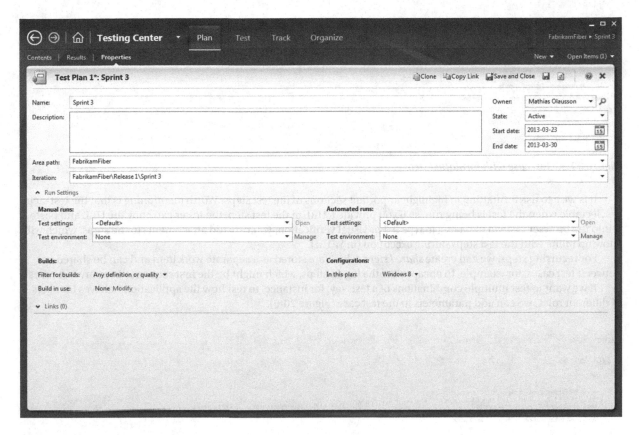

Figure 20-4. *Test plan properties*

Designing Test Cases

Now that we have reviewed the test plan and the different types of suites, we can look at adding test cases to the test plan suites.

What Is a Test Case?

A *test case* represents the test instructions for a tester. It is implemented as a TFS work item, which means we can customize it so it contains the information the tester needs to complete the test run. The test case can be viewed in any TFS client, but to edit it we have to use either MTM or WTM. Let's walk through the core elements of a test case.

Test Steps

The Steps section is of course the central part of the test case, as shown in Figure 20-5. We add steps for the test instructions and provide expected results. The expected results are particularly important to spend some time thinking about because these are the validation points we use to assert that the test case is testing the right thing. If the expected results are well formulated, we can use them to validate the test step in a manual test as well as if we automate them, saving time and making the test runs more repeatable.

| STEPS | SUMMARY | TESTED USER STORIES | ALL LINKS | ATTACHMENTS | ASSOCIATED AUTOMATION |

	Action		Expected result		Attachments
1.	Go to the Fabrikam service site at http://intranet.fabrikam.com				
2.	Login as **Andy** and password **Qwerty**		Andy's name is shown in the top-right corner.		
3.	Add a new ticket with a good title and description				
4.	Select a customer.				
5.	Submit the ticket		The ticket info is displayed with a new ticket id.		
	Click or type here to add a step				

Figure 20-5. *Test case with formatted steps*

It is wise to use formatting to highlight important sections of the test steps. Worth mentioning is that the test step is selectable when the test is being run, so if you provide a URL in the test step, the tester can copy the URL and paste it into the browser instead of having to type it. For visual verification, you can add attachments to the steps, which will show up inline with the test steps during execution (in WTM).

For recurring steps, we can create *shared steps*, which are stored as a separate work item and can be shared between test cases, for example, to encapsulate the log-in steps, which might be the first sequence in many test cases.

If we want to test multiple combinations of a test, say, for instance, to test how the application behaves for users of different roles, we can add parameters to the test case (Figure 20-6).

| STEPS | SUMMARY | TESTED USER STORIES | ALL LINKS | ATTACHMENTS | ASSOCIATED AUTOMATION |

	Action		Expected result		Attachments
1.	Go to the Fabrikam service site at http://intranet.fabrikam.com				
2.	Login as **@User** and password **@Password**		User's name is shown in the top-right corner.		
3.	Add a new ticket with a good title and description				
4.	Select a customer.				
5.	Submit the ticket		The ticket info is displayed with a new ticket id.		
	Click or type here to add a step				

Parameter values

User	Password
Andy	Qwerty
Jane	Qwerty

Figure 20-6. *Test case with parameters*

Each set of parameters shows as test iterations when the test case is run, and in MTM we also get the nice effect that each data value is copied into the Windows clipboard so we can paste it into the target UI element, something that also makes it possible to fast forward the rest of the test iterations.

Test Case Summary

The test case summary contains a description field that is useful for documenting the purpose of the test case (Figure 20-7). This field is also shown in the MTM Test Runner when the test is run later, so use it to write reminder notesf ort het ester.

Figure 20-7. *Test case summary*

CreatingT estC ases

In our scenario we want to add test cases to our first requirement:

> *As a service repair I want to be able to view ticket details from the dashboard so the tickets are easy to access when we're with our customers.*

The requirement has acceptance criteria defined for it, which is great input to our test case design. As a start, we can create one test case for each acceptance criteria and later, as we find need to, we can add more test cases for edge cases.

Let's start by creating a test case for the acceptance criteria:

> *A service representative should be able to assign the service ticket to another service repair.*

When adding a test case for a requirement, a link is automatically created to the requirements under the Tested Backlog Items tab. Figure 20-8 shows a completed test case.

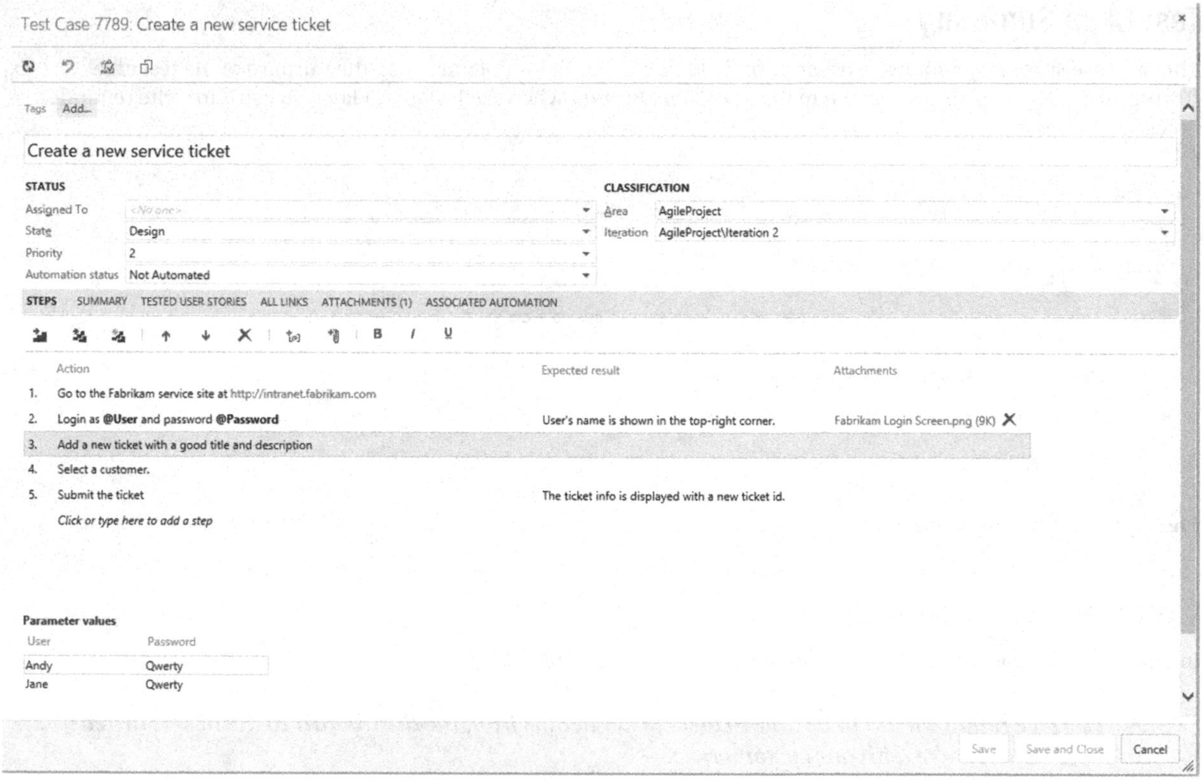

Test Case 7789: Create a new service ticket

Tags Add...

Create a new service ticket

STATUS

Assigned To	<No one>
State	Design
Priority	2
Automation status	Not Automated

CLASSIFICATION

Area	AgileProject
Iteration	AgileProject\Iteration 2

STEPS SUMMARY TESTED USER STORIES ALL LINKS ATTACHMENTS (1) ASSOCIATED AUTOMATION

	Action	Expected result	Attachments
1.	Go to the Fabrikam service site at http://intranet.fabrikam.com		
2.	Login as @User and password @Password	User's name is shown in the top-right corner.	Fabrikam Login Screen.png (9K) ✗
3.	Add a new ticket with a good title and description		
4.	Select a customer.		
5.	Submit the ticket	The ticket info is displayed with a new ticket id.	
	Click or type here to add a step		

Parameter values

User	Password
Andy	Qwerty
Jane	Qwerty

Save   Save and Close   Cancel

Figure 20-8. *Test case for assigning the service ticket to another service repair*

After adding test cases to cover the acceptance criteria, we can take a look at the product backlog item again. A small but effective feature of the Scrum work item design is that we can view the list of test cases at the same time we view the list of acceptance criteria, as shown in Figure 20-9. This is a great way to check whether we've added test cases to cover the requirements.

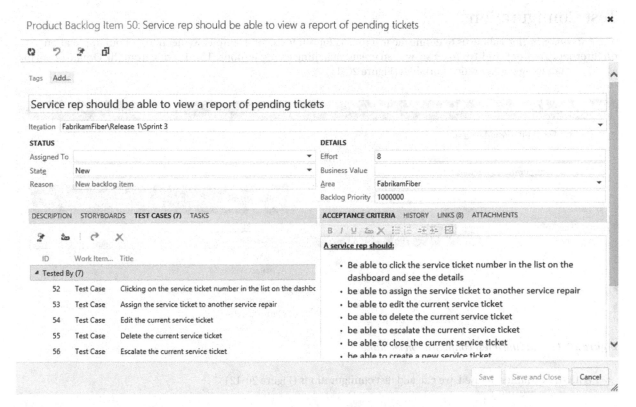

Figure 20-9. *Requirement with acceptance critera and test cases*

With the test cases in place, we now have a test plan ready to start testing (Figure 20-10).

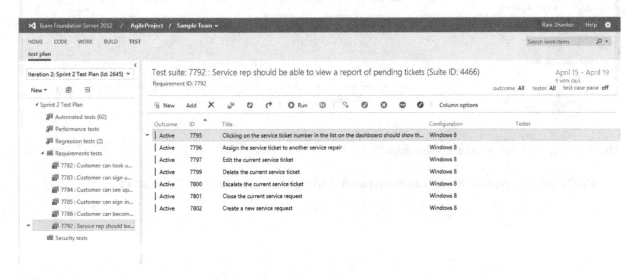

Figure 20-10. *Sprint 2 test plan with test cases*

Test Configurations

The *test configurations* allow us to define the test matrix for our tests, for example, we need to test our application on Internet Explorer 9 and 10. To do so, we can create matching configurations. This is done from the Organize tab in MTM by managing configuration variables (Figure 20-11).

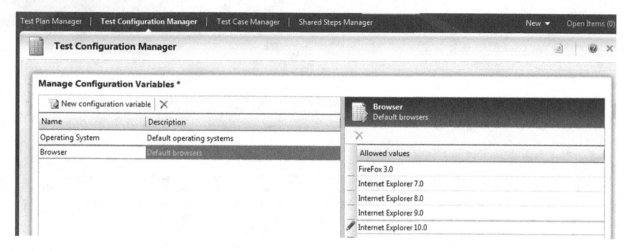

Figure 20-11. *Adding a test configuration variable*

With the variables defined, we can add test configurations (Figure 20-12).

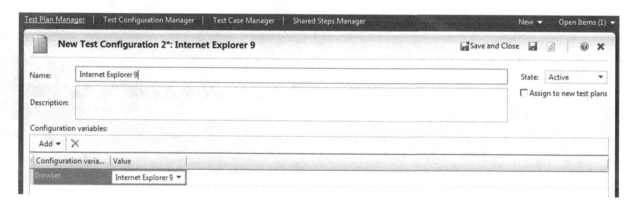

Figure 20-12. *Adding a new test configuration*

Finally, we can assign each test to the corresponding configurations, as shown in Figure 20-13.

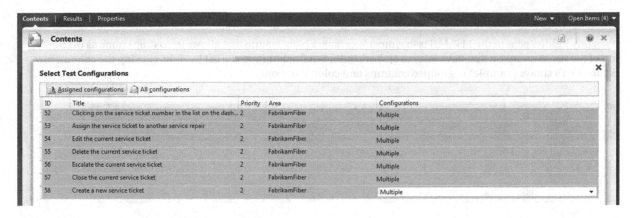

Figure 20-13. *Mapping test cases to test configurations*

Assign to Tester

If we have many test cases and many testers, it can be effective for the test manager to assign test cases to the designated tester. One way to divide the work can be to assign tests to users by configuration (Figure 20-14).

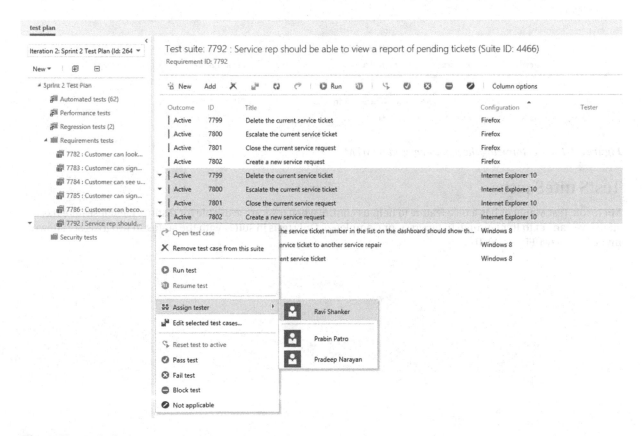

Figure 20-14. *Assign test cases to tester*

Groupinga ndA ddingF ields

A slightly hidden gem in the MTM UI is that most lists have a pivot feature that allows us to drag columns over the top of the list to group on that field. We can also add additional columns to the list by right-clicking the column row. Figure 20-15 shows examples of grouped columns and column options.

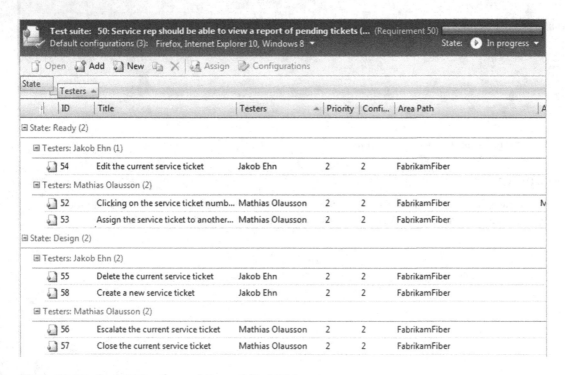

Figure 20-15. *Customizing the work item grid in MTM*

TestS uiteS tatus

Microsoft Test Manager has a nice feature to help us control when tests are available for testing. Each test suite has a status we can set to In planning, In progress, or Completed. Only tests in suites with the status In progress are shown int heT estv iew(Figure 20-16).

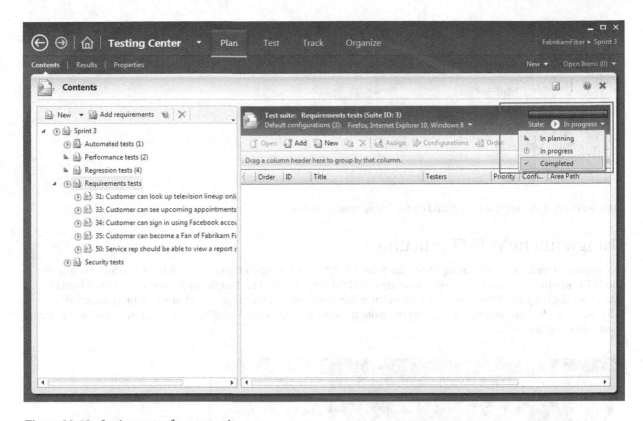

Figure 20-16. *Setting status for a test suite*

Running Tests

Before we start running texts, it's good to have an understanding of how the Test view works. From the Test view we can:

- *Run the test* (with options to override the plan default settings): We can select tests to run in many ways, for instance, by suite or by multiselecting the tests to run.

- *Open the test case*: We can read up on the details before starting the test.

- *Change the test status*: We can set the test to blocked, reset, passed, or failed without starting a testr un.

Filtering Tests to Run

Previously we explained how a test planner can assign tests to testers and configurations. When a tester wants to use that information, we can create a filter in the Run view so we only see the relevant set of tests (Figure 20-17).

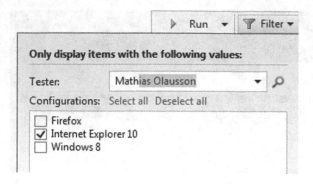

Figure 20-17. *Filtering test runs based on tester and configuration*

Usingw itht heM TMT estR unner

In Chapter 19 we looked at running a test case from the WTM. This chapter looks at the richer experience when we use MTM to run tests. Starting the test opens up the MTM Test Runner. The Test Runner starts in a mode where it takes over the left part of the screen and scales the other area, which is nice if you want to test your application in full-screen mode. You can change docking behavior if you want to so you can position the window in a different way, as shown in Figure 20-18.

Figure 20-18. *Selecting the Test Runner screen position*

When starting a new test, we get to choose if we want to create an *action recording*, which is a recording of all user interactions for the test and is a script we can use later for automatic test playback in MTM or to generate an automated test in Visual Studio.

The Test Runner displays the test steps so we can mark them as passed or failed as we go through the test case (Figure 20-19). If the test step contains parameters, we can bind those to the application we are testing by pasting the data value from the clipboard, which speeds up testing multiple iterations. The parameter value is copied into the clipboard by default when you move to the test step containing the parameter. If you want to copy the parameter explicitly, you can do so by just clicking the Data link.

Figure 20-19. *Working with a test case in the Test Runner*

If the test step has a validation point, it is also displayed in the test step description.

When we are running multiple tests or iterations, we can easily switch between them using the navigation control in the upper-left part of the Test Runner (Figure 20-20).

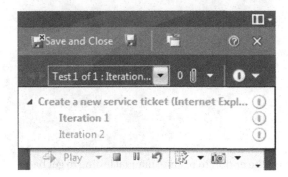

Figure 20-20. *Moving between tests and iterations in the Test Runner*

One feature in the Test Runner that can be difficult to spot is the test case summary. If you want to read the summary, there is a little expander link just above the list of test steps (Figure 20-21).

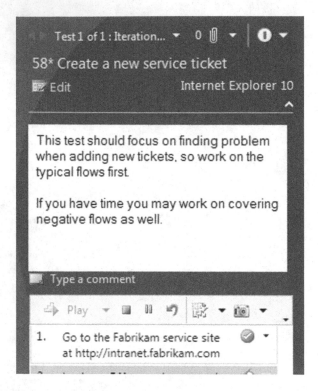

Figure 20-21. *Viewing the test case summary when running the test*

Another nice feature is the possibility to quickly switch between the running test and MTM by clicking the little window icon in the top toolbar, as shown in Figure 20-22. Switching from the test run back to MTM pauses the current test but only for the length of the MTM session. If you close MTM, the test run will be marked as failed if that test has any Expected Results (i.e., it has one or more Validation steps), otherwise, it will be marked as Passed.

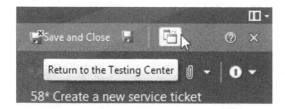

Figure 20-22. *Switching between Test Runner and MTM*

The test run in Figure 20-23 is shown as In progress, and we have the option to resume manual testing to get back to the Test Runner window.

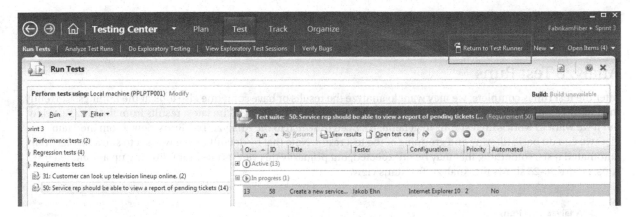

Figure 20-23. *Resume manual testing*

This feature can also be used if you want to pause the test and come back at a later time or let someone else continue running the test. Figure 20-24 shows how a paused test can be resumed from the test list.

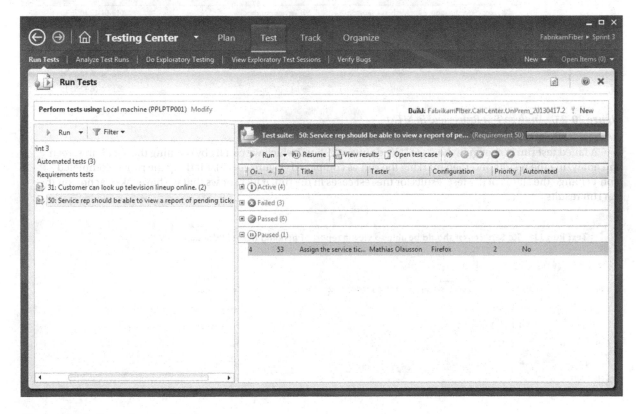

Figure 20-24. *Resume paused test*

When the test is completed, we go back to the test view. If we want to view the data from the test run later, we can just click the View result button to go back to the details from that particular run for the test case.

Analyze Test Runs

After the test run is complete, we may want to analyze the results or have someone else look at the findings. Currently, the tools to analyze test runs are only available in MTM. We can always go to the latest results from the Run Test view, but if we want to work with test runs in general, we need to switch to the Analyze Test Runs view. From the Main view we can do basic filtering and grouping of the test result. Note that by default the view is set to show results from automated tests, something that may be unexpected, but primarily this view is used for following up automated test runs. Figure 20-25 shows the Analyze Test Runs view.

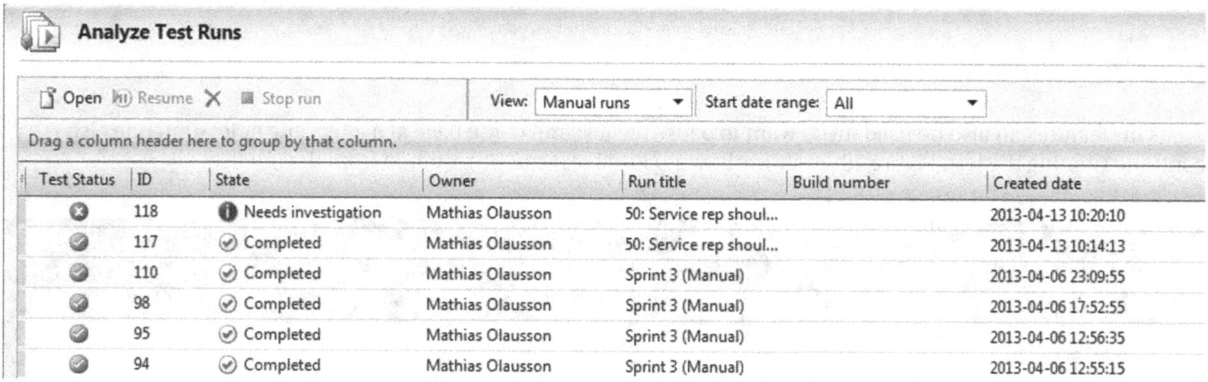

Figure 20-25. *Analyze Test Runs view in MTM*

A failed test run is shown in the state "Needs investigation," which we can fix by opening the Test Run screen and analyzing the results and then marking the run as completed (Figure 20-26). Marking the run as completed won't change the status of the test results for the test cases in the run, it just shows that we have taken action on the test run results.

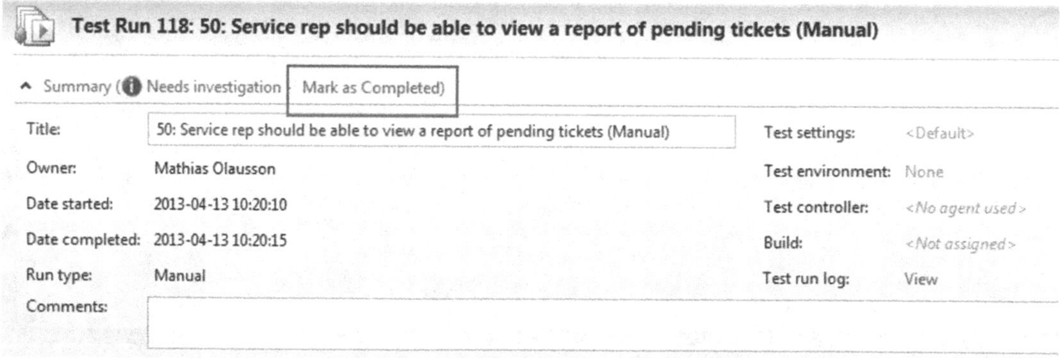

Figure 20-26. *Working with Test Run details*

If we scroll down to the Tests section in the report, we get a list of the tests that were run in this test run (Figure 20-27). Here we can drill down and look at the details of a test run and raise a bug afterward. We can also make a decision about the cause of a problem by selecting the failure type and a resolution.

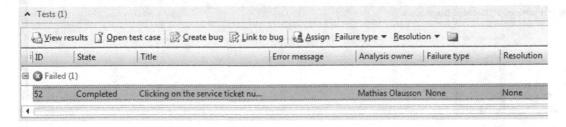

Figure 20-27. *Tests analysis actions in MTM*

Opening the results of a particular test shows the details of that test run. One detail to pay a little extra attention to is the Result History list. The result history is a good way to learn more about the test when troubleshooting. If the test works all the time, we probably have introduced an error. If the test sometimes passes and sometimes fails, we could have a regression issue, or there may be a problem with the test case, and perhaps we need to add more information in the test case so we can make sure it is run the same way every time.

■ **Note** Test results are stored per test plan. If you want to track test results consistently, it usually works best to have small test plans, each with a distinct purpose.

Test Settings

When we run tests, we can manually add content to the test results, such as attaching files, including screenshots, or writing comments. This is great for traceability and for test run analysis, but for bug fixing it is also practical to get detailed information about the system under testing so a developer can reproduce the problem quickly.

The default settings for test runs can be assigned to the test plan on the Test Plan Properties view. We also can override the default by choosing Run with Options when starting a test run. Either way, we get the test framework to locate a test setting we configured earlier.

To manage test settings, we switch to the Lab Center in MTM and select Test Settings. For manual tests, it is very straightforward to create a new test setting; first, we give the test settings a unique name, then we select the environment where the tests are run (Chapter 21 for more information about test environments), and finally we add the diagnostic data adapters to use in the test run.

DataC ollection

The central part of a test setting in MTM is the Data and Diagnostics section where we can specify which data collectors we want (Figure 20-28). Most of the data adapters are configurable to help us fine tune the data collection for best results.

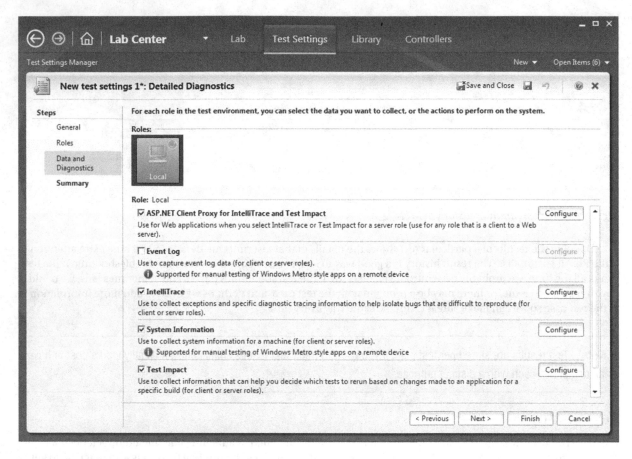

Figure 20-28. *Creating a new test setting*

The built-in data adapters in MTM 2012 are:

- *Action log*: Used to collect UI interactions when the test is run.

- *ASP.NET Client Proxy for IntelliTrace and Test Impact*: Used to collect IntelliTrace and Test Impact data from a web server.

- *Event Log*: Captures events from the event log, which event to capture, as well as how many events to collect, which can be configured.

- *IntelliTrace*: Used to collect runtime and exception information from the system under test, which can be used by developers to speed up the time it takes to understand the cause of a problem.

- *System Information*: Gathers system information from a machine, such as the amount of random access memory and operating system and browser type.

- *Test Impact*: Collects test coverage data used to calculate test impact so we can determine which tests to rerun based on code changes.

- *Screen and Voice Recorder*: Records the desktop where the tests are run. This can be configured to only store video recordings on failed test, which can help reduce the amount of data stored int hed atabasec omingf romt estr esults.

Most of the adapters also let us configure how the data collection should work, for instance, by controlling whether a screen recording should be saved for successful test passes.

Once the test settings have been defined, they can be associated to the Test Plan from the Test Plan Properties window. You can also choose to verify the test settings at runtime by either assigning it to the test plan or choosing the test setting when we start a test run by selecting Run Options (Figure 20-29).

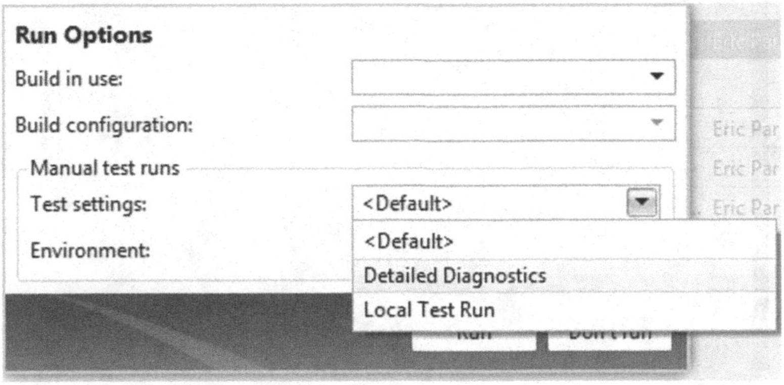

Figure 20-29. *Specifying test settings when starting a test*

Typically we will create one test setting per type of test scenario, for instance, local testing, detailed diagnostics, and remote testing. The recommendation is to use as inexpensive a test setting as possible. This way we can speed up testing and reduce the amount of diagnostic data that get collected and when needed we can rerun tests using a different setting to gather more information.

■ **Note** The test results stored in TFS can quickly fill up the TFS database, so be conservative with which data you save from test runs. The size of the TFS database not only affects the operational performance, but may also slow down maintenance jobs such as backups. The TFS Power Tools contain a test attachment cleaner tool that can be used to remove unnecessary test artifacts (http://msdn.microsoft.com/en-us/vstudio/bb980963.aspx).

Reporting Bugs and Validating Fixes

Chapter 19 explained how we can create bugs from the WTM. With MTM we have the same capability but we also get integration with the data collectors, which helps us capture valuable information from the test session. MTM also has a nice feature for verifying bugs. Information from the test run where the bug was reported can be used to quickly rerun the test session from the point where the problem occurred.

Creatinga B ug

First, let's start by creating a bug from MTM. We can easily create a bug from Test Runner anytime during the test session, as shown in Figure 20-30.

Figure 20-30. *Creating a bug when running a test*

When a bug is created, data from the diagnostic data adapter are collected and added to the bug report. The test steps are also copied into the bug form, which makes it really simple and quick to report a new bug. In fact it is so easy to do that we can report a bug for any problem we encounter, be it during development or testing. Figure 20-31 shows an example of a bug report with rich test run–data attached.

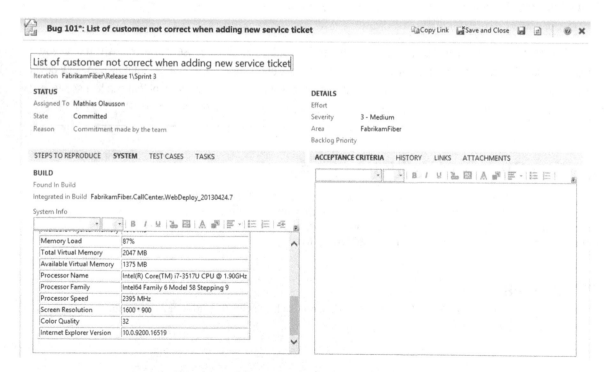

Figure 20-31. *A bug report created from a test run in MTM*

It is sometimes argued whether it is a good practice to report bugs in a sprint where the tested feature is still under development. Our recommendation is that it is better to report the bug and let the team decide when to deal with it rather than distracting a developer with the issue right away.

■ **Note** How does MTM know which work item type is a bug? MTM uses the Bug work item category to find the default type for a bug and open that form. If your work item type for bugs is called Defect instead of Bug, you can update the work item category to reflect this.

Reporting bugs directly from the test run is of course the most common way to do it. But what if we forget or didn't think it really was a bug and want to add one later? Rather than having to create a bug report from scratch, we can instead use the test run results (Figure 20-32).

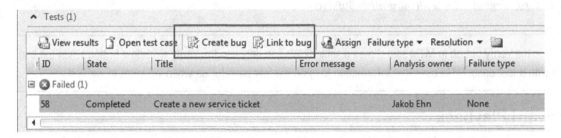

Figure 20-32. *Create a bug report from the test run results*

VerifyingB ugs

After a bug has been filed, it will go through the process of triage and development until it is eventually fixed and ready for testing. To make the process of finding the state of a bug easy, we can use the Verify Bugs view in MTM (Figure 20-33).

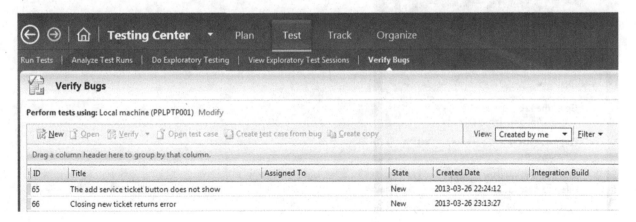

Figure 20-33. *Verify Bugs view in MTM*

A good way to work with this view is to look at the State and Assigned To columns to track the progress of the bug. In Figure 20-33, we can see that the bug has been approved and the team has committed to fix it. No one is working on it yet because the Assigned To field is empty. When the developer fixes the bug, the check in should eventually become part of a TFS build, which in turn can update the Integration Build field on the bug, as shown in Figure 20-34.

Figure 20-34. Verify bugs in MTM with Integration Build set

> ■ **Note**   Why is the Verify button in MTM sometimes disabled? We can only use the Verify workflow button when the bug is associated with a test case. MTM uses that information to open the test case for us when we what to verify it.

Fast-Forward Playback

When we verify a bug fix, we can either run the test case again or we can use a feature in the test runner called *fast-forward playback*. As the name implies, this feature allows us to replay a test session, and it does so by using an existing action recording associated with the test case (as described earlier when we discussed running tests). As you can see in Figure 20-35, each test step with an associated action recording is shown with an orange line next to it. This information also tells us a little about how the actions were recorded. To use the feature with the best results, we recommend you focus on getting a clean recording and make sure to mark each step correlated with the action log. There is no way to edit the action recording later, so the only option is to rerun the test and save a new action log.

Figure 20-35. Fast-forward playback using MTM

The playback feature is of course just as useful (perhaps more) during normal testing. Isn't it great to be able to run a regression test with the click of a button!

■ **Note**   Action recordings are saved per test plan, which means that a test case can have a different action recording in different scenarios.

Summary

This chapter covered how to do test planning with TF Service, the WTM, and the MTM. Many of the features are available in both the web and the desktop clients. MTM has additional capabilities for test planning, exploratory testing, and data collection. MTM also gives us custom views for managing test results and bugs, so we will likely want to use both of these clients for different scenarios.

The next chapter will complete the testing section by examining how we can use TF Service to create lab environments. We can use these environments for manual testing, but also to integrate the build and deployment process to create a build-deploy-test workflow that lets us implement a continuous delivery process for our product.

■ ■ ■

LabMan agement

It is desirable for most projects today to have short cycles and transparent development processes that allow us to change the plan after every cycle. This typically means that in two to four weeks a set of features needs to go from developers to testers to stakeholders and perhaps even to customers. To support this we need lots of different test environments to validate the development work. There is also a lot of work to keep the environment ready for testing, which includes not only making sure the right version of the product is there but also including test data and dependent services. If we want to succeed with agile projects, we must make sure to manage this complexity well. Unfortunately, it is often far from a simple process to implement in a project.

Visual Studio Lab Management was introduced with TFS 2010 as a platform to build a lab infrastructure to support these new requirements. It has many features that can be used to speed up the process for managing the test environments used. As a result it also improves the overall experience around testing and bug fixing with tooling for automated deployment and testing as well as collection of data from machines in the lab environment.

Perhaps the best improvement in TFS 2012 is the notion of standard environments, with which we can create a lab environment based on any existing machine we want to use in a test environment.

This chapter explains how to leverage Visual Studio Lab Management to implement a solution for test lab management, which can be used for manual testing, as well as automated processes such as deployment and testing.

Architecture

To set up Visual Studio Lab Management requires knowledge of the features it offers. The next sections will explain the capabilities and components in the product that enable us to define the architecture for Lab Management configuration.

Capabilities

First, let's take a look at the capabilities Visual Studio Lab Management offers. Lab Management is all about making testing easier. We can use Lab Management to create labs to run manual and automated tests. Lab Management also extends the TFS Build system with deployment and remote testing capabilities.

Improved Manual Testing

Perhaps the most tangible capability of Visual Studio Lab Management is doing manual testing more effectively. With Lab Management and virtualization it is now possible to create lab environments to allow for testing of complex test systems (database and web servers, integration services) as well as testing multiple configurations (operating systems, platforms, languages).

Environments for Automated Testing

It is also possible to use lab environments to run automated tests. The lab environment is then controlled by the Test Agent installed on machines in the environment. How tests should be executed on the target environment is controlled by settings in MTM and Visual Studio. The Test Agent can be configured to run both interactive and noninteractivet ests.

Framework for Build-Deploy-Test Workflows

As mentioned at the beginning of the chapter, one of the key elements of an effective test process is to manage environments effectively. Apart from creating and using the environments, implementing automated build-deploy-test (BDT) workflows that can virtually rebuild a complete environment in minutes is a killer feature of Lab Management. BDT workflows is implemented using the standard build definitions in TFS Build and can be customized and extended to support the deployment needs of your application.

Cloning Environments

Working within a complex environment can be challenging work. How many times have we found ourselves struggling to get a test environment with all components set up? Wouldn't it have been great if it were possible to take a copy of the environment when you have gotten it working and reuse it for future testing? Lab Management environments can do just that; if we want to create a copy of an environment, we can create a template and then use that to create clones for other testers, other configurations, or whatever our needs may be.

Of course cloning machines can have side effects, particularly when it comes to starting up several instances of the same type of environment. The solution for this is to use network isolation to create isolated environments.

Network Isolation

To solve the problem with cloned environments, Lab Management allows us to create isolated environments. An isolated environment is, simply put, a lab environment with managed networking. When an environment is created with network isolation, the machines in the environment are placed on a private subnet so that additional running environments with conflicting components can work independent of one another. Figure 21-1 shows an example where an original environment has been cloned. Using network isolation, the internal addresses (and all other configuration data) are identical but the external addresses are unique.

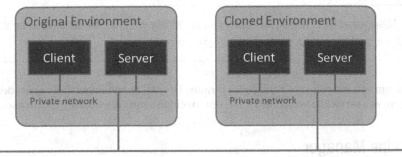

Figure 21-1. *Isolated environments*

■ **Note** At the time of writing, Lab Management does not support cloning environments and network isolation when running on TF Service. These capabilities require Microsoft System Center Virtual Machine Manager, which is not available with TF Service.

Components

Now with the main capabilities of Lab Management covered, let's take a look at the components used to support those capabilities.

Test Controller

The *test controller* is a service responsible for controlling test execution. It can be used for controlling load tests and also for managing automated test runs, which is what we use it for in lab environments. Each test controller used with Lab Management is bound to a TFS Team Project Collection but can be used by any project in that project collection.

Test Agent

A *test agent* is a service installed on a test machine and enables three things:

- *Test execution*: Tests run on the machine are managed by the test agent (including things such as downloading test assemblies and test dependencies).

- *Data collection*: The test agent collects data as configured for a test run.

- *Deployment workflow execution*: If a machine is part of a BDT workflow, the test agent will execute the deployment part of the workflow.

■ **Note** With Visual Studio 2012 Lab Management, the test agent deploys automatically when a new lab environment is created from Microsoft Test Manager. A test agent is always connected to a test controller.

The test agent can be configured to run tests interactively (typically for running UI tests) or noninteractively as needed. If possible, you should run the test agent as a service to avoid having the test machine running with a logged on user.

System Center Virtual Machine Manager

System Center Virtual Machine Manager (SCVMM) is the component required if we want to create new virtual machines for lab environments directly from MTM.

The SCVMM client also has to be installed on the TFS Application Tier to enable the SCVMM Lab Management functionality.

Lab Management 2012 supports the 2008 R2 and 2012 versions of SCVMM.

Standard Environments

With Visual Studio 2012 Lab Management, it is possible to create an environment based on existing infrastructure without installing SCVMM. This is great because we can now start using Lab Management without any additional installation required. The lab machines in a standard environment can be physical or virtual (or both), and the virtual machine does not have to be managed by SCVMM or Hyper-V.

To create a standard environment, you only need to know the names of the machine you want to add to the environment and a user account to be used to log in and deploy the test agent service onto the machine.

A standard environment can be connected to directly from MTM and the Test Runner, making the integration with lab environments really smooth.

SCVMM Environments

The alternative to standard environments is to use a SCVMM environment. The key features of a SCVMM environment include:

- *Create new machines from templates*: New lab machines can automatically be created by anyone (having permissions) running MTM. It is no longer required to send a request to the operations department to get machines created for a new environment or to do other maintenance operations such as starting, stopping, snapshotting, or restoring machines.

- *Support for snapshots*: It is possible to work with snapshots from MTM, which enables testers to save state during testing. This is a powerful feature both to unlock the tester if a test case fails (no need to block an environment while waiting for a resolution) and to give a developer a fixed point in time to reproduce a bug.

- *Connection inside MTM*: A SCVMM environment can be connected to MTM and the Test Runner, just like with the standard environment.

■ **Note** Using SCVMM environments is not an option when using TF Service because it's not possible to configure SCVMM with TF Service.

Setting up the Lab

Currently, we're somewhat limited in what's possible to set up in Lab Management when working with TF Service. We cannot use SCVMM and SCVMM environments. But we can create standard environments, which does give us the ability to keep track of our environments, run manual and automated tests, as well as implement BDT workflows using the out-of-the-box template. The matrix in Table 21-1 shows how the combinations of Cloud service and on-premises components add up.

Table 21-1. *Matrix showing the support for different capabilites and hosting options*

Capability	On-PremisesT FSw ith On-Premises Build	TF Service with On-Premises Build	TF Service with Hosted Build
Standarde nvironment On-premises lab	Supported	Supported	Doesn otw ork
Standard environment Azure IaaS VM lab	Unsupported	Unsupported	Doesn otw ork
SCVMM Environment	Supported	Does not work	Does not work

So when implementing Lab Management with TF Service today, we can only create a standard environment and we have to use on-premises machines for build services and the lab machines.

Topology

Now let's look at the environment we can set up with TF Service without making any customizations or requiring complicated configurations. What we have to resort to is an on-premises solution for our test lab, with an optional on-premises build service if we want to enable an automatic BDT workflow. The illustration in Figure 21-2 shows the components required to set up an on-premises standard lab environment.

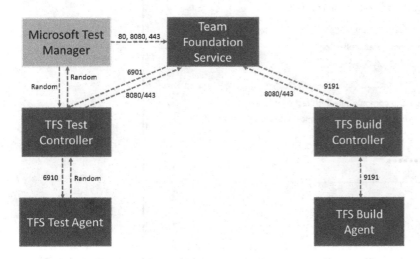

Figure 21-2. *TF Service and standard environment topology*

Next we will walk through the process of setting up the lab environment.

Installing the Test Controller

First, we need to install a test controller. We recommend installing the test controller on a dedicated machine that's not part of any lab environment. If you are going to install an on-premises build service, the test controller can be installed on the same machine.

Here's how to set up the test controller:

1. Install the Test Controller from the Agents for Visual Studio 2012 installer media available at http://www.microsoft.com/visualstudio/eng/downloads.

2. After the installation completes, configure the test controller. It's recommended to use a domain account for the controller and lab service accounts.

3. Connect the test controller to TF Service's DefaultCollection. When adding TF Service you will be prompted for your Microsoft account to authenticate with the service. This credential will be stored and used when communicating between TF Service and the lab environment. Figure 21-3 shows a completely configured test controller.

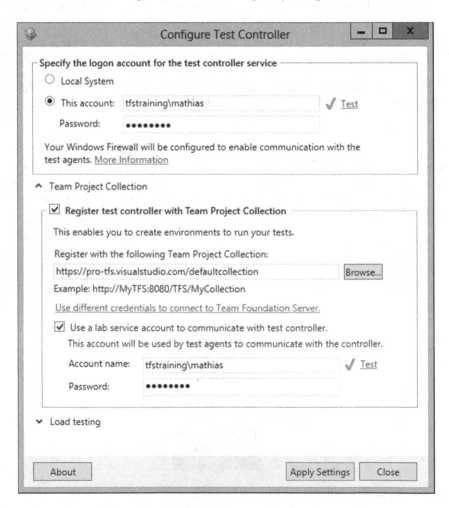

Figure 21-3. *Configuring a test controller*

Installing an On-Premises Build Service

If we want to use the out-of-the-box build templates for BDT workflows, we need to install an on-premises build service. How to set this up was covered in Chapter 15.

Creating a Standard Environment

With the test controller installed, we can now create a standard lab environment. Because a standard environment is more or less a grouping of existing (physical or virtual) machines, we need to install and configure the machines for use in our lab. We also need to make sure the firewall is configured to allow communication between the different components in the topology, as discussed earlier in this chapter. Follow these steps to set up the lab environment:

1. To create a new lab environment, start the Microsoft Test Manager and go to the Lab Center activity.

2. Then go to the Environments tab and click New to start the wizard to create an environment.

3. Select to create a Standard Environment. Name the environment and optionally add tags to attribute the environment. Figure 21-4 shows an example where a tag KeepUntil is created, which can be used to indicate how long this environment is valid.

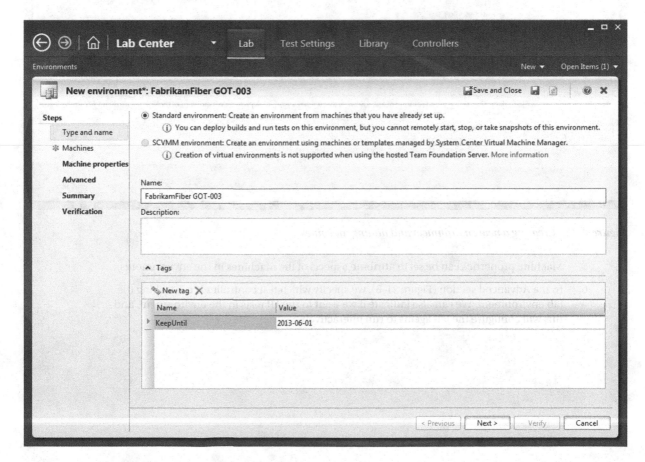

Figure 21-4. *Creating a new environment and giving it a name and tags*

4. Add the machines to the environment (Figure 21-5). Here we type in the names of the machines and the logical machine type. We also specify an account to be used to install and configure the test agent in the environment.

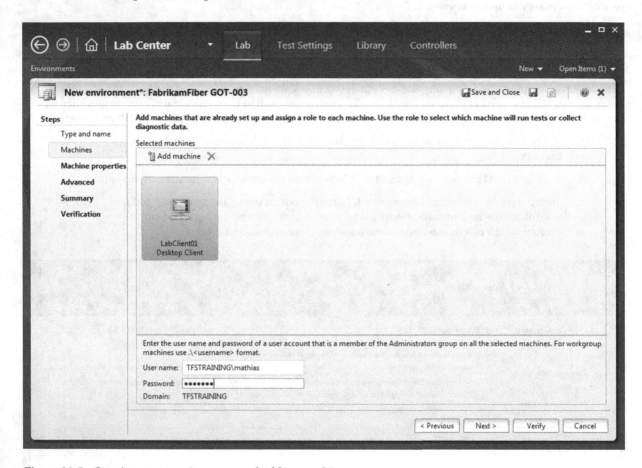

Figure 21-5. *Creating a new environment and adding machines*

5. Machine properties can be set to attribute aspects of the machines in the environments.

6. In the Advanced section (Figure 21-6), we specify which test controller is controlling the lab environment. We can also indicate if we want to run UI tests in the environment, and this will configure the lab agents to run interactively.

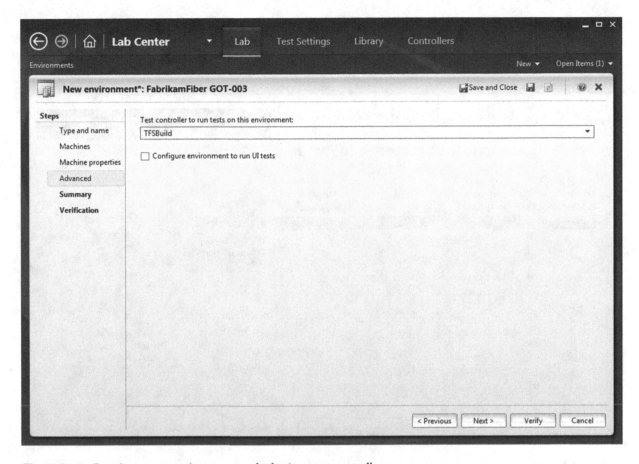

Figure 21-6. Creating a new environment and selecting a test controller

7. Finally, we validate the configuration and start the environment creation (Figure 21-7). The test controller will now deploy the test agent onto the machines in the environment and configure them according to the settings in the wizard.

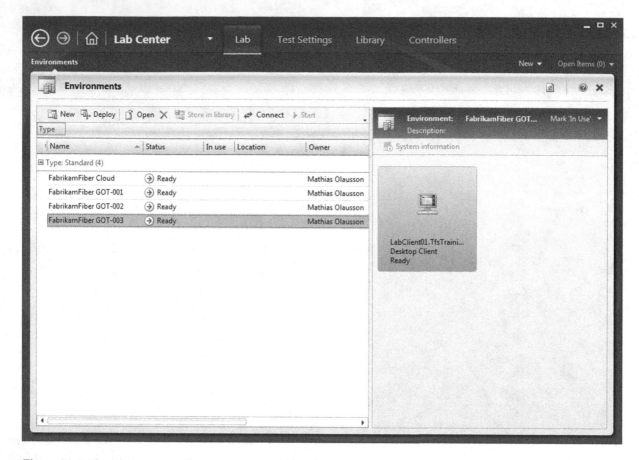

Figure 21-7. Creating a new environment, now completed

Testing with Lab Management

With the test lab topology in place, we can immediately take advantage of this and start using the lab for testing. This is great because it is important to show the effect of any change quickly to get confidence and continued support from the stakeholders. This next section will first explain how to do manual testing in the lab followed by examples of how to set up the environment to run automated tests.

RunningM anualT ests

Manual testers can take advantage of the lab infrastructure in several ways:

- Connecttoa ne nvironment
- Collectda taf rome nvironment
- Start and stop environment for test (SCVMM environments)
- Snapshote nvironment(SCVMMe nvironments)

So why waste time? Let's go testing!

Selecting an Environment to Use

The first step is to find the environment to use and make sure it's available for testing. A virtual machine may be stopped and need to be started or an environment may be in use by someone else running tests on it. Fortunately, MTM will help us get control of this so we can pick our environment and start testing. For the Lab Center in MTM you can manage the environments and use the "In Use" marker to tag an environment as in use, as shown in Figure 21-8.

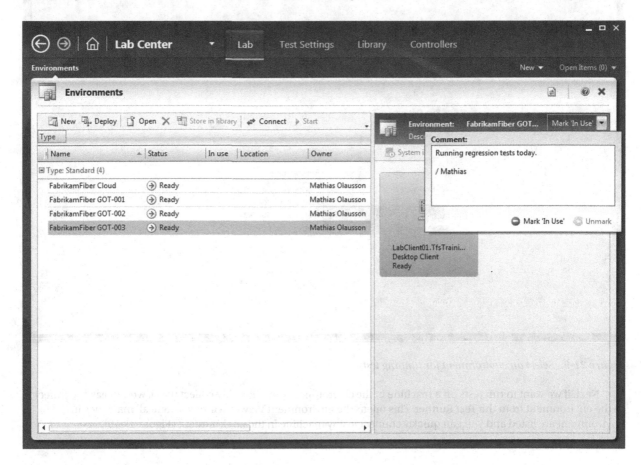

Figure 21-8. Setting the "In Use" marker

Connecting to an Environment for Testing

After we have made sure the environment is started and reserved for us, it is time to run some tests on it. Select Run Tests when starting a test run and select the Environment to use under Run Options (Figure 21-9).

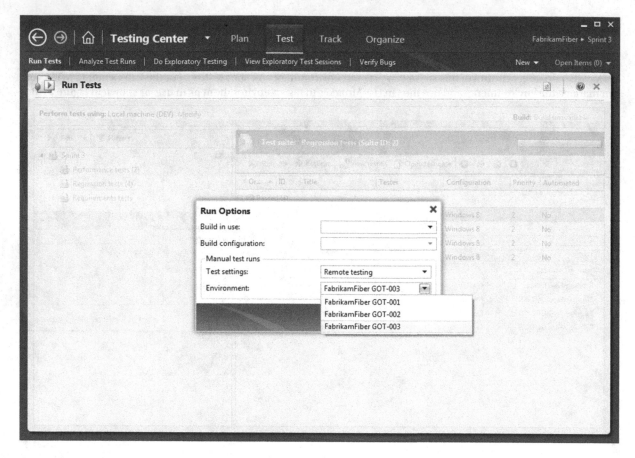

Figure 21-9. *Select an environment for running tests*

Next, if we want to run tests on a machine in the environment (and not only collect data), we can easily connect to the environment from the Test Runner. This opens the Environment Viewer window where all machines in the environment are listed and you can quickly connect to any machine in the environment (Figure 21-10).

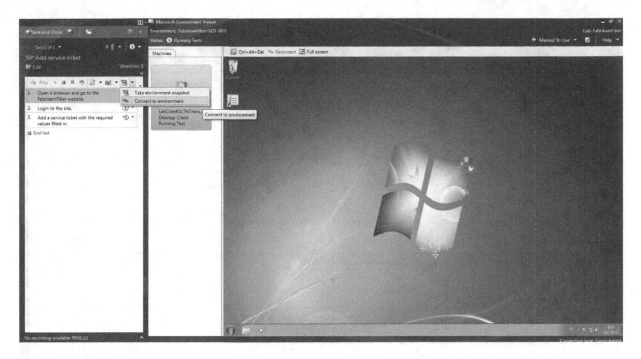

Figure 21-10. *Using the Environment Viewer from the Test Runner*

■ **Note** The Environment Viewer uses the Remote Desktop protocol (RDP) to connect to the environment so the port for RDP must be open (default 3389).

By default the owner of the environment connects using a host-based connection; others may use guest-based connections. A host-based connection is routed using the Hyper-V virtual machine connection protocol, which will let you interact with the machine even when it does not have an IP address. This can be very valuable if you need to do low-level tasks, such as install the operating system.

You can also right-click the machine in the environment and connect using the standard Remote Desktop protocol client. This is typically something you do if you want to bring local resources to the test machines (such as printers, discs, or USB devices) or to use the clipboard to copy and paste stuff between machines.

Manual testing can be performed both outside and inside an environment. Testing from the outside is often the choice for applications where the client can be run on the local machine and simply connects to sites and services in a test environment. If the client should be run inside the environment, then you many want to install and run MTM on the machine where the test is run, typically for the possibility to create an action recording.

AutomatedT esting

In Chapter 20 we saw how automated tests can be associated with a test case. The connection between automation and test case allowed us to track how and where test cases have been automated. Figure 21-11 shows a test case with an associated automated test, and creating the association will set the automation status to Automated.

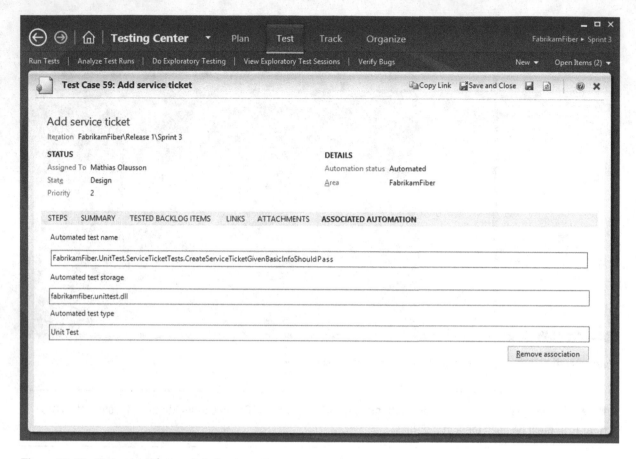

Figure 21-11. *Test case with associated automation*

To run an automated test in a lab environment from MTM, we must select the following when starting the test:

- *A build*: The build is used to find the automation component specified on the test case.

- *A test settings definition*: Test settings define properties for the test run, such as deployment items and data collectors.

- *The target environment*:T hisi sw heret het estss houldr un.

Just as for a manual test run, it is possible to define all of this on the test plan, as shown in Figure 21-12.

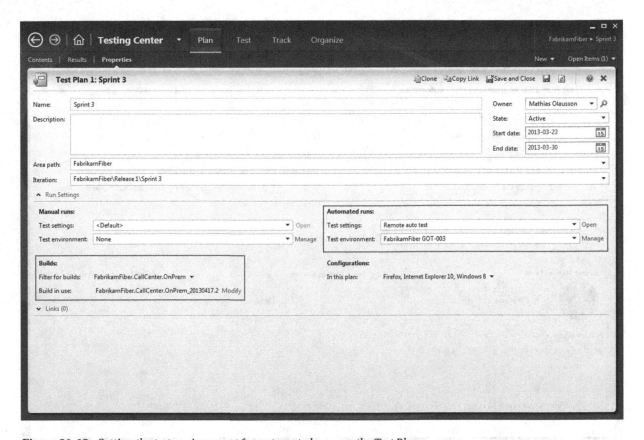

Figure 21-12. *Setting the test environment for automated runs on the Test Plan*

When executing automated tests in MTM, we should pick the environment the same way we would for manual testing to make sure others know the environment is in use. This can be automated in BDT workflows by customizing the default lab workflow; we will look at how to do this later in the chapter when we discuss automating deployment to lab environments.

Running Automated Tests from MTM

Now let's look at running the automated tests directly from MTM. It turns out that running an automated test is very similar to running a manual test, we just have a different view for monitoring the test progress (Figure 21-13).

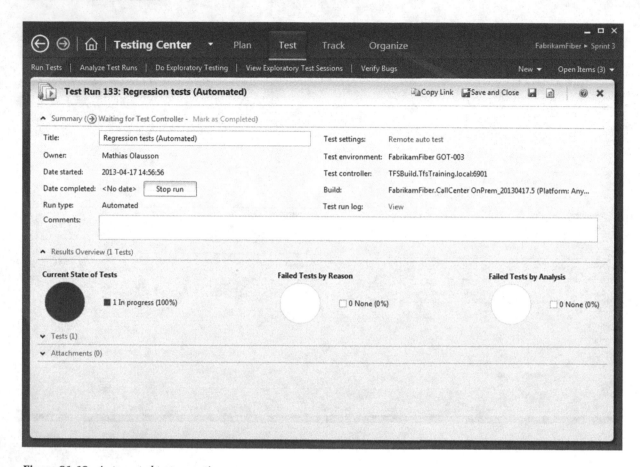

Figure 21-13. Automated test execution

If we want to view the execution steps for the test run, we can click Test to view the test run log (Figure 21-14). This is a good place to start looking when troubleshooting failing tests.

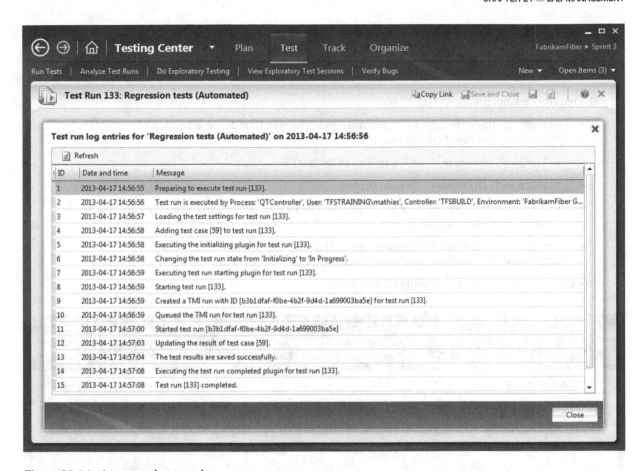

Figure 21-14. *Automated test run log*

Running Automated Tests from the Command Line

A third option for starting automated tests is to run them from the command line. This may sound like an edge case, but it actually quite nice to be able to start a test run without having to open up MTM. `tcm.exe` is the tool to do this, and we can use the same settings as in MTM when starting a test run. This is provided in Listing 21-1.

Listing 21-1. Settingsf orT estR un

```
tcm run /create
      /title:title
      /planid:id
      /collection:teamprojectcollectionurl
      /teamproject:project
      (/suiteid:id /configid:configid | /querytext:query)
      [/settingsname:name]
      [/owner:owner]
      [/builddir:directory]
      [/testenvironment:name]
      [/login:username,[password]]
      [/include]
```

With our manual example this would translate to:

```
tcm.exe run /create /title:"Sprint 3" /planid:1 /collection:https://pro-tfs.visualstudio.com/
DefaultCollection /teamproject:FabrikamFiber /suiteid:4 /configid:2
```

The required arguments are:

- planid: The ID for the test plan to run tests from. The plan ID is displayed under Organize ➤ Test Plan Manager in MTM.

- collection: The name of the TFS project collection.

- teamproject: The name of the team project.

- suiteid: The ID of the test suite to run tests in. The suite ID is displayed when selecting a suite in the Plan or Test views in MTM.

- configid: The ID of the test configuration to run tests on. We find this ID on the Organize ➤ Test Configuration Manager tab in MTM.

An example of a running test is shown in Figure 21-15.

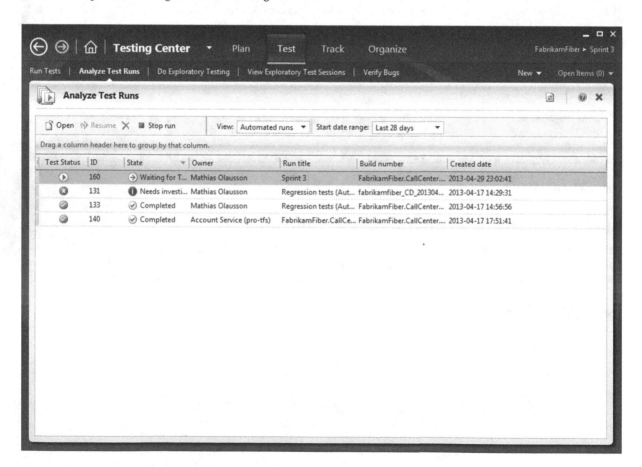

Figure 21-15. *Automated test running*

Build-Deploy-Test Workflow

Now that we've looked at options for our deployment and we've gone through the ways to run automated tests, we're ready to combine our skills of creating automated tests, creating test environments, and setting up automated build processes to create a complete end-to-end scenario for the complete BDT workflow.

We'll focus on using as much of the existing infrastructure in Visual Studio 2012 as possible, so we'll base our implementation of a BDT workflow on TFS Build and Visual Studio Lab Management. A good BDT process allows us to quickly manage a large number of environments because the whole deployment process is now automated, and with the validation from automated tests, we can feel confident that the machines get updated in a controlled way. In other words, we are ready to go into continuous delivery of software!

Implementinga B DTW orkflow

Although it can be a complex task to implement a BDT workflow, a lot of work has been done for us with Visual Studio Lab Management. A BDT workflow in Lab Management is mostly implemented using shared infrastructure such as the build and test services. This means we can focus on what needs to be done and not so much on how to do it. Figure 21-16 illustrates the built-in workflow in Lab Management.

Figure 21-16. *A build-deploy-test workflow in Visual Studio 2012 Lab Manager*

To make it easy to get started with a continuous deployment workflow, TFS Build comes with a build template tailored for Lab Management that implements a BDT process.

The Lab Management template (`LabDefaultTemplate.11.xaml`) contains the following core components:

- Capability to revert a lab environment to a known state.

- Select or run a compile build to get a version of the application to deploy and test. This is a normal TFS build that would include running unit tests if appropriate.

- Run scripts to deploy the application. Test agents are used to run the scripts locally on each machine in the environment.

- Take a snapshot of the environment so we can revert to a clean state whenever we want without having to do a new deployment.

- Run tests on the machines in the lab environment.

- Createa b uildr eport.

In the sections that follow we will set up a BDT process to be used for deployment to the team's test environment. Physical or virtual machines not managed by SCVMM can still be used to create a lab environment and use the LabDefaultTemplate, except for snapshot functionality, which will be disabled (again, for TF Service, only standard environments are available).

We will use as many of the existing Visual Studio 2012 features as possible to implement the BDT process. To implement the process we need to:

1. Create a standard environment for testing.

2. Create automatic tests to run as part of the build.

3. Create a build definition to create a new version of the application (covered in Chapter 16).

4. Create a build definition for the deployment and testing part of the workflow.

We will consider steps 1-3 complete and focus on step 4 to create the BDT workflow.

Create a BDT Build Definition

To create a BDT build definition, we follow the procedure for a default build with the following exceptions:

- *Workspace*: This may not be necessary as the BDT workflow will only deploy and test. If the BDT workflow has dependencies that the BDT build uses (for instance, deployment scripts), then we may need to set up the workflow as well.

- *Build defaults*: No drop folder is needed as the BDT workflow normally will not produce any output.

- *Process:*S elect LabDefaultTemplate.11.xaml as the build process template.

Figure 21-17 shows our BDT workflow being set up.

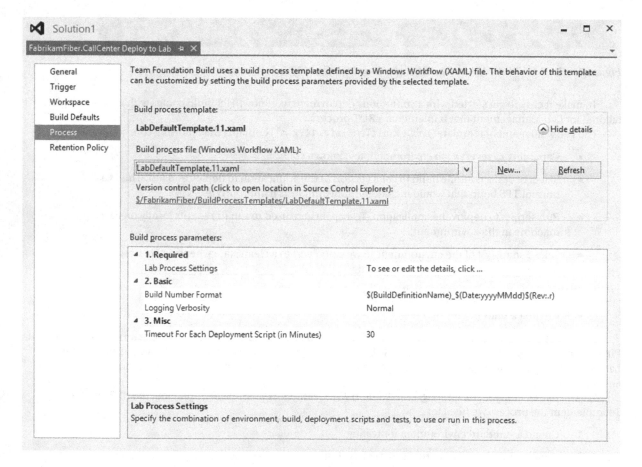

Figure 21-17. Creating a BDT build definition

A special requirement to run Visual Studio Lab Management BDT workflows that queue a compile build as part of the workflow is that there needs to be at least two agents available. If we only have one build agent, then the deployment build will be blocked by itself waiting for the build workflow to begin. Figure 21-18 shows a build controller with two build agents.

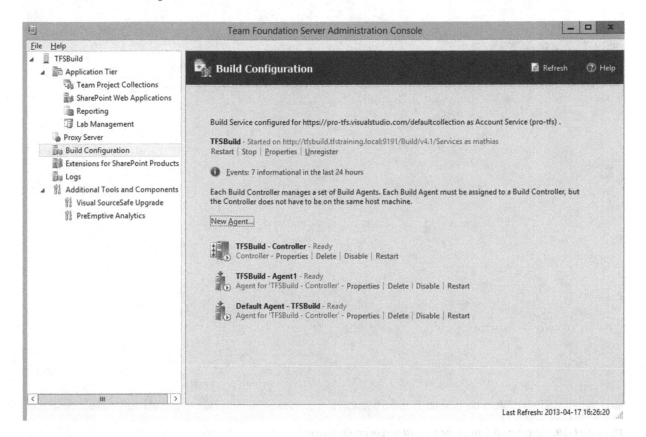

Figure 21-18. *Configuring the build service to have at least two agents*

The only required argument in the LabDefaultTemplate is that we open the configuration wizard and configure the build as described in the following section.

Selecting the Target Environment

The first step in the Lab Workflow wizard is to select the lab environment. We need to select an existing Lab Management environment, and we can optionally configure the workflow to revert the environment to a specific state before the deployment is done, given that the environment is using SCVMM (Figure 21-19).

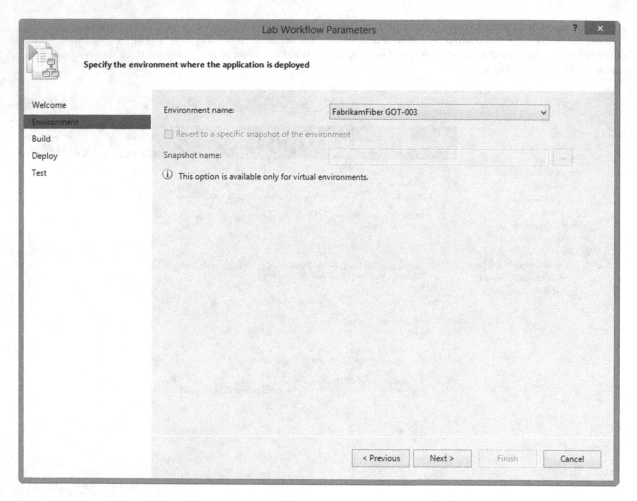

Figure 21-19. *Selecting a Lab Management target environment*

Selecting Application Build to Deploy

Next we select the build to deploy. We have the following options for picking a build that the workflow should use:

- *Use a Team Foundation build*: Here we can either queue a new build as part of the BDT workflow or we can pick an existing build.

- *Use a build from a specified location*: We can also choose to deploy a build from a selected location; this is useful if other tools are used to produce builds to deploy.

Figure 21-20 shows the build to deploy configuration dialog box.

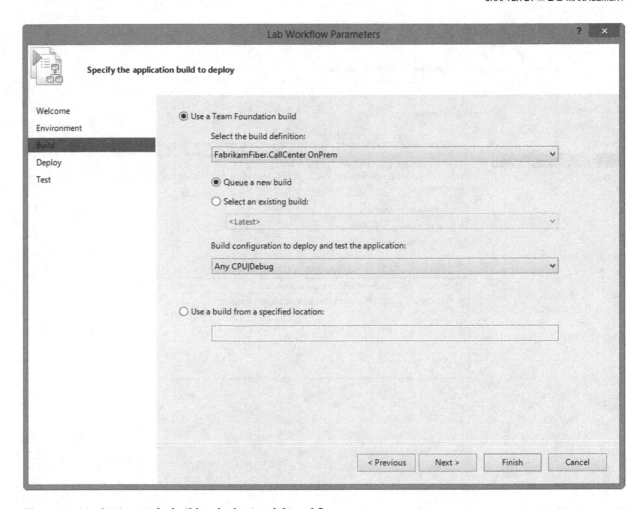

Figure 21-20. *Setting up the build to deploy in a lab workflow*

Defining the Deployment Steps

With target environment and build to deploy selected, we can now add the deployment steps (Figure 21-21). The Lab Workflow is very generic; it allows us to run commands or scripts on each of the machines in the environment. We can address the machines either by role or by name, whichever is most suitable.

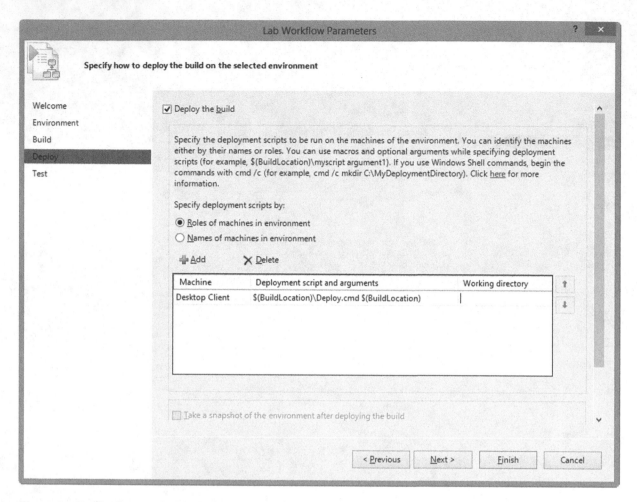

Figure 21-21. *Configuring deployment for a lab workflow*

The scripts are run locally on the target machine so it needs to be available as specified on the target machine. If necessary, we can also specify a working directory.

When we add deployment commands, we may need to pass in arguments from the build process. Currently, we can use the following properties:

- $(BuildLocation): This is the location of the build. If you specified to use the build from a shared location, then this variable represents that path. For the other options, this is the full path for the build based on the configuration you selected to build and the build drop location in the build definition. If you build your application as part of your workflow, you can use this to access the latest files that were created by that build.

- $(InternalComputerName_<VM Name>): This is used to obtain the computer name for a virtual machine that is part of a virtual environment. You might know the virtual machine name, but not the computer name. If you have a deployment script to set up a web server that requires the computer name, you can pass this as an argument to the script. For example, if the virtual machine name for the web server was VM1 and the computer name was MyWebServer, you would type $(InternalComputerName_VM1) as the argument for your script and this would pass the value MyWebServer to your script.

- $(ComputerName_<VM Name>): This is the fully qualified domain name of the virtual machine. This can be used to access the computer even from outside the virtual environment. You might want to pass this as an argument to set up a web server. For example, if the virtual machine name for the web server was VM1, you would type $(ComputerName_VM1) as the argument for your script to pass the fully qualified domain name of the virtual machine.

In the example in Figure 21-21, we locate the deployment script on the drop folder of the build. We also pass in the build location (drop folder) as an argument to the deployment script so the script can find the application to deploy.

The simple deployment script in Listing 21-2 is sufficient to deploy the built application to the app server.

Listing 21-2. DeploymentS cript

```
REM ---
REM --- Map arguments passed from build
REM ---
SET DropPath=%1
SET DeploymentPath=c:\FabrikamFiber

REM ---
REM --- Deploy application
REM ---
RD %DeploymentPath% /S /Q
XCOPY %DropPath%\_PublishedWebsites %DeploymentPath% /S /Y /I
```

Adding Tests

Finally, we add the tests we want to run as part of the BDT workflow (Figure 21-22). The tests to run need to be defined in a test plan in Microsoft Test Manager and we can then filter out tests to run by test suite and configuration, for instance, to specify that for this BDT workflow we will only run Windows 8 tests.

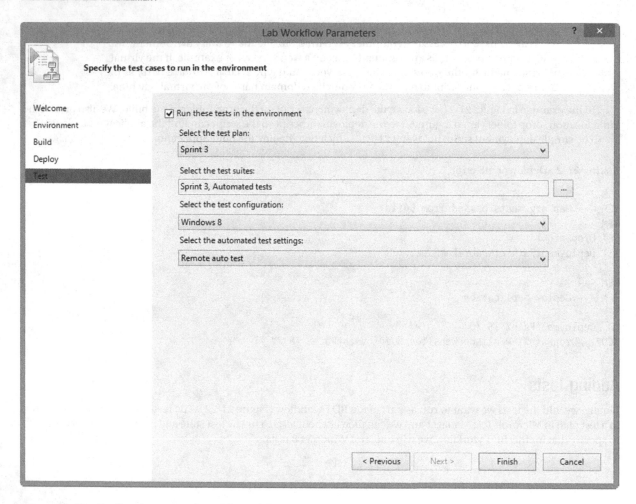

Figure 21-22. *Configuring testing for a lab workflow*

Running the BDT Workflow

Running the BDT workflow is just like running any other build in TF Service: we can use the Team Explorer Builds to queue a new BDT build manually or we can set the build definition to trigger based on other criteria. Figure 21-23 shows a build report for a completed lab workflow build.

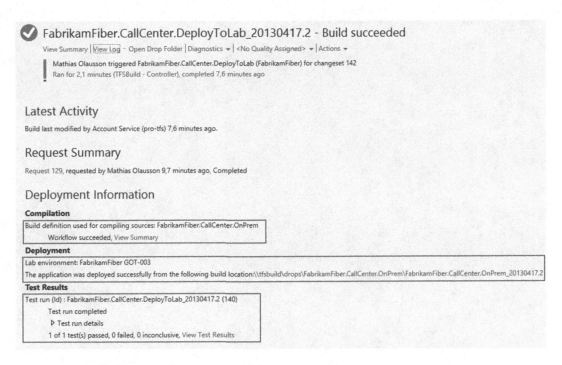

Figure 21-23. *Build report for a completed BDT workflow*

Note how nicely we get information about which build was deployed to which environment. We also get a good view of the test results.

This completes the setup of a BDT workflow. As you can see, it really ties together the work we've already done, which means little extra work is needed to get a continuous delivery process in place. This is just what TFS and ALM are all about; adding separate practices is good but integrating them can really create an impressive process!

Summary

This chapter explained how Visual Studio Lab Management can be used to enable a more efficient test process. Lab Management makes it possible to create test environments for manual and automated testing. The agents in the infrastructure also simplify data collection during testing, which helps developers better troubleshoot reported bugs. We have also seen how to use the capabilities of Lab Management to implement a complete automated BDT workflow. Although we're currently limited to on-premises standard environments, it is still a very powerful capability that we should take advantage of today.

Index

A

ActiveD irectory,6 1
AdvancedAle rtsM anagementpa ge,6 7
Agilep rojectm anagement
    agilet esting,1 8
    backlog,1 6–17
    developmentt eam,1 2
    DoD,1 2
    estimation,1 5–16
    FabrikamF iber,43
    PBIa ndS BI, 10
    pilotp roject,4 4
    PO,10– 12
    project startup phase
        backlogb uilding,5 2
        backlogg rooming,5 7
        backlogi tems,a dding,5 2
        backlogo rderu pdating,5 7
        DoDd efinition,53
        expense report project, 49
        PBI,5 5
        pokerp lanning/storyp oints,5 5
        requirements,51
        riska ssessment,5 6
        teamb uilding,4 9,5 7
    requirements,13– 15
    RUP,10
    scrum master (SM), 10, 12
    scrump rocess,9
    scrum process template
        built-inW IQLE ditor,4 8
        burndown chart, 46–47
        Kanbanb oard,48– 49
        weba ccesspor tal,46
        worki temt ypes,4 5
    SP,1 0
    XP,17– 18

Agilet esting
    acceptancec riteria,2 93–294
    evolvingt ests,2 95
    exploratoryt esting,3 06
        acceptancec riteria,3 11
        bugr eport,3 08
        testc ase, 308–309
        worki tem,3 10
    MicrosoftT estM anager,2 96
    Microsoft Web Test Manager, 297
        testc ases,2 99
        testp lan,3 00
        testr un,3 01–305
AlertsE ditor,6 5–66
Application Lifecycle Management (ALM)
    competences
        agilep ractice,1
        architect,3
        businessa nalyst,3
        businessm anager,2
        businessn eeds,1 –2
        DBAs,3
        developers,3
        operations and maintenance
            staff,3
        PMO,2
        projectc ollaboration,2
        projectm anager,2
        testers,3
        unifiedv iew,4
        user experience (UX) design, 3
    2.0+c oncept
        agilep ractice,6
        collaboration,7
        features,6
        Microsoft,6
        Timeis r ight,6– 7
        workp lanning,7

Application Lifecycle Management (ALM) (*cont.*)
 modernb usinessc hallenge,1
 threep illars,4
  automation,5
  traceability,5
  visibility,d evelopmentp rogress,5
 tools,5
Architecture,L abM anagement
 capabilities,3 39
  automated testing, 340
  BDTw orkflows,340
  cloninge nvironments,3 40
  manual testing, 339
  networki solation,3 40
 components
  SCVMM,3 42
  testa gent,3 41
  testc ontroller,3 41
Automatedt esting
 commandline
  collectiona rgument,3 56
  configida rgument,3 56
  planida rgument,3 56
  runningt est,3 56
  settings for test run, 355
  suiteida rgument,3 56
  teamprojecta rgument,3 56
 MTM
  automatedt este xecution,3 54
  testr unl og,3 54–355
 targete nvironment,3 52
 testca se,351– 352
 testp lan,3 53
 tests ettings,3 52
Automatic deployment, Windows Azure
 activities in workflow,281
 authorizingT FSc onnection,2 75
 AzureContinuousDeployment.11.xamlp rocess
   parameters,2 78–279
 buildw orkflowde tails,280
 compatibilityG DR,271
 deployment build definition,276
 deploymenth istory,2 78
 deployments ummary,2 77
 Fabrikam Fiber web solution, 271
 publishingp rocessp arameters,2 79
 saving build definition,277
 selectingt eamp roject,2 75
 solution tob uild,27 7
 sourcecon trolpr ovider,274
 sources ettings,2 76
 SQLd atabases ettings,2 73
 troubleshooting
  Configuret ab,2 82
  diagnosticl ogs,2 82–283
   Diagnosticss ection,2 82
   ResetD eploymentC redentials,2 82
 VisualS tudio 2012,2 71
 webs itec reation,2 72
 webs ited etails,2 72
 WindowsA zureM anagementP ortal,2 72

B

Backlog grooming, 11, 89
BDTw orkflow. *See* Build-deploy-test (BDT) workflow
Builda utomation
 artifacts,215
 automatingr epetitivet ask,2 02
 buildl og,2 22
 changesets and work item, 225
 continuousi ntegration,2 01
 definition
  name,217
  newb uild,2 16
  parameter,2 19–220
  retentionp olicyt ab,2 21
  sourcec ontrol,216
  templatep rocess,2 19
  trigger,2 17
  workspace,218
 enforcingt raceability,2 02
 Git team project
  branchs election,2 33
  configuration and platform, 234
  GitTemplate.xaml,2 33
  new team project creation, 232
  solutionp ath,2 34
  summaryp age,2 35
 hostedb uilds erver,2 03
  architecture,2 03
  builda gentp roperties,2 05
  buildc ontrollerp roperties,2 04
  limitation,206
  manageb uildc ontroller,2 03
  software,2 05
 machined evelopment,2 01
 magicm achines yndrome,2 02
 managingd ependency
  customization,2 09
  NuGet restore packages, 207
  sourcec ontrol,207
 MSBuild,2 23
 newb ugc reation,2 24
 output,2 24
 premises build server
  assigningb uildc ontroller,2 14
  build agent configuration,2 11–212
  builds ervicea ccount,2 12–213
  manageb uildc ontroller,2 13

operations ystem,2 10
teamp rojectc ollection,2 11
queue,22 2
summarys creen,2 23
teamf oundationb uild,2 02
test execution
Add/Edit test run dialog box, 226
automated tests dialog box, 226
MSTest.exer unner,2 27
testa dapter,2 29
test case filter,2 27
test metadata file,227
visual studio test runner, 227
testi mpacta nalysis,2 23
tracking build status
actions,237
alert,239
Community TFS build manager, 237
explorer,2 36
favorites, 237
notification power tool, 242
WindowsW orkflowb uildp rocess,2 23
Build-deploy-test(BDT)w orkflow,340,357
addingt ests,3 63
application,3 60–361
buildd efaults,3 58
buildr eport,3 64–365
buildse rvice,35 9
deployments teps,3 61
BuildLocation,3 62
ComputerName_<VMN ame>,3 63
deployments cript,3 63
InternalComputerName_<VMN ame>,3 62
lab workflow,362
frameworkf or,3 40
implementationo f,3 57–358
Lab Management target environment, 359–360
process,358
setu p,3 58
workspace,358
Buildp rocesst emplates
custom activities development
BuildActivitya ttribute,2 65
code,2 64–265
CustomBuildProcessTemplate.xaml,2 65
errorm essage,2 69
new custom build activity, 264
NumberOfMillisecondsi nputa rgument,2 65
runningc ustoma ctivity,2 68
solution,2 64
sourcecon trol,268
toolbox,2 63,2 66
workflow,267
XAML,2 62

customa ctivitya dding,2 49–250
customized build summary section, 251
customt emplatec reation,2 47–248
DefaultTemplate.11.1xaml template, 246
editing,2 47
external custom activities
AssemblyInfo custom activity, 255, 259–260
AssemblyVersion,2 60
FindMatchingFilesa ctivity,2 60
finished workflow,261
HostedB uildS erver,258– 259
RunOnAgenta ctivity,2 59
sequencea ctivity,2 60
versiona ssemblies,2 62
VisualS tudio,2 55–257
new input parameters
arguments tab, 252
DeploymentOutputTexta rgument,2 52
FabrikamFiber.CallCenter.CIb uild,2 54
metadata,2 52
process parameter metadata editor, 252–253
refresh build definition,254
Showd etailsb utton,2 54
WriteCustomSummarya ctivity,2 53
newt emplatea ssigning,2 48
Team Foundation Build Activities toolbox, 249
WindowsW orkflowf oundation,2 45–246
WriteCustomSummaryInfoa ctivity,2 50
Businessp rocesses,1

■ C

Capability Maturity Model Integration
(CMMI)pr ocess,32
Clienta ccessl icense(CAL),1 09
Continuousd eployment
SSDT database projects
ina utomatedb uilds,2 90
MSBuilda rguments,2 89
publish profile,289
Visual Studio 2012 Professional, 289
WebD eploy
ina utomatedb uilds,2 88
definition,283
installation,2 84
publishp rofilec reation,2 85
WindowsA zure(see Automatic deployment,
WindowsA zure)
ContinuousI ntegration(CI),1 8
Customer
feedback
e-mail,110
feedbackr esponse,1 13
feedbacks ession,110

Customer (*cont.*)
    providingf eedback,1 11
    requestf eedback,1 08
    requestf eedbackw izard,1 09
    submittingf eedback,1 12
  mockups
    deletec ustomerm ockup,1 04
    delete customer user story, 102
    MicrosoftP owerPoint,1 03
    reusables toryboards hape,1 07
    sketchys hape,1 04
    storyboardl inkt ool,1 05

D

Databasea dministrators(DBAs),3
Definitiono fD one(DoD),1 2

E

Eclipse
  buildsp age,1 88–189
  Fabrikam Fiber team project, 177
  sourceco ntrol
    FabrikamFiber,1 81,183
    pending changes,1 84–185
    repositoryt ype,1 83
    ShareP roject,1 81–182
    sourcec ontrolh istory,1 86
    TFS ervicew orkspace,181– 182
    Visual Studio Team Explorer, 184
    workspacem appings,1 84–185
  TeamE xplorerE verywhere
    (*see* Team Explorer Everywhere)
  Teamprise,177
  WorkI tems,186– 187
eXtremeP rogramming(XP),1 7–18

F

FabrikamF ibers olution,1 81
FabrikamF ibert eamp roject,1 77
Fast-forward playback, 336
ForresterR esearch,6 –7
Forwardin tegration(F I),145

G

Git,1 19
  advantages of, 122
  annotatedt ags,1 20
  branching,1 20
    conflicts,170
    merging,1 69
    newl ocalb ranch,1 68
    non-MicrosoftG itt ools,1 74

publisheda ndu npublished,1 67
    serverr epository,174
    switchingb ranch,1 69
    TeamW ebA ccess,1 73
  branchv isualization,1 21
  commandl ineutil ity,176
  cross-platformc lients,1 21
  disconnectedw ork,1 19
  distributedd evelopment,1 19
  extensions,1 57
  lightweight tags, 120
  rebasing,1 20
  rewritingh istory,1 19
  TeamE xplorer
    Difft ool,1 64
    history,1 63
    localr epository,1 62,1 65
    pullingc hange,1 66
    pushingc hange,1 66
    serverr epository,1 61–162
    sourcec ode,1 63
    sourcec ontrols ystem,1 58
    TeamM embersh ub,1 59
    teamp roject,1 59
  workflows,120
Gitc ommandl ineutil ity,176
Git-TF,1 96–198

H, I, J

Hostedb uilds erver
  architecture,2 03
  buildc ontrollerp roperties,2 04
  limitation,206
  manageb uildc ontroller,2 03
  software,2 05
Hosteds ervice
  decision,2 5
  on-premises TFS installation
    customization,2 2
    datam igration,2 3
    dependencies to local environment, 24
    identitiesa nda uthentication,2 3
    legal requirements and policy, 23
    operationc ontrol,2 3
    reporting, 24
    SharePoint,24
  organizationd ependentf actor,2 5
  TFs ervice
    Azured eployment,2 2
    builds erver,2 2
    externalu ser,2 2
    On-premise/cloudr esource,22
    trouble-freeope ration,21
    updates,2 1
    zerof rictions tart,2 1

K, L

Kanbanm ethod
  boards
    book-writingp roject,9 7
    editor,9 7
    setup,9 6
    teamw eba ccess,9 6
    visual graph, 98
  corep roperties
    collaborativea pproach,9 5
    manage flow,94
    processp olicy,9 4
    WIP limit,94
    workflowv isualization,9 2
  incrementale volutionaryc hanges,9 2
  job titles, roles, and responsibilities, 92
  profoundk nowledge,9 5
  rolesa ndp rocesses,9 2
  sprintp lanning,9 1
  TFS ervice
    boards,9 5
    Scrump rocesst emplate,9 6
  theoryof constr aints,95
  Toyotap roduction system,9 1
  WIPl imitedp ulls ystem,9 1

M, N, O

Magicm achines yndrome,2 02
MicrosoftS olution Framework(MSF),3 2
MicrosoftT estM anager(MTM),2 96
  bugc reation,3 34–335
  datacolle ction,331– 333
  VerifyB ugsvie w,335– 336
MicrosoftV isualS tudioS crum,32
Microsoft Web Test Manager (WTM)
  testc ases,2 99
  testp lan,2 98,3 00
  testr un,3 01–305
Mockups
  deletec ustomerm ockup,1 04
  delete customer user story, 102
  MicrosoftP owerPoint,1 03
  reusables toryboards hape,1 07
  sketchys hape,1 04
  storyboardl inkt ool,1 05
MTM. *See* Microsoft Test Manager (MTM)

P, Q

Productb acklogi tems(PBIs),1 0,5 5
Producto wner(PO),1 0–12
Projectde livery,1 1
Projectm anagemento ffice(PMO),2

R

RationalU nifiedP rocess(RUP),1 0
Returno ni nvestment(ROI),1 1
Reversei ntegration(RI),1 45

S

Server Data Tools (SSDT) database projects
  ina utomatedb uilds,2 90
  MSBuilda rguments,2 89
  publish profile,289
  VisualS tudio2 012P rofessional,2 89
Sourcec ontrols ystem
  Git
    advantages of, 122
    annotatedt ags,1 20
    branching,1 20
    branchv isualization,1 21
    cross-platformc lients,1 21
    disconnectedw ork,1 19
    distributedd evelopment,1 19
    lightweightt ags,1 20
    rebasing,1 20
    rewritingh istory,1 19
    workflows,120
  TFVC
    advantageso f,1 22
    atomicc heck-in,1 16
    branching,1 17
    branch visualization and tracking, 117–118
    check-inpol icies,116
    cross-platforms upport,1 18
    disconnectedw ork,1 18
    labeling,1 17
    lockfi les,116
    shelving,1 16
    teamv isibility,1 16
    TrackW orkI tem,1 18
Sprint
  scrump rocess
    backlogg rooming,7 9,8 9
    dailys tandup,7 9,8 5–86
    retrospective,79,90
    sprintp lanning(*see* Sprint planning meeting)
    sprintr eview,7 9,8 9
    TFS ervice,87– 89
Sprintb acklogi tems(SBIs),1 0
Sprintb acklog(SP),1 0
Sprintp lanning
  availablet imec alculation,6 9
  capacityp lanning,7 0–71
  dropdownc ontrol,7 2–73
  expense report, 72
  groomedb acklog,7 3

Sprint planning (*cont.*)
    projectcoste stimation,77
    projectr eleasep lanning,7 5
    sprintb acklog,7 1–73
    storyp oints,7 1–72
    TFS,7 3–74,7 6–77
Sprintp lanningm eeting
    boardv iew,8 4
    burndownc hart,8 1–82
    ControlP anel,8 2
    definition,79
    Linkst ab,8 4
    newt askf orm,8 0
    Remaining Work field,81
    tagfi lter,8 3
    users tory,8 0
    Visual Studio 2012 update, 82
    worki tem,8 3
SSDT. *See* Server Data Tools (SSDT)
    databasepr ojects
Stakeholderm anagement,1 1
Staticcode a nalysis,201
System Center Virtual Machine
    Manager(SCVMM),3 42

■ T

TeamE xplorerE verywhere,177
    accessing,1 80
    Add Repository dialog box, 179
    InstallN ewS oftware,1 78
    plug-in,1 78
    TeamF oundationS erver,179– 180
    TeamP roject,1 81
    TFS ervicea ccount,1 78
TeamE xplorervie w,158
Teamf oundationb uild, 202
TeamF oundationS erver,1 79
TeamF oundationS ervice
    account
        creation,2 9–30
        naming,2 8
        structureo f,2 8
        teamp rojectc ollection,2 7
    invitingp eople
        manage team members window, 39
        rolesa ndpe rmissions,40– 41
        usera ddition,4 0
    new team project
        Connectp age,3 6
        creation,3 0
        development process templates, 32, 34
        names election,3 1
        new TF server addition, 38
        sourcec ontrols ystems,3 2
        TeamE xplorer,3 6

    TFd ialogb ox,3 7
    TFs ervers election,3 8
    VisualS tudiol ink,3 5
Team Foundation Version Control (TFVC), 32, 115
    advantageso f,1 22
    atomicc heck-in,1 16
    branching,1 17
        creation,1 39
        rules,138
        visualization,1 40
    branch visualization and tracking, 117
    check-inpol icies,116
        buildsp olicy,1 16
        commentp olicy,1 16
        worki temp olicy,1 16
    coder eviews
        codes ection,1 54
        filel evel,1 54
        finalization,156
        overallc omment,154
        request,1 52
        viewa ndr esponse,1 54
    cross-platforms upport,1 18
    disconnectedw ork,1 18
    labeling,1 17
    lockfi les,116
    merging
        forwardi ntegration,1 45
        limitation,142
        Merget oolw indow,1 43
        Mergew izard,1 41
        PendingC hangesp age,1 44
        Pendingc onflictw indow,142
        reversein tegration,145
        TFS ervice,140
    shelving,1 16,1 35
    Source Control Explorer
        annotate,1 32
        centralw indow,1 27
        file Compare version, 131
        history, 130
        Pending Changes page, 133, 135
        shelveset,1 36
        sourcec ontrolo peration,1 26–127
        toolw indow,1 32
    workspaces(*see*W orkspaces)
    TeamE xplorer
        hub,124
        sourcec ontrols ystem,1 23–124
        TeamM embersh ub,1 25
        teamp roject,1 25
    teamv isibility,1 16
    visualization and tracking
        inp rogress,1 51
        resuming, 152
        TrackC hangeset,1 45

Work Item tracking, 147
Workp age,1 50
worksuspe nsion,1 51
Teamm embers
add/removet eamm embers,6 0
managingm embers,5 9
newt eam,6 1–63
TF Service groups
builda dministrators,6 4
contributors, 64
projecta dministrators,64
projectv alidu sers,6 4
TFS ervices ecurity,6 1
userp ermissions,6 4
WindowsL iveI D,6 0–61
Teamprise,177
Test-drivend evelopment(TDD),6
Testm anagement
assign test cases to tester, 323
grouping and adding fields,324
reporting bugs and validating fixes,3 33–337
runningt exts
AnalyzeT estR uns,3 30–331
datacolle ction,331– 333
filteringt est,3 25
MTMte str unner,326– 330
tests ettings,3 31
test case
acceptancec riteria,3 19,3 21
servicer epresentative,3 19
Sprint 2 test plan, 321
testc ases ummary,3 19
tests teps,3 17–318
testc onfigurations,3 22–323
testp lan,3 13
testp lanp roperties,3 16–317
tests uites
query-baseds uite,3 14
requirements-baseds uite,3 14–315
Sprint 2 test plan, 316
statics uite,3 14
status, 324–325
TFS erverE ventS ervice,67
TFVC. See Team Foundation Version Control (TFVC)

U

Users tories,1 3

V

Visual Studio Lab Management
BDT workflow (see Build-Deploy-Test (BDT) workflow)
capabilities,3 39
automated testing, 340
cloninge nvironments,3 40
manual testing, 339
networki solation,3 40
components
SCVMM,3 42
standarde nvironments,3 42
testa gent,3 41–342
testc ontroller,3 41
settingu p,3 43
on-premisesb uilds ervice,3 45
standarde nvironment,3 45–348
testc ontroller,3 44
topology,3 43
testing
automatedt esting(see Automated testing)
EnvironmentV iewer,3 50–351
host-basedc onnection,3 51
"InU se"m arker,3 49
manualt ests,3 48
runningt ests,3 50

W

WebD eploy
definition,283
installing,2 84
publishp rofile
connection,2 86
FabrikamFiber.Webpr oject,286
name,286
settings,2 87
ins olution,2 88
WindowsI ntegratedS ecurity,2 87
WindowsL iveI D,6 1
WindowsW orkflow foundation
activities,245
arguments,2 45
variables,2 45
Work-in-progress(WIP)l imitedp ulls ystem,9 1
WorkI temQ ueryL anguage(WIQL),4 8
Workspaces
localw orkspace,1 29
mapping,1 28
private,1 30
public, 130
serverw orkspace,1 29
WTM. See Microsoft Web Test Manager (WTM)

X, Y, Z

Xcode
Gitin tegration,189
iOSd evelopment,1 89
sourcec ontrol,193– 196
TFS ervicer epository,190– 191,193